250 Classic Movies

250 Classic Movies

by George McManus

BearManor Media
2013

250 Classic Movies

© 2013 George McManus

All rights reserved.

All rights reserved. No part of this publication may be reproduced or transmitted in any form or by any means without written permission of the publisher.

For information, address:

BearManor Media
P. O. Box 71426
Albany, GA 31708

bearmanormedia.com

Typesetting and layout by John Teehan

Published in the USA by BearManor Media

ISBN — 1-59393-742-3
978-1-59393-742-3

Table of Contents

Introduction	1
Silents	9
British Classics	37
Foreign Classics	59
Action-Adventure	83
Animation	113
Comedy	127
Romantic Comedy	149
Romance	171
Comedy-Drama	191
Costume Drama	209
Drama	231
Epics	265
Family Films	289
Film Noir	305
Mystery-Thrillers	325
Horror	355
Science Fiction	377
War Films	397
Westerns	419
Musicals	447
About the Author	475
Acknowledgments	477
Photo Credits	479
Bibliography	481

Introduction

Here are 250 Classic Movies in twenty categories, all examples of great filmmaking, presented for the newest generation of movie fans. Included are data, awards, trivia, reviews, back stories, posters, and photographs. Are these 250 the greatest movies ever made? Not necessarily, though they are certainly among the best.

I come from a time in the 1940s and 1950s when double features were regular fare. This has allowed me to see more than my share of pictures, and since my mother once worked behind the candy counter of a local movie house, I visited the theater often. In fact, I met my wife at a movie theater—she was a ticket-seller.

I began my broadcast career in Louisiana but spent most of my 40 years in radio/TV in California. I actually covered the Academy Awards backstage for two years (Cloris Leachman let me hold her Oscar, and I was there the night they honored Charlie Chaplin in person), and I served as MC at the premiere of the James Bond movie *You Only Live Twice*.

Most significantly, I met and interviewed, mostly in-studio, dozens of the larger-than-life stars, writers, and directors I had so long admired on-screen. Among them: William Wyler, Jean Renoir, Elia Kazan, Charlton Heston, Lauren Bacall, Kirk Douglas, Carroll Baker, Karl Malden, Debbie Reynolds, John Carradine, Agnes Moorehead, William Goldman, Mercedes McCambridge, Darryl Ponicsan, Shirley MacLaine, Mark Rydell, Peter Bogdanovich, Paul Williams, Anita Loos, Jule Styne, Bruce Dern, Philip Kaufman, Alan Arkin, Michael Ritchie, Red Skelton, Andy Griffith, Lloyd Bridges, Dale Evans Rogers, Elvis Presley, Johnny Cash, Pat Boone, Lowell Thomas, and Louis L'Amour.

While I didn't get to interview him at length, I did actually meet the great John Ford on the set of one of his John Wayne Westerns (*The Horse Soldiers*) shot in Louisiana. We chatted for several minutes about that day's shoot. For a man who was often referred to as grumpy and non-talkative, he was very gracious—I think because I was a fellow Irishman.

At first, I had trouble talking with director William Wyler (*Ben-Hur*) until I remembered he was hard-of-hearing in one ear. Wyler had lost hearing while filming *The Memphis Belle* in WWII. Loud gunfire and aerial explosions had cost him as he shot footage from the belly of the aircraft. Wyler was a visionary. I asked him about the future of special effects and he advised all young screenwriters "not to worry because nowadays these guys can create anything you can imagine." That was four years before *Star Wars*. But he admitted he wasn't always right. He urged Vivien Leigh to take the part of Isabella in *Wuthering Heights* though she insisted on playing Cathy, opposite her boyfriend Laurence Olivier. But Goldwyn wanted Merle Oberon for the lead. Wyler told Vivien, "You're not known in the United States. You'll never do better than this for your first American film." He was wrong, of course. Six months later she became Scarlett O'Hara in *Gone With the Wind*.

Elia Kazan, director of two Marlon Brando classics (*A Streetcar Named Desire, On the Waterfront*), told me he believes "In the not-too-distant future, the sex act itself will be portrayed in major feature films. They're already close to that now with soft-porn making its way into TV soaps." I hope he's wrong. I think the explicitness in Brando's *Last Tango in Paris* influenced Kazan's thinking. Personally, I believe there are still many new directors with enough sense to realize that sexual innuendo is more provocative than watching the real thing. Also, Kubrick has already tried it with *Eyes Wide Shut* which flopped at the box-office for the very reason that it showed too much. Kazan said something else that shocked me. He directed James Dean in *East of Eden* and said "He wasn't much of an actor when I got him." Wow.

I asked Charlton Heston which person had the most influence on his career. "DeMille," he answered without missing a beat, and added, "If an actor can't make it in this business after playing leads in two DeMille films, he might as well give up." Charlton, called "Chuck" by DeMille, starred in *The Greatest Show on Earth* and *The Ten Commandments*. Heston went on to star in Wyler's *Ben-Hur*. Heston tells a funny story about that classic. Yakima Canutt, the famous stuntman, was second-unit director on the film and worked with Heston on the chariot race. Charlton told Canutt he didn't know if he could win the race. Canutt replied,

"You just stay in the chariot, Chuck, and I guarantee you'll win the race." Heston also likes to spin the yarn about DeMille making one of his epics, which had four cameras set at different positions to catch the action of an important scene. After DeMille yelled "Action!" and the scene ended, the great director called out to camera one, "How'd it go?" "Sorry, boss," came the response, "the horses and explosions knocked the camera over; didn't get anything." DeMille turned to camera two: "It was too dusty, it's a complete loss." DeMille then checked on camera three: "I know you're not going to believe this, but the camera malfunctioned." So on to camera four up on the hill, the all-reliable master shot. DeMille cried out: "How'd it look, Charlie?" The shouted reply? "I'm ready when you are C.B."

I think the most fun I ever had during an interview was with Kirk Douglas, years before his stroke; incidentally, he has been a tremendous inspiration to other actors for the way he has dealt with his physical handicap. He's even made movies with that condition. We began our chat by kidding one another and continued that way through the half-hour. When I met the superstar, who was bigger than life to me, I blurted "Hey, you're not as tall as I thought!" To which he quipped, "Yeah, but I'm taller than you!" And he was. As we walked to the recording studio, I dug my index finger into my chin like impersonator Frank Gorshin used to do to imitate Kirk; Douglas spotted it right away and said, "You have to do more than that to imitate me." Douglas admits to being brash and cocky, like his pal Burt Lancaster, both of whom had humble beginnings and, to be noticed, had to fight their way to the top. Kirk is one of those rare Hollywood celebrities who knows who he is and is very comfortable with himself, and doesn't have to prove anything to anybody. He was a star almost from the start and played in nearly every genre, including heavy drama, comedies and Westerns. I learned he was very proud of his film *Spartacus*. He also liked a little-known, low-budget film called *Lonely Are the Brave*. When we finished our talk, I accompanied him down the elevator to street level while he waited for his limo. We talked some more with Kirk leaning against a sidewalk tree. I couldn't help but notice dozens of people walking by and not noticing this great star in their midst, and he wasn't wearing sunglasses. Douglas just smiled; he wasn't fazed by it in the least.

I interviewed Debbie Reynolds in her dressing room backstage at the Nugget in Sparks, Nevada. Between shows, she spent her time knitting and receiving a phone call from her mother. I kept asking her if I was taking up too much of her time but she insisted she didn't mind because "It gets boring back here waiting for the next performance." And what performances they were! – singing, dancing, doing skits and telling anecdotes about her life in Tinseltown. And she still sings "Tammy" in her shows, and why not—it sold a million records! Her favorite film? *Singin' in the Rain*, which she also thinks is the best musical ever made. I particularly admire Debbie for two aspects of her colorful life: one of her husbands was a gambler and lost nearly all of her fortune. But she refused to file backruptcy, feeling personally responsible for the debts. So she worked extra-hard and increased the number of roadshows to make up the losses. Secondly, I admire her efforts to try and save MGM. Debbie begged the management of MGM not to sell off the property, but instead to turn it into an amusement park with tours of the old soundstages and workshops. They refused and turned it over to the redevelopment folks who tore it all down. What a shame. However, Debbie was able, at auction, to obtain many of the costumes, props and artifacts. Her goal is to establish a museum to keep the legend of Hollywood alive for future generations. This beautiful and talented lady loves her work and loves the history of filmmaking.

Lowell Thomas, the great CBS correspondent (who invented the term "Lawrence of Arabia" and introduced Cinerama), upon meeting me said, "George McManus?" Why I knew the cartoonist George McManus in Chicago; he drew Maggie and Jiggs (the strip was called "Bringing Up Father"); he was a great guy, wonderful man!" Mr. Thomas, also famous as the narrator on movie newsreels, told me he had hoped to restore the Cinerama three-screen process in the future. Unfortunately, he died before he could try. I quite liked Cinerama, despite the connecting seams. I saw the original *Seven Wonders of the World* in Cinerama in Hollywood and, later, *How the West Was Won* on the giant wrap-around screen.

My name also became a point of conversation when I interviewed the famous Western novelist Louis L'Amour. He wasn't interested in writing screenplays but much of his historical research was fodder for lots of movie Westerns. I interviewed him about his newly-released book and, upon learning my name, he immediately informed me that he had found, in his extensive study into Wild West lore and legend, a gunfighter named "George McManus." I was afraid to ask how the fellow died, but one can imagine.

I got up-close with moviemaking when I let a movie company use part of my house for a film: *Tell Me a Riddle* starring Melvyn Douglas, directed by Lee Grant. The cast and crew came by the house very early every day for a week, turning the property into a veritable movie studio. They even rebuilt my garage into a set for a scene for the picture. There were takes and re-takes, actors and actresses going over lines, stand-ins standing by, and assistants yelling "Quiet on the set!" The set was my house! My wife suddenly realized that one day when she came home early with a bag of groceries and Grant, quietly recording post-production lines in our living room, screamed at her to "Get the hell out of here!" Ms. Grant apologized later, not realizing that the mysterious intruder had been the lady of the house.

I interviewed Karl Malden on the set of his TV police series *The Streets of San Francisco*. I brought up the fact that he had worked three times with the great Brando (*A Streetcar Named Desire, On the Waterfront, One-Eyed Jacks*); I wondered if things always went well. Malden said, "Absolutely," and he had been "thrilled to have known and worked with Marlon" and they got along just fine. Of course, they went back to Broadway where they had appeared together in *Streetcar* before it was made into a film, "But the producers," said Malden, "were nervous about the transition from stage to Hollywood. Brando wasn't well-known at the time and Jessica Tandy was not a box-office star. So when it was announced they had signed Vivien Leigh for the part of Blanche, everybody knew they had a winner." And win it did! Vivien won the Academy Award for Best Actress, Malden won the supporting Oscar for his role as Mitch, and the film was nominated for Best Picture. Malden, real name Mladen Sekulovich, honored his Yugoslavian parents during his career by always including his last name in every picture. For example, when he played Omar Bradley in *Patton*, he called out to a soldier, "Hey, Sekulovich!"

I wished I had had more time to talk to director Peter Bogdanovich. He arrived late through no fault of his own—traffic and bad weather as I recall. He came in puffing on a big Churchill cigar, long before radio stations posted "no smoking" signs in studios. Peter not only made a niche for himself in filmmaking, but he also got more than his share of pop-culture attention. His mistress, *Playboy* centerfold Dorothy Stratten, was murdered; and Peter also had a long-standing relationship with actress Cybill Shepherd. Bogdanovich is a member of an exclusive club—former critics who later made movies. It happens in Europe a lot—notably, Godard and Truffaut, and others—but it doesn't happen much in America. In the 1960s, Peter went to work as an assistant director to low-budget genius Roger Corman. It was great on-the-job training. It led to Bogdanovich's creating two black-and-white classics:

The Last Picture Show and *Paper Moon*. But Peter, as a journalist, did something else I admired and envied: he interviewed, on film, five giants: John Ford (Peter admits it was a stop-and-start exercise because the great director didn't want to be interviewed in the first place), John Wayne, James Stewart, Henry Fonda, and Orson Welles. In fact, his Welles interview, an hour-long chit-chat done in a restaurant booth (a copy of which I have), was probably the last interview Welles did.

A superstar I always admired was Edward G. Robinson. I got hold of his home address and sent him a letter on company stationery requesting an interview. One day in the newsroom, the desk editor called me across the room: "Hey, McManus, there's a guy on the phone who claims he's Edward G. Robinson and wants to talk to you." It *was* Eddie G. His very distinguishable voice, reminiscent of his familiar gangster roles, crackled across the phone line: "Mr. McManus, this is Edward G. Robinson. I understand you'd like to interview me." He didn't want to do a telephone interview, so we made plans to talk at the upcoming Academy Awards. Sadly, it didn't happen. Mr. Robinson died before the event. He received a posthumous Oscar and I did interview his widow that night.

Amazingly, the first celebrity interview I ever did was with the man that *TV Guide* later picked as "Entertainer of the Century," and he appeared in thirty-three movies. I was working at KTLD in Tallulah, Louisiana. One day I pulled up to the Trailways Bus Station café to pick up a sandwich on my way to work. Parked in front was a pink Cadillac with the name "Elvis Presley" scrawled in small lettering on the driver's side door. I went inside and there he was, the man who would become "The King of Rock-and-Roll." Elvis was sitting with his musicians, Scotty Moore and Bill Black, at a table eating hamburgers and drinking Cokes. They were on-the-road, dropping off free copies of their Sun records at radio stations. I told him where the station was, located next to the radio tower just outside of town. Sure enough, about a half-hour later, here comes that Cadillac kicking up dust while bouncing down the dirt road to the box-like building. Elvis came in, nice as could be, sat down with me at the microphone and talked about his records, his upbringing in Tupelo, and how much fun he was having making music and performing. No, I didn't get his autograph; I was in too much of a shock to think about it, but I still remember the incident like it was yesterday.

Dale Evans was in San Francisco to give an inspirational talk with

Christian songs at a local church. I interviewed Dale in a restaurant booth at the Holiday Inn where she was staying. Dale started out as a pretty nightclub singer before she got a movie contract at Republic Pictures. The studio became famous for its serials and Westerns. She made dozens of B-Westerns with "The King of the Cowboys," Roy Rogers, whom she would marry. Roy proposed one evening just before he and Dale would ride out into an arena at a rodeo; Roy and Dale had to do rodeos between pictures to make enough to pay the bills. They were paid very little at the studio, despite the fact that they were Republic's most popular stars. They got so much fan mail Roy and Dale couldn't handle it, and the studio wouldn't provide a secretary. So Roy stacked it in the bed of his pickup truck and dumped it at the door of studio boss and miser Herbert J. Yates. Roy and Dale knew their share of hard times, losing three of their children in tragic circumstances. Over the years, Dale wrote fifteen books detailing their ups and downs. As she said, "Life is a series of peaks and valleys. You have to go through the valleys to appreciate the mountaintops." Before we left each other, I said to her, "Dale, I want you to know, when I was a kid I was in love with you." She smiled and said, "I can't tell you how many men have told me that."

I also did broadcast interviews with twelve authors and film historians who knew a great deal about old movies: Bob Thomas, Clive Hirschhorn, Steven H. Scheuer, Jesse Lasky, Jr., Ralph Rosenblum, Patrick Agan, Richard Alleman, James Bacon, Joe Hyams, Hector Arce, Pauline Kael, and Sheilah Graham.

For some perspective, here is a list of the top twenty-five American films of all time as chosen by the American Film Institute (1998), all of which are included in this book. In order, they are: *Citizen Kane, Casablanca, The Godfather, Gone With the Wind, Lawrence of Arabia, The Wizard of Oz, The Graduate, On the Waterfront, Schindler's List, Singin' in the Rain, It's a Wonderful Life, Sunset Boulevard, The Bridge on the River Kwai, Some Like It Hot, Star Wars, All About Eve, The African Queen, Psycho, Chinatown, One Flew Over the Cuckoo's Nest, The Grapes of Wrath, 2001: A Space Odyssey, The Maltese Falcon, Raging Bull,* and *E.T. The Extra-Terrestrial.*

As to the top-grossing films, in 1996 *USA Today* enlisted Exhibitor Research Company to determine the top moneymakers, adjusted for inflation. Again, in order: *Gone With the Wind, Star Wars, E.T. The Extra-Terrestrial, The Ten Commandments, The Sound of Music, Jaws,* and *Doctor Zhivago*. Each made over half a billion dollars and *Gone With the Wind* grossed nearly one billion dollars worldwide.

The cut-off for the classics included in this collection is 1999, which means three more recent super-hits—which became instant classics—are included: *Titanic* (1997), *Toy Story* (1995), and *Jurassic Park* (1993). So now, let's take a ride on, as Frank Capra once called it, a "magic carpet of film" and turn the spotlight on the incredible first century of filmmaking. Let us all, young and old, honor and enjoy these remarkable movie memories.

Silents

The Birth of a Nation

1915, USA, Epoch, 187 minutes, B&W, Silent
Producer/Director: D.W. Griffith
Cast: Henry B. Walthall, Lillian Gish, Mae Marsh, Ralph Lewis, George Siegmann, Elmer Clifton, Joseph Henaberry, Raoul Walsh

> "The most beautiful single shot I have seen in any movie is the battle charge in *The Birth of a Nation.*"
> —James Agee.

This landmark epic drama, about the Civil War and its aftermath, was the birth of modern cinema as we know it with montages, cross-cuts, fades, and close-ups. Griffith didn't invent the processes, but he was the first to put them all together in one feature film. There would be a sad ending for Hollywood's first master filmmaker however, Griffith died in 1948 at the old Knickerbocker Hotel, lonely and alcoholic, victim to a cerebral hemorrhage. Ezra Goodman wrote, "At Griffith's funeral, the sacred cows of Hollywood gathered to pay him homage. A week before, he probably could not have gotten any of them on the telephone."

Some of the ideas in the film Griffith took from real-life: he was the son of a Confederate colonel who was ruined by the Civil War. But the crux of the story is taken from Rev. Thomas Dixon's play *The Clansman*. The film depicts anarchy in the black-ruled South after the Civil War. The film was made for less than a million dollars and grossed $100 million; nevertheless, it came under fire and remains controversial even to this day. Despite criticisms of the film (some of the black characters are played by white actors in make-up and the KKK is shown as benevolent by pro-

tecting white families from vengeful black leadership), the picture continues to show up among lists of the greatest films of all time.

The story focuses on the relationship between a Southern family and a Yankee family, the Camerons and the Stonemans. Henry B. Walthall plays Col. Ben Cameron who is in love with a pretty Northern girl, Elsie Stoneman (Gish). Elsie is the daughter of Austin Stoneman (Lewis), a congressman ambitious for power in the New Reconstructionist South. Stoneman's political ally is a leader of a party of mulattoes, Silas Lynch (Siegmann). Marsh plays Flora Cameron, Clifton plays Phil Stoneman, Henaberry plays President Lincoln, and Walsh is his assassin, John Wilkes Booth.

- Austin Stoneman is based on a clubfooted, wig-wearing Congressman named Thaddeus Stevens.
- Battle scenes were filmed by cameramen Billy Bitzer and Karl Brown on hillsides that are now Forest Lawn Memorial Park in Hollywood Hills.
- Some Civil War veterans were used as extras.
- Erich von Stroheim was one of the assistant directors.

- Walsh later became a director. His films include *White Heat, High Sierra, They Drive by Night,* and *The Roaring Twenties*.
- President Wilson said of the film: "It is like writing history with lightning, and my one regret is that it is all so terribly true."

The Cabinet of Dr. Caligari

1919, Germany, Famous Films, 69 minutes, B&W, Silent
Producer: Erich Pommer. Director: Robert Wiene
Cast: Werner Krauss, Conrad Veidt, Lil Dagover, Friedrich Feher

> "Like a steel spring responding to violent compression, *The Cabinet of Dr. Caligari* sprang onto the post-war scene of filmmaking…a triumph of style expression."
> —Parker Tyler, *Classics of the Foreign Film*

Though now considered a silent classic, many international critics of the time refused to commend the film because it was made in Germany and its release was so close to the end of WWI, when the whole world felt

Conrad Veidt and Werner Krauss in *The Cabinet of Dr. Caligari*.

victimized. German films, for the most part, had fallen prey to censorship, so had it not been for the pragmatic Sam Goldwyn, it would not have found its way into America. Goldwyn believed the plot might make audiences see that they'd been asleep to what was happening in Europe. *The Cabinet of Dr. Caligari* is now seen as one of the great expressionistic films of all time and its influence on fantasy, illusion, and imagination remains inestimable.

Veidt, who would later portray Nazi Major Strasser in *Casablanca*, plays a somnambulist named Cesare, a poor soul who has allegedly been asleep for 25 years. The sleepwalker is under the hypnotic influence of a mad magician in a traveling show, Dr. Caligari (Krauss), who keeps his victim on display in an upright cabinet. Dagover plays Jane, a lovely young woman who also falls under Caligari's spell and wanders about in a trance-like state. Her suitor Francis (Feher) tells the tale—one of murder, abduction, and mind control. Yet, in the end, it appears that it is the storyteller himself who is insane, for Dr. Caligari is head of the asylum—and the narrator emerges as the madman!

- The simple sets were made of heavy paper and cardboard.
- Pommer had wanted Fritz Lang (*Metropolis*) to direct but he wasn't available.
- Writer Hans Janowitz wanted his girlfriend, actress Gilda Langer, to play the part of Jane, but Langer fell ill and died.
- Janowitz got the idea for the plot when he visited a carnival and saw a strange man hanging around. The next day he heard that a girl had been murdered there. Janowitz attended her funeral and was surprised to see the same man in attendance.

City Lights

1931, USA, United Artists, 87 minutes, B&W, Silent
Producer/Director: Charles Chaplin
Cast: Charles Chaplin, Virginia Cherrill, Harry Myers, Florence Lee, Hank Mann

> "…an unqualified commercial success as well as an artistic triumph."
>
> —Ephraim Katz

A silent romantic comedy/melodrama that was both a critical and box-office hit at a very tough time; when Hollywood was converting to sound. But Chaplin's "Little Tramp" character made it work, preserving the silence just a little longer. The film incorporated mere bits of the new element of sound into the film, like gunshots, a boxing ring bell, and the gibberish of a politician giving a speech.

Chaplin plays an optimistic homeless man who salvages a girl's eyesight. Cherrill plays the pretty but blind flower girl whom Charlie loves. Lee plays the girl's grandmother. In order to come up with the rent owed by the girl

Charles Chaplin and Virginia Cherrill in *City Lights*.

and her grandmother Charlie enters a boxing match to win the prize money. In what turns out to be the funniest sequence in the picture Chaplin fancy dances around the ring to avoid the punches of the prizefighter (Mann), while hiding behind the referee. It is surely this scene that caused fellow comic W.C. Fields to opine that Chaplin was "a damned ballet dancer."

Among the other antics are: Chaplin nearly stepping into a sidewalk hole left by a street elevator, his falling into water next to a drunken millionaire (Myers) trying to commit suicide, and Charlie drunkenly slipping and sliding on a slick dance floor.

Famous dialogue…
The Tramp: Can you see now?
The Girl: Yes, I can see now.

- It was Chaplin's most involved work, taking three years to make, though actual shooting took six months.
- There were some inactive weeks until Chaplin could get inspired. Cherrill was even fired at one point, later to be re-hired.
- Look for Jean Harlow as an extra in the nightclub scene.
- Chaplin wrote both the script and the music and edited the film.
- In an astonishing oversight by the Motion Picture Academy, *City Lights* received no Oscar nominations, though the picture is now considered a silent classic.

The General

1927, USA, United Artists, 107 minutes, B&W, Silent
Producer: Joseph M. Schenck, Director: Buster Keaton
Cast: Buster Keaton, Marion Mack

> "No movie chase has ever been sustained so long, so successfully, or with such an expert intermingling of genuine thrills and hilarious comic situations."
> —Joe Franklin, *Classics of the Silent Screen.*

The year was 1927. Baseball was the national pastime, dominated by the New York Yankees and their "murderer's row" led by Babe Ruth

Buster Keaton in *The General*.

and Lou Gehrig. The Bambino hit 60 homers that year. The president was "Silent Cal" Coolidge. At the movies, silent pictures reigned; filmmakers did not suspect that later that year, on October 6, Al Jolson's *The Jazz Singer* would usher sound into the industry and change the shape of Hollywood forever. But for now, two years ahead of the stock market crash, they talked baseball—and Buster. Buster Keaton had just made one of the funniest pictures in years, *The General*.

The General is the name of a locomotive and the story, written by Keaton with Clyde Bruckman, is based on an actual Civil War event. The exploit took place in Georgia when Union spies tried to steal a train and sabotage Confederate rail lines. Keaton plays engineer Johnnie Gray, a fumbling but zealous "Johnny Reb" who is denied enlistment but becomes one of the South's most valiant soldiers. Annabelle Lee (Mack), whom Johnnie loves, happens to be in the baggage car when the train thieves arrive but Keaton comes to the rescue.

Keaton, a former vaudeville acrobat, does his own stunts and takes incredible risks during the making of the movie including sitting on the drive shaft of train wheels and balancing a chunk of lumber while leaning against the train's front scoop; both feats accomplished while the train was *in motion*. And there's more, he takes a dangerous tumble from a big-wheeled bicycle and does a tricky routine with a loaded snub-nosed cannon; while he picks up a sword the cannon fires just over his head.

- Keaton had to film in Oregon. Neither Georgia nor Tennessee had the right tracks; Civil War trains were narrow-gauge. He also liked Oregon's countryside with valleys, little lakes, and mountain streams.
- The film has the most expensive stunt ever done in silent pictures: a real train, not a model or miniature, drops into a river off a collapsing burning bridge.
- In reality, the Southerners who caught the eight train-jackers hanged them.

The Gold Rush

1925, USA, United Artists, 72 minutes, B&W, Silent
Producer/Director: Charles Chaplin
Cast: Charles Chaplin, Mack Swain, Georgia Hale

"Often accepted as Chaplin's greatest comedy..." —Leslie Halliwell, *Halliwell's Filmgoer's Companion*

One of Chaplin's three greatest feature films along with *City Lights*, and *Modern Times*, the comedy was listed among the 12 best films of all time in a poll of critics by the British Film Institute in 1952. The movie contains two of Chaplin's most famous scenes as The Little Tramp: starving in the Klondike gold rush of 1898, Charlie cooks his shoe, eats the sole, relishes the laces as if they were spaghetti and sucks the nails like bones; later Charlie improvises the dance of the dinner rolls on two forks.

With a script written by Chaplin, the film begins with hundreds of gold seekers trekking up snowy Chilkoot Pass. Charlie plays The Little Tramp as a Lone Prospector. After navigating a narrow mountain ridge, he's followed by a bear into the Yukon Territory and happens upon the snowbound cabin of Big Jim McKay (Swain). The spot serves as the focus of two more humorous scenes: the delirious and hungry McKay imagines the Tramp as a big chicken that Jim wants to eat (for the scene Chaplin dons a chicken suit and perfectly acts out the mannerisms of a chicken), chasing him outside the cabin with a gun and an axe; then, after a snow-

Charlie Chaplin in *The Gold Rush*.

storm, the cabin teeters on the side of a cliff with the twosome running from end to end to keep the wobbly building from going over the edge.

At nearby Dawson, the Tramp finds the love of his life, a dance hall queen named Georgia (Hale). In the most touching and poignant scene in the film, she invites herself to dinner and Charlie goes all out for her—but she fails to show. Sadness, however, turns to joy after Big Jim and Charlie find a lucky strike and Georgia, opportunist that she is, reenters the life of the millionaire gold miner.

- Both Chaplin and Swain got sick repeatedly eating licorice shoe soles and candy nails.
- The film took 14 months to shoot, often in cold weather, around Truckee, Nevada.
- Chaplin's long-suffering cameraman was Rollie Totheroh, who shot most of Chaplin's greatest films, including *City Lights, Modern Times* and *The Great Dictator*.
- Over 1,000 extras were used for the opening scene in which prospectors form a long line up the snow-covered mountain.

Greed

1924, USA, MGM, 135 minutes, B&W, Silent
Producer: Sam Goldwyn, Director: Erich von Stroheim
Cast: Gibson Gowland, Jean Hersholt, ZaSu Pitts

"It remains not only a movie milestone, but Stroheim's own lasting monument." —Joe Franklin, *Classics of the Silent Screen*

This is the only major feature film in the history of cinema that has dared so thoroughly to show the innate carnality of man. A picnic on a concrete sewer is the metaphor for the life that unfolds for San Francisco dentist John "Doc" McTeague (Gowland), based on Frank Norris's novel entitled *McTeague*. Shot entirely on location in San Francisco, Oakland, and Death Valley, von Stroheim's lengthy classic was originally nine hours long. MGM's new production boss Irving Thalberg ordered it cut to two hours, 15 minutes.

The silent images are, in some ways, even more powerful without sound. For example, McTeague's ill-fated marriage to Trina (Pitts) begins with a funeral procession in the street outside while the wedding takes place; Trina, on her wedding night, stares at a caged canary, fearful that she too is now a prisoner—despite winning a $5,000 lottery. But the jackpot becomes the root of evil for her, McTeague, and their supposed friend Marcus (Hersholt). The frightful conclusion in the heat and sand of Death Valley is classic filmmaking.

The film effectively ended von Stroheim's directing career, though he continued to act (*Grand Illusion, Sunset Boulevard*). He reportedly said, "The man who cut my film had nothing on his mind but a hat" (said edi-

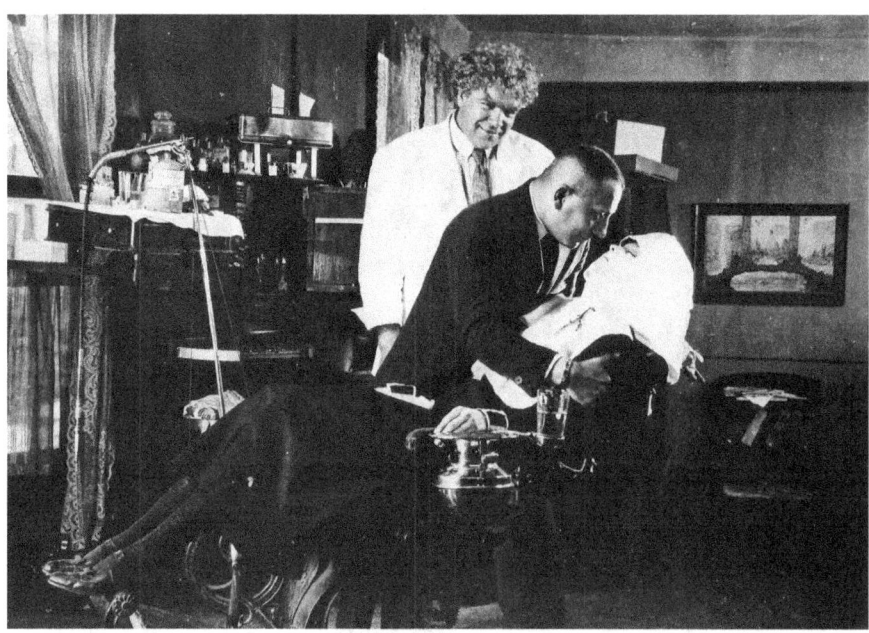

Director Erich Von Stroheim shows Gibson Gowland (left) how to handle the abuse scene with ZaSu Pitts in *Greed*.

tor was Joseph Farnham, acting on orders from Thalberg). All edited reels were melted down for the silver.

- A cook died in the 125-degree desert heat and an over-wrought cameraman was sent home. Cameras had to be soaked in ice-water which evaporated in minutes.
- Many scenes were shot at the actual locations mentioned in Norris's book. It was the first feature film to be shot completely on location.
- Jean Renoir called it "the film of films."

The King of Kings

1927, USA, Pathé Exchange, 158 minutes, B&W, Silent
Producer/Director: Cecil B. DeMille
Cast: H.B. Warner, Jacqueline Logan, Dorothy Cumming, Joseph Schildkraut, Ernest Torrence, Victor Varconi

H.B. Warner as Christ, Dorothy Cumming as the Virgin Mary, Ernest Torrence as Peter in *King of Kings*.

"The most ambitious film of the silent period."
—Charles Higham

A few years after the success of *The Ten Commandments* (1923), DeMille undertook what seemed to be the ultimate risk: a portrayal of the life of Christ. It turned out to be no risk at all—the film was a sensation, opening in April to huge crowds in New York, and in May as the premier show at Hollywood's Grauman's Chinese Theater. The popularity of the film continued into the 1930s and 1940s with reissues and churches sponsoring 16mm showings for their congregations. (As a child I saw it at a church viewing—the impression it made on me remains to this day; it was like watching newsreel footage of Jesus.)

The film was photographed by Peverell Marley who had joined Famous Players/Lasky right out of Hollywood High School. Marley, a camera bug, was a quick study of cinematography and shot the silent version of *The Ten Commandments*. (Marley would be one of the cameramen to work on DeMille's sound/color version of *The Ten Commandments* in 1956.) Marley studied many Biblical paintings and chose nearly 300 on which to base his scenes. A few sequences, including the resurrection, were shot in the early Technicolor process. The set designer was Mitchell Leisen (*The Squaw Man, The Sign of the Cross*) who built a cyclorama for the crucifixion scene, using ten big arc-lights revolving on wheels to depict drifting clouds. DeMille's long-time associate Jeanie Macpherson wrote the screenplay after researching hundreds of books about the life of Christ.

Jesus was portrayed by H.B. (Henry Byron) Warner, who was kept from the cast and crew between scenes and driven to and from the set in a car enclosed with curtains. Logan portrays Mary Magdalene, the courtesan. Cumming is the Virgin Mary, Schildkraut is Judas, Torrence is Peter, and Varconi is Pontius Pilate.

- DeMille said he kept Warner isolated to help keep him in character, but some on the set believed it was to shield Warner from criticism for his alcoholism.
- The film used about 3,000 extras.
- The scenes for the Sea of Galilee were shot at Catalina Island.
- William Boyd, who would later become B-Western hero Hopalong Cassidy, played Simon of Cyrene, the man who helped Jesus carry the cross.

Metropolis

1926, Germany, UFA, 123 minutes, B&W, Silent
Producer/Director: Fritz Lang
Cast: Brigitte Helm, Alfred Abel, Rudolph Klein-Rogge, Gustav Frohlich

"**** Classic silent-film fantasy…startling set design and special effects…"
—Leonard Maltin, *Leonard Maltin's Movie and Video Guide*

Hitler liked this film but Lang didn't like Hitler and left Germany—quickly. The plot is about dehumanization of the working-class under tyranny. Lang's futuristic sci-fi classic is brimming with symbolism like church iconography and memorable images—not the least of which is an evil robot made in the likeness of the heroine.

Based on the novel by Thea von Harbor (Lang's wife), the screenplay depicts a city 100 years into the future, an ultra-modern metropolis of skyscrapers, airships, shuttle cars and high-speed trains. The trouble is—the whole mechanized contraption is being run by slave laborers living underground!

Fiendish industrialist John Frederson (Abel) rules the city from lavish penthouse quarters while stressed-out workers toil below the streets to create his perfect world. However, his naïve son, Freder (Frohlich), discovers the truth and tries to stop the injustice. Meanwhile, a respected and saintly young woman named Maria (Helm) becomes a threat when

Gustav Frohlich and Brigitte Helm, surrounded by children, as director Fritz Lang (seated on the front of the camera cart) shoots a scene for *Metropolis*.

she leads a revolt among the workers. To head it off, a mad scientist, Dr. Rotwang (Klein-Rogge), creates a false Maria—a robot (also played by Helm)—to mislead the enslaved people.

- Probably a quarter—possibly a third—of the original film has been lost. The running time at the premiere was over three hours, but Lang later cut more than an hour himself; since that time numerous versions of varying lengths have been released.
- Over 1,000 extras were used over a production period of two years.
- The special effects were created by Eugene Schufftan who developed the "Schufftan Process" (by which live action is combined with reflected mirror images of miniatures).
- Lang fled to Paris, London, and Hollywood after the Nazis came to power.

Modern Times

1936, USA, United Artists, 85 minutes, B&W, Silent
Producer/Director: Charles Chaplin
Cast: Charles Chaplin, Paulette Goddard, Henry Bergman, Chester Conklin, Allan Garcia, Murdoch McQuarrie

> "**** One of the all-time greats, a sensational one-man show by Chaplin, writing, directing, producing, scoring, and starring in this eternal saga of everyman in all times."
> —Steven H. Scheuer

In this silent comedy classic, Chaplin plays The Little Tramp for the last time. He attacks the machine age, providing one of cinema's most famous scenes: Charlie as a factory worker trying to keep up with the assembly line, even tumbling into the cogs and ratchets of the machinery…a metaphor of how modern man has been eaten up by the work of his own hands. The movie ends with the now-famous shot of Charlie and Goddard walking away, hand-in-hand, down the middle of the highway.

This is the only major feature film whose creator was producer, director, writer, lead actor, editor, and composer of the score (including the familiar theme "Smile"). While it is a silent film, there are some sound

Charles Chaplin and Paulette Goddard in *Modern Times*.

effects (a radio, videophone, etc.) and background voices. One of the best bits is Charlie being forced by his boss to be a guinea pig for a new feeding machine invention which goes totally haywire.

Chaplin plays a Depression-era unemployed man who meets up with a pretty homeless girl, Ellen Peterson (Goddard), and together they set out to find happiness in a weary world. Conklin (a former Mack Sennett Keystone Kop with a trademark walrus mustache) is the mechanic. Bergman plays the café manager. Garcia is the president of the steel company and McQuarrie is the inventor of the feeding machine.

- The factory machinery was made of wood and rubber made to look like steel.
- This was the last silent film with title cards.
- Goddard became Chaplin's third wife.
- Chaplin said the film's purpose was to entertain, not to make a political statement.
- It was this film, with its alleged criticism of capitalism, that convinced the House Un-American Activities Committee that Chaplin was a Communist, a charge he denied. Nevertheless, Chaplin left for Switzerland where he remained until return-

ing to America in 1972 to receive an Honorary Oscar. He got the longest standing ovation in the history of the Academy Awards.

Nosferatu

1922, Germany, Prana Films, 104 minutes, B&W, Silent
Producer/Director: F.W. Murnau
Cast: Max Schreck, Greta Schroder, Gustav von Wangenheim

> "(A) silent masterpiece."
> —Mike Clark, *USA Today*

Max Schreck as the vampire in the silent classic *Nosferatu*.

This classic silent-film version of the famous Bram Stoker novel is only somewhat similar to the most famous version of the vampire story, Tod Browning's *Dracula* (1931) starring Bela Lugosi. Schreck as Count Dracula is infinitely more hideous: skeleton-thin, whitened face, sunken eyes, pointy teeth, bald head, and elongated fingernails.

Jonathan Harker (Von Wangenheim) is a real estate agent sent from Bremen to a castle in Transylvania to attempt to sell the Count's land near the Harker house. From a photograph, the Count is overcome with the beauty of Harker's wife Nina (Schroder) and makes the deal, in order to get close to her. Later, during his seduction of Nina, she realizes she must sacrifice herself, sexually, to destroy the embodiment of evil.

Highlights: the visit to the Carpathian castle, rats leaving the earthen-filled coffin, the contaminated ship, the phantom ship entering the harbor, the plague in the city, Nosferatu carrying his coffin through the streets, the vampire overtaking Nina, Nosferatu's disappearance at daybreak.

- Nosferatu is Romanian for "undead."
- Schreck's name reportedly means "terror." Max made about a dozen films but never exceeded his triumph as the vampire.
- Friedrich Wilhelm Murnau (*Sunrise*, 1927) died in a car wreck in 1931; he had been in the midst of contract negotiations with Paramount.
- The Munich Film Museum believes they have fully restored the print with the original color tints, 28 lost shots, and 115 titles.

Pandora's Box (Lulu)

1929, Germany, Nero Film, 110 minutes, Silent
Producer/Director: G.W. Pabst
Cast: Louise Brooks, Fritz Kortner, Franz Lederer, Carl Goetz, Alice Roberts, Gustav Diesel, Krafft Raschig

> "Above everything else in this film, one remembers the exceptional personality of Louise Brooks."
> —Georges Sadoul, *Dictionary of Films*

After appearing in 13 rather insignificant films for Paramount, Brooks walked out on her contract and was taken to Europe by German

Louise Brooks, star of *Pandora's Box*, was one of the most fascinating screen personalities of the 20s and 30s.

director G.W. (Georg Wilhelm) Pabst who had been impressed with her work in Howard Hawks' *A Girl in Every Port* (1928). Pabst wanted her for writer Frank Wedekind's sexually-free spirit in *Pandora's Box*. (In Greek mythology the gods created the first woman, Pandora, who carried a box containing all evil intentions and maladies; she opens the box and unleashes the afflictions on the human world.)

After 24 films, Brooks became a recluse but then a cult figure in the 60s and 70s when she wrote articles about moviemaking and a book about her experiences (*Lulu in Hollywood,* 1974). Andrew Sarris, critic for *The Village Voice,* called her "One of the most enduringly fascinating women ever to appear on the screen." She died in 1985.

In this strange tale of carnal lust and murder, Lulu (Brooks), a nymphomaniac, makes her wealthy lover Dr. Ludwig Schon (Kortner) marry her but his son Alwa (Lederer) falls in love with her. Ludwig is accidentally killed by Lulu in a struggle with a gun. Soon she descends into poverty and prostitution. She accepts payment for sex to take care of Alwa and a pimp named Schigolch (Goetz).

Roberts plays Countess Anna Geschwitz who is sexually drawn to Lulu and engages her in an erotic dance. Raschig is muscle builder Rodrigo and Diesel is Jack the Ripper.

- After *Pandora's Box* and *Diary of a Lost Girl* (1929), also for Pabst, Brooks returned to Hollywood but found that breaking her contract with a major studio had poisoned her career which eventually faded to black by 1939. Her last film was a B-Western with John Wayne, *Overland Stage Raiders.*
- The part of the Countess is believed to be the first on-screen lesbian role. Roberts was not a lesbian and was reluctant to play the part.
- Lulu's outfit at the end was really Brooks' but Pabst had it soiled and scuffed up to make her appear down-and-out.
- The "bob" hairstyle is still referred to as a "Lulu."

The Phantom of the Opera

1925, USA, Universal, 79 minutes, B&W, Silent
Producer: Carl Laemmle, Director: Rupert Julian
Cast: Lon Chaney, Mary Philbin, Norman Kerry, Arthur Edmund Carewe

> "One of the greatest of horror films, and certainly the pinnacle of the genre in the silent era."
> —Clive Hirschhorn, *The Universal Story*

Even today, though parts of the film seem hokey by modern standards, the unmasking scene is viewed by many as brilliant. Chaney, a master of make-up, is Erik: a mistreated musician who becomes Erik the Phantom, residing in the catacombs and dungeons underneath the Paris Opera House during the 19th century. The hideously disfigured madman, who falls in love with operatic understudy Christine (Philbin), devises a diabolical plot as revenge against those he believes are responsible for his miserable existence in the bowels of the earth.

Lon Chaney as *The Phantom of the Opera*.

Kerry plays Raoul, Mary's fiancé. Carewe is Ledoux of the secret police. The plot is taken from Gaston Laroux's 1910 novel of the same name. The film was reissued in 1930 with a few sound portions added. Though Julian directed the bulk of the picture, he and Chaney didn't get along well, and by the end Edward Sedgwick (uncredited) came aboard to film the final chase sequence. The story was remade by Universal, in color, with Claude Rains as Erik in 1943; Nelson Eddy co-starred.

- Chaney's grotesque, skull-like make-up consisted of a wire clip to push up his nostrils, celluloid filler for his cheeks and drops to dilate his eyes.
- Set designer Charles Hall (*Frankenstein, Dracula*) built an exact replica of the Paris Opera House (seating 3,000) on the back-lot at Universal.
- Some scenes are in Technicolor.
- Chaney, son of deaf-mutes, was billed as "The Man of a Thousand Faces." He was the subject of a film by that title in 1957 with James Cagney as Chaney.

Safety Last

1923, USA, Hal Roach Studios/Pathé, 65 minutes, B&W, Silent
Producer: Hal Roach, Directors: Fred Newmeyer, Sam Taylor
Cast: Harold Lloyd, Mildred Davis, Bill Strother, Noah Young, Westcott Clarke

> "Harold Lloyd's first complete masterpiece and one that made him world-famous as the timid 'ordinary guy' in spectacles who is always inadvertently getting involved in dangerous stunts."
> —Georges Sadoul, *The Dictionary of Films*

The comedy was made at a time when daring men called "human flies" would scale tall buildings, drawing street crowds. Lloyd saw one, Bill Strother, and was so impressed with the stunt and the reaction it got that he decided to do a picture around just such an incident. He later hired Strother to double for him in the wall climb in this film, though Lloyd did his own stunt atop the building, a gag that has become famous.

Harold Lloyd in *Safety Last*.

Harold plays a small-town guy who leaves his fiancée (Davis) to make his fortune in the big city and gets a job as a clerk in a department store. He gets involved in a publicity stunt for the store that sends him up a skyscraper. The stunt takes up a third of the picture.

There is no trick photography here, and processed backgrounds had not been figured out yet. Lloyd *really* hangs off the side of a building, or the façade of a building he had built on top of a real building. There was a wooden platform with a mattress 15 feet below him but had he fallen he might have bounced off—as a dummy did during one of the tests. What made it all the more dangerous and impressive was that Lloyd had lost his right thumb and index finger in 1919 when a bomb accidentally exploded during a photo shoot. In each of his post-1920 films, including this one, he wore a five-fingered rubber glove housing a prosthetic device. This made his climb that much harder since his left hand did most of the work, and Lloyd was born right-handed.

The highlight of the stunt is when a giant clock cracks open leaving Harold dangling from the clock hands. But there's still a 'topper:' catching his foot in the rope sent down to save him, Lloyd swings wide, upside down, to the top of the building. Even today, in the age of special effects, the gag draws gasps.

Strother plays Harold's pal, Young is the cop, and Clarke is the floorwalker.

- Mildred Davis became Mrs. Lloyd after this film wrapped shooting.
- Harold made over 200 films, more than Chaplin and Keaton combined, and received an Honorary Academy Award in 1952.
- Lloyd became a millionaire, hitting the big-time when he created a straw hat wearing college-boy character in horn-rim glasses without lenses.
- His Greenacres estate (now 1740 Greenacres Place) remains one of the showcase properties in Beverly Hills. The 44-room mansion was built in 1929 and Lloyd lived there until his death in 1971. Once a venue for tourists, the estate is now privately owned.

Sherlock Jr.

1924, USA, Metro, 45 minutes, B&W, Silent
Producers: Buster Keaton, Joseph Schenck; Director: Buster Keaton
Cast: Buster Keaton, Kathryn McGuire, Ward Crane, Ford West, Joseph Keaton, Erwin Connolly, Jane Connelly

> "Keaton's *tour de force* and perhaps his most perfect exercise in the 'comedy of objects' of which he was a master…"
> —John Baxter, *Sixty Years of Hollywood*

In *Sherlock Jr.*, Keaton is a movie projectionist who dreams of becoming a detective. Some of the gags include Keaton standing between two train boxcars as they slam together, just missing him (Keaton really did this dangerous stunt himself after measuring exactly how much space he had to work with); while sleeping in the projection room, he dreams he's on the screen and his "soul" jumps into the picture with every change the setting becomes real and he's suddenly participating in a new situation like leaping off a rock into water in one scene and landing in a snowdrift in the next; later, as a sleuth, he leaps into a suitcase carried by a woman in a long dress—all done entirely without camera tricks.

Buster Keaton in *Sherlock Jr.*

West plays the theatre manager and doubles as the old woman with the suitcase. Crane plays the villain. McGuire is The Girl, Jane Connelly is her Mother, Joseph Keaton (Buster's real father) plays The Father, and Erwin Connelly is the butler and the handyman.

Keaton's films found a new generation in the 1960s, first in Europe, then back in the States. His last public appearance was at the Venice Film Festival in 1965, where he received a standing ovation. He died a few months later.

- In the suitcase illusion, the man holding the suitcase actually only has his head showing through a hole in the fence. Underneath is a trapdoor concealed by the dress. Buster leaps into the stomach of the dress and simply goes through another larger hole in the fence.
- Young Joe Keaton got his nickname from neighbor Harry Houdini, the famous magician, who called the youngster "Buster" because he likened the busy kid to a tornado; Buster often ran around doing somersaults and handstands. He later became a member of his parents' vaudeville acrobatic comedy act.

- "Only an artist aware of the complex appeal to fantasy in cinema could have conceived *Sherlock Jr.,* the most philosophically eloquent of silent comedies."—David Thomson, *A Biographical Dictionary of Film*

Sunrise

1927, USA, Fox, 97 minutes, B/W, Silent
Producer: William Fox, Director: F.W. Murnau
Cast: Janet Gaynor, George O'Brien, Margaret Livingston

> "Lyrical melodrama, superbly handled: generally considered among the finest Hollywood productions of the twenties."
> —Ruth Halliwell and John Walker, *Halliwell's Film Guide*

Produced just ahead of *The Jazz Singer*, but with far fewer sound elements, *Sunrise* has the right to claim that it's Hollywood's first sound film, though the Al Jolson classic generally claims that honor. The difference is, *Sunrise* is far superior to *The Jazz Singer* in plot, acting, and production techniques. There is little sound in *Sunrise* but it *is* in there, mainly as sound effects—traffic noise, voices of the crowd and, particularly, the voice of one driver in the midst of downtown traffic as the lead players emerge in the big city.

But that is not the only technical achievement for *Sunrise*. The film won the first Academy Award for cinematography, done by cameramen Charles Rosher and Earl Struss. "Its style is dominated by fluid camera movements that are so masterfully handled that they also seem invisible."—Georges Sadoul, *Dictionary of Films*.

Gaynor won the first Academy Award for Best Actress for her role as the wife of a rural man (O'Brien). He gets seduced by an evil city woman (Livingston) who persuades him to murder his wife.

Opening title: "This story of a man and his wife is of nowhere and everywhere, you might hear it anywhere and at any time. For everywhere, *the sun rises and sets*—in the city's turmoil or under the open sky on the farm, life is much the same, sometimes bitter, sometimes sweet, tears and laughter, sin and forgiveness."

George O'Brien and Margaret Livingston in the seduction scene from *Sunrise*.

- In 1989 the film was one of the first 25 named to the National Film registry, which was created by the Library of Congress to promote film preservation.
- Gaynor starred in the 1937 classic *A Star is Born*.
- O'Brien became a popular B-Western star in the thirties.
- Livingston later became the fourth and last wife of bandleader Paul Whiteman.
- Murnau gained fame in his native Germany by directing the horror classic *Nosferatu* in 1922. In 1931, at age 42, he died in a car crash in California.
- William Fox began with a penny arcade in Brooklyn and turned it into a chain of movie theaters which became Fox Film Corporation. In 1935 Fox merged with 20th Century. His name also lives on today in television as the Fox Cable Channel and the Fox News/Business channels.

British Classics

Black Narcissus

1947, UK, The Archers, 100 minutes, Color
Producers/Directors: Michael Powell, Emeric Pressburger
Cast: Deborah Kerr, David Farrar, Sabu, Kathleen Byron, Jean Simmons, Flora Robson

> "...one of the cinema's most beautiful films, a visual and emotional stunner..."
> —Ruth Halliwell and John Walker, *Halliwell's Film Guide*

It's such a striking film; it's as if it were colored with colored chalks. It won Oscars for the work done by cinematographer Jack Cardiff and art director Alfred Junge. The New York Film Critics named Deborah Kerr Best Actress for her role as Sister Clodagh. The film, based on the novel of the same name by Rumer Godden, is backed by the emotionally-charged music of Brian Easdale (*The Red Shoes*).

The spellbinding plot of this atmospheric horror-thriller compresses the torment of isolation, the struggle between carnal and spiritual, and the unbalanced perception that comes from seeing things as one wishes them to be. Five Anglican nuns are assigned the task of establishing a mission and clinic in the hidden Himalayas. The building however has an inauspicious past; it formerly housed the harem for a potentate. Serenity is not to be as the lives of the nuns and the others in the mountain community are hindered by an oppressive climate—and their very inner beings are soon shattered among the mists, flowers and sunsets, and the brooding routine of work and heavy darkness.

Kathleen Byron and David Farrar in *Black Narcissus*.

Clodagh is the leader of the group from Calcutta. Byron is the neurotic and mad Sister Ruth. Robson is Sister Philippa. Simmons is Kanchi, a bewitching adolescent orphan. Farrar is the handsome but stoic British agent, Mr. Dean. Sabu plays the Young General Dilip Rai, who wears a strange, alluring scent called—Black Narcissus.

- Powell, Pressburger and their Archers production company produced about two dozen unusual films between 1942-1957, including *The Red Shoes,* an internationally popular hit in 1948.
- The whole amazing set, with buildings overlooking a cliff and forest, was built in a production studio in England.
- Sabu was working as a stable boy in India when he was discovered by Alexander Korda for his film *Elephant Boy.*

Dead of Night

1945, UK, Ealing, 104 minutes, B&W
Producer: Michael Balcon, Directors: Basil Dearden, Alberto Cavalcanti, Robert Hamer, Charles Crichton

Cast: Michael Redgrave, Mervyn Johns, Googie Withers, Sally Ann Howes, Roland Culver, Frederick Valk, Ralph Michael, Anthony Baird, Judy Kelly, Michael Allan, Basil Radford, Naunton Wayne, Barbara Leake, Mary Merrall, Miles Malleson

> "Much has been written about Michael Redgrave's brilliant, hair-raising performance as the schizophrenic ventriloquist."
>
> —Jerry Vermilye, *The Great British Films*

This picture is one of the finest British horror films of the forties and actually consists of five supernatural tales linked by one set-piece. The "linking story" features a little middle-aged architect, Walter Craig (Johns), who has a recurring nightmare. He is awakened by a phone call from a man named Eliot Foley (Culver) who says a mutual acquaintance has recommended Craig to do some work on Foley's country home, Pilgrim's Farm. Craig accepts the invitation to come down for the weekend to look the place over. Upon arriving, Craig meets several people also

Michael Redgrave as the mad ventriloquist in *Dead of Night*.

staying at the country home and finds he knows the guests *even though he has never met them before!* Craig tells them about his feeling of *déjà vu* and, subsequently, each person volunteers his own strange experience. As it so happens, one of the guests is a psychiatrist named Dr. Van Straaten (Valk) who offers his interpretation of each episode.

Two of the stories are directed by Cavalcanti: "The Ventriloquist's Dummy" and "The Christmas Ghost." In "The Ventriloquist's Dummy" a small-time vent, Maxwell Frere (Redgrave), believes his dummy talks back to him. "The Christmas Ghost" is about an encounter with a spirit from the past.

The other three segments are: "The Haunted Mirror," "The Hearse Driver," and "The Golfers." The various characters are: Joan Cortland (Withers), Peter Cortland (Michael), Sally O'Hara (Howes), Mrs. O'Hara (Leake), Mrs. Foley (Merrall), Hugh Grainger (Baird), Joyce Grainger (Kelly), Jimmy Watson (Allan), George Parratt (Radford), Larry Potter (Wayne), and the hearse driver (Malleson).

- Dearden does the linking narration.
- Ealing Studios, created by Michael Balcon and writer T.E.B. Clarke, is now occupied by the BBC.
- Radford and Wayne, featured in "The Golfers," first played their comedic characters in Hitchcock's *The Lady Vanishes* (1938). They reprised the characters previously in *Night Train to Munich* (1940).
- U.S. distributors cut out the golfing story because they felt that the comedy segment didn't fit with the rest of the film.
- The 1978 film *Magic* with Anthony Hopkins is a rip-off of "The Ventriloquist's Dummy."

Great Expectations

1947, UK, Cineguild, 118 minutes, B&W,
Producer: Ronald Neame, Director: David Lean
Cast: John Mills, Valerie Hobson, Francis L. Sullivan, Finlay Currie, Martita Hunt, Jean Simmons, Anthony Wager, Alec Guinness

> "Dickens' novel has been filmed several times, but never with such definition, pace, and attention to detail as in the deluxe version directed by David Lean…"
> —Leslie Halliwell, *Halliwell's Filmgoer's Companion*

British Classics   41

Alec Guinness and John Mills in *Great Expectations*.

This mysterious Charles Dickens tale concerns an orphan boy named Pip (Wager) who becomes enchanted by a beautiful but mean-spirited young girl named Estella (Simmons) who is the adopted daughter of a rich but vengeful spinster-recluse Miss Havisham (Hunt). For no apparent reason, Pip becomes the recipient of a great deal of financial assistance from a secret benefactor, someone who has told officiating attorney Jaggers (Sullivan) that Pip is seen as "a young man of great expectations."

Pip soon moves to London to learn to be a gentleman. (Pip as a young adult is played by Mills.) Estella too, goes to become a lady. (Hobson plays her as a young woman.) After returning from their youthful studies, Pip and Estella meet again. Pip has always loved her despite her horrible demeanor. Estella continues to live in Miss Havisham's deteriorating mansion.

It is Pip's friend Herbert Pocket (Guinness) who informs Pip about the secret of the Havisham household. Miss Havisham had continued living in the house 25 years after her fiancé walked out on her on the day of their intended marriage. The broken-hearted woman left her main room intact all those years, even the wedding cake and decorations, dusty and decaying. Out of revenge she adopted Estella and taught her to hate and despise men. It is into this implausible situation that Pip brings his love for Estella, a woman he has so strangely come to adore.

The opening scene is one of the best ever filmed, as young Pip walks on a wintry night through a graveyard to place flowers on his mother's grave, when suddenly he is confronted by an escaped convict he comes to know as Abel Magwitch (Currie).

The film was nominated for Best Picture, Lean was nominated for Best Director, and Guy Green won the Academy Award for his photography. John Bryan and Wilfred Shingleton won for sets/art direction.

- Neame also worked on the screenplay with Lean and Anthony Havelock-Allan. In fact, they received an Oscar nomination for their effort.
- Hobson was married to Havelock-Allan.
- Simmons was 17 when the picture was filmed.
- This was the first of six films Guinness made with Lean.
- Hunt originally played the role on-stage, which Lean saw and liked.
- If you think you've seen the very unusual face of Currie before, you have: he was one of the magi in Wyler's *Ben-Hur*.
- That's really St. Paul's Cathedral in the background when Pip arrives in London. Lean felt it was easier to shoot in front of the famous old church rather than reproduce it in a studio.

Hamlet

1948, UK, J. Arthur Rank, 155 minutes, B&W
Producer/Director: Laurence Olivier
Cast: Laurence Olivier, Jean Simmons, Eileen Herlie, Basil Sydney, Felix Aylmer

> "Be you 9 or 90, a PhD or just plain Joe, *Hamlet* is the movie of the year."
> —*The Washington Times*

> "To be, or not to be: that is the question." – Act 5, Scene 1

Sir Laurence Olivier, who was knighted in 1947, as *Hamlet*.

The Shakespearean tragedy won both the British Academy and the U.S. Academy Award for Best Picture. Olivier won the Oscar for Best Actor as the pensive, introspective Prince of Denmark in addition to an Academy Award nomination for Best Director. The film also won Oscars for costumes and art direction.

The plot in a nutshell: a ghost haunting Elsinore Castle turns out to be the former king and Hamlet's father. He returned to tell his son that he was murdered by Claudius (Sydney), now the new king. Not surprisingly, the former king seeks to have his death avenged. Hamlet's mother Gertrude (Herlie) has married the new king, further complicating matters. In the midst of all this, Hamlet has fallen in love with the beautiful but mad Ophelia (Simmons), daughter of the Lord Chamberlain Polonius (Aylmer). The story culminates in a duel at the end which includes a rapier with a poisoned tip and a poisoned cup of wine. Who gets the wine and who gets the rapier thrust is where it all leads.

Many, if not most, Shakespeare buffs place *Hamlet* at the top of the Bard's best works. The drama was written circa 1600 and first published in 1603. As to the film presentation, it is quite possibly Olivier's finest performance. Charlton Heston called Sir Laurence the greatest stage and screen actor of the twentieth century. Examining Olivier's record of awards, it is easy to suggest the Old Vic Theatre veteran did bypass all others with numerous stage awards, the Oscar for *Hamlet*, one for Best Supporting Actor (*Marathon Man*), and nine other nominations.

- *Hamlet* was the first non-American film to win the Oscar for Best Picture.
- The film played successfully in the U.S. at selected theaters on a reserved-seat basis with increased ticket prices.
- The characters Rosencrantz and Guildenstern were cut.
- Simmons was only 18 at the time of filming.
- Olivier has distinctive corn silk hair. For the film he bleached it so people "would forget it was Olivier they were seeing and only see Hamlet."

The Lady Vanishes

1938, UK, Gaumont British, 97 minutes, B&W
Producer: Edward Black, Director: Alfred Hitchcock
Cast: Margaret Lockwood, Michael Redgrave, Dame May Whitty, Paul Lukas, Naunton Wayne, Basil Radford, Catherine Lacey, Mary Clare, Philip Leaver

> "A classic of its kind."
>
> —*TV Guide*

Hitchcock won the New York Film Critics Award for Best Director for this spy-thriller set on a moving train. An American girl, Iris Henderson (Lockwood), is on a sightseeing trip on a trans-European train from the Balkans to England when a snowstorm delays the trip at a village.

Michael Redgrave and Margaret Lockwood in *The Lady Vanishes*.

Staying overnight at a lodge, Iris encounters a bevy of strange people, including a kindly English governess named Miss Froy (Whitty) who befriends her. The next morning Iris receives an unknown knock on the head while about to board the train. Once the train is underway again, Iris' bump causes her to fall asleep with Miss Froy sitting across from her in a train compartment. Upon awakening from the nap, Iris learns that the elderly lady has vanished and nobody knows what happened to her. In fact they all say they never even saw her.

The plot is heavy with Nazi spies—and a good English spy in their midst. The rigmarole includes a musicologist (Redgrave), a magician (Leaver), a nun (Lacey), a baroness (Clare), a brain surgeon (Lukas), and two cricket fans (Wayne and Radford) for comedic relief.

Redgrave, as Gilbert (his screen debut in a leading role), is the only person on the train willing to help Iris find out what's going on. However he has an ulterior motive; he wants to become romantically involved with the pretty Miss Henderson.

- The film was shot in the, as Lockwood described it, "cramped" Islington Studios in London. The whole set was only 90 ft. long.
- The story, taken from Ethel Lina White's novel "The Wheel Spins," was based on an actual incident in 1880—of course, the script was updated with the Nazi aspect.
- The project was originally planned for director Roy William Neill as part of the Sherlock Holmes series. Neill still used the germ of the idea in his Holmes film *Terror By Night*.
- Wayne and Radford reprise their bits in *Dead of Night* (1945).
- Selznick saw the film and offered Hitchcock a Hollywood contract.
- Orson Welles saw the film about a dozen times.
- French critic/director Francois Truffaut said it was his favorite Hitchcock film.

Oliver!

1968, UK, Romulus/Columbia, 146 minutes, Color
Producer: John Woolf, Director: Carol Reed
Cast: Ron Moody, Mark Lester, Oliver Reed, Shani Wallis, Jack Wild, Harry Secombe, Joseph O'Conor, Hugh Griffith, Leonard Rossiter

> "…a brash, colorful, and boundlessly energetic expansion of Lionel Bart's popular stage musical based on the novel by Charles Dickens…*Oliver!* was a healthy box-office success and it remains a lasting favourite."
> —Clive Hirschhorn, *The Columbia Story*

Winner of seven Academy Awards, including Best Picture and Best Director, *Oliver!* was the perfect film to top off the golden age of movie musicals. It was so good and so successful that one wonders why Hollywood gave up producing musicals; the best guess is that musicals were part of an age of fantasy and innocence that the 1960s generation shattered.

Moody, the finest Fagin of all time, was nominated for Best Actor and 15-year-old Wild, as the Artful Dodger, was nominated for Best Supporting Actor. Everybody and everything in this film is first-rate. Onna White received a Special Academy Award for her outstanding choreography. Two remarkable production pieces, "Consider Yourself" and "Who

Carol Reed directing Mark Lester as *Oliver!*

Will Buy?" set the highest standards for future musicals. The latter piece, set in a market garden, is a seven-minute array of everything from prancing parsons and acrobats to vegetable vendors and a steam train!

Ten-year-old Lester is Oliver Twist, the boy brought up in a nineteenth century London workhouse (with the temerity to ask for more food), who is sold to work in a funeral parlor, but escapes and falls in with a gang of young pickpockets—led by Fagin. Reed is the most menacing Bill Sikes you'll ever see and Wallis, as girlfriend Nancy, develops her character with spunk and gusto. All of the supporting players are extremely good: Secombe as Mr. Bumble, Griffith as the inebriated Magistrate, Rossiter as Mr. Sowerberry, the equally-drunk undertaker; and O'Conor as Mr. Brownlow, the man who saves Oliver from future tragedy.

Some of the great songs include: "Food, Glorious Food," "Boy For Sale," "Where Is Love?," "Pick A Pocket Or Two," "As Long As He Needs Me," "It's A Fine Life," "Reviewing The Situation," "I'd Do Anything," and "Be Back Soon."

- Bart couldn't read music! He sang his created melodies to a pianist who set them to music.
- The cast included more than 80 boys who variously appeared in selected scenes.
- Lester became a doctor in England.
- Reed was the nephew of the director.
- Moody played Fagin on-stage in England and America. At the end of the show, while still in costume, he would take the dog "Bulls-eye" for a stroll through the audience with turned-up hat asking for hand-outs, much to the delight of the crowd.

The Red Shoes

1948, UK, The Archers/Eagle-Lion Films, 136 minutes, Color
Producer: J. A. Rank, Directors: Michael Powell, Emeric Pressburger
Cast: Moira Shearer, Anton Walbrook, Marius Goring, Robert Helpmann, Albert Basserman, Leonide Massine

> "...a visually splendid and captivating film...striking imagery...exciting color cinematography...beautiful dancing... exotic behind-the-scenes atmosphere..."
> —Frank N. Magill, *Magill's Survey of Cinema*

Based on the fairytale by Hans Christian Andersen, the film was both a critical success and a box-office smash, running for two years to packed houses at New York's Bijou Theater. It was Oscar-nominated for Best Picture. It is *the* essential movie about ballet.

Jack Cardiff's photography (and Hein Heckroth's art direction) provided one of the screen's finest color films. *The Great British Films* called it "artful, paint-box Technicolor." Natalie Kalmus of the Technicolor Company said it was the best example of three-strip Technicolor. Mike Clark, *USA Today*, called it "the most beautiful color film ever." (However, there

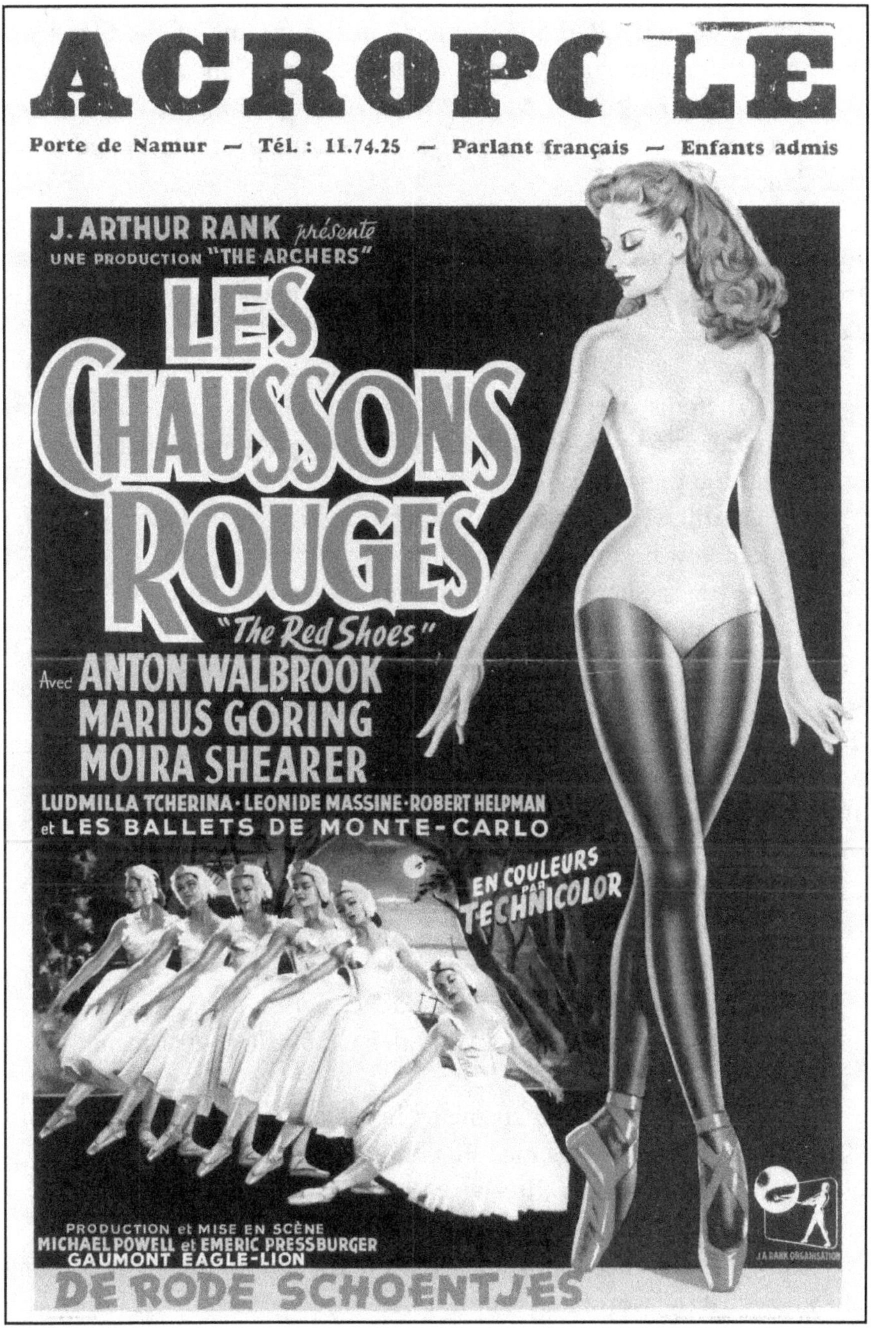
ACROPOLE
Porte de Namur — Tél. : 11.74.25 — Parlant français — Enfants admis
J. ARTHUR RANK présente
UNE PRODUCTION "THE ARCHERS"
LES CHAUSSONS ROUGES
"The Red Shoes"
Avec ANTON WALBROOK
MARIUS GORING
MOIRA SHEARER
LUDMILLA TCHERINA · LEONIDE MASSINE · ROBERT HELPMAN
et LES BALLETS DE MONTE-CARLO
EN COULEURS PAR TECHNICOLOR
PRODUCTION et MISE EN SCÈNE
MICHAEL POWELL et EMERIC PRESSBURGER
GAUMONT EAGLE-LION
DE RODE SCHOENTJES

is another film to challenge it: Jack Cardiff's *Black Narcissus*, also directed by Powell and Pressburger.)

The 15-minute "Red Shoes Ballet" in the middle of the film used more than 50 dancers and is pure cinematic magic: Shearer, as Victoria Page, with dark red hair and milky white skin—and marvelous dancing skill—is glorious to watch as the ballerina wearing the fantastic red shoes that dance her to death.

Walbrook is the martinet impressario, Boris Lermontov. Goring is Julian Craster, Vicky's composer-husband, who wants to take her away from the dance before it's too late. Helpmann plays Ivan, Basserman is Sergei and Massine is Grischa.

- When discovered, Scottish-born Shearer was a 21-year-old dancer in the Sadler's Wells Ballet Company, and second to Margot Fonteyn.
- Cardiff went to many ballet shows over several weeks to figure out how best to shoot the film.
- At times, Shearer was suspended in a harness for hours to provide some of the more uncanny dance moves for the film.

Things to Come

1936, UK, London Films, 93 minutes, B&W
Producer: Alexander Korda, Director: William Cameron Menzies
Cast: Raymond Massey, Ralph Richardson, Cedric Hardwicke, Margaretta Scott, Pearl Argyle, Ann Todd, Edward Chapman

> "The result is a visually superb science fiction film."
> —Robin Karney and Joel W. Finler, *Chronicle of the Cinema*

Korda was really quite visionary in choosing the H.G. Wells story "The Shape of Things to Come." England was still in depression with war clouds on the horizon just three years away. The film begins with a peaceful Christmas scenario when suddenly the world is plunged into war.

But the Wells vision looked far beyond the immediate crisis, looking ahead to what the world might be like a hundred years into the future—to 2036. Keep in mind, this was before World War II, before the United Nations, before the atom bomb, before the moon landing and space explora-

tion, and long before computer technology. Consequently, some scenes appear tame and inconsequential by comparison with the real world. In the film, people worry about not having gas masks (not underground shelters to shield them from nuclear attack). The end of the film has scientists concerned about whether they can make it to the moon, which seems obtuse by comparison. And, in his final speech, Massey—as critic Danny Peary rightly observes—appears more like a lunatic than a benevolent dictator.

In spite of its archaic prose, *Things to Come* has much to offer and has been an inspiration to sci-fi writers and movie special effects people worldwide. The space-age city and crafts are captivating. There are battle scenes about as good as it gets. The five-minute industrial production/march of progress montage is remarkable even today. Credit, mostly, special effects expert Ned Mann who did the silent version of *The Thief of Bagdad*; but also credit Menzies who went on to become a very good production man in Hollywood. Menzies worked on *Gone with the Wind*; he filmed the burning of Atlanta and handled the high crane-camera shot of bodies in the streets.

Massey plays confederation leader John Cabal and, later, Oswald Cabal. "Cabal" is a most appropriate word choice since it means a number of persons secretly united for some private purpose: an intrigue, a plot. Massey's character would have you believe the purpose is world peace. But at what price? Some see the story as communistic in theory; others perceive it as the making of another secret society, promoting international globalism. It is doubtful that either Wells, Korda, or Menzies had such ideas in mind.

Richardson plays The Boss, a tyrant. Scott does dual roles as Roxana and Rowena. Hardwicke is Theotocopulos, Todd is Mary Gordon, Argyle is Catherine Cabal, and Chapman is Passworthy.

- Wells, who also wrote the sci-fi classics *The Time Machine* and *War of the Worlds*, didn't like the film, even though he worked on the screenplay with Lajos Biro.
- Over a quarter-million dollars was spent on the movie, quite a lot in those days.
- Ernest Thesiger (Dr. Pretorius in *The Bride of Frankenstein*) was originally assigned the role of Theotocopulos but Korda decided they needed a more familiar name and brought in Hardwicke.

The Third Man

1949, UK, British Films, 104 minutes, B&W
Producers: Alexander Korda, David O. Selznick; Director: Carol Reed
Cast: Joseph Cotten, Orson Welles, Trevor Howard, Alida Valli, Bernard Lee, Wilfred Hyde-White

> "...Reed, in the best Alfred Hitchcock tradition, has wrought a complex masterpiece, adding layers of subtlety and suggestion, as well as characteristic imaginative Reed touches in the movie's visual imagery."
> —Jerry Vermilye, *The Great British Films*

The British Academy voted it Best Picture while in America Reed got an Oscar nomination for Best Director and cameraman Robert Krasker won the Academy Award for Best Cinematography. Graham Greene's original story and screenplay about corruption in postwar Vienna was shot on location in five weeks with day and night units in Vienna.

Orson Welles, Carol Reed and Joseph Cotten, on the set of *The Third Man*.

Cotten narrating the opening line: "I never knew the old Vienna before the war, with its Strauss music, its glamour and easy charm…Constantinople suited me better."

The devastation of the militarily divided city was the perfect atmosphere for a mystery-thriller about moral decay. Krasker's angled shots added just the right dimension for the crooked Harry Lime (Welles) who doesn't appear until halfway through the picture. His hideaway and demise in the baroque sewers of Vienna is symbolic of a rat. Holly Martins (Cotten), a broke American writer of Westerns, is called to Vienna to do some work for his old friend, Lime, who—unbeknown to Holly—has sunk into the black market…and has been—allegedly—killed!

Harry, talking to Martins on the great Ferris wheel, trying to explain why he, Lime, chose a life of crime: "In Italy for 30 years under the Borgias they had warfare, terror, murder, bloodshed. They produced Michelangelo, Leonardo da Vinci and the Renaissance. In Switzerland they had brotherly love, 500 years of democracy and peace. And what did that produce?—the cuckoo clock! So long Holly." (Welles wrote the speech himself.)

Howard is Major Calloway, a military investigator; his aide is Sergeant Paine (Lee). Hyde-White (Pickering in *My Fair Lady*) is Mr. Crabbin, head of the local book club. Anna Schmidt (Valli) loves Harry; soon Holly falls in love with her, too.

- Anton Karas' "The Third Man Theme," played on a zither, became a hit recording. Reed and Howard stumbled upon Karas playing his instrument outside a Viennese café; Karas made so much money on the tune that he bought the café!
- There was no train: it was a cardboard silhouette, with added steam and train sounds.
- In the final scene, Cotten lights a cigarette as Valli does a long walk past him, toward the camera, with autumn's leaves falling from a corridor of lifeless trees. Cotten literally didn't know if she would stop and talk to him, Reed told her not to. And prop men on high ladders, out of view, tossed the leaves.
- Lee became "M" in the James Bond series.
- Welles, needing cash to finance *Othello*, took $100,000 instead of 20% of the profits, a decision he later regretted. The film was a major international hit.

The 39 Steps

1935, UK, Gaumont-British Pictures, 82 minutes, B&W
Producer: Michael Balcon, Director: Alfred Hitchcock
Cast: Robert Donat, Madeleine Carroll, Lucie Mannheim, Godfrey Tearle, Peggy Ashcroft, Wylie Watson, John Laurie

> "The extraordinarily fast pace, tensions and surprises of the plot, mingled with black humour, add up to one of the most amazing British films of the period."
> —Joel W. Finler, *All-Time Movie Favorites*

Hitchcock used this device a lot: an innocent man caught up in treachery. In this case, Canadian tourist Richard Hannay (Donat) visiting London helps a woman out of a riotous situation in a music hall only to learn she is on the run from spies—members of a secret society known as "The 39 Steps." Her name is Annabelle Smith (Mannheim). To escape two men on her trail, the attractive Miss Smith asks Hannay if she may come home with him, and does. But after spending the night, she ends up with a knife in her back, laden by a killer who sneaked through a window.

Madeleine Carroll and Robert Donat in *The 39 Steps*.

Hannay finds a map in her grasp with a place encircled in Scotland. When Hannay sees the strange men outside his flat, obviously waiting for him, Richard makes his getaway. The trouble is, when police find the body of the dead woman, the search is on for the running man.

The chase begins on a train and ends up in the Scottish Highlands where Hannay encounters an overbearing and jealous farmer (Laurie) and his pretty young wife, Margaret (Ashcroft). Hannay receives lodging for the night—and in one of the most fascinating scenes, Margaret learns Richard is a wanted man but instead of rejecting him, she decides to help him.

Hannay is caught by police at one point and is locked by handcuffs to a witness, the very lovely Pamela (Carroll), who gets dragged around by Hannay when he gets the chance to escape; they even have to share a bed at an inn masquerading as newlyweds.

Tearle is Prof. Jordan, the man with a missing joint finger, leader of the cabal trying to transfer weapons secrets out of the country. Watson is Mr. Memory, the stage entertainer who knows the secret and has committed the whole thing to memory.

- It was partly shot on location in Scotland, at Edinburgh and at Glen Coe Highlands.
- In his appetite for malice, Hitch, at the end of one day's shooting, pretended he couldn't find the handcuff key and had Donat and Carroll locked together for another half-hour.
- The plot, based on the spy novel by John Buchan, is a rare look at secret societies. Few films have ventured into that realm: *Network* and *Eyes Wide Shut* are two others.

Zulu

1964, UK, Diamond Films Ltd./Embassy Pictures, 138 minutes, Color
Producers: Stanley Baker, Cy Endfield; Director: Cy Endfield
Cast: Stanley Baker, Michael Caine, Jack Hawkins, Ulla Jacobsson, James Booth, Nigel Green, Patrick Magee

> "A tremendous hit in Britain, its production source, *Zulu* also drew all lovers of gung-ho excitement in America and elsewhere."
> —John Douglas Eames, *The Paramount Story*

Stanley Baker and Michael Caine in *Zulu*.

An excellent dramatization of the defense of a British outpost in Colonial South Africa in 1879. In the Army's last stand defending Rorke's Drift, 130 British soldiers held off 4,000 Zulus for 24 hours after the Empire's most ignominious defeat: the loss of 1,200 troops. Following the bloody battle, eleven soldiers were honored with Victoria Crosses.

Shot on location in Natal, South Africa, utilizing real Zulus, the battle sequences with the Zulu warriors are some of the most amazing pieces of film footage ever exhibited. How Mr. Baker and company even managed to get these strong and proud, independent-minded natives to participate, as well as act, is an astonishing accomplishment in itself.

Baker plays Chard, the courageous British mission's Commander, Caine is Bromhead, Chard's impudent Lieutenant; Booth is Private Hook, a reluctant soldier who feigns sickness—yet becomes one of the heroes of the fight. Hawkins is Witt the post missionary and Jacobsson is his daughter. Green is Sgt. Bourne and Magee is Reynolds, the unit surgeon.

John Barry (of the James Bond theme) did the stirring music. Paramount released the film in America. In 1979, Endfield wrote the screenplay for a prequel: *Zulu Dawn*, a Dutch production.

- Richard Burton narrates the foreword.
- This was Caine's first major film, the picture that brought him to the attention of producers in both England and the U.S.
- Sir Stanley Baker was knighted by the Queen in 1976, just weeks before he died of lung cancer at the age of 49.

Foreign Classics

Alexander Nevsky

1938, Russia, Mosfilm, 112 minutes, B&W
Producer/Director: Sergei Eisenstein
Cast: Nikolai Cherkasov, Nikolai Okhlopkov, Dmitri Orlov, Vasili Novikov, Andrei Abrikosov, Vladimer Yersho, Vera Ivashova, Aleksandra Danilova

"...a masterpiece..."
—Roger Ebert, *Roger Ebert's Video Companion*

Russia's greatest director was a master of the montage, and uses it well in this thirteenth century story about Russia's victory against invading Teutonic Knights. The highlight is the 28-minute "Battle on the Ice."

David Thomson calls it Eisenstein's "most spectacular film and his most plainly American in style." Leslie Halliwell sees Eisenstein as a "cinema giant." The director is most famous for this film and *Potemkin* (1925) and *Ivan the Terrible Parts 1 and 2* (1945, 1946).

Filmed just ahead of WWII, the conflict between the forces actually parallels the upcoming confrontation between Russia and Germany. Briefly, Eisenstein was embarrassed when his country signed a pact with the Nazis, but eventually *Alexander Nevsky* was used as a source of patriotism when the Nazis broke the pact and attacked Russia.

Cherkasov plays Nevsky, the prince of princes. Yershov is the grand master of the Teutonic Order. Orlov is Ignat, the master armorer. Novikov is Pavsha, governor of Pskov. The characters include; Vasili (Okhlopkov), Gavrilo (Abrikosov), Olga (Ivashova), and Vasilisa (Danilova).

A scene from the "Battle on the Ice" sequence in *Alexander Nevsky*.

- Sequences, filmed by cameraman Eduard Tisse, were shot to correspond with the already composed Prokofiev score.
- It is reported that over 2,000 warriors participated in the famous battle but historians are still not sure where the actual battle took place.
- A voracious reader as a child, by the time he was ten Eisenstein was fluent in Russian, German, French, and English. Later, he began learning Japanese.
- As a young film fan, Eisenstein was inspired and influenced by the work of D.W. Griffith.
- Eisenstein became famous for the three-head, three-figure composition, something John Ford admittedly used from watching Eisenstein's films.
- "*Alexander Nevsky* is a classic because of Eisenstein's intellectual and artistic integrity."—Parker Tyler, *Classics of the Foreign Film*.

The Bicycle Thief (Bicycle Thieves)

1949, Italy, P.D.S./De Sica Productions, 90 minutes, B&W
Producer/Director: Vittorio De Sica
Cast: Lamberto Maggiorani, Enzo Staiola, Lianella Carell

> "...an unchallengeable peak of what we may take to be the art of motion pictures."
>
> —Parker Tyler

Sometimes referred to by film historians as the best foreign film ever made, the neo-realist drama won the New York Film Critics Award for best foreign film, Best Picture from the British Academy, and a Special Academy Award (Oscars were not handed out for Best Foreign Film until 1956). Georges Sadoul (*Dictionary of Films*) calls it "the most important film of the immediate post-war period."

The screenplay is by Cesare Zavattini (*Yesterday, Today and Tomorrow*), and though simple in plot and execution, the picture adeptly carries us, over 24 hours, through the life-and-death struggles of a poor Italian

Lamberto Maggiorani and Enzo Staiola in *The Bicycle Thief.*

family in war-devastated Rome. A man loses his bicycle, his livelihood, used to support himself, his wife, their little boy, and a baby, and in the frustration he surprisingly finds he, too, could become a thief to survive. Maggiorani is the father, Antonio Ricci; Carell is the wife, Maria; Staiola is their son, Bruno.

The poverty and anxiety of life had caused unemployed Antonio to hock his bicycle to buy food and pay the rent, but now he has a chance to get a job, but it requires that he own a bicycle. He and his wife pawn their bedsheets to get enough money to retrieve the bicycle. They are able to get it out of the pawn shop and the father happily goes to work pasting up posters—until a thief changes everything.

- Practically everybody in the film is an untrained actor; even the adult leads are professionally inexperienced.
- The posters Antonio is putting up are of the movie *Gilda* with Rita Hayworth.
- De Sica directed several classics, including *Umberto D, Two Women,* and *The Garden of the Finzi-Continis;* but he also appeared as an actor in more than 150 films, including the romantic comedy *It Started in Naples* with Sophia Loren and Clark Gable.

The Blue Angel

1930, Germany, Classic Films, 103 minutes, B&W
Producer: Erich Pommer, Director: Josef von Sternberg
Cast: Marlene Dietrich, Emil Jannings, Kurt Gerron

"**** Excellent."

—Steven H. Scheuer

Dietrich, in the film that made her an international star, is Lola-Lola, seductive cabaret vamp singing at The Blue Angel, warbling her now-famous "Falling In Love Again." Jannings is the teacher who falls under her spell—and ends up in the gutter.

How does it happen? Innocently enough. Professor Roth, an aging bachelor and high school teacher, chases some of his students out of Lola's second-rate music hall only to become infatuated with her beauty and

Josef von Sternberg and Marlene Dietrich.

charm. He ends up losing his job to become a sad assistant to the magician (Gerron) in Lola's troupe. On the side, he sells dirty pictures of his paramour. At the end, disgusted with what he has become, Roth staggers back to his old schoolroom, sits behind his former desk, clutching it with all his might in the dying hope that he can recover the world that has slipped through his fingers.

The legend of Dietrich began with this classic, a somber tale of a sexual slave. And just as Lola manipulated Roth, Dietrich herself was created in the image of the exotic woman of mystery by her mentor-Svengali: Josef von Sternberg with whom she made seven films. Straddling a chair, in white top hat and black silk stockings, Dietrich—guided by Sternberg—forevermore establishes the persona of the sultry femme fatale. The fact that she was overweight in her debut didn't matter. Lee Garmes, the Paramount cinematographer, would later add to the image with his imaginative use of lighting and poses. Nevertheless, it is Dietrich herself who sells the vision, with her peaked cheekbones, smoky German-accented voice, lovely legs, and an innate ability to look glamorous and alluring in any kind of costume.

- Dietrich combined the first part (Mar) of her real first name (Maria) with the last part (lene) of her middle name (Magdalena) to get half of her stage name.
- Ernest Hemingway: "If she had nothing but her voice, she could break your heart with it. But she also has that beautiful body and the timeless loveliness of her face."
- The story, based on the novel by Heinrich Mann, was remade in 1959 with May Britt and Curt Jurgens but without much success; the problem with the film was—it didn't have Dietrich.

Diabolique

1954, France, Seven Arts, 107 minutes, B&W
Producer/Director: Henri-Georges Clouzot
Cast: Simone Signoret, Vera Clouzot, Paul Meurisse, Charles Vanel

> "Surprises that explode like shotgun blasts!"
> —*The New York Times*

One of the most famous and popular cult films of the mid-50s. The horror-thriller with plot twists takes place at a school for boys on the outskirts of Paris: two women, the wife and the mistress, murder the schoolmaster…the

Vera Clouzot and Simone Signoret in *Diabolique*.

man they've been sharing. But the body keeps popping up! The film won the award for Best Foreign-Language Film from the New York Film Critics.

Vera Clouzot, a Portuguese actress and wife of the director, plays Christina Delassalle, wife of abusive and oppressive teacher Michel Delassalle (Meurisse). Signoret is the other woman, Nicole Horner, who has also come to despise her vitriolic lover. Vanel plays detective Alfred Fichet, the dogged investigator who uncovers the evil murder plot.

H.G. Clouzot, who had received rave notices for his earlier thriller, *The Wages of Fear* (which starred Signoret's husband Yves Montand), bought the rights to the novel by Pierre Boileau and Thomas Narcejac just before Alfred Hitchcock put in his bid.

- Though Hitchcock failed to secure the screen rights for this film, Boileau and Narcejac so desired to work with the famed director that they wrote a special screenplay for him, which he used with great success: *Vertigo*.
- The two women drive from the outskirts of Paris to Niort, which just happens to be the birthplace of the director.
- After the film ends, Clouzot urges the audience, "Don't be diabolical yourself. Don't spoil the ending for your friends by telling them what you have just seen."

8½

1963, Italy, Cineriz, 138 minutes, B&W
Producer: Angelo Rizzoli, Director: Federico Fellini
Cast: Marcello Mastroianni, Claudia Cardinale, Anouk Aimee, Sandra Milo, Rossella Falk, Barbara Steele, Guido Alberti, Tito Masini, Neil Robinson, Ian Dallas

> "Fellini's beautiful, irresponsible, sometimes incomprehensible but highly cinematic extravaganza for our times, about a film director with doubts"
> —Leslie Halliwell, *Halliwell's Filmgoer's Companion*

Winner of the Oscar for Best Foreign Film, 8½ is—as critics have claimed—self-indulgent and quite often baffling. But it's more, much more. The film is a great example of free-form filmmaking: it is well-act-

ed, it is perfectly edited (Leo Gatozzo) and wonderfully photographed (Gianni Di Venanzo) with an inventive score (Nino Rota). Plus, the film won the Oscar for Costume Design (Piero Gherardi). Does the script (by Fellini and Tullio Pinelli) make any sense? Of course. It's a terrific examination of a man's fears and fantasies, strung together in a mixture of dreams and reality. And the bottom line is: there's the need for the protagonist to learn how to love.

The somewhat autobiographical film is about a movie director, Guido Anselmi (Mastroianni), creatively stuck in neutral during his midlife crisis. From the opening stress attack in the enclosed car, through an assortment of clowns, strange people and beautiful women, to the gathering of all the characters in Guido's life in a circus ring at the end, the film is filled with fascinating episodes and imagery.

Cardinale plays a sex goddess, appropriately named Claudia. Aimee is Luisa Anselmi. Alberti plays Pace the producer, Masini is the cardinal, Dallas is the mind-reader, Robinson is Guido's agent. Among a plethora of women, Milo plays Carla, Falk is Rossella, and Steele is Gloria.

- Fellini gave it this title because he had done that many films, seven features, and three shorts; he counts each short as half a film.
- Not unlike Guido, Fellini had creative block prior to making the film and he visited a psychoanalyst. But both experiences inspired him to write a script about a director who can't think of what to do next.
- Fellini seriously considered Laurence Olivier for the lead.

Grand Illusion

1937, France, World, 117 minutes, B&W, France
Producer/Director: Jean Renoir
Cast: Jean Gabin, Pierre Fresnay, Erich von Stroheim, Marcel Dalio, Dita Parlo

> "If I had to save only one film in the world, it would be *Grand Illusion*."
>
> —Orson Welles

Nominated for an Academy Award for Best Picture, this foreign classic about a WWI POW camp was voted by critics in 1957 among the 12 greatest movies of all time. It's an anti-war film, a prison escape adventure, and—at the end—a love story. Renoir fashioned the war drama without a single battle scene. The theme is chivalrous warfare.

Three Frenchmen are prisoners-of-war of the Germans: Marechal (Gabin), Boieldieu (Fresnay), Rosenthal (Dalio). Von Stroheim plays the prison camp commandant, Von Rauffenstein, a monocled gentleman who despises his position as a bureaucratic policeman. Parlo plays a German peasant girl who falls in love with Marechal.

The grand illusion is the world within an escape plan, a world of hope—and love for the families left behind; the war is reality. The other side of the

coin is the German dream—their grand illusion—of world domination. But there are other illusions within the grand illusion: the pretense covering the escape, German youth playing at being soldiers, Von Rauffenstein acting out his role as hard overseer, the POWs dressed as women for the prison revue with stupefied Germans looking on (and a sudden return to reality with POWs singing the "Marseillaise" upon learning the French had retaken some home soil). But, in the main, the title is summed up by Gabin at the end when he hopes there will never be another war. Illusion indeed.

- Renoir was the son of famous impressionistic artist Auguste Renoir.

- The script is partially based on Renoir's own experiences as a pilot in the war; he was wounded in the leg by a German bullet that left him with a limp for the rest of his life.
- Later, Renoir said he was greatly discouraged to see a new world war break out just a few years after he made his highly praised anti-war film.

Jules and Jim

1962, France, Films du Carosse/SEDIF, 105 minutes, B&W
Producer/Director: Francois Truffaut
Cast: Jeanne Moreau, Oscar Werner, Henri Serre

> "Will rank among the great lyric achievements of the screen."
> —Pauline Kael

There was never a more appropriate film for the free-love Sixties Generation. The subject is a *menage-a-trois*. Truffaut's controversial classic is at the top of France's *New Wave* of filmmaking. His screenplay is

Jeanne Moreau, Henri Serre and Oskar Werner in *Jules and Jim*.

based on Henri-Pierre Roche's novel.

The story is set in Paris and extends from 1912 and WWI to WWII. Two men, a Frenchman and an Austrian, love the same woman, an unforgettable Parisian, and she loves them back—in a frolicking but tragic love story. It is, to be sure, a hopeless romance for all; Catherine even has a daughter by Jules. It's a 25-year relationship (in which nobody seems to age), an on-again off-again love triangle, that ends in madness. It all comes together in the senseless climax.

Moreau is the impulsive and manic Catherine. Werner is Jules who must fight on the side of the Germans in WWI. Serre is tall Jim who becomes enslaved—immortally—by Catherine's charms and whims.

- Several French organizations, supporting the two-parent family, came out against the film on moral grounds.
- Truffaut, a former film critic, plays the French ufologist in Spielberg's *Close Encounters of the Third Kind*.
- Moreau, a veteran of more than 70 films, was born in Paris where her father ran a French restaurant in the Montmartre section, a district often visited by actors.
- Paul Mazursky did an unsuccessful remake, *Willie and Phil*, in 1980.

La Dolce Vita

1960, Italy, Astor Pictures/Riama Film Roma Cinecitta, 174 minutes, B&W
Producers: Giuseppe Amato, Angelo Rizzoli; Director: Federico Fellini
Cast: Marcello Mastroianni, Anita Ekberg, Anouk Aimee, Yvonne Furneaux, Alain Cuny, Walter Santesso, Magali Noel

> "**** Staggering...Masterfully directed...absorbing...elements of greatness."
>
> —Steven H. Scheuer

La Dolce Vita means "the sweet life" but it might as well be called "the carnal life," because that's what this popular Sixties film is about: searching for happiness and the meaning of life within the world of wild parties and sex. The film won the Grand Prize at the Cannes Film Festival

Marcello Mastroianni and Anita Ekberg in *La Dolce Vita*.

and Fellini received an Oscar nomination for Best Director. The story and screenplay are by Fellini.

This fascinating view of decadence inside Rome's high society features Mastroianni as a tabloid reporter, Marcello Rubini, seeking scandals, gossip and lifestyle stories about movie stars and celebrities—the rich and famous, the bored, the drunk and the drugged, the dreamers, the unfaithful, the suicidal, the religious and the criminal underworld… all looking for thrills and excitement and that elusive something beyond their all-too-real environment. Marcello, not surprisingly, gets too close and winds up a member of the party animals.

Photographed by Otello Martelli, the film opens with a helicopter transporting a statue of Christ over the city, over beautiful girls in bikinis on the beach, to the Vatican. The film closes with a pretty girl trying but failing to lure Marcello out of his three-day drunken stupor into her world of innocence but his brain is too vacuous to accept her gentle, angelic invitation.

Ekberg portrays a movie star named Sylvia. Aimee is Maddalena. Furneaux is Emma. Noel is Fanny. Cuny plays Steiner.

- The Vatican strongly opposed the film.

- The paparazzi, the modern horde of press photographers, gets its name from a character in the film: Paparazzo (Santesso), Marcello's photographer.
- The tune "Patricia," played to the striptease, became a big international hit recording.
- Ekberg was Miss Sweden in the 1951 Miss Universe pageant.

La Strada (The Street)

1954, Italy, Trans-Lux, 115 minutes, B&W, Italy
Producers: Dino De Laurentiis, Carlo Ponti; Director: Federico Fellini
Cast: Anthony Quinn, Giulietta Masina, Richard Basehart

Director Federico Fellini.

"An altogether beautiful movie, both touching and amusing, magnificently acted by Masina and Quinn."
—Steven H. Scheuer, *Movies on TV*

The first non-English film to win the Academy Award, the first to win in the newly-created category of Best Foreign Film. It also won the Grand Prize at Venice. *La Strada* is simple yet complex, a powerful but sensitive story of loneliness and brutality. Quinn is Zampano, a one-man traveling circus act, a strongman who drives a motorcycle-wagon around the countryside, entertaining for money through every small town he finds. Masina is his clown-assistant/concubine, a dim-witted waif named Gelsomina, bought by Zampano from the young girl's poverty-stricken mother. Basehart plays an acrobat referred to as The Fool.

Nino Rota did the very effective score. The story and screenplay are by Fellini and Tullio Pinelli. The poignancy of the film comes from the very relationship itself. The girl does everything she can to win his approval; he, on the other hand, is indifferent and mean and hateful to her.

The film very nearly was not distributed outside Italy. Critics of the movie felt it gave the world a poor impression of what Italy was like following the war. Fellini took his case for unfettered art to the Roman Catholic Church and it was Cardinal Siri of Genoa who gave his blessing to the project, short-circuiting those who, at the very least, had called for certain scenes to be censored.

- Quinn originally wanted a percentage of the profits but his agent wanted a salary deal instead. The decision cost Quinn a million dollars.
- Masina was Mrs. Fellini: they were married for over 50 years.
- There are circus tableaus in several Fellini films, probably because as a very young boy he ran away from home and joined a circus, only to be returned to his parents within a few days. Nevertheless, the experience left an indelible impression on him.

Picnic at Hanging Rock

1975, Australia, South Australia Film Corp., 115 minutes, Color
Producers: Jim McElroy, Hal McElroy; Director: Peter Weir
Cast: Rachel Roberts, Anne Lambert, Dominic Guard, Margaret Nelson, Vivean Gray, Karen Robson, Jane Vallis

> "The first part of the film is absolutely spellbinding. No picture I can think of has a more sinister atmosphere ... Casting is impeccable."
> —Danny Peary, *Cult Movies 2*

Based on Joan Lindsay's book, and the best of the metaphysical films, the movie takes place on St. Valentine's Day in 1900 at Appleyard College, a finishing school in the state of Victoria near Australia's Hanging Rock, a 500 ft. high volcanic formation. The girls and their female chaperones go for a picnic at the Rock but three of them and an instructor mysteriously vanish!—sucked into the stony bowels by the Rock itself? Or could it have been a UFO abduction?

The film is overflowing with sexual symbolism, unsolved secrets, and mysterious metaphors: all the clocks and watches get stuck at high noon (magnetic influence), the phallic Rock is borne of volcanic (orgasmic)

A scene from *Picnic at Hanging Rock*.

eruption, a homage to St. Valentine (pagan fertility), rite of passage into sexuality with the virgin girls (in white) bursting with sexuality (held in check by corsets), the sacrificial element (the growling sound from the Rock), the nap (under watchful eyes), Miranda (Lambert)—seen as a sexual goddess: "What we see and what we seem are but a dream, a dream within a dream."

Robson plays Irma, one of the missing girls who returns but can't remember what happened. Vallis is Marion Quade, the other missing girl. Gray is Greta McCraw, the teacher who vanished. Nelson is Sara, who is in love with Miranda. Roberts portrays Mrs. Appleyard. Guard is Michael Fitzhubert, who becomes totally obsessed with the disappearance and seeks to unlock the mystery.

- The Rock is a popular tourist site and many think the film is based on a true story but there is no record of such a case.
- Strangely, by accident, they started shooting on Feb. 14th, Valentine's Day, the day of the story's event.
- Cinematographer Russell Boyd put yellow-orange veils over the camera lens for the other-worldly effect at the Rock.
- The ominous pipes of pan music is by Gheorghe Zampir.
- At the time of its release, it was the first Australian film to achieve international success.

Rashomon (In the Woods)

1951, Japan, Daiei, 83 minutes, B&W
Producers: Jingo Minoru, Masaichi Negata; Director: Akira Kurosawa
Cast: Toshiro Mifune, Machiko Kyo, Masayuki Mori, Takashi Shimura

> "This brilliant film's forthright unvarying pictorial loveliness, its perfect acting, its use of subjectivity to make a richly complex image of truth, not only make it a classic among foreign films but also ripe for inclusion among the greatest films of all time."
> —Parker Tyler, *Classics of the Foreign Film*

This drama was a breakthrough for the Japanese film industry in the West and introduced Kurosawa, Japan's greatest filmmaker, to West-

Director Akira Kurosawa.

ern audiences: winner of the Oscar for Best Foreign Film and winner of the Grand Prize at the Venice Film Festival. Based on two short stories by Kyunosuke Akutagawa, the film is a tale of rape and murder as seen through the eyes of four witnesses, each with a different point-of-view.

Rashomon uses the flashback process to probe guilt, truth and reality. The location for the exposition is Rashomon, one of the gates of Kyoto. The time is the eighth century in medieval Japan. The incident takes place in a forest. A man and his wife are attacked there by a bandit (Mifune). The man (Mori), a samurai, is killed and his wife (Kyo) raped. Or so it would seem. Because later, in a courtroom setting, a woodcutter (Shimura) who witnessed the episode has a different version. The murdered man, speaking through a medium, also has an opposing account, as does the woman. Four different sides coming into conflict. The woman was apparently violated with her tied-up husband watching. Or, did she give in without a fight? The woman says she was raped. She also claims she stabbed her husband after he refused to forgive her for engaging in the sexual act. The bandit said she gave into him willingly after he killed her husband in a fair fight. The corpse said he committed suicide after seeing his wife let herself be so easily taken. The woodcutter describes a scene of cowardice by all parties.

- Akutagawa, depressed over the world's immorality, committed suicide at the age of 35.
- The story was updated and remade as *The Outrage* (1964) with Paul Newman and Claire Bloom.
- Kurosawa's *Yojimbo* was a model for the "spaghetti Western" *A Fistful of Dollars*, his *Seven Samurai* was remade in America as *The Magnificent Seven*, and *The Hidden Fortress* was one of the inspirations for George Lucas' *Star Wars*.

Seven Samurai

1954, Japan, Toho Studios, 197 minutes, B&W
Producer: Shojiro Motoki, Director: Akira Kurosawa
Cast: Takashi Shimura, Toshiro Mifune, Yoshio Inaba, Seiji Miyaguchi, Minoru Chiaki, Daisuke Kato, Isao Kimura, Keiko Tsuhima

> "A raging sensuous work—it leaves you both exhilarated and exhausted...Kurosawa is perhaps the greatest of all contemporary film craftsmen."
> —Pauline Kael

Kurosawa's classic received a Special Honorary Oscar from the Academy of Motion Picture Arts and Sciences and the Silver Lion Award of the Venice Film Festival. Kurosawa, who became famous for his battle scenes, does an extraordinary job both artistically (spending painstaking hours with several novice actors) and technically: in split-second editing, effective slow-motion sequences, and use of the telephoto lens. The plot is about farmers in a sixteenth century village, terrorized by 40 bandits, hiring seven transient samurai warriors to defend them.

Shimura is Kambei, the wise leader of the samurai fighters. Mifune, who became a mainstay for Kurosawa, appearing in 16 of his films, is energetic Kikuchiyo. Miyaguchi, who never even held a sword before making the movie, plays Kyuzo. Inaba is Gorobei. Chiaki plays Heihachi. Kato is Shichiroji, Kambei's fellow warrior from the past. Kimura is Katsushiro and Tsuhima is Shino, the girl from the village who falls in love with Katsushiro.

- The epic was originally over 200 minutes long but was cut to 160 for international distribution, but it was such a hit that most of the remainder was restored.
- The story was actually based on a legend that a small village did hire a group of unemployed samurai to protect them.
- Filming on the horseback battle in the rain and mud was delayed for several days in order for the crew to find more horses.
- Budgeted at $500,000, it was the most expensive Japanese film to date.
- The movie took a year to make.
- In 1961, American director John Sturges used the plot for his popular Western, *The Magnificent Seven*.

The Seventh Seal

1956, Sweden, Svensk Filmindustri, 96 minutes, B&W
Producer/Director: Ingmar Bergman
Cast: Max von Sydow, Bibi Andersson, Gunnar Bjornstrand, Nils Poppe, Bengt Ekerot, Inga Gill, Inga Landgre, Gunnel Lindblom, Ake Fridell, Maud Hansson, Anders Ek

> "Ingmar Bergman's most fascinating and infuriating film... Its meaning probably can't be fully analyzed, even by Bergman himself, but almost every scene is in some way memorable, and the film stands as a textbook of filmcraft."
> —Leslie Halliwell.

This strange black comedy-drama-allegory, set during the Black Plague in the fourteenth century, was written by director Bergman himself, based on medieval morality plays. At the center of the plot (such as it is) there's a Knight, in effect Bergman's Everyman. Von Sydow plays the depressed and confused Knight, Antonious Block, back from the Crusades.

Max von Sydow and Bengt Skerot in *The Seventh Seal*.

Different people get different ideas and questions from the film: Does God exist? If He does, why does He allow suffering? Because God permits such misery and death, is God worth our respect, devotion, and obedience? Is there really a purpose to life? Is life meaningless? Does God simply want us to procreate and form families? Why doesn't God talk to us? Where is God? We see Death, in person, but not God—why?

And this is one of the hallmarks of the film, the very questions it raises in times of great difficulty.

In the story, the Knight has lost his faith though his wife, Karin (Landgre), has not. Death (Ekerot), in the form of a whiten-faced specter, comes for the Knight but Block tries to divert the black-robed Grim Reaper with a game of chess. Cinematographer Gunnar Fischer's famous longshot at the end of film shows the Dance of Death with six of the characters in the story being led away by Death; the longsuffering Karin, however, is not one of them. And some see this as the answer to the film's mystery: Faithfulness to God to the very end is all that matters.

Bergman also uses an acting troupe as a centerpiece, reminding us of Shakespeare's line that all the world's a stage and we are its players, its actors, its fools. Why does Jof the juggler (Poppe) work with just two balls? Could it be that things that seem expert and intricate to man, like the art of fast, complex juggling, really appear simplistic to God?

Bjornstrand is the squire, Jons. Andersson is Jof's wife, Mia. Fridell is the blacksmith, Plog. Gill plays Lisa, the blacksmith's wife. Hansson is The Witch. Ek is The Monk. The Girl is played by Lindblom.

- The Dance of Death inspired Woody Allen's climax in *Love and Death* (1975).
- The Dance was shot at sunset using technicians and assistants since the actors had left for the day.
- Bergman's visuals were inspired by murals on church walls where his father, a minister, preached.
- The title is from the Bible's Book of Revelation.

The Wages of Fear

1952, France/Italy, Era Film/Fono Roma/Cinedis, 156 minutes, B&W
Producer/Director: Henri-Georges Clouzot

Cast: Yves Montand, Charles Vanel, Peter Van Eyck, Folco Lulli, Vera Clouzot

> "...one of the first French films to obtain a wide showing in English-speaking countries..."
> —David Thomson, *A Biographical Dictionary of Film*

Clouzot's companion thriller to *Diabolique* is a take-off on the Biblical warning: the wages of sin is death. Four down-and-out men from France, Italy, and Germany are running from the law and find themselves hiding away in a vapid village somewhere in South America. They are: Mario (Montand), a Corsican; Jo (Vanel), a Parisian; Bimba (Van Eyck), a German, and Luigi (Lulli), an Italian. Vera Clouzot plays Linda, a barmaid at the only watering hole in the muddy outpost, and she thinks she's fallen in love with Mario.

The men arrived by small plane separate of one another, but come together when they learn that an American-owned oil company is hiring truck-drivers. Here's the chance for each man to possess enough money to fly out of the hell-hole; but these wages will come with fearful conse-

Charles Vanel and Yves Montand in *The Wages of Fear*.

quences. The company is offering four men $2,000 each for driving two truckloads of nitroglycerine 300 miles to a jungle oil field to blast out an oil well fire.

The desperate experience for the truckers over bumpy dirt roads, up and down mountains and through jungle brush, is one of the most harrowing adventures in cinema history. Any sudden shaking of the explosives could mean death. In one scene, the drivers must ease their way over rotting boards nearly hanging off a cliff; in another scene, Mario and Jo have to get through a pond of oil that has escaped from a broken pipeline, and Jo gets injured when he gets caught under the wheels of the truck. Director Clouzot wrote the screenplay based on the novel by George Arnaud. The British Academy awarded the film Best Picture.

- Bill Friedkin did a remake in 1977, *Sorcerer,* which provides more insight as to who the men were prior to escaping to South America.
- Vera Amado Clouzot, a Brazilian actress, is the wife of the director; she's also in her husband's other classic, *Diabolique,* with Simone Signoret, wife of Montand.
- While the setting looks exactly like some rundown, third-world village in South America or Latin America, the fact is—the picture was shot at several locations in the South of France; and the village was built from the ground up!

Action-Adventure

The Adventures of Robin Hood

1938, USA, Warner Bros., 102 minutes, Color
Producer: Hal B. Wallis, Directors: Michael Curtiz, William Keighley
Cast: Errol Flynn, Olivia de Havilland, Basil Rathbone, Claude Rains, Eugene Pallette, Alan Hale, Ian Hunter, Patric Knowles

"…gorgeous and exciting…"
—Albert R. Leventhal, *The Movie Makers*

Nominated for Best Picture, Flynn's green-clan Robin is one of the screen's most energetic and durable characters. Even today, it looks totally fresh, thanks to the silver-based Technicolor of the era; it outlasts virtually everything else made in 1938. Just as only Gable could play Rhett in *GWTW*, Flynn was born to be the arrow-shooting English romantic who stole from the rich to give to the poor. Legend has it that Sir Robin of Locksley actually did roam Sherwood Forest with his Merry Men about 1191. De Havilland, only 19 at the time, is lovely and perfect as the virginal Maid Marian.

The film won three Academy Awards: score (Erich Wolfgang Korngold), art direction (Carl Weyl), editing (Ralph Dawson).

Rains, always good in everything, is Prince John, the treacherous brother of King Richard the Lion Heart (Hunter), trying to steal the throne from his kidnapped sibling. His accomplice in this devious deed is Sir Guy of Gisbourne, excellently played by Rathbone in one of his two most famous roles; the other, of course, is Sherlock Holmes. The sword-fight, without doubles, between Gisbourne and Robin at the climax is classic.

Errol Flynn in *The Adventures of Robin Hood*.

Froggy-voiced Pallette, tipping the scales at 300 lbs., plays Friar Tuck. Hale is Little John and Knowles portrays Will Scarlett.

- James Cagney was originally considered for the part of Robin.
- Sherwood Forest was really Bidwell Park in Chico, Calif.
- Keighley directed most of the outdoor action sequences.
- Stuntmen really took arrows in the chest and back due to heavy padding, a steel breastplate and a slab of balsa wood.
- Professional archer Howard Hill doubles for Robin in the tournament; he was actually able to split an arrow with a second arrow!

- Olivia's golden horse is Roy Rogers' Trigger.
- Hale also played Little John in the silent version (1922) with Douglas Fairbanks as Robin.

The African Queen

1951, USA, Romulus-Horizon, 106 minutes, Color
Producer: Sam Spiegel, Director: John Huston
Cast: Humphrey Bogart, Katharine Hepburn, Robert Morley

> "...a splendidly successful mixture of comedy, character and adventure."
> —Ruth Halliwell and John Walker, *Halliwell's Film Guide*

Bogart, as a boozing river-rat, won the Oscar for Best Actor and Hepburn, as a spinster-missionary, was nominated for Best Actress in this comedy-romantic adventure shot on location in Africa. Huston won for Best Director.

It has to do with German infiltration into the jungles of East Africa in 1914; the German plan was to try to make soldiers out of the natives. As a result of the German takeover of the area, Methodist minister Sam Sayer (Morley) loses his life and his sister, Rose (Hepburn), is left to fend for herself. Alcoholic Charlie Allnut (Bogart) saves Rosie following a burn-out of her village. Heading downriver in Charlie's boat, the two ride the rapids, duck bullets, and fight off leeches. During their ordeal, they grow very fond of each other in their effort to find safe-haven. Then Rosie gets the brilliant idea that they should blow up a German battleship harbored off the coast!

The story, which is both patriotic and spiritually based, is from C.S. Forester's novel; film critic James Agee was one of several who adapted the screenplay. The title is really a play on words: the old boat is named "The African Queen" and Kate's Rosie is also a sort of African queen.

- Bogart and wife Lauren Bacall, who accompanied her husband on the shoot, were the only two who didn't come down with dysentery; Bogie brushed his teeth with Scotch.
- The part of Rose was originally offered to Bette Davis but she was pregnant.

Humphrey Bogart and Katharine Hepburn in *The African Queen*.

- The leeches were made of rubber.
- The vessel was an old boat that had been used in the area for years; it's now docked next to the Holiday Inn in Key Largo, Florida.
- It was filmed in Uganda, the Congo, Turkey, and England.

Captain Blood

1935, USA, Warner Bros., 119 minutes, B&W
Producer: Hal B. Wallis, Director: Michael Curtiz
Cast: Errol Flynn, Olivia de Havilland, Lionel Atwill, Basil Rathbone, Guy Kibbee, Henry Stephenson, Donald Meek, Jessie Ralph, Holmes Herbert, J. Carrol Naish

> "The classic swashbuckler that made Flynn a superstar…"
> —Jay A. Brown & Consumer Guide, *Rating the Movies*

Errol Flynn as *Captain Blood*.

Nominated for Best Picture, the pirate adventure takes place in the late seventeenth century between England and France and is based on the 1922 novel by Rafael Sabatini. Erich Wolfgang Korngold did the fine score (*The Adventures of Robin Hood*).

Called to assist a man who turns out to be a rebel to the British crown, Dr. Peter Blood (Flynn) is convicted of high treason without a fair trial and sent into slavery on a remote island colony in the West Indies of the Caribbean Sea. Col. Bishop (Atwill), a cruel plantation owner, buys Blood, at the urging of his beautiful niece, Arabella (De Havilland), who is drawn to him romantically and even shields his daring escape plans. Blood and his band of slaves take a Spanish pirate ship during their attack on the port city. Blood then becomes a pirate himself and soon confronts French pirate Capt. Levasseur (Rathbone), pillager of the open seas. As fate would have it, Blood must save the woman he loves from the hands of the brutal Levasseur.

The film is loaded with notable character actors, all WB contract players: Stephenson plays Lord Willoughby, Kibbee is Hagthorpe, Meek portrays Dr. Whacker, Ralph is Mrs Barlow, Herbert is Capt. Gardner, and Naish is one of Levasseur's henchmen.

- Robert Donat was originally set to play Blood but dropped out at the last minute over a contract dispute. Jack Warner looked around his stock players and decided on Flynn for the lead. Errol, very nervous at the start, was making only $300 a week but after the success of the film, he insisted on a raise, which he got, in four figures.
- Flynn and Curtiz did 12 films together.
- Errol and Olivia (19 at the time of the film) did nine films together.
- All the ships were miniatures.

Dirty Harry

1971, USA, Warner Bros./Malpaso, 103 minutes, Color
Producer/Director: Don Siegel
Cast: Clint Eastwood, Andy Robinson, Harry Guardino, Reni Santoni, John Vernon, John Larch

Clint Eastwood as *Dirty Harry*.

"Brilliantly filmed and edited for maximum impact."
—Leonard Maltin

From TV's *Rawhide* and a bit part in *Revenge of the Creature* in the 50s through his "spaghetti Westerns," Eastwood gradually became a star. But it wasn't until *Dirty Harry* that the tall, lean, and handsome actor would become an international superstar. This police-action film may be the best ever made; it spawned four sequels with Eastwood as the lead character, "Dirty Harry" Callahan, a tough San Francisco police inspector who believes the law shows too much sympathy for criminals and hardly any for their victims. Why do they call him "Dirty Harry?" Because he does every dirty job that comes along.

And this job is as dirty as they get. Callahan is assigned the task of tracking down a serial killer who calls himself Scorpio, played with all the gusto and meanness he can engender by Robinson. Scorpio shoots and kills a young woman and sends a note to the Mayor (Vernon) and Police Chief (Larch) telling them he wants $100,000 or he'll kill a citizen every day until he gets the ransom. Before the Mayor, Chief and Police Lieutenant (Guardino) can get their act together, Scorpio shoots another person, ups his demand to $200,000 and kidnaps a young girl and buries her; she has only a few hours before suffocating. Callahan and his partner, Chico Gonzales (Santoni), are on a quest against time to find this low-life murderer who, as Harry sees it, will soon kill again simply because "he likes it."

As part of the film's good vs. evil symbolism, Harry and Chico track the killer on a rooftop next to a "Jesus Saves" neon sign—and the killer, dressed in a stocking ski-mask, lures Harry to the foot of the giant Mt. Davidson Cross where he beats and kicks the cop, breaking two of his ribs. The most famous scene is in Kezar Stadium where Harry, mid-field, holds his .44-Magnum over the wounded Scorpio as a helicopter-camera pulls away into the fog.

Early in the film there's the now-famous line Harry uses on a downed bank-robber who thinks about reaching for his gun as Harry stands over him. "Do you feel lucky?" asks Callahan. "Well, do you punk?" Harry uses that line again at the end of the film when Scorpio has the same chance.

- Frank Sinatra was first offered the part but had to turn it down because of a wrist injury.
- The movie marquee shows Eastwood's *Play Misty for Me*.
- The story was based on a real San Francisco killer who called himself Zodiac who was never caught; speculation is that he either died or ended up in an insane asylum.

The French Connection

1971, USA, 20th Century-Fox, 104 minutes, Color
Producer: Philip D'Antoni, Director: William Friedkin
Cast: Gene Hackman, Roy Scheider, Fernando Rey, Tony Lo Bianco, Marcel Bozzuffi, Frederic de Pasquale, Harold Gary. Eddie Egan

> "The film is a masterpiece of editing and suspense, with a classic chase as its highlight."
> —Tony Thomas and Aubrey Solomon,
> *The Films of 20th Century-Fox*

Gene Hackman in *The French Connection*.

Adapted from Robin Moore's bestseller about an international drug ring, the film won five Academy Awards: Best Picture, Best Actor (Hackman), director, screenplay (Ernest Tidyman), editing (Jerry Greenberg). Owen Roizman shot most of the film with a hand-held camera, giving the picture a documentary look.

Hackman is Jimmy "Popeye" Doyle, a crude New York City detective on the heels of French drug trafficker Alain Charnier (Rey). Scheider plays Doyle's partner, Buddy Russo. The story intimately describes the biggest narcotics seizure in police history, the 1962 drug bust of 120lbs. of pure heroin worth about $30 million on the street.

The exciting 26-block car vs. overhead commuter-train chase took five weeks to shoot and Hackman did a lot of the driving, along with stuntman Bill Hickman (who also appears in the film as a federal agent). The chase sequence, the best since *Bullitt,* takes place through Bensonhurst beneath the West End subway line.

Lo Bianco plays Sal Boca, the small-time middle man for the drug deal. Bozzuffi is Pierre, the hit-man; de Pasquale is Henri Devereaux, the French TV star who gets paid to transport his car and its rocker panels full of heroin to America. Gary plays the New York moneyman, Joel Weinstock, who closes the deal.

- The actual detectives are in the film: Doyle in real life was Eddie Egan who plays Lt. Simonson; partner Sonny Grosso has a small part as Officer Klein.
- Irv Abrahams, Irv the police garage mechanic who tears the "hot" car apart, is real.
- Subway conductor Bob Morrone was the real motorman.
- The Three Degrees lounge act sing the Jimmy Webb song "Everybody Gets To Go To The Moon."
- D'Antoni also produced *Bullitt.*

Jaws

1975, USA, Universal, 124 minutes, Color
Producers: Richard D. Zanuck, David Brown; Director: Steven Spielberg
Cast: Roy Scheider, Richard Dreyfuss, Robert Shaw, Lorraine Gary, Murray Hamilton

> "…one of the top-grossing films of all time."
> —Clive Hirschhorn, *The Universal Story*

The first summer blockbuster, based on Peter Benchley's bestseller, was nominated for Best Picture and John Williams' music became famous for its suggestion of impending invisible horror: a marauding Great White Shark. The 25 ft. man-eater makes life a living hell for the visiting swimmers at the summer resort of Amity Island in New England. The adventure-thriller is among the Top 10 Moneymakers in cinema history. Williams won the Oscar for his theme.

Filmed at Martha's Vineyard, off Cape Cod, Mass. (a former whaling village), the plot has the massive shark killing and menacing tourists and

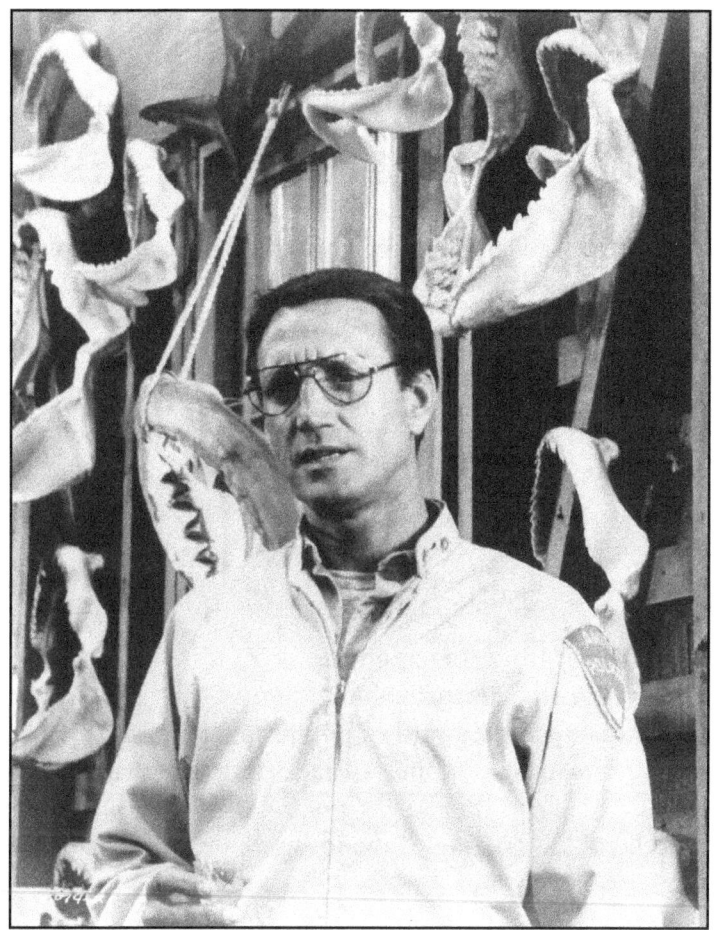

Roy Scheider in *Jaws*.

townspeople as Mayor Vaughn (Hamilton) tries to keep the bad publicity from ruining local business. Caught in the tug-of-war between the township and the need to save people's lives is Police Chief Martin Brody (Scheider) who wants the beach put off-limits. In an effort to solve the problem, the town hires a rough-and-tumble shark hunter named Quint (Shaw), a modern Captain Ahab, to kill the killer from the sea. Dreyfuss plays Matt Hooper, an oceanographer with keen knowledge about sharks. Gary is Brody's supportive wife, Ellen.

Famous line (from Scheider): "You're gonna need a bigger boat!"

- The mechanical shark was named Bruce after Spielberg's lawyer.

- The first time they used the fake shark it sunk 30 feet to the bottom.
- A replica of the shark is a fixture on the Universal City amusement park tour.
- The nude bather, the shark's first victim, is Susan Backlinie who reprises the role at the start of Spielberg's *1941* (1979).
- Underwater shark footage was shot off Australia's Great Barrier Reef by shark photographers Ron and Valerie Taylor.
- The added scene in which a head pops out of the bottom of a boat was shot in the backyard swimming pool of editor Verna Fields.
- Benchley, who also appears in the film as a TV reporter, is the grandson of humorist and character actor Robert Benchley.

Key Largo

1948, USA, Warner Bros., 101 minutes, B&W
Producer: Jerry Wald, Director: John Huston
Cast: Humphrey Bogart, Edward G. Robinson, Lauren Bacall, Lionel Barrymore, Claire Trevor, Thomas Gomez, Marc Lawrence

> "Excellent! Electrifying! A moody and intense gangster drama!"
>
> —*The Hollywood Reporter*

Warning, a hurricane is heading for the Florida Keys, but the biggest storm is brewing inside the Key Largo Hotel where a mobster waits and three people are held hostage. Eddie G reprises his gangster image one more time.

Johnny Rocco (Robinson) has been deported; he waits to meet up with another racketeer (Lawrence) to make a counterfeit money deal. Cigar-chomping Rocco often lies in a cold bath with a fan on him to beat the heat. Meanwhile, held at gunpoint by Rocco's henchman Richard Curly Hoff (Gomez), are the disabled proprietor of the hotel, James Temple (Barrymore); his widowed daughter-in-law Nora Temple (Bacall), and former army major Frank McCloud (Bogart) who has dropped by to pay his respects to Mr. Temple whose son died in battle under McCloud's command. But Frank has had his fill of fighting…until now…when he

John Huston, Edward G. Robinson and Humphrey Bogart discuss the boat scene for *Key Largo*.

must confront Rocco to save Nora and James—plus his own life.

The film is based on the play by Maxwell Anderson. Trevor, as Rocco's alcoholic gun moll, Gaye, won the Oscar for Best Supporting Actress.

- Bacall said making the film was great fun; she served tea and cookies during a break in shooting every afternoon and Lionel would regale everybody with theatre stories. She also said Robinson was "a lovely, funny man."
- Rocco was based on Al Capone who retired to Florida and Trevor's character was based on Gay Orlova, Lucky Luciano's girlfriend.
- This was the fourth and final pairing of Bogart and Bacall.
- In 1981, Bertie Higgins had a hit recording, "Key Largo," about the film.
- Barrymore was disabled by arthritis and required the wheelchair (which he also used in *It's a Wonderful Life*, as Mr. Potter, his most famous role).

Little Caesar

1930, USA, Warner Bros., 77 minutes, B&W
Producer: Hal B. Wallis, Director: Mervyn LeRoy
Cast: Edward G. Robinson, Douglas Fairbanks, Jr., Glenda Farrell

> "The first talking gangster film…caused a long-lasting controversy but sold a lot of tickets and produced a host of imitators."
> —Leslie Halliwell, *Halliwell's Filmgoer's Companion*

Edward G. Robinson as *Little Caesar*.

The granddaddy of all gangster movies built bulldog-faced Eddie G's tough-guy image and set the stage for Cagney's *The Public Enemy* (1931), Paul Muni's *Scarface* (1932), Bogart's *The Petrified Forest* (1936), Pat O'Brien's *Angels With Dirty Faces* (1938) with Cagney and Bogart, Raoul Walsh's *The Roaring Twenties* (1939) also with Cagney and Bogart, George Raft's *They Drive By Night* (1940) with Bogart, and Bogie's *High Sierra* (1942). Robinson essentially reprised his role in *Key Largo* (1948) also with Bogart, and Cagney blew up the early-gangster genre in *White Heat* (1949).

Based on the novel by W.R. Burnett, Robinson plays Chicago gangland boss Cesare Enrico Bandello, a "Little Caesar" to the underworld. Fairbanks is Joe Massara, Rico's associate in a widespread operation of illegal booze, crooked gambling joints, whorehouses, and secret speakeasies. Farrell is nightclub queen Olga Strasssoff.

Rico's death scene underwent a key script change. At the end, Rico utters the line, "Mother of Mercy, is this the end of Rico?" It was changed to that because of complaints about the original line seen by preview audiences: "Mother of God, is this the end of God?" Francis Faragoh and Robert E. Lee received an Academy Award nomination for their screenplay. The fine photography is by Tony Gaudio (*The Letter*) with outstanding art direction by Anton Grot (*Captain Blood*).

- Robinson's character is not based on Al Capone, as many supposed, but on Salvatore Cardinella, a violent Chicago gangster during Prohibition.
- The role of Joe is a character allegedly based on George Raft.
- Clark Gable was originally considered for the Massara part.
- There is speculation that the Rico Law (Racketeering Influence Corrupt Organization Act) got its acronym from Rico.
- Mervyn LeRoy: "I had the pleasure of directing Mr. Robinson in *Little Caesar* and we have been great friends for many years. He is one of the finest actors living, and one of the finest gentlemen it has been my good fortune to know. I cannot say enough about him as an actor or as a person."

Lost Horizon

1937, USA, Columbia, 132 minutes, B&W
Producer/Director: Frank Capra
Cast: Ronald Colman, Jane Wyatt, John Howard, Sam Jaffe, H.B. Warner, Margo, Thomas Mitchell, Edward Everett Horton, Isabel Jewell

> "Using (James) Hilton's visionary novel as a starting point, he (Capra) explores the promise and implication of perfect existence with a depth and poetry the original never achieved."
> —John Baxter

Nominated for Best Picture, the Capra classic about the discovery of Shangri-La won Oscars for editing and art direction. Stephen Goosson spent a year building the sets. An entire Tibetan village was built at Sherwood, 40 miles from Hollywood.

Escaping a Chinese revolution, British diplomat Robert Conway (Colman) and four others crash-land their plane in icy Tibet's Himalayan mountains where they trek through snowy landscape to find refuge in an

Ronald Colman and Jane Wyatt in *Lost Horizon*.

unknown city—where the inhabitants don't age! They are treated royally but when the group decides to leave, Conway finds he's in a quandary: he has fallen in love with a young woman in the city—the beautiful Sondra Bizet (Wyatt). Adding to his dilemma, most of the people there are very, very old. What would happen if Sondra were to leave this sheltered environment?—a special hideaway where a high altitude has frozen out elements promoting the aging process.

Jaffe, with caked-on make-up to make him appear 200 years old, plays the Grand Lama. Warner is Chang the sage. Jewell is Gloria and Margo is Maria. Howard portrays George Conway, Mitchell plays Chalmers, and Horton, as usual for comic relief, is Lovett.

- Snow scene close-ups were shot in a Los Angeles ice house to get the cold breath effect.
- Bleached corn flakes were used in the blizzard.
- The model doubling for Wyatt in the nude bathing scene had her breasts uncovered but was not visible because of the long shot.
- The film opened to a poor response from a preview audience in Santa Barbara; an alarmed Capra rushed the film back to the editing room where he and editors Gene Havlick and Gene Milford cut and chopped for hours, including removing 12 minutes from the front. Their efforts saved the film.

Manhattan Melodrama

1934, USA, MGM, 93 minutes, B&W
Producer: David O. Selznick, Director: W.S. Van Dyke
Cast: Clark Gable, William Powell, Myrna Loy, Mickey Rooney

> "Colorful, well-acted underworld tale of two boyhood friends who end up on opposite sides of the law."
> —*TV Guide*

It was this film that was playing at Chicago's Biograph Theater in 1934 when FBI agents, tipped off by "the lady in red," cut down notorious bank robber John Dillinger in a hail of bullets in front of the movie house; Dillinger loved watching Gable and made a date to see this movie though he should've stayed out of sight.

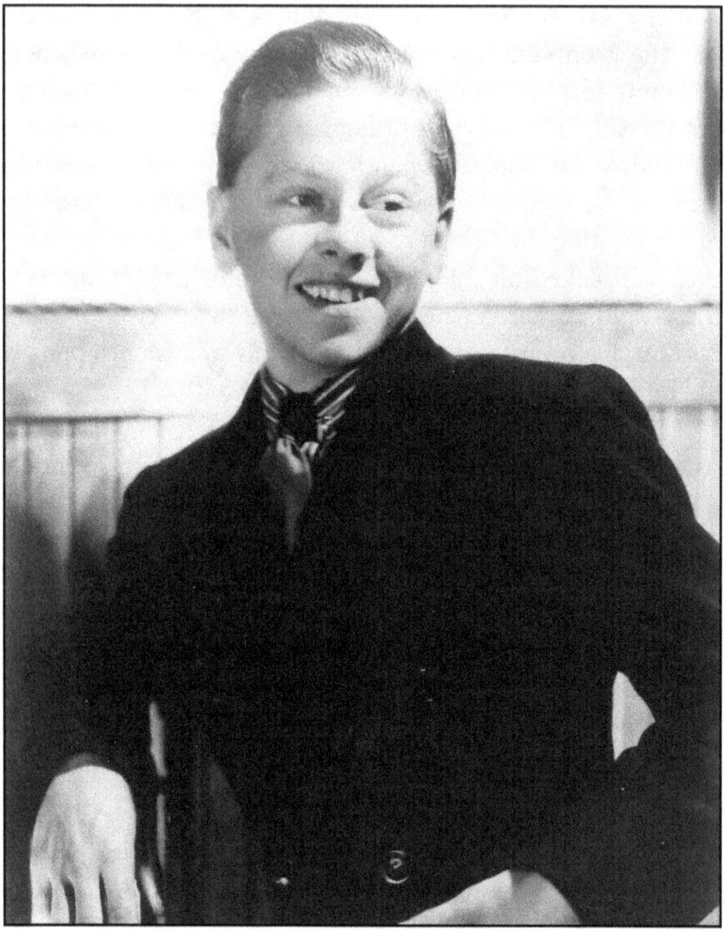

Mickey Rooney portrays Blackie as a boy in *Manhattan Melodrama*.

The story begins with the arrival of immigrants, including a spectacular boat fire, at turn-of-the-century New York City, through the speakeasy-gambling days of the turbulent Twenties. The plot follows the lives of two pals from childhood, one who becomes a slick gambler and the other who is elected to the office of District Attorney. Gable plays casino boss Edward J. "Blackie" Gallagher; Powell is D.A. James W. "Jim" Wade. Loy is Eleanor Packer who loves them both. Arthur Caesar won the Oscar for Best Original Story.

There's excellent support from Rooney as "Blackie" as a boy, Leo Carrillo as Father Joe, Samuel S. Hinds as the prison warden, and Shirley Ross as the singer in the Cotton Club.

- The fire is a good re-creation of the General Slucum Steamer disaster in New York harbor, killing over 1,000 people.
- The shooting at the Biograph on July 22, 1934, was set up by Anna Sage, a brothel madam, to help the FBI and prevent her deportation, which didn't work—they shipped her back to Romania anyway.
- Loy and Powell did 14 films together.
- George Cukor shot additional scenes because Van Dyke was already filming *The Thin Man*. Van Dyke was known as "One Take Woody" because he didn't like to re-shoot scenes.
- Carrillo became Pancho on the TV series "The Cisco Kid."
- Hinds was a lawyer for over 30 years before becoming an actor.
- Rodgers and Hart's "Oh Love, The Bad In Every Man" later became "Blue Moon."

Moby Dick

1956, USA, Warner Bros., 116 minutes, Color
Producer/Director: John Huston
Cast: Gregory Peck, Richard Basehart, Leo Genn, Orson Welles, Friedrich Lederbur, James Robertson Justice, Harry Andrews, Bernard Miles, Mervyn Johns, Noel Purcell, Royal Dano, Tamba Alleney

> "A true epic…unforgettable…a masterpiece."
> —*The Los Angeles Examiner*

As Herman Melville's famous novel begins, so this marvelous 1841 adventure film begins: "Call me Ishmael." Basehart is Ishmael, teller of the sea tale about a peg-legged ship captain seeking revenge on a great white whale that took his leg and left his face scarred. But the mighty whale, called Moby Dick, left the captain more than just physically scarred, for he is emotionally scarred for life in his never-ending quest to administer justice against this leviathan of the seas.

Peck, in one of his finest roles, plays the madman, Captain Ahab, in pursuit of Moby Dick at all costs. And pay they do, Ahab, Ishmael and all the crew of the *Pequod*, as Moby Dick turns his powerful strength against the very ship itself.

Gregory Peck as Captain Ahab in *Moby Dick*.

Also aboard the New England whaling ship are: Starbuck (Genn), the second-in-command, who calls it "an evil voyage" and talks of mutiny; Queequeg (Lederbur), the tattooed heathen; Elijah (Dano) who prophesizes the fate of the *Pequod*, Boomer (Justice), Stubb (Andrews), Manxman (Miles), Peleg (Johns), the Carpenter (Purcell), Pip (Alleney). On land, in New Bedford in a pulpit made in the shape of a ship's bow, Father Mapple (Welles) prays for the doomed journey. The screenplay is by Huston and sci-fi writer Ray Bradbury.

- Welles, who wrote his own dialogue, had trouble with the scene until Huston provided him with a bottle of brandy to put his nerves at ease.
- Peck, tied to an 85-ft. fake whale, got lost in the fog for several minutes when the launch tow-line snapped. A frantic stunt crew finally dragged Peck and the rubber device to safety.

- Peck thought Huston would've been a better Ahab. Actually, Huston had wanted his father, Walter, to play the part but he had died four years earlier.
- The water sequences were shot off the coasts of Wales and Ireland in the Irish Sea and off the Canary Islands.

Mutiny on the Bounty

1935, USA, MGM, 132 minutes, B&W
Producer: Irving Thalberg, Director: Frank Lloyd
Cast: Charles Laughton, Clark Gable, Franchot Tone

> "**** Magnificent version."
>
> —*TV Guide*

It was the only time in Hollywood history when three men from the same film were all nominated for Best Actor: Laughton, Gable, Tone (and none won; Victor McLaglen took the Oscar for *The Informer*). Laughton

Charles Laughton as Captain Bligh in *Mutiny on the Bounty*.

is sadistic Captain Bligh, Gable is first-mate Fletcher Christian, Tone is Midshipman Roger Byam. Despite the film's losses in the acting category, the adventure-drama won Best Picture.

Based on an actual event on a voyage from England to Tahiti in 1787, the *HMS Bounty* sets sail with its contemptible Captain at the helm. The goal of the voyage was to get a supply of breadfruit plants to be removed to the Caribbean where they would be transplanted for food for slaves on those colonies. But the crew couldn't take anymore of William Bligh's hatred and unjust acts. Twelve crewmembers mutiny. Christian sets the Captain and 18 sailors adrift in a lifeboat.

That would seem to be the demise of the austere Mr. Bligh—but remember this is a true story. The surprise of the film is that Bligh and his men, in a tiny boat, survive and return to England as heroes, bringing the wrath of the King and his navy upon the mutineers. The film is based on the Nordhoff-Hall book.

- The story was remade in 1962 with Marlon Brando and Trevor Howard and again in 1984, *The Bounty,* with Mel Gibson and Anthony Hopkins.
- The company built an exact replica of the real Bounty; thanks in great part to art director Cedric Gibbons, one of Hollywood's finest set-creators.
- The mutineers with native women settled on Pitcairn Island where there are less than 100 descendants today.
- Bligh's voyage to the Dutch East Indies and safety, without a sail or compass, is still considered one of England's most remarkable feats of seamanship.

The Public Enemy

1931, USA, Warner Bros./Vitaphone, 96 minutes, B&W
Producer: Darryl F. Zanuck, Director: William A. Wellman
Cast: James Cagney, Jean Harlow, Mae Clarke, Joan Blondell, Edward Woods, Beryl Mercer, Donald Cook

> "The bleak reality and cold nihilism of this film still have the power to impress the thoughtful student of society."
> —Richard Griffith, *The Movies*

Mae Clarke gets a grapefruit in the face from James Cagney in *The Public Enemy*.

The little rips and splotches on copies of this film from the original now add to its authentic look, transporting us back to the early years of the twentieth century; the camera lens taking viewers through Prohibition, its secret world of the speakeasy, and its underworld of crime bosses. The foreword of the film makes a plea to the movie-goers to try to do something about the nation's immorality and criminal element. Obviously, the plea fell on deaf ears because crime and corruption seem just as prevalent in the modern world as a hundred years ago. Nevertheless, this was one of the objects for Zanuck and Wellman to make this movie, to show how young people get into trouble and turn into bad guys. But as far as the movie goes, Cagney (whom we see grow up in a loving family) was so likeable, even in his errant ways, many in the audience were sad to see him get what's coming to him. His end, and the end of the picture, is classic: Cagney's body, bound in bandages, delivered to the home of his mother and propped outside against the front door; when it's opened, the corpse falls inside.

The film made Cagney a star. It was almost not to be. Woods began with the lead, but Zanuck and Wellman smartly switched them and

Cagney started a famous career in motion pictures while Woods is all but forgotten. Cagney plays Tom Powers, a Chicago hood who becomes a ruthless gangster battling rival gangs. Woods is Tom's pal, Matt Doyle. Harlow, in her next big role after *Hell's Angels,* plays gun-moll Gwen Allen. Clarke is Kitty, Tom's mistress. Blondell is Mamie, a saloon-keeper. Mercer is Tom's Irish mother. Cook is Tom's straight-and-narrow brother who fails to make his younger brother see the light.

- The film is famous for Cagney, at the breakfast table, shoving half a grapefruit into Clarke's face; she didn't know it was coming.
- To add realism, Wellman placed a marksman with a submachine gun, out of the view of the camera, firing real bullets against the stone wall of a building, within a few feet of Cagney's head!
- Jack Warner wanted the last scene, with the falling bandaged body, removed; he said it made him sick. Zanuck and Wellman literally fought to keep it in. When director Mike Curtiz, who was in the room at the time, agreed with Warner, Zanuck punched Curtiz in the mouth. Warner quickly gave in.

Raiders of the Lost Ark

1981, USA, Paramount, 115 minutes, Color
Producers: George Lucas, Frank Marshall; Director: Steven Spielberg
Cast: Harrison Ford, Karen Allen, Paul Freeman, John Rhys-Davies, Denholm Elliott

> "The most incredible series of action and stunt set pieces I've ever seen in a movie."
> —Roger Ebert, *Roger Ebert's Movie Home Companion*

One of the greatest adventure films ever made and a box-office blockbuster: the top-grossing film of the year. It's a throwback to the movie serials of the 30s and 40s when cliffhangers kept kids and parents alike coming back for the next chapter every Saturday. Filled with humor, fast action, and exotic locations, the film was nominated for Best Picture and won several technical Oscars. Its success spawned two hit sequels: *Indiana Jones and the Temple of Doom* (1984) and *Indiana Jones and the Last Crusade* (1989).

Harrison Ford as Indiana Jones in *Raiders of the Lost Ark*. © Lucasfilm LTD.

Indiana Jones (Ford) is a fedora-clad, leather-jacketed, whip-cracking archaeologist-adventurer who gets the chance of a lifetime: the U.S. Government will pay him to search for the age-old Ark of the Covenant, a powder keg of spiritual invincibility, missing since the days of Old Testament prophets. Lawrence Kasdan's screenplay, from an idea by Philip Kaufman, takes place in 1936 with the Nazis ascending to power; they're also looking for the lost Ark, hoping to harness its energy to provide their armies with superhuman strength.

Jones' partner in the search is a hardy former love interest, Marion Ravenwood (Allen), whose romantic flames get fanned again. Sallah (Rhys-Davies) is Indy's friend and helper in the quest. Indy's nemesis, Dr. Belloq (Freeman), is working for the Nazis. Dr. Marcus Brody (Elliott) is the university curator of artifacts.

A five-minute climactic sequence in the desert is one of the most fantastic special effects displays ever screened—manifesting the power and nature of the Ark. Likewise, the 12-minute opening is unparalleled: Indy retrieving a golden idol from a booby trapped jungle tomb then being chased by a giant boulder.

- The boulder was made of fiberglass.
- 6,000 snakes were used for the Well of Souls sequence; a slab of plexiglass kept the creatures from the stars.
- It was shot in Tunisia, Hawaii, France, and at Elstree Studios in England. The campus was the University of the Pacific in Stockton, Calif.
- Stuntman Terry Leonard is the Ford-double for the dangerous slide under the truck; the film used 14 stunt people overall.
- Tom Selleck was originally considered for the Jones role.

The Roaring Twenties

1939, USA, Warner Bros., 104 minutes, B&W
Producer: Hal B. Wallis. Director: Raoul Walsh
Cast: James Cagney, Priscilla Lane, Humphrey Bogart, Frank McHugh, Gladys George, Jeffrey Lynn, Paul Kelly

> "Among the last of the Warner gangster cycle, this was perhaps the best production of them all, despite the familiar plot

line; stars and studio were in cracking form."
—Ruth Halliwell and John Walker, *Halliwell's Film Guide*

The best crime drama depicting the Prohibition-era underworld and the last Cagney-Bogart pairing. This is the one in which Cagney's death scene has him wounded and staggering down the street and up the steps of a church where a speakeasy gun moll tells an inquiring cop, "He used to be a big shot."

Cagney and Bogie play fellow soldiers from WWI who can't find work following the war and turn to the bad side to survive. Eddie Bartlett (Cagney) falls hard for nightclub singer Jean Sherman (Lane) but loses

Frank McHugh, James Cagney and Humphrey Bogart in a publicity pose for *The Roaring Twenties*.

everything in the stock market crash of 1929. Jean then finds safety in the arms of their pal, Lloyd Hart (Lynn), a struggling lawyer who works his way up to district attorney. Bogart plays gun-toting bootlegger George Halley. McHugh is Eddie's buddy, Danny Green; George plays Panama Smith and Kelly is Nick Brown.

- Panama is based on nightclub hostess Texas Guinan.
- Bartlett is based on the life of bootlegger Larry Fay.
- This was the last of Cagney's gangster roles for 10 years until *White Heat*.
- McHugh, one of Cagney's personal friends, appeared in 11 Cagney movies.
- Director Anatole Litvak began the picture.
- Walsh played John Wilkes Booth in D.W. Griffith's *The Birth of a Nation*.

Unconquered

1947, USA, Paramount, 147 minutes, Color
Producer/Director: Cecil B. DeMille
Cast: Gary Cooper, Paulette Goddard, Howard DaSilva, Boris Karloff, Mike Mazurki, Ward Bond, Katherine DeMille, Victor Varconi, Cecil Kellaway

> "…the public went to it in droves…it paid off in spectacle and some superb color photography, and the quality of the historical detail was high…a good visual impression of the colonial frontier."
>
> —George MacDonald Frazer,
> *The Hollywood History of the World*

One of the greatest adventure films of all time with all the essential elements in place…action, excitement, drama, suspense, humor, and romance. And the screenplay is based on fact: Indian war parties in 1763 besieging farms and forts, killing colonists and British redcoats for a month until they came upon Fort Pitt (now Pittsburgh), commanded by Capt Ecuyer (Varconi). The 300 soldiers and frontiersmen (plus another 300 women and children) hold out for 30 days until they are saved by a splen-

Paulette Goddard and Gary Cooper in *Unconquered*.

did corps of settlers and the Black Watch—many of whom were already dead though propped up in wagons to frighten the marauding Indians.

Cooper is Capt. Chris Holden who falls in love with indentured slave Abigail "Abby" Hale (Goddard). DaSilva is the villain, Martin Garth, trying to steal Abby from Chris. Garth is a trader supplying illegal arms to the Indians in an attempt to remain kingmaker West of the Allegheny Mountains. Holden, on behalf of Gen. Washington, is out to break Garth's stranglehold to open up the frontier for the good of the new country.

Bond plays Holden's friend, John Fraser. Kellaway is Jeremy Love, Abby's surrogate father. Mazurki is Garth's henchman, Bone. Karloff portrays Guyasuta, Chief of the Senecas. K. DeMille is Hannah, Guyasuta's daughter pledged in blood to Garth.

- Outdoor scenes were shot at Cook Forest, Pennsylvania by Ray Rennahan (*Gone With the Wind*); the canoe sequence was filmed on the Snake River in Idaho.
- In the siege of Fort Pitt, 2,000 arrows were used, 500 with flaming points.

- Katharine is the adopted daughter of C.B.
- During production the crew jokingly referred to the shoot as "The Perils of Paulette."

Animation

Bambi

1942, USA, RKO, 69 minutes, Color
Producer: Walt Disney, Director: David Hand

> "*Bambi* is the gentlest of Disney's animated features…It stands unique among the Disney cartoons in its style and atmosphere, and indeed, it would be quite some time before the studio would again go to such lengths to achieve the realistic detail found in this film."
> —Leonard Maltin, *The Disney Films*

From its compelling opening, with the camera moving left to right through the forest in a 3-D effect (using the multiplane process), to the forest fire finale, *Bambi* has had more positive affect on small children than any other film in the history of cinema.

The key to the continual success of this little movie is how children see it and very soon, in their own lives, learn to react to animals as if they were human. The animals in the film talk and react to one another, like two and three-year-olds, as if they were little children. Tiny tots watching the film get it right away. From the start, the mother and all other animals in the forest teach the young Bambi about things, about life and its dangers.

To adults who had never seen the film, the tendency would be to pass it off as kid-stuff, and it is; but for those who enjoyed the film as a child, they have been taught—subconsciously—to love and respect all animals, they now have ingrained within themselves a feeling of love for animals that lasts a lifetime. Beyond that, one must admit that experiencing the death of a parent is a sobering and frightening thing and is about as adult as you can get. The positive influence of this film cannot really be measured.

Faline and Bambi in *Bambi*. © Walt Disney Productions.

The stars are a fawn named Bambi, his mother, a young rabbit called Thumper, and a cute little skunk—Flower. The story was based on the book by Felix Salten. The film's music is by Frank Churchill; the chorus conducted by Charles Henderson.

- Two live fawns, sent by the State of Maine, were used as models for Bambi.
- Human models, including Ice Capades star Donna Atwood, were used for the ice-skating scene.
- Hundreds of pictures of Maine forests were taken by Disney photographer Jake Day and animators studied them in detail.

Cinderella

1950, USA, RKO, 74 minutes, Color
Producer: Walt Disney, Directors: Wilfred Jackson, Hamilton Luske, Clyde Geronimi
Cast (the voices of): Ilene Woods, William Phipps, Eleanor Audley, Rhoda Williams, Lucille Bliss, Verna Felton

"It is a work of genuine charm, thanks to skillful characterizations and story work, and, most importantly, an especially winning score."
—Leonard Maltin, *The Disney Films*

This was Disney's first full animated feature since the war and it turned out to be a big hit. But Walt was taking a big risk. Disney spent $3 million on the project—the most time and money since *Snow White*; had it failed, some believe the studio would have gone under. The film also made additional profits from the copyrighted songs and soundtrack. The picture was such an early success that Disney immediately launched into *Alice in Wonderland* using the same three directors. *Cinderella* has become one of the all-time Disney classics. The company made another $64 million on DVD release sales in 2005.

In designing the creation, the studio went back to the popular fairy tale genre of *Snow White* but writers and animators spruced up the glass slipper story by adding animal friends for Cinderella (Woods). And catchy songs (by Mack David, Jerry Livingston, and Al Hoffman) add to the zestfulness of the movie: "Bibbidi Bobbidi Boo," "A Dream is a Wish Your Heart Makes," "Cinderella," and more.

Cinderella and the Fairy Godmother in *Cinderella*. © Walt Disney Productions.

Phipps is the voice of Prince Charming. Audley is the wicked stepmother. Williams and Bliss are the hateful stepsisters. Felton provides the voice for the Fairy Godmother. Special cinematic processes were the work of Ib Iwerks.

- Woods was the best of 300 girls who tried out for the part.
- Most of the animation work was done with artists using live-action models. Even the carriage and its pumpkin counterpart had been models.
- Felton also plays the Queen of Hearts in *Alice in Wonderland*. Felton was Junior's grandma on the Red Skelton Radio Show in the 40s.

Dumbo

1941, USA, RKO, 64 minutes, Color
Producer: Walt Disney, Director: Ben Sharpsteen
Cast: (the voices of) Edward Brophy, Verna Felton, Sterling Holloway, Cliff Edwards

> "A film you will never forget."
> —*The New York Times*

The shortest of the Disney animated classics is also one of the very best. Veteran Disney animator Ward Kimball said, "I think the Disney cartoon reached its zenith with *Dumbo*." The little movie won the Oscar for Best Scoring of a Musical Picture and the surrealistic sequence, "Pink Elephants on Parade," with Dumbo accidentally getting drunk on champagne, remains one of the most memorable parts of any animated film.

Let's face it, a story about a flying baby elephant in a circus has got to be a sure winner, and it was and remains so. Several songs stand out including the one about a little circus train that could, "Casey Junior," "Look Out for Mr. Stork," "Baby Mine," and the crows on the telephone line singing "When I See An Elephant Fly" (recall Robert Stack crying while watching it in Spielberg's 1979 comedy *1941*).

Brophy is the voice of Timothy Q., the mouse that keeps Dumbo on the straight and narrow. Felton is the voice of Mrs. Jumbo. Holloway,

Dumbo and Timothy in *Dumbo*. © Walt Disney Productions.

familiar as the voice of Winnie the Pooh, is the voice of the stork. And Edwards, most famous as Jiminy Cricket in *Pinocchio*, is the voice of the Black Crow.

- It was one of the lowest budgets in Disney animation history, coming in at under a million dollars, while most animated features ran two or three million.
- The plot design, from a story by Helen Aberson and Harold Pearl, took six months and the animators took just another year to produce the concept.
- Sharpsteen was also one of the supervising directors on *Pinocchio, Cinderella, Alice in Wonderland, The Living Desert, The Vanishing Prairie, Melody Time,* and *The Adventures of Ichabod and Mr. Toad.*

Fantasia

1940, USA, RKO Radio, 126 minutes, Color
Producer: Walt Disney, Production Supervisor: Ben Sharpsteen
Host: Deems Taylor

> "**** A rare, innovative animated feature from Walt Disney that combines classical music with cartoons."
> —Jay A. Brown & Consumer Guide, *Rating the Movies*

Disney's most creative and challenging work, earning Special Oscars for Disney, musical conductor Leopold Stokowski, and recording engineers William Garity and John Hawkins. Nevertheless, some critics were not too generous at first: a few classical devotees felt Disney took too many liberties with interpreting the music. Taylor, voice of the New York Philharmonic radio broadcasts, introduces the program. The film features eight segments of classical music depicted by colorful animation:

"Toccata And Fuge In D Minor" by Johann Sebastian Bach is illustrated by abstract patterns.

"The Nutcracker Suite" by Peter Ilich Tchaikovsky is in two parts: "The Dance of the Sugar-Plum Fairies" has fireflies turning into luminescent ballerinas; "Chinese Dance" shows mushrooms whose tops appear as Oriental hats.

"The Sorcerer's Apprentice" by Paul Dukas stars Mickey Mouse.

"The Rite of Spring" by Igor Stravinsky features the creation of the Earth.

"Pastoral Symphony" by Ludwig von Beethoven is shown through characters of Greek mythology.

"Dance of the Hours" by Amilcare Ponchielli uses elephants, hippos, ostriches, and crocodiles.

"Night on Bald Mountain" by Modest Mussorgsky is a startling celebration of evil by the Black Demon.

"Ave Maria" by Franz Schubert pictures good overcoming evil.

- The film lost money upon its original release but was a major hit when reissued in 1969, due to the Sixties Generation experiencing its psychedelic imagery. Home video sales were also excellent in 1991.
- This was the first American film to use stereophonic sound.

Animation ○ 119

Walt Disney—producer of *Fantasia*—and creator of Mickey Mouse, Donald Duck and Disneyland. © The Walt Disney Company.

- Bela Lugosi spent several days at the Disney Studios as one of the models for the Demon in "Night on Bald Mountain."
- The set-up for the "Ave Maria" sequence was 200 feet long.
- The Sorcerer's name is "Yen Sid" which is "Disney" spelled backwards.
- Igor Stravinsky was the only one of the composers still living at the time of the film's release. He reportedly didn't like the fact that bits of his work had been slightly altered or adapted to fit the animation.

Pinocchio

1940, USA, RKO Radio, 88 minutes, Color
Producer: Walt Disney, Directors: Ben Sharpsteen, Hamilton Luske
Cast (the voices of): Dickie Jones, Christian Rub, Cliff Edwards, Evelyn Venable, Walter Catlett, Charles Judels, Frankie Darro

> "…one of Disney's most visually innovative films and also his 'meatiest' animated feature…a film of amazing detail and brilliant conception."
> —Leonard Maltin, *The Disney Films*

Carlo Lorenzini's nineteenth century children's story about the marionette who became a boy is one of Disney's three greatest animated films (*Snow White and the Seven Dwarfs, Fantasia*). Walt's staff of over 60 artists worked on the project for three years with the quality enriched by use of the Multi-plane camera: a dozen Multi-planes were used, for example, in the town panorama.

The movie won Oscars for Best Score and Best Song: "When You Wish Upon a Star" (Leigh Harline, Ned Washington, Paul J. Smith). The

Geppetto and Pinocchio in the animated classic *Pinocchio*.
© Walt Disney Productions.

songs include "Give A Little Whistle," "I've Got No Strings," and "Hi-Diddle-Dee-Dee."

Among the highlights: the singing march through the town, Pinocchio swallowed by a whale, and Pinocchio's transformation into a donkey (what William K. Everson calls "surely one of the screen's supreme moments of horror").

Jones is the voice of Pinocchio. Rub is Geppetto the puppet maker. Edwards plays Jiminy Cricket. Venable is the voice of the Blue Fairy. The characters include Figaro the cat, Cleo the goldfish, and Monstro the whale. Judels is both the coachman and Stromboli, the evil puppet master who takes Pinocchio captive. Catlett is Honest John, the sly fox. Darro is Pinocchio's young friend, Lampwick.

- Jones appeared in a few other films, notably *Destry Rides Again* and *Young Mr. Lincoln*, then retired with his wife and four children to a ranch in Salinas, Calif.
- Edwards, nicknamed "Ukulele Ike," played Harmony, Charles Starrett's sidekick in B-Westerns.
- The film was made for about $2½ million and grossed nearly $39 million. It made millions more in video releases in the 80s and 90s.
- One of the cut scenes was Geppetto telling Pinocchio about his grandfather, an old pine tree.

Snow White and the Seven Dwarfs

1937, USA, RKO Radio/Disney, Animation, 83 minutes, Color
Producer: Walt Disney, Director: David Hand
Cast: (the voices of) Adriana Caselotti, Lucille LaVerne, Harry Stockwell, Pinto Colvig, Billy Gilbert

> "How does one begin to talk about *Snow White*—the first full-length animated feature, the turning point in Walt Disney's career, a milestone in film history, and, as more and more people realize with each passing year, a great film"
> —Leonard Maltin, *The Disney Films*

After announcing to his stunned staff that their first animated feature would be from *Grimm's Fairy Tales*, Walt Disney sat his artists in a circle

Snow White and the Witch in *Snow White and the Seven Dwarfs*.
© Walt Disney Productions.

around him and proceeded to act out the plot for the next two hours. For the film, to give the characters a more life-like appearance, the Disney team created the Multi-plane camera, its lenses pointing down on four or five layers of background and animation. (Disney first tested the Multi-plane system in a Mickey Mouse cartoon, *The Old Mill*.) Over three years in the making, the film got a standing ovation from its preview audience in Los Angeles and went on to break box-office records everywhere. For their extraordinary efforts, Disney Studios received a Special Academy Award in the form of seven miniature statuettes plus one regular-sized Oscar. (In 1941, director Hand would oversee *Bambi*.)

For the voice of Snow White, Walt chose an opera-trained 18-year-old, Adriana Caselotti, over the popular Deanna Durbin: Walt said he thought Deanna's voice was too mature. LaVerne, the old hag in *A Tale of Two Cities*, was the choice for the second-most important part in the picture, the Wicked Queen/Old Witch. Colvig, the voice of Disney's famous cartoon character Goofy, is both Grumpy and Sleepy. Gilbert is Sneezy. Dopey didn't require a voice. The other three Dwarfs are Happy (Otis Harlan), Bashful (Scotty Mattraw) and Doc (Roy Atwell). Stockwell is Prince Charming.

Highlights: the Magic Mirror ("Who is the fairest of them all?"), Snow White's run through the forest, Snow tidying up the cottage ("Whistle While You Work"), the Dwarfs working in the diamond mine ("Heigh-Ho"), the Queen's transformation, the Witch's trip from the castle to the forest, Snow singing "Someday My Prince Will Come," the animals rushing to get the Dwarfs, and Snow White's death scene. There are scary moments, to be sure; as Danny Peary points out—when the Witch presents the poisoned apple to Snow, it's symbolic of Satan the serpent giving Eve the apple in the Garden of Eden.

- Among the 32 animators and layout artists was Art Babbitt; his pretty young wife, Marge, was used as the model for Snow White (she would later become a partner in the dance team of Marge and Gower Champion).
- Hollywood critics, thinking the movie would fail, referred to it as "Disney's Folly."
- It was the first film to ever have a soundtrack recording album released.
- The first film to tie-in merchandising memorabilia.
- Some of the names originally considered for the Dwarfs: Awful, Blabby, Gabby, Gloomy, Jumpy.
- How was LaVerne able to change her voice from the beautiful Queen to the Old Witch? By removing her false teeth.

Toy Story

1995, USA, Walt Disney Pictures/Pixar, 87 minutes, Color
Producers: Ralph Guggenheim, Bonnie Arnold; Director: John Lasseter
Cast: (the voices of) Tom Hanks, Tim Allen, Annie Potts, Don Rickles, Jim Varney, John Ratzenberger, Wallace Shawn, John Morris, Erik von Detten

"Miraculous!"
—*Entertainment Weekly*

The #1 box-office hit of the year was also the first fully computer-generated full-length feature film, a clever milestone in movie animation. Director Lasseter received a Special Oscar for his creation. And Randy New-

Woody the pull-string cowboy and Buzz Lightyear in *Toy Story*. © The Walt Disney Company.

man got nominated for Best Original Song ("You've Got A Friend In Me"). The popular family film also spawned a whole series of collectible toys.

It's all about toys that come alive when kids and grown-ups aren't around. The toys belong to a kind and lovable six-year-old named Andy (Morris). The leader of the toy room is a pull-string cowboy (minus a six-shooter in his holster) named Woody (Hanks). Take-charge Woody also happens to have a face like Tom Hanks. New to the toy world is a square-jawed space ranger named Buzz Lightyear (Allen). Buzz ("To infinity and beyond!") was given to Andy at his birthday party. But the addition causes anxiety for Woody who feels his role as leader of the toys is challenged. The rivalry produces a lot of laughs and adventure.

Also in the cast as toys are Potts as Bo Peep, Rickles as Mr. Potato Head, Varney as Slinky Dog, Ratzenberger as Hamm the Piggy Bank, and Shawn as Rex the Dinosaur. Von Detten is Sid, the bad boy next door who likes to torture toys by taking them apart, but Sid meets his match when Woody and Buzz confront the boy's hateful ways.

- Each frame took 4 to 13 hours to create depending on the complexity of the scene.
- Billy Crystal turned down the part of Buzz; he later said it was the worst career decision he ever made.
- Pixar also wanted to use a Barbie Doll as one of the characters but Mattel said no. However, after the huge success of the film, they allowed Barbie to be used in *Toy Story 2* (1999).

Comedy

The Bank Dick

1940, USA, Universal, 73 minutes, B&W
Producer/Director: Edward Cline
Cast: W.C. Fields, Cora Witherspoon, Una Merkel, Evelyn Del Rio, Jessie Ralph, Franklin Pangborn, Grady Sutton, Russell Hicks, Pierre Watkin, Richard Purcell

> "*The Bank Dick* contains the fullest measure of Fields' humour."
>
> —John Baxter

W.C. Fields has become one of Hollywood's most legendary figures. In a movie-memorabilia shop, it would not be unusual to find plaster statues of Fields in a crumpled high hat and selling just as well as representations of Marilyn Monroe, Chaplin, Laurel and Hardy, James Dean, or Bogart. Fields is much imitated and beloved, despite his screen image of being a henpecked boozer who hates kids and dogs. It's the Fields voice, though, that endears us the most: a gravelly whine like air eased from a tire tinged with cynicism and sarcasm.

Fields wrote the screenplay under the pseudonym Mahatma Kane Jeeves. Fields is Egbert Sousé (Soo-say) who spends much of his day at the Black Pussy Cat Saloon and Café, mostly because he needs to get out of his house where nagging wife Agatha (Witherspoon), mother-in-law Brunch (Ralph), daughters Myrtle (Merkel) and Elsie (Del Rio) make life miserable for him. At the bar, Sousé meets movie producer Mackley Q. Green (Purcell) who is looking for a replacement for drunken director A. Pismo Clam (played by Jack Norton, the screen's most famous inebriated charac-

W.C. Fields as *The Bank Dick*.

ter). Souse talks his way into taking over the picture. But this three-ring circus changes fast as Egbert accidentally captures a bank robber and gets a hero's attention from the bank president (Watkin) who hires Souse as a bank guard. Now the fun really begins when Souse, again at the saloon, meets shyster J. Frothingham Waterbury (Hicks) who sells Egbert worthless shares in a gold mine, though Souse had to talk Myrtle's boyfriend, Og (Sutton), a teller at the bank, into secretly "borrowing" $500 to make the deal. Are you following this? Well, who should suddenly appear on the scene but prissy bank examiner J. Pinkerton Snoopington (Pangborn) and the race is on to cover the shenanigans. It all ends with one of the screen's wildest car chases, something Cline was very versed in doing since he directed many of the Keystone Kops comedies for Mack Sennett.

- Joe the bartender is played by Shemp Howard, one of The Three Stooges. When Joe comes on the screen, the song "Listen to the Mockingbird" is played. It was the Stooges' theme.
- The setting is Lompoc (Lompoke), Calif., a temperance town during prohibition. Fields, known for his enjoyment of the forbidden beverage, picked the location for that reason.
- Author Jay Robert Nash says Fields got his bulbous nose because he was once a pool hustler and was often beaten up by angry pool hall victims. His nose was broken so often it became red and swollen. As to how he became a drinker, he used to work as an ice man early in the morning. When he got off at noon, he would kill the afternoon in the local saloon drinking nickel beer.

Dr. Strangelove
Or: How I Learned to Stop Worrying and Love the Bomb

1964, UK, Columbia, 93 minutes, B&W
Producer/Director: Stanley Kubrick
Cast: Peter Sellers, George C. Scott, Sterling Hayden, Slim Pickens, Keenan Wynn, Peter Bull, James Earl Jones, Tracy Reed

> "...classic nightmare comedy..."
> —Danny Peary, *Guide for the Film Fanatic*

The best black comedy ever made! But how can a movie about near-nuclear annihilation be funny? You have to see it to believe it. It's a *tour de force* for Sellers in three roles: American President Muffley, RAF Capt. Mandrake, and Dr. Strangelove—a weird nuclear scientist patterned after a concoction of international figures: Werner von Braun, Edward Teller and Henry Kissinger. Strangelove has enough trouble controlling his nearly-human artificial arm, let alone handling a nuclear arsenal. Sellers received an Academy Award nomination for Best Actor. Kubrick and the film also got Oscar nominations. The British Academy voted it Best Picture.

Based on Peter George's book *Red Alert*, Kubrick turned it into a satire when he found so much of the serious stuff was really laughable. Besides the dominant acting of Sellers, there are three other very memorable performances: Hayden as paranoid U.S. Air Force Commander Jack D.

Peter Sellers in *Dr. Strangelove*.

Ripper, Scott as gum-chewing Chief of Staff "Buck" Turgidson and Pickens as bomb-riding Major T.J. "King" Kong.

The cigar-chomping Ripper, convinced that fluoridation is a Communist conspiracy, launches a nuclear attack on the Russians, sealing his base off so Muffley can't stop him. Expecting a retaliatory strike, Muffley phones the Soviet Premier to apologize, explaining that one of his generals "went and did a silly thing." The Russian Ambassador (Bull), invited to the urgent meeting of the Joint Chiefs, gets into a tussle with Turgidson who catches the enemy envoy taking secret photos, prompting Muffley to exclaim: "Gentlemen! You can't fight in here! This is the War Room!" Pickens, meanwhile, is airborne reading the contents of the B-52 survival kit: "Shoot. A fella could have a pretty good time in Vegas with all of that stuff!"

Wynn plays dunderhead Col. "Bat" Guano. Jones (later the voice of Darth Vader in *Star Wars*), in his film debut, plays Lt. Lothar Zogg. Reed, the only woman in the film, plays Turgidson's secretary, Miss Foreign Affairs.

Vera Lynn, a popular British singer during WWII, is heard in a recording of her ballad, "We'll Meet Again (Don't Know Where, Don't Know When)," at the end of the film over continuous shots of atomic and nuclear bomb explosions.

- Sellers was actually cast in four roles, also as Major Kong, but couldn't develop a good Texas accent. Kubrick remembered Pickens from *One-Eyed Jacks* and asked him to take over the part.
- The U.S. Air Force refused to let Kubrick study the interior of a B-52 bomber so the intricate control panel was made up. Shots of the bomber in flight are of a model on strings.
- Terry Southern's script called for a custard pie fight in the War Room (that's why the food table was set up) but Kubrick thought it too crazy for the satirical plot and scrapped it.

Duck Soup

1933, USA, Paramount, 68 minutes, B&W
Producer: Herman J. Mankiewicz, Director: Leo McCarey
Cast: Groucho Marx, Harpo Marx, Chico Marx, Zeppo Marx, Margaret Dumont, Louis Calhern, Edgar Kennedy, Raquel Torres

> "The Marx Brothers' most striking film is a satire on fascism and war."
> —Georges Sadoul, *Dictionary of Films*

This is the one that contains the famous mirror bit when Groucho and Harpo, in long nightshirts, nightcaps, and moustache/glasses/cigar, act out each other's "reflection" (Groucho gave McCarey credit for the gag, an old vaudeville bit).

Chico, Zeppo, Groucho and Harpo, the Marx Bros., stars of *Duck Soup*.

Groucho plays Rufus T. Firefly, president/dictator of Freedonia, sponsored in his new position by wealthy widow Mrs. Gloria Teasdale, played by Dumont, the wonderful dowager foil in seven of their films. Calhern, attempting a revolution, hires two spies, Chico and Harpo, to assist his sabotage. Chico, in typical Marxian logic, explains their surveillance of Firefly: "Monday we watcha Firefly's house but he no come out, he wasn't home; Tuesday we go to the ballgame but he fool us, he no show up; Wednesday *he* go to the ballgame but we fool him, *we* no show up; Thursday it was a doubleheader, nobody show up; Friday it rained all day, it was no ballgame—so we stayed home and listened to it on the radio."

The screenplay is by Bert Kalmar and Harry Ruby with additional dialogue by Arthur Sheekman and Nat Perrin.

At one point in the film, Groucho and Chico face the music in a courtroom…

> Groucho: Gentlemen. Chicolini here may talk like an idiot and look like an idiot, but don't let that fool you. He really is an idiot. I implore you, send him back to his father and brothers who are waiting for him with open arms in the penitentiary. I suggest that we give him ten years in Leavenworth or eleven years in Twelveworth.
>
> Chico: I tell you what I'll do. I'll take five and ten in Woolworth.

Their non-stop zaniness includes Edgar Kennedy, famous for the slow-burn, as a lemonade street vendor; he and Chico and Harpo do the three-hat-switch routine.

Torres is Vera, Calhern's pretty helper. Harpo has a field day with a blowtorch, a pair of scissors, and a motorcycle-with-sidecar that keeps leaving Groucho behind.

- It was Zeppo's last screen appearance; he became a Hollywood agent.
- It was their last film before moving to MGM in a deal with producer Irving Thalberg.
- Their real first names: Groucho is Julius, Harpo is Adolph, Chico is Leonard, and Zeppo is Herbert. There was a fifth brother, Milton (Gummo), who didn't follow the brothers into movies.

His Girl Friday

1940, USA, Columbia, 92 minutes, B&W
Producer/Director: Howard Hawks
Cast: Cary Grant, Rosalind Russell, Ralph Bellamy, Gene Lockhart, John Qualen, Helen Mack, Billy Gilbert

> "…the brilliant feminist role-reversal remake."
> —Ken Wlaschin

Hawks' fast-talking screwball comedy, famed for its overlapping dialogue, is a first-rate remake of *The Front Page* (1931) from the play by Ben Hecht and Charles MacArthur. In the original, the role of ace reporter Hildy Johnson is a man but Hawks turns the Hildy character into a female part: Russell.

Grant is Walter Burns, Hildy's ex-husband and former boss at the newspaper, a scheming editor whose latest scheme is to get Hildy to return to the paper—and to marry him again! Hildy, who's just divorced Walter, is considering giving up her madcap career for a quiet life with

dull insurance man Bruce Baldwin (Bellamy). But Burns knows better; he knows she has printer's ink for blood and is the best in the business, not to mention the fact that he still loves her. And Walter hits upon a murder story to lure her back.

There's a host of terrific supporting characters including Lockhart as Sheriff Pinky Hartwell, Qualen as the confused murderer, Mack as streetwalker Mollie Malloy, Gilbert as process-server Joe Pettibone, and the best bunch of crazy news reporters that ever entered a city hall press room.

- There are inside-joke references to Bellamy and Grant. Cary, in one scene, says Baldwin resembles "that actor Ralph Bellamy." And, in another place, Grant ad libs, "The last person who said that to me was Archie Leach, just a week before he cut his throat." Archibald Leach was Grant's real name.
- How did Hawks hit upon the idea? "I asked a girl to read Hildy's part, I read the editor and I stopped and said, 'Hell, it's better between a girl and a man than between two men.' I called Ben Hecht and said, 'What would you think of changing it so that Hildy is a girl?' And he said, 'I think it's a great idea', and he came out and we did it."
- Ginger Rogers, Irene Dunne, and Jean Arthur all turned the Hildy part down.

It's a Gift

1934, USA, Paramount, 73 minutes, B&W
Producer: William Le Baron, Director: Norman McLeod
Cast: W.C. Fields, Kathleen Howard, Charles Sellon, Jean Rouveral, Tom Rupp, Baby LeRoy, T. Roy Barnes

> "Fields' best film!"
>
> —Leslie Halliwell

Famous for two classic scenes: the cranky blind man, Mr. Muckle (Sellon), accidentally smashing light bulbs in the Fields' grocery store while a customer demands kumquats…and Fields trying to sleep on the porch-swing while a passerby (Barnes) looks for neighbor Carl LaFong ("Capital L, small a, capital F-o-n-g").

W.C. Fields takes a tumble in a garbage can in *It's a Gift*.

Fields plays a small-town New Jersey grocer, Harold Bissonette (pronounced Bis-o-nay), whose inheritance allows him to buy, against the wishes of nagging wife Amelia (Howard), an unseen California orange grove. Ah yes, we see it coming—will this plot of ground really produce oranges? Nonetheless, they take off in an old car to enjoy their dream gift, whatever it might be.

The screenplay is taken from a 1925 play by Fields and J.P. McEvoy. Rouveral plays daughter Mildred, Rupp is son Norman, and Baby LeRoy (real name LeRoy Overacker) is Baby Dunk.

- The film's credits say it was based on a story by Charles Bogle, but Bogle is a pseudonym for Fields. Fields, who was co-writer on his films, often put up outlandish name credits in place of his own.
- Demonstrating his distrust of banks, Fields stuck his money in dozens of different banks, some accounts which still can't be traced because they're under different names.
- Fields reportedly had on-set fights with co-star Baby LeRoy. Once, after spiking the baby's milk with booze, he shouted, "Walk the lush around, that boy's no trouper!"

- William Claude Dukenfield (1879-1946) learned to juggle at the age of 9, had a fight with his father, left home at 11 and spent time in pool halls, where he also learned the game of billiards. At 14, he began in show business by getting a job as a juggler at an amusement park. He was a vaudeville headliner before the age of 20. Fields made his first film in 1915, a short called *Pool Sharks*.
- Fields made 14 films at Paramount. Bing Crosby, who also worked at the studio, knew Fields well: "His comedy routines appeared spontaneous and improvised, but he spent much time perfecting them. He knew exactly what he was doing every moment, and what each prop was supposed to do."

A Night at the Opera

1935, USA, MGM, 94 minutes, B&W
Producer: Irving Thalberg, Director: Sam Wood
Cast: Groucho Marx, Chico Marx, Harpo Marx, Kitty Carlisle, Allan Jones, Margaret Dumont, Sig Rumann

"Thoroughly inspired."
—*The New York Times*

The biggest Marx Bros. hit at the box-office—and the first of their pictures for MGM, their first under the tutelage of "Boy Wonder" Thalberg, and the first without Zeppo (who quit to become a Hollywood agent, and a good one). It's also the film that contains their famous crowded stateroom scene: 15 people jammed into Groucho's tiny cabin.

Groucho is Otis B. Driftwood, financial and social advisor to a rich widow, Mrs. Claypool (Dumont). Driftwood convinces her to invest in the New York Opera in order to get into high society. Groucho's scheme is to transfer some of Italy's finest opera stars to America, but, as you might imagine, everything doesn't go as planned.

Rosa (Carlisle) and Ricardo (Jones) are singers transported from Italy, Harpo and Chico are stowaways on the ship. Harpo is Tomasso, a harp-playing dresser, and Chico is Fiorello, a pianist who plays with as few fingers as possible. Chico does a dandy rendition of Nacio Herb Brown's "All I Do Is Dream of You." He's also the receptacle for one of the film's best

Chico Marx, director Sam Wood, Groucho Marx and Harpo Marx, taking a break on the set of *A Night at the Opera*.

lines…when Groucho explains the sanity clause of the contract they just signed, Chico responds, "You can't fool me, there ain't no Sanity Claus." German-accented Rumann is along as Gottlieb, the business manager.

Each of the brothers, rambunctious anarchists, had his own special characterization: Groucho with painted-on mustache, horn-rimmed glasses and stooped-over walk; Harpo in fluffy wig, silent except for a taxi-horn, always chasing pretty girls; Chico, inveterate gambler, with Italian hat and accent, interpreting for Harpo.

- Carlisle became a panelist on the popular TV game show *What's My Line?*
- Groucho became host of the long-running TV game show *You Bet Your Life*.
- Jones (who took Zeppo's part) was the father of pop singer Jack Jones.
- Gummo was one of the original four Marx Bros. in vaudeville but left before their Broadway success and was replaced by Zeppo.

- As a talent agent, Zeppo represented Clark Gable, Carole Lombard, Barbara Stanwyck and Robert Taylor.
- $55,000 was offered to Harpo if he would utter just one word, "Murder!" in their 1946 film *A Night in Casablanca*. He refused.
- Jack Benny on the Marx Bros.: "If you ever sat at the Hillcrest Country Club and Groucho is there you'll find he'll make you laugh in the same way he does on screen. Chico, I would say, loved women and gambling, period. Harpo was probably the sweetest man you would ever want to meet."

Raising Arizona

1987, USA, 20th Century-Fox, 94 minutes, Color
Producer: Ethan Coen, Director: Joel Coen
Cast: Nicolas Cage, Holly Hunter, Trey Wilson, John Goodman, Randall "Tex" Cobb, William Forsythe

> "Formidably flaky comedy…Aggressively wacked-out sense of humor may not be for all tastes, but if you're attuned to it, it's a scream—a heady mix of irony and slapstick."
> —Leonard Maltin,
> *Leonard Maltin's Movie and Video Guide*

One of the truly *avant-garde* films of the 80s, with innovative filmmaking and a style all its own, made by two inventive brothers: Joel and Ethan Coen who wrote the very funny screenplay. All of their offbeat films have the same look about them: *Blood Simple, Fargo; Oh, Brother, Where Art Thou?*

Joel studied film at New York University; Ethan was a philosophy student at Princeton. They both loved movies and decided to put their talents together, setting out to create new techniques. One of their ingenious methods involves attaching a camera to the middle of a plank of wood—as they hold each end—and running with it, later speeding up the action in the editing room.

This Coen entry is about two babynappers, an ex-con and an ex-cop. H.I. McDunnough (Cage) can't seem to stop robbing convenience stores and continually ends in prison where he meets a pretty officer named

Holly Hunter and Nicolas Cage in *Raising Arizona*.

Edwina (Hunter), Ed for short. The next time he gets out, they decide to marry but they find they can't have children. While in a state of depression, they learn of a rich furniture store-chain dealer, Nathan Arizona (Wilson), whose wife has recently given birth to quintuplets. H.I. and Ed figure that's just not fair: the Arizonas with five kids, they with none. So they kidnap one of the boys. But complications arise when two goofy jail-bird-brothers, Gale (Goodman) and Evelle Snoats (Forsythe), H.I.'s former inmates, bust out of prison (appropriately through a sewer pipe) and come to visit the newlyweds; the Snoats re-kidnap Nathan, Jr. And adding to everyone's woes, a bounty-hunting motorcyclist from Hell (Cobb) sets out to retrieve the baby.

- The film was shot in several Arizona locales: Scottsdale, Phoenix, Valley of the Sun, and Tonto National Forest.
- The opening credits appear 11 minutes into the film.
- Holly's character was written especially for her.
- Fifteen babies, some twins, were used for the quints.
- Cobb couldn't ride a motorcycle when he started the movie.

Road to Morocco

1942, USA, Paramount, 83 minutes, B&W
Producer: Paul Jones, Director: David Butler
Cast: Bing Crosby, Bob Hope, Dorothy Lamour, Anthony Quinn, Dona Drake

> "…until the advent of the James Bond canon in the sixties the *Roads* were the most successful film series…(*Road to Morocco*) considered to be the best of the batch…"
> —Peter van Gelder

The *Road* pictures pushed Bing and Bob into the Box-Office Top 10 from 1943-1953. One big reason for the success of the films is the additional dialogue each actor put into the movies, each hiring their own gagmen to create extra lines, usually personal barbs and topical jokes.

In this journey to the land of Arabian Nights, Jeff Peters (Crosby) and Orville "Turkey" Jackson (Hope) are shipwrecked and find themselves in Morocco. Then fast-talking Jeff sells Orville into slavery so they can escape prison for not paying their restaurant bill. But the slavery isn't so bad after all; Jackson must marry the beautiful Princess Shalmar (Lam-

Dorothy Lamour, Bing Crosby and Bob Hope in *Road to Morocco*.

our) which he is more than willing to do. Jeff finally catches up to "Turkey" who doesn't want to be rescued. Quinn plays Kasim who intends to marry Shalmar himself. As you might expect, by the end, Lamour prefers Bing and Hope has to look elsewhere to find love, which he does in one of Shalmar's lovely handmaidens (Drake).

Bing sings "Moonlight Becomes You" and "Ho-Hum" and both he and Bob do the title tune: "We're off on the road to Morocco, this taxi (a camel) is tough on the spine. Where we're going, why we're going, how can we be sure. I'll lay you eight to five we meet Dorothy Lamour." Lamour sings "Constantly."

- The other *Road* pictures: *Road to Singapore* (1940), *Road to Zanzibar* (1941), *Road to Utopia* (1945), *Road to Rio* (1947), *Road to Bali* 1952), *Road to Hong Kong* (1962).
- *Road* ingredients include the "Patty-cake routine" that turns into a punch in the jaw for the villain.
- Hope always made a joke out of wanting to win an Oscar and never getting one but, in fact, Bob won five Special Academy Awards.
- Hope's visits to American servicemen throughout the world are legendary; he became the #1 entertainer of troops abroad.
- Crosby was one of Hollywood's biggest stars. Ken Wlaschin calls Bing, "The most popular American entertainer of the twentieth century, with equally big careers in radio, music and cinema, Crosby is one of the major movie stars—even if film historians have rarely accorded him his rightful place."

Some Like It Hot

1959, USA, United Artists, 121 minutes, B&W
Producer/Director: Billy Wilder
Cast: Marilyn Monroe, Tony Curtis, Jack Lemmon, Joe E. Brown, George Raft, Pat O'Brien, Joan Shawlee

> "Wacky, clever, farcical comedy that starts off like a firecracker and keeps on throwing lively sparks."
>
> —*Variety*

Undoubtedly, the greatest comedy ever made, starring Marilyn Monroe in her finest role. The film was the #3 moneymaker of the year, and Wilder received Oscar nominations for directing and writing (with Izzy Diamond). Lemmon also got nominated for Best Actor.

But make no mistake about it: the film belongs to Monroe. Marilyn, again, is cast as a victim—trampled by men, tragic, secretly nipping booze from a flask and seeking solace in the care of a millionaire. Up pops Curtis, posing as a Shell Oil heir and sounding like Cary Grant. Marilyn Monroe is reeled-in once more.

Director Billy Wilder (in white cap leaning on the camera) prepares Tony Curtis and Marilyn Monroe for a shot in *Some Like It Hot*.

Curtis and Lemmon are two out-of-work hot-jazz musicians in Chicago in the "Roarin' 20s." They accidentally witness the Valentine's Day Massacre and are spotted by Spats (Raft) and his mobsters and our boys are forever on the lam—chased to a resort in Florida. To escape, Joe (Curtis) and Jerry (Lemmon) dress as female musicians and join an all-girl orchestra whose lead singer is Sugar Kane, played by the voluptuous Monroe. Joe changes his name to Josephine and Jerry, who hates the name Geraldine, calls himself Daphne.

Monroe had to learn to play the ukulele for the part and sings "I Wanna Be Loved by You," "I'm Through with Love," and "Runnin' Wild." The film shows off Marilyn's amazing talent, as an actress and doing comedy, and it also shows off her amazing body in a see-through dress—which, in one smoky, nightclub scene, gives the appearance of being completely topless!

Brown plays Osgood Fielding III, a rich old guy who wants to marry Daphne. Brown has one of the screen's most famous closing lines—after Lemmon, in frustration, reveals he's really a man: "Well, nobody's perfect!"

O'Brien is Mulligan, the cop tailing Spats and his gang. Shawlee plays the leader of Sweet Sue's Society Syncopaters.

- Monroe only made 27 films but has emerged, after the first century of filmmaking, as Hollywood's most famous and legendary star; her untimely and mysterious death at the age of 36 probably had a lot to do with it.
- Marilyn was pregnant during production and had a miscarriage soon after.
- There's a gag between Raft and a young gangster, the latter flipping a coin—a bit begun in the early crime pictures by Raft...who says to the fellow, "Where'd you pick up that cheap trick?" And who's the young man? Edward G. Robinson, Jr., son of the famous actor who played crime bosses in Raft's prime.
- Wilder's original choices for the leads: Mitzi Gaynor, Danny Kaye and Bob Hope.
- The resort is Hotel Del Coronado in San Diego.
- The film's working title: *Not Tonight, Josephine*.

Sons of the Desert

1933, USA, Hal Roach Studios, 68 minutes, B&W
Producer: Hal Roach, Director: William A. Seiter
Cast: Stan Laurel, Oliver Hardy, Mae Busch, Dorothy Christie, Charley Chase, Lucien Littlefield

> "The quintessential Laurel and Hardy comedy."
> —Leslie Halliwell, *Halliwell's Filmgoer's Companion*

They were the perfect pair: Stan—thin, innocent, British; Ollie—fat, quick-tempered, Southern. Laurel looking regularly confused in bow-tie, breaking into tears in a bewildering world; Hardy gallant with a square little mustache, fingering his necktie; both in bowlers, the little guy bungling and smiling stupidly from ear-to-ear while the big guy takes the falls—always blaming the head-scratching Stanley for their dilemma: "Here's another fine mess you've gotten me into!" Their highly-successful formula included a bit where Ollie, as an aside of disgust, looks directly into the camera.

Oliver Hardy and Stan Laurel in *Sons of the Desert*.

In this comedy, considered by many of their fans to be their best, Stan and Ollie, as themselves, play members of a men's club, lodge-brothers in fezzes known as "Sons of the Desert." The boys try to trick their wives by saying they're going to Hawaii for a phony doctor-prescribed rest (the doctor is a vet) when they're really going to Chicago for the lodge convention—and a weekend of big city nightclubbing. "Why did you get a veterinarian," Ollie asks Stan. "Well," Laurel replies, "I didn't think his religion would make any difference." Naturally, the girls catch on to their ploy and a wild melee ensues.

Busch plays Lottie Hardy, Christie is Betty Laurel. Chase is the irritating brother-in-law and Littlefield is the doctor. The boys sing "Honolulu Baby."

- The Laurel and Hardy Fan Club is named "Sons of the Desert."
- The twosome made over 100 films together and won an Oscar for their comedy short *The Music Box* (1932).
- Stan created most of their gags.
- Ollie's real name was Norvell Hardy but his family and friends called him "Babe."
- Laurel, who was married five times, received a Special Academy Award in 1960; Ollie had died three years earlier. Stan passed away in 1965.
- In his last years, Stan kept his name and address in the Santa Monica phone book so he could be visited by fans—and they often did arrive at the door unannounced, much to his delight.

Young Frankenstein

1974, USA, 20th Century-Fox, 108 minutes, B&W
Producer: Michael Gruskoff, Director: Mel Brooks
Cast: Gene Wilder, Peter Boyle, Marty Feldman, Madeline Kahn, Cloris Leachman, Teri Garr, Kenneth Mars, Gene Hackman

"A monster riot."

—*The New York Times*

While Brooks' comedy, on the surface, appears to be simply making fun of all the Frankenstein movies, in truth it's Mel's loving tribute to the Universal Picture classics, movies he enjoyed as a young boy in Brooklyn.

Gene Wilder and Peter Boyle in *Young Frankenstein*.

He even shot his film in black-and-white so it resembles his favorite horror flicks of the 30s and 40s.

Wilder plays Dr. Frederick Frankenstein, grandson of the notorious creator of a Monster from dead human parts, who determines to make a Monster that works. Inga (Garr) is Frederick's lovely German assistant and Frau Blucher (Leachman) is the crazy keeper of the Frankenstein castle.

Based on Mary Shelley's famous novel, the Brooks and Wilder screenplay/parody imitates some of the most famous scenes from *Frankenstein, The Bride of Frankenstein* and *The Son of Frankenstein*: this new Monster (Boyle) not only learns to talk but sings and dances (to "Puttin' On The Ritz"); Elizabeth (Kahn), the bride of the Monster, ends up with those lightning-like streaks in her hair; the Police Inspector (Mars) jabs darts in his wooden arm just like Lionel Atwill in sequel #2, the Blind Hermit (Hackman) who feeds the Monster seems as oblivious as James Whale's first one, and Igor the hunchback assistant (Feldman) is just as much a bungler as the original.

To be sure, there are new inventive situations, chief among them a candle bit in which Frederick and Inga get baffled over a secret door to a passageway; and there's a play on words at the Transylvania train station based on the big-band song "Chattanooga Choo-Choo."

- Brooks uses the same old laboratory equipment from the original films. He found that Kenneth Strickfaden, who put the stuff together, still had it stored in his garage.
- Garr was set to do Elizabeth but Kahn insisted on doing that part so they switched roles.
- The movie was adapted into a Broadway musical in 2007; it played for more than 400 performances.

Romantic Comedy

Adam's Rib

1949, USA, MGM, 101 minutes, B&W
Producer: Lawrence Weingarten, Director: George Cukor
Cast: Katharine Hepburn, Spencer Tracy, Judy Holliday, Tom Ewell, Jean Hagen

> "It isn't solid food but it certainly is meaty and juicy and comically nourishing."
> —*The New York Times*

Tracy and Hepburn did nine films together and this courtroom comedy has to be their best. It's written by the husband-and-wife team of Garson Kanin and Ruth Gordon. The film, about litigious lawyers married to each other, promoted women's rights long before the feminist movement became vogue.

Amanda Bonner (Hepburn) defends a rather dumb blonde (Holliday) who shoots her adulterous husband (Ewell) and Adam Bonner (Tracy) is the district attorney. The story opens with Holliday trailing her unfaithful spouse to the apartment of Hagen; Judy shoots Tom while he's in the arms of Jean, but Judy doesn't kill him. What follows is a very funny trial with Tracy as prosecutor and his lawyer-wife as recalcitrant legal opponent.

The trial begins with confident Spencer and determined Kate exchanging grins under the courtroom table. But by trial's end, their glowing glances have turned to scowls; then, at home, a routine massage for the wife by the mate ends with a smack on her backside:

Katharine Hepburn and Spencer Tracy in *Adam's Rib*.

> TRACY: Whatsamatta, don't you want your rubdown? What, are you sore about a little slap?
> HEPBURN: You meant that—didn't you?
> TRACY: No…
> HEPBURN: I can tell!
> TRACY: Whadya have back there—radar equipment?!

The closing scenes (including a tearful role reversal by Tracy) complete this clarion comedy: there's no difference between the sexes, and hooray for that little difference!

- The song "Farewell Amanda" was written by Cole Porter at Kate's personal request.
- The original title for the film was *Man and Wife*.
- Marilyn Monroe tested for the Holliday role but Columbia boss Harry Cohn never bothered to see the test.

- The film includes a charming home-movie sequence of Tracy and Hepburn and the footage was used several times at tribute banquets for the actors.
- Tracy and Hepburn had a 25-year affair that Hollywood reporters knew about but never wrote about.
- Spencer's Catholic wife, Louise, alternated with Kate in a deathbed vigil for Spencer who died two weeks after completing *Guess Who's Coming to Dinner* (1967) in which Tracy and Hepburn co-starred.

Annie Hall

1977, USA, United Artists, 95 minutes, Color
Producer: Charles H. Joffe, Director: Woody Allen
Cast: Woody Allen, Diane Keaton, Tony Roberts, Carol Kane, Paul Simon, Shelley Duvall, Janet Margolin, Colleen Dewhurst, Christopher Walken

> "**** This is an absolutely marvelous film...Some of their scenes together are amongst the wittiest, tenderest and most romantic scenes ever captured on film."
> —Steven H. Scheuer, *Movies on TV*

Allen's semi-autobiographical romantic comedy won the Academy Award for Best Picture (beating *Star* Wars) and made Keaton a star: she, as ditsy but charming Annie Hall, won the Oscar for Best Actress. Allen also won for Best Director and he and Marshall Brickman won for Best Original Screenplay.

The film is alive with innovative cinematic techniques: not only flashbacking but then stepping into the scene to talk to the characters from the past. In a sidewalk shot, New York comedian Alvy Singer (Allen) and his friend Rob (Roberts) are heard talking but it's 45 seconds before they clearly walk into view; waiting in a movie line, Alvy settles an argument by producing the subject of the discussion. Subtitles tell what Alvy and Annie are really thinking during a nonsensical conversation. Annie's soul walks away as an apparition during love-making; there's a real clip of Dick Cavett interviewing Woody on TV; suddenly feeling Jewish, Alvy appears as an orthodox rabbi with beard; several asides are made directly to the

Diane Keaton after receiving the Oscar for Best Actress for *Annie Hall*.

audience. There are split-screen effects; Alvy stops a stranger on the street to discuss his troubles and the woman reacts calmly with knowledge about his problems; Alvy appears as a cartoon character with the wicked queen from *Snow White*; Allen and Keaton improvise a very funny scene with a lost lobster.

Then there are the biting Allen one-liners: "They (Californians) don't throw their garbage away, they make it into television shows;" "I can't get with any religion that advertises in *Popular Mechanics*."

Kane, Duvall and Margolin play three of Alvy's former girlfriends. Simon is singer/record producer Tony Lacey. Dewhurst is Mrs. Hall and Walken plays Annie's weird brother, Duane.

- Working title: "Anhedonia" which means the inability to feel pleasure.
- Keaton's real name is Diane Hall.
- Keaton's clothes, which became an "in" fashion, were her own.
- Alvy's sneezing into the cocaine tin got so many laughs at private screenings that editor Ralph Rosenblum had to keep adding extra footage without dialogue after the scene so the audience wouldn't miss the next lines.

Bringing Up Baby

1938, USA, RKO, 102 minutes, B&W
Producer/Director: Howard Hawks
Cast: Cary Grant, Katharine Hepburn, May Robson, Charles Ruggles, Barry Fitzgerald, Virginia Walker, George Irving

> "A near-perfect example of that whole genre known as screwball comedy."
> —Robert Osborne, *Turner Classic Movies*

While this is one of the best comedies of its kind, such was not the case when it was first released: it bombed. And it was over two decades before it found its audience, via TV reruns in the Sixties. Part of the reason for not clicking with fans in the Thirties was because of Hepburn herself. Exhibitors had dubbed her "box-office poison" after several early flops.

Cary Grant and Katharine Hepburn in *Bringing Up Baby*.

Hepburn's first comedy, scripted by Dudley Nichols and Hagar Wilde, is true zaniness with snippets of slapstick. Kate stars as a scatter-brained heiress, Susan Vance, who, at first sight, falls for a bespectacled paleontologist, Dr. David Huxley (Grant). She draws him closer through the help of a leopard named "Baby." It seems her brother, a zoologist, has sent her a leopard from South America and Susan calls Huxley for advice on how to handle the cat. Through it all, Huxley is engaged to be married to a straitlaced co-worker named Alice (Walker) but that's not stopping Susan once she sets her sights on the absent-minded professor. Kate accidentally rips off the backside of her dress at a nightclub and Cary tries to hide the tear by walking close behind her out the door. And that dress! It's one of the weirdest ever on-screen, silvery with some sort of plastic ribbons floating around the head. Costumer Howard Greer wanted to show just how eccentric the rich of that day could be.

Robson plays Huxley's rich aunt, Elizabeth Random; Irving is Alexander Peabody, the aunt's legal advisor. Ruggles is explorer Major Horace Applegate and Fitzgerald plays another nut-case, Aloysius Gogarty.

- During all the antics, Grant ends up wearing a woman's dressing gown; when Aunt Elizabeth asks him why—he ad libs, "Because I just went gay all of a sudden!" This was the first use of the homosexual term in a major movie.
- Three familiar character actors have uncredited parts: Billy Benedict (from The Bowery Boys) is David's caddy, Jack Carson is a circus worker, and Ward Bond plays a motorcycle cop.
- There is no musical score besides the opening/closing titles.
- Skippy played the terrier named George. It was also Asta in *The Thin Man* (1934).
- The film used split-screen, rear-screen projection and other optical tricks in the scenes where the actors had to be near the leopard. Special effects by Linwood Dunn and Vernon Walker.
- Peter Bogdanovich, with an endorsement from Hawks, did a successful remake in 1971; *What's Up, Doc?* with Barbra Streisand and Ryan O'Neal.

The Graduate

1967, USA, United Artists, 105 minutes, Color
Producer: Lawrence Turman, Director: Mike Nichols
Cast: Dustin Hoffman, Anne Bancroft, Katharine Ross, Murray Hamilton, William Daniels, Buck Henry

> "For the college-age audience of 1967, this was the film of the year, one that everyone saw several times and that became integral to everyday conversation."
> —Danny Peary

Oscar-nominated for Best Picture, *The Graduate*, about the trepidation of youth transitioning to adulthood, was the top grossing film of 1968. The romantic-comedy received seven Academy Award nomina-

Katharine Ross and Dustin Hoffman in *The Graduate*.

tions and Nichols won for Best Director. Simon and Garfunkel's inventive soundtrack ("Mrs. Robinson," "The Sounds of Silence," "Scarborough Fair") won three Grammy trophies.

Hoffman, in his first starring role, plays college graduate Benjamin Braddock who gets seduced by the wife of his father's business partner. Bancroft is Mrs. Robinson, the older and alcoholic woman, involved in a summer-long secret romance with Ben.

Conflict comes when Ben suddenly falls hopelessly in love with Mrs. Robinson's lovely daughter, Elaine (Ross), a student at the University of California at Berkeley. To try to make things right, Ben admits the affair to Elaine who, not surprisingly, says she never wants to see him again. Not taking no for an answer, Ben pursues her in Berkeley—turning up wherever she goes.

All three stars, Hoffman, Bancroft, and Ross, got Oscar nominations. Hamilton plays Mr. Robinson, Daniels plays Ben's father.

The screenplay is by Buck Henry and Calder Willingham from the novel by Charles Webb. Part of the memorable dialogue results from executives, friends of the Braddock family, offering business advice to the young graduate: "Ben, I want to say one word to you, just one word—plastics." Possibly the funniest scene is when Ben goes to rent a room at a quality hotel for himself and Mrs. Robinson, only to feel embarrassed and self-conscious in front of the suspicious desk clerk (Henry).

- The cocked leg, framing Hoffman, on the movie poster belongs to Linda Gray, not Bancroft. Gray would later play Mrs. Robinson in the musical version of the film on the London stage.
- Patty Duke was offered the role of Mrs. Robinson but turned it down.
- Charles Grodin was originally considered for the role of Ben.
- When Ben goes to Berkeley, he's on the top deck of the Bay Bridge (which is easier for the camera to shoot) but is actually heading to San Francisco.
- After Elaine screams in Ben's rooming house, that's Richard Dreyfuss in a bit part shouting, "I'll get the cops!"
- Hoffman got only $17,000 for the part and went on unemployment right after making the film.

Hannah and Her Sisters

1986, USA, Orion, 103 minutes, Color
Producer: Robert Greenhut, Director: Woody Allen
Cast: Mia Farrow, Barbara Hershey, Dianne Wiest, Michael Caine, Woody Allen, Max Von Sydow, Maureen O'Sullivan, Lloyd Nolan, Carrie Fisher

> "Woody Allen's *Hannah and Her Sisters,* the best movie he has ever made, is organized like an episodic novel, with acute self-contained vignettes adding up to the big picture."
> —Roger Ebert, *Roger Ebert's Video Companion*

Allen won the Oscar for Best Screenplay, was nominated Best Director, and the film—an excellent romantic comedy—got nominated Best Picture. Caine and Wiest both won supporting Academy Awards.

Farrow is Hannah, the eldest and reliable sibling; her husband, Elliot (Caine), thinks he's fallen in love with Hannah's younger sister, Lee (Hershey), who lives with an older, eccentric, reclusive artist, Frederick (Von

Mia Farrow, Barbara Hershey and Dianne Wiest in *Hannah and Her Sisters*.

Sydow). The other sister, Holly (Wiest), is a neurotic would-be actress who borrows $2,000 from Hannah to start a catering service with her friend, April (Fisher). Mickey Sachs (Allen), Hannah's ex-husband, is a hypochondriacal TV producer who runs a comedy show that resembles "Saturday Night Live." Norma (O'Sullivan) and Evan (Nolan), a theatrical couple, are the mother and father of the sisters, all of whom live in Manhattan.

Allen, an expert at hallway/doorway shots, takes Carlo Di Palma's photography one step beyond with an ingenious scene with the troubled sisters having lunch in a restaurant; the slowly swirling camera leaves one person's comment, picks up another's reaction, traveling in search of an expression here and look there.

To show just how good Caine is, he does his big scene, pouring his heart out to Lee on a street corner, with his back to the camera. In the fumbling part of the incurable romantic, Caine is an ersatz for Allen, who would have played the part himself had he not needed to be Mickey.

- Many scenes were filmed in Farrow's actual apartment.
- O'Sullivan really was the mother of Farrow; Mia's father was director John Farrow.
- Nolan never saw the film, he died shortly before its release.

It Happened One Night

1934, USA, Columbia, 105 minutes, B&W
Producer: Harry Cohn, Director: Frank Capra
Cast: Clark Gable, Claudette Colbert, Walter Connolly, Roscoe Karns, Alan Hale, Jameson Thomas

> "…when it was first released, the critics were largely unimpressed. It was the public that had the good taste. They loved *It Happened One Night*, came to see it time and again, told their friends about it."
> —Peter Van Gelder, *That's Hollywood*

It was the first film to win all four major Oscars: Best Picture, Director, Actor (Gable), Actress (Colbert). Gable plays Peter Warne, a reporter who finds a spoiled, rich runaway girl, Ellie Andrews (Colbert), and in one

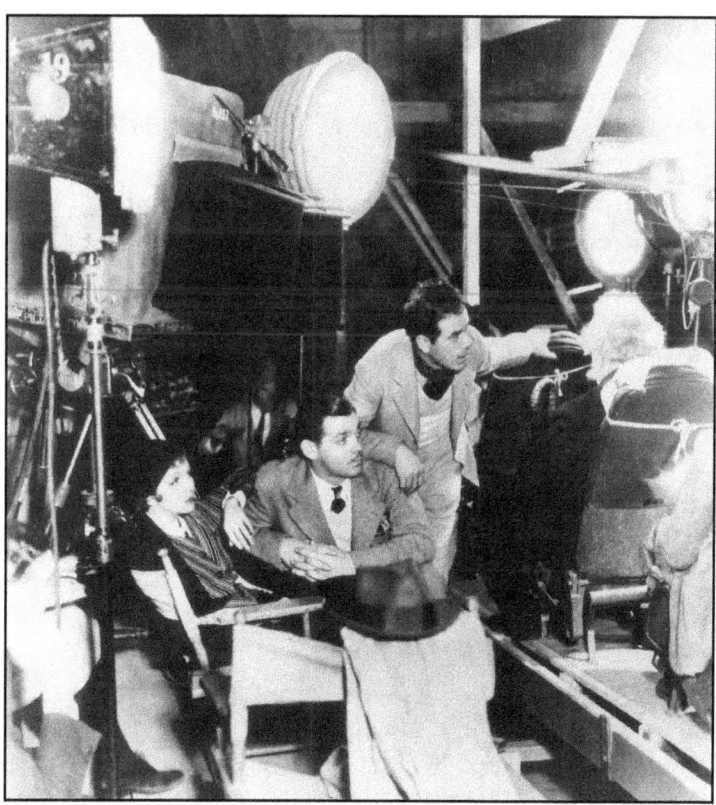

Claudette Colbert, Clark Gable and Frank Capra on the set of *It Happened One Night*.

of the funniest scenes in the comedy they have to share a motel room.

It was one of the first screwball comedies during the Depression and was based on the story "Night Bus" by Sam Adams in *Cosmopolitan*. MGM loaned Gable to Columbia, allegedly because some at the studio thought he'd gotten too big for his breeches and they figured if they made him work at a minor studio it would keep him in line. No one, including Harry Cohn, ever suspected he'd win an Oscar! The success of the film turned Columbia's fortunes around.

The motel scene has Gable hanging a blanket on a stretched rope dividing their sleeping spaces. When Ellie stubbornly refuses to move from his side, he starts to disrobe—one article of clothing at a time, causing her to run to safety. Another very funny scene happens while they're trying to hitchhike. He fails to get a car to stop, then she shows him up by revealing her leg to the next driver who screeches to a halt!

Connolly plays Alexander Andrews, Ellie's rich father. Thomas is King Westley, Ellie's fiancé. Karns is Oscar Shapeley and Hale plays Danker.

- Myrna Loy turned down the role of Ellie and Robert Montgomery rejected the Gable role.
- There wasn't another major Oscar sweep until *One Flew Over the Cuckoo's Nest* in 1975.
- Because of Gable's bare-chested scene in the motel, sales of men's undershirts declined.

The Lady Eve

1941, USA, Paramount, 97 minutes, B&W
Producer: Paul Jones, Director: Preston Sturges
Cast: Barbara Stanwyck, Henry Fonda, Charles Coburn, William Demarest, Eugene Pallette

> "One of the most intoxicating comedies ever made."
> —James Harvey, *Romantic Comedy*

Stanwyck once said, "Put me in the last 15 minutes of a picture and I don't care what happened before. I don't even care if I was in the rest of the damned thing—I'll take it in those 15 minutes!" In *The Lady Eve*, Stanwyck is there from the start and owns it from the start.

Barbara Stanwyck as *The Lady Eve*.

It's hard to imagine anyone but Stanwyck as the luxury-liner con-artist who, assisted by her card-shark father, takes a bachelor millionaire for a ride. Stanwyck has a dual role: Eugenia "Jean" Harrington—and an English lady named "Eve." After getting caught early on, Eugenia transforms herself into this other person to try again at capturing the affections of unassuming explorer and snake expert Charles "Charlie" Poncefort Pike (Fonda), son of rich beer manufacturer Horace Pike (Pallette). Coburn plays Jean's duplicitous father, Colonel Harry Harrington. Ambrose "Muggsy" Murgatroyd (Demarest), Charles' personal assistant, knows a con job when he sees it and warns his young, inexperienced boss to watch his back.

The comedy was a box-office hit for Paramount—and for Sturges, who then was able to convince the studio to let him try some more of his offbeat ideas: *Sullivan's Travels, The Palm Beach Story, The Miracle of Morgan's Creek, Hail the Conquering Hero.*

- Richard Schickel: "Sturges was the only truly comic mind to emerge in American film in the late thirties and early forties, a deep-dyed eccentric who made some of the oddest, and (in their erratic way) funniest movies of the period."
- Uncharacteristically, Fonda does five pratfalls.

- Henry Fonda: "Stanwyck can act the hell out of any part, and she can turn a chore into a challenge. She's fun, and I'm glad I had a chance to make three movies with her. *The Lady Eve* was the best….She's a delicious woman."

Ninotchka

1939, USA, MGM, 110 minutes, B&W
Producer/Director: Ernst Lubitsch
Cast: Greta Garbo, Melvyn Douglas, Ina Claire, Sig Rumann, Bela Lugosi

> "It remains a favorite Hollywood example of this genre."
> —Ruth Halliwell and John Walker, *Halliwell's Film Guide*

In the 30s, these romantic comedies were referred to as "sophisticated comedies." And Lubitsch was their best director. Garbo's last great film is a model of Lubitsch's escapist comedies with ancillary sexual innuendo. Throughout the genre, it's understood that at least one partner under-

Greta Garbo and Melvyn Douglas in *Ninotchka*.

stands the meaning of sexual activity, that it is the height of love-making; or has actually had experience with sex, or—at the very least—wants very badly to have that experience. In this film, it is Douglas who can't wait to teach the stoic but beautiful Garbo a thing or two.

Sadly, this was the only time that Lubitsch and Garbo had the chance to work together. In fact in two years, Garbo would leave Hollywood and become a recluse—and a legend. *Ninotchka,* advertised as "Garbo laughs," showed the Swedish star's range of acting; she had already proved her talent in drama and tragedy; she was often the doomed protagonist.

For this picture, Garbo received an Academy Award nomination for Best Actress and the film was nominated for Best Picture. The script, a rare spoof of the Soviet system of Communism, was co-authored by Billy Wilder, Charles Brackett and Walter Reisch, and Garbo's long-time cameraman William Daniels was behind the lens.

Garbo plays a duty-bound Russian agent named Ninotchka who is sent by her government to France to sell czarist jewels. In Paris, she meets a suave Frenchman, Count Leon D'Algout (Douglas), who makes her aware that there's more in this world to think about than Red Square. Claire is the Grand Duchess Swana. Rumann is Iranoff and horror star Lugosi is Commissar Razinin.

- Other titles considered: *A Foreign Affair* and *We Want to be Alone.*
- The story was remade in 1957 as the musical *Silk Stockings.*
- In retirement, Garbo continued her famous screen mystique. She never allowed photographs or personal interviews. She spent most of her time in an apartment on the Upper East Side of New York, though she also made trips to Switzerland and the French Riviera. Reportedly, she told a friend that the one thing she regretted was not having children. She died at 84 in 1990.

Nothing Sacred

1937, USA, United Artists, 75 minutes, Color
Producer: David O. Selznick, Director: William A. Wellman
Cast: Carole Lombard, Fredric March, Charles Winninger, Walter Connolly, Sig Ruman, Margaret Hamilton, Hattie McDaniel

Carole Lombard, Walter Connolly and Fredric March in *Nothing Sacred*.

"...a wildly hysterical comedy presenting some of the most insane moments ever captured on film...a film so courageous it has become a landmark of screwball comedy."
—Frank N. Magill, *Magill's Survey of Cinema*

With the screenplay by a former newspaperman, Ben Hecht, who wrote *The Front Page* (1931), this story is about callous reporters and an exploitative press. Hecht's opening line for the film: "New York, skyscraper champion of the world, where the slickers and know-it-alls peddle gold bricks to each other—and truth, crushed to earth, rises more phony than a glass eye."

The popular comedy stars Lombard as Hazel Flagg, a small-town Vermont girl who is dying of radium poisoning, and March as a cynical New York City reporter, Wally Cook, who brings her to the Big Apple to boost circulation...the trouble is, she isn't dying! In the meantime, while Wally shows Hazel around the city, he falls in love with her.

Winninger plays Dr. Enoch Downer, the goofy doctor who misdiagnosed Hazel. Ruman is Dr. Emil Eggelhoffer, the physician who smells a rat. Connolly is the paper's distraught editor, Oliver Stone. Hamilton plays a rather strange Vermont local in a drugstore. McDaniel is Mrs. Walker.

- Ring Lardner, Jr. and Budd Schulberg were uncredited co-writers with Hecht.
- This is one of Billy Barty's early films. Barty, famous for his role as the Bible salesman in *Foul Play* (1978), is the little guy who bites Wally's ankle in Vermont. Barty founded Little People of America in 1957.
- This was Lombard's only color film.

Pillow Talk

1959, USA, Universal, 110 minutes, Color
Producers: Ross Hunter, Martin Melcher; Director: Michael Gordon
Cast: Doris Day, Rock Hudson, Tony Randall, Thelma Ritter

> "It all worked delightfully…a quality cast…"
> —Clive Hirschhorn, *The Universal Story*

Day was the #1 box-office star and Hudson was second, both on the strength of this hit sophisticated sex-comedy. Day was also nominated for an Oscar for Best Actress.

Rock Hudson and Doris Day in a publicity photo for *Pillow Talk*.

Adorable Doris plays Jan Morrow, a Manhattan interior decorator who shares a telephone party-line (yes, they actually had such things for a while) with bachelor songwriter Brad Allen (Hudson). And it seems every time she wants to use the phone, there's Brad—with his sexy voice wooing a woman. He thinks of Jan as just an old maid until he finally meets her, and then to shield his identity as a womanizer he pretends to be a shy, rich Texan named "Rex Stetson."

Stan Shapiro and Maurice Richlin won an Academy Award for their fine screenplay that makes good use of a split-screen: Doris and Rock, while taking separate baths and talking on the phone, touch the bottoms of their feet together.

Randall is great as Brad's rich friend Jonathan Forbes. Ritter plays Alma, Jan's boozing but very funny housekeeper. Day sings the title song over the credits. Miss Day's terrific outfits are by Jean Louis.

- Doris and Rock followed with two more romantic comedies: *Lover Come Back* (1961) and *Send Me No Flowers* (1964), both quite successful.
- Rock didn't want to do *Pillow Talk* because he had never done comedy before and wasn't sure he could pull it off; Day and Hunter talked him into it.
- Melcher was Day's husband.
- In the diner scene, Tony was actually knocked out, accidentally, by the extra who was to fake a punch but missed and really hit Tony. What you see on-screen is an unconscious Randall slumping down into the booth.

Play It Again, Sam

1972, USA, Paramount, 87 minutes, Color
Producer: Arthur P. Jacobs, Director: Herbert Ross
Cast: Woody Allen, Diane Keaton, Tony Roberts, Jerry Lacy, Susan Anspach

> "Hilarious comedy was the picture that really established Allen's screen persona...Picture is consistently funny—Allen's date attempts are all classics."
> —Danny Peary, *Guide for the Film Fanatic*

Diane Keaton and Woody Allen in *Play It Again, Sam*.

The film opens with the last great scene from *Casablanca* when a gallant Bogart gives up Ingrid. Woody's glasses reflect the sequences as he sits in a movie theater, enthralled by his favorite actor; but as the theater lights come up and Woody snaps out of his vicarious dream world, he realizes he's no Bogie—or is he?

Allen is at his comedic best as Allan Felix, a San Francisco pill-popping hypochondriac who has trouble dating since his wife, Nancy (Anspach), walked out on him. At the heart of the screenplay, by Allen, are appearances by Bogart (Lacy) acting as a conscience.

Along the way are some very funny situations and dialogue. Downcast Woody: "I'm so depressed. Maybe if I took two more aspirins it would help. That makes six aspirins. I'm turning into an aspirin junkie. Next thing I'll be boiling the cotton at the top of the bottle to get the extra." And trying to pick up a pretty but strange girl (Diana Davila) at the Berkeley Museum, he asks: "What are you doing Saturday night?" She calmly replies, "Committing suicide." To which he responds, "What about Friday night?"

Keaton and Roberts are Allan's closest friends, Linda and Dick Christie; and they're always setting up Allan with dates. Dick, a high-powered investment broker, in an effort to make Allan forget his ex-wife, says to Felix, "Allan, you have invested your emotions in a losing stock, it was wiped out, it dropped off the board. Now what do you do, Allan? You reinvest maybe in a more stable stock. Something with long term growth possibilities." Felix says, "Who are you going to fix me up with, General Motors?"

- The script is taken from the Broadway play of the same title which ran for 453 performances in 1969. Allen, Keaton, Roberts and Lacy were all members of the stage cast.
- Jacobs produced *Planet of the Apes* (1968).
- Ross directed *The Goodbye Girl* (1977).
- Roberts is the cousin of Everett Sloane of Orson Welles' Mercury Theatre.

Risky Business

1983, USA, Warner Bros./Geffen Co., 98 minutes, Color
Producers: Jon Avnet, Steve Tisch; Director: Paul Brickman
Cast: Tom Cruise, Rebecca DeMornay, Joe Pantoliano, Richard Masur, Janet Carroll, Nicholas Pryor

> "A classic American comedy."
> —*US Magazine*

A breakthrough film about high school teenage erotic dreams in a perfect mix with surrealism. The most unusual romantic comedy of the 80s, reminiscent of *The Graduate* of the 60s. The film gently pokes fun at some of our traditional values: parenting, bureaucratic education, sexual guilt and illegal prostitution—with a compelling score by Tangerine Dream. Two rock hits also dress up the background, "Every Breath You Take" by The Police, and "Old Time Rock and Roll" by Bob Seger, the latter done in pantomime by Cruise in long shirt, bare legs and socks, sliding into movie mythology on a slick wood hallway floor.

Joel (Cruise) is a nice high school senior who, as a member of the school's Future Enterprisers of America, has to design a business project. He accidentally stumbles upon a highly profitable though highly risky business: a call-girl operation at his home while his parents (Carroll, Pryor) are away for a few days. It all starts innocently enough when Joel dates Lana (DeMornay), a sexy hooker trying to escape her pimp, Guido (Pan-

Rebecca DeMornay and Tom Cruise in a promotion photo for *Risky Business*.

toliano). (DeMornay comes across as one of the sexiest screen goddesses since Bardot.) After Joel wrecks his father's car, Lana gets her friends together to help Joel pay for the damages. And who are the customers? Joel's friends. All of this is going on while Joel is supposed to be studying to get into Princeton. Masur does a good job as the university interviewer.

The surrealism comes in three fascinating scenes. Joel contemplates telephoning a call-girl listed in a sex magazine and considers the consequences, acted out on-screen with vice-cops and his father using a bullhorn outside on the lawn trying to lure Joel out of the house; and when Joel (as Ralph) does make the call—he envisions a catcher's mask slipping down over his face to hide the guilt. Another very effective surreal scene is when Lana arrives ("Are you ready for me, Ralph?"). Finally, the seduction on a moving train is incredulous erotica.

- It was shot on location in Chicago.
- Thomas Cruise Mapother had only done some acting in high school when he landed a part in *Endless Love* (1981).
- Cruise, a prominent Scientologist, was introduced to the belief by his first wife, actress Mimi Rogers.

Romance

Blood and Sand

1941, USA, 20th Century-Fox, 125 minutes, Color
Producer: Darryl F. Zanuck. Director: Rouben Mamoulian
Cast: Tyrone Power, Linda Darnell, Rita Hayworth, Alla Nazimova, Anthony Quinn, J. Carrol Naish, John Carradine, Laird Cregar

> "Great entertainment…romance, action, great performances and inspired direction."
> —*The Hollywood Reporter*

Zanuck remembered, as a lad of 20 in 1922, the effectiveness and popularity of Valentino's silent picture *Blood and Sand;* and when he became a producer he commissioned Jo Swerling (*The Westerner*) to write a sound screenplay. It was a great idea, particularly since casting would include three rising stars.

The mysticism and sensuality of the matador and the bull-ring are backdrops for the story based on the novel by Vicente Blasco Ibanez. Power is Juan Gallardo, a boy from Seville who becomes one of Spain's most popular bullfighters. Darnell plays his longsuffering wife, Carmen Espinosa, his childhood love. Hayworth is Dona Sol—brazenly sexy and fascinating, dominating Juan's heart, mind and body. Half of the film's title derives from Juan's mother, Senora Gallardo (Nazimova), who says to him, "You can't build a house on sand."

Quinn is Juan's rival, Manola; Carradine is his brother, Nacional; Naish plays friend Garabato and Cregar is Natalio, critic of the ring. Rex Downing is Juan as a boy and Ann Todd plays Carmen as a child. The film won the Oscar for color photography by Ray Rennahan and Ernest Palmer.

Rita Hayworth and Tyrone Power in *Blood and Sand*.

- The costumes worn by the bullfighters are authentic; noted tailor Jose Perez made copies of matador suits worn by famous bullfighter Francisco Delgado.
- The bullfighting sequences were shot in Mexico City.
- The film is spectacularly colored, due partly to Mamoulian personally spray-painting the sets—making the reds redder, the greens greener, etc. Zanuck thought the director mad as Rouben rushed around, spray-gun in hand. But the result was so amazing that Zanuck didn't bother to sneak preview the picture and sent it straight into release.

Camille

1937, USA, MGM, 110 minutes, B&W
Producer: Irving Thalberg, Director: George Cukor
Cast: Greta Garbo, Robert Taylor, Lionel Barrymore, Henry Daniell

"Garbo's best performance."
—*The New York Times*

She has been called "The Swedish Sphinx" and "The Divine Garbo" and this romantic tragedy is a fine illustration of her titles. The beautiful and mysterious Garbo was almost always better than the scripts she had to work with, though this one—based on the 1848 French classic "The Lady of the Camellias"—provides the star with plenty of room to work. It

Greta Garbo as *Camille*.

may well be the greatest romance the screen has ever known, and it most certainly contains one of the most memorable death scenes in the history of cinema, as the doomed heroine slumps into extinction in the arms of her lover.

The luminous Garbo received an Oscar nomination for Best Actress and the New York Film Critics presented her with their award for Best Actress.

With her favorite cameraman William Daniels on-set, Garbo portrays a Parisian prostitute, more kindly referred to as a courtesan or court lady, named Marguerite Gautier, called Camille because of her love of the camellia flower. Her two most prominent lovers are aristocrat Armand Duval (Taylor) and the cold and callous Baron de Varmille (Daniell), though the one she truly grows to love is Armand. Duval, in fact, wants to accept his share of the family fortune early to take Camille away to another country to become his wife. His father, Monsieur Duval (Barrymore), has other ideas and worries that his son is throwing his life away. Consequently, the elder Duval importunes Marguerite to drop Armand—out of love for the young man. Realizing that consumption has taken over her fragile body, she finds it within herself to make the fatal decision.

- This was Garbo's favorite of all her own films.
- Thalberg, called "The Boy Wonder," was the model for F. Scott Fitzgerald's "The Last Tycoon." He died of pneumonia at the age of 37, before *Camille* was released.
- Verdi's opera "La Traviata" is adapted from the original story by Alexander Dumas Fils.
- The story was played on-stage by Sarah Bernhardt and on-screen by Theda Bara, Pola Negri and Norma Talmadge.

Casablanca

1943, USA, Warner Bros., 102 minutes, B&W
Producer: Hal B. Wallis. Director: Michael Curtiz
Cast: Humphrey Bogart, Ingrid Bergman, Paul Henreid, Claude Rains, Conrad Veidt, Dooley Wilson, Sydney Greenstreet, Peter Lorre

> "A picture which makes the spine tingle…they have so combined sentiment, humor and pathos with taut melodrama

and bristling intrigue that the result is a highly entertaining and even inspiring film."

—*The New York Times*

A super-classic that won the Oscar for Best Picture and went on to legendary status. Curtiz won for Best Director and a trio of writers, Howard Koch and brothers Julius and Philip Epstein, won for Best Screenplay. The script was written day-by-day with Koch delivering new pages each

Michael Curtiz looks on as Ingrid Bergman and Humphrey Bogart practice dance steps for *Casablanca*.

morning to Curtiz and the cast. The story is based on an unproduced play, *Everybody Comes to Rick's,* by Murray Bennett and Joan Alison. In an interview, Bennett said he was weeping when he wrote the singing battle of the French and German national anthems.

The bittersweet romantic/adventure stars Bogart—in his greatest role—as American Rick Blaine, neutral proprietor of Rick's Place in French Morocco's Casablanca at the outset of WWII. The city is a drop-off point for refugees fleeing Europe because of the Nazis. New complications arrive for Rick when a former love, beautiful Ilse Lund (Bergman), re-enters Blaine's life on the arm of her husband—an escapee from a concentration camp: Victor Laszlo (Henreid), an underground anti-fascist leader. Veidt is the villainous Nazi Major Strasser, out to capture Laszlo. Rains is wonderful as Captain Louis Renault, the French prefect and *bon vivant* to Rick. Wilson is Sam, Rick's closest friend and piano player at Rick's Café Americain. Greenstreet plays a black marketeer and owner of the rival café, The Blue Parrot. Lorre is a thief hiding some elusive letters of transit. Laszlo and Lund would like to get their hands on those letters so they can safely get out of town. As fate would have it, the letters fall into the possession of Rick. The question is: Will Rick give them up or is he still too angry at Ilse for walking out on him in Paris?

The film, backed by the remarkable score of Max Steiner, is loaded with memorable lines: "I'm shocked—shocked to find that gambling's going on in here;" "Round up the usual suspects," "I remember every detail—the Germans wore blue, you wore gray;" "Of all the gin joints in all the towns in all the world, she walks into mine;" "Louie, I think this is the beginning of a beautiful friendship;" "Play it again, Sam" is never said; Ilse says, "Play it once, Sam" and "Play it, Sam, play 'As Time Goes By'" and "Here's looking at you, kid."

- The film was rushed into theaters to take advantage of the Allied landing in North Africa. Churchill, Roosevelt and Stalin held a summit in Casablanca and that also benefited the film's receipts.
- The script began as a B-picture to star George Raft and Hedy Lamarr but Wallis saw the potential and upgraded it.
- The cast didn't know the ending, indeed, neither did the writers. They were going to shoot two endings, to test at previews, but after the first one everybody knew it was right and the alternate was scrapped.

- Wilson didn't really play the piano; he was a drummer.
- Greenstreet and Lorre had just worked with Bogie in *The Maltese Falcon*.

Mogambo

1953, USA, MGM, 115 minutes, Color
Producer: Sam Zimbalist, Director: John Ford
Cast: Clark Gable, Ava Gardner, Grace Kelly, Donald Sinden, Philip Stainton

> "Lusty remake of *Red Dust*. Gable repeats his role, Ava Replaces Harlow, Kelly has Mary Astor's part."
>
> —Leonard Maltin

Ava Gardner and Clark Gable co-star in *Mogambo*.

Gable was affectionately labeled "King of Hollywood" in an Ed Sullivan readers' poll during Clark's long reign in the Box-Office Top 10 (1932-1943). But after the tragic death of wife Carole Lombard, he joined the Air Force, leaving his career behind. After the war, he did return briefly to the Top 10 (1947-1949) before another lull in popularity. *Mogambo* put him back in the Top 10 for the last time. Gable died in 1960.

Mogambo, which means, among the African natives, "the greatest," is about a great white hunter on the dark continent: Victor Marswell (Gable) who gets involved in a romantic triangle with two beautiful women. Gardner plays Eloise "Honey Bear" Kelly, a Manhattan party-girl who somehow gets stuck between planes—and stuck on Victor. The other woman is Linda Nordley (Kelly), bored and naïve wife of British anthropologist Donald Nordley (Sinden). Linda finds it impossible to resist Victor, a one-of-a-kind he-man, able to stand perfectly still while natives throw spears around his body in a fear test. Both Gardner and Kelly received Oscar nominations; Ava for Best Actress (the only nomination in her career) and Grace for Best Supporting Actress. Brownie the guide is played by Stainton.

The scenes in this romantic-adventure are very similar to the original version, that's because the screenwriter was the same man, John Lee Mahin. The color scenery makes the big difference. And there's a reason why the photography is so good; Ford brought along two of Hollywood's greatest cinematographers: Robert Surtees (*Ben-Hur*) and Freddie Young (*Doctor Zhivago*). Nevertheless, despite the Technicolor, there are those who think *Red Dust* (1932) is the better film—mainly because of Jean Harlow. In any event, this film continues to gain in cult status because of its three main stars. Also the real gorilla sequence is fascinating to watch.

- It was shot on location in Kenya, Tanganyika, Uganda, and French Equatorial Africa, using actual tribes from those areas.
- Gardner was once voted "The Most Beautiful Woman in the World." She was married thrice: Mickey Rooney, Artie Shaw, and Frank Sinatra; Sinatra accompanied her to Africa.
- Some gossip columnists suggested Gable and Kelly might have had an affair during the shoot. Author James Spada quotes Gore Vidal, an MGM screenwriter at the time: "Grace almost always laid the leading man" and had a strong sexual desire for Clark but failed in her quest.

Morocco

1930, USA, Paramount, 92 minutes, B&W
Producer: Adolph Zukor, Director: Josef von Sternberg
Cast: Marlene Dietrich, Gary Cooper, Adolphe Menjou

> "Marlene Dietrich emerged as an absolute sensation in *Morocco*."
>
> —*The Paramount Story*

This unusual romantic-adventure was a box-office smash-hit and actually saved the studio from bankruptcy. Dietrich, in her first American

Marlene Dietrich in *Morocco*.

film, received an Academy Award nomination for Best Actress, her only Oscar nomination.

The film is famous for three things: Dietrich, as an entertainer, planting a kiss on a surprised female member of the audience; Dietrich dressed in men's clothes: a black tux, top hat and white bow-tie while smoking a cigarette; and Dietrich, in evening gown and high heels, trailing her lover into the Sahara desert. Dietrich plays Amy Jolly, a cabaret singer, based on the novel *Amy Jolly* by Benno Vigny. Singing "What Am I Bid For My Apple?," and showing her famous shapely legs, she becomes an enchantress and Cooper as Tom Brown, a member of the French Foreign Legion, can't get enough of her. But the legionnaire is challenged by a wealthy socialite, Monsieur La Bessiere (Menjou), who is also quite taken with Amy and wants to marry her, and the romantic race is on for her affections.

Dietrich, the same year, had already turned heads with her portrayal of the vamp in Germany's *The Blue Angel,* also directed by her mentor, von Sternberg. Paramount brought the duo to Hollywood for six films. Lee Garmes is Dietrich's photographer, and was so for several of her films, stressing the correct use of light and shadow to emphasize her cheekbones.

- Dietrich on the break-up with von Sternberg: "I didn't leave Sternberg. He left me. That's very important. In my life, he was the man I wanted to please most. He decided not to work with me anymore. And I was very unhappy about that."
- The desert sequence was shot along a small sand-dune beach at Guadalupe, Calif., below San Luis Obispo.
- Dietrich said it was she who came up with the idea of kissing another woman in the cabaret.

Now, Voyager

1942, USA, Warner Bros., 117 minutes, B&W
Producer: Hal B. Wallis, Director: Irving Rapper
Cast: Bette Davis, Paul Henreid, Claude Rains, Gladys Cooper, Bonita Granville, John Loder

> "The quintessential wish-fulfillment weepie..."
> —Clive Hirschhorn, *The Warner Bros. Story*

"Oh, Jerry, we have the stars, let's not ask for the moon."—Davis as Charlotte Vale in the most famous line from the melodrama. Davis plays a repressed young woman who finally finds love in the person of a married man, Jerry Durrance (Henreid). Davis received an Oscar nomination for Best Actress and Cooper, as her overbearing and possessive mother, got nominated for Best Supporting Actress.

The story is taken from the novel by Olive Higgins Prouty about a Boston family and the matriarch who insists on having her own way, even at the risk of destroying her daughter, physically and emotionally.

There's a famous bit of business with two cigarettes; Henreid was to light Bette's, hand it to her then light his own with the same match but it kept going out before the switch, so he placed both cigs in his mouth at the same time and lit each one with the same match.

Rains plays Dr. Jacquith, the psychiatrist who encourages Charlotte to step out on her own; Granville is Charlotte's sister June Vale, and Loder is wealthy suitor Elliot Livingston.

The title of the film is taken from the Walt Whitman poem "The Untold Want": "Untold want, by life and land 'nere granted, Now, Voyager, sail thou forth to seek and find."

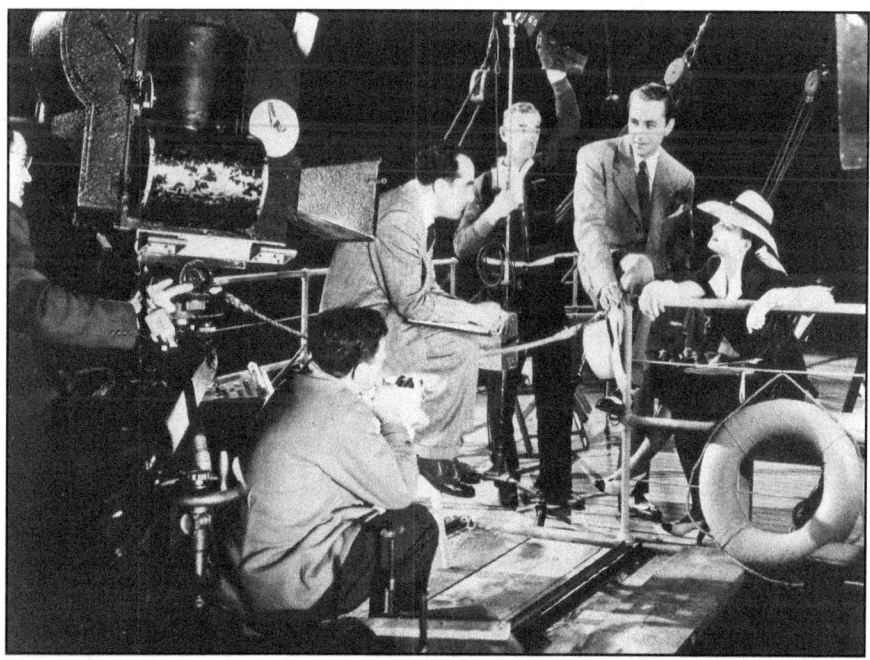

Irving Rapper directing Paul Henreid and Bette Davis for *Now, Voyager*.

- This was the biggest box-office hit of Davis' career.
- The shoot went over schedule by one day which left Rains rushing to the set of *Casablanca* the very next morning.
- A clip of the film was used in a movie theater sequence of *Summer of '42* (1970).
- Davis said the fan mail she received after the release of *Now, Voyager* was most rewarding: "Truly hundreds of letters from children of possessive mothers, whose lives had been ruined as was Charlotte's before meeting Jacquith; also many from mothers admitting their similar mistakes with their children."

Out of Africa

1985, USA, Universal, 161 minutes, Color
Producer/Director: Sydney Pollack
Cast: Meryl Streep, Robert Redford, Klaus Maria Brandauer, Malick Bowens, Michael Kitchen, Joseph Thiaka

> "Magnificent…the most memorable movie love story since *Doctor Zhivago.*"
> —Michael Medved

Based on the books by Isak Dinesen, with the breathtaking Oscar-winning photography of David Watkin, the romantic-drama won seven Academy Awards including Best Picture and Best Director. Streep received an Oscar nomination for Best Actress. Shot in 101 days in Kenya, the story, set just ahead of WWI, follows the life of Danish Baroness/author Karen Blixen who wrote under the pseudonym Isak Dinesen. The plot covers Blixen's true-life adventures from her arrival in Africa to her departure in 1931.

Karen (Streep) marries her cousin, an Austrian aristocrat, Baron Bror Blixen (Brandauer), whom she doesn't love; the union was to get her a title. She soon has an affair with a big-game hunter and pilot, Denys Hatton (Redford). Karen is determined to make her life in Africa a success: she runs a coffee plantation and endures the heat, lions, and Masai warriors of East Africa.

Bowens is the faithful Somali servant, Farah, Karen's companion and friend. Kitchen plays Berkeley Cole and Thiaka is Kamante.

Meryl Streep and Robert Redford in *Out of Africa*.

- Judith Thurman, who wrote a biography of Dinesen, served as an advisor and co-producer on the film.
- Audrey Hepburn was originally offered the role of Karen.
- Trained lions were brought in from California.
- Streep developed her accent by listening to tape recordings of Dinesen's voice.

The Philadelphia Story

1940, USA, MGM, 112 minutes, B&W
Producer: Joseph L. Mankiewicz, Director: George Cukor
Cast: Katharine Hepburn, Cary Grant, James Stewart, Ruth Hussey, John Howard, Roland Young, Virginia Weidler, Mary Nash, John Halliday

> "...stands out as by far the most adult and successful film of its type."
>
> —Leslie Halliwell

Nominated for Best Picture, the popular romance—featuring three superstars—is most famous for its opening scene in which an angry Grant, who really wants to hit his ex-wife, instead puts his hand on Hepburn's face and shoves her back through the door to the floor! Hepburn, in the role she played on Broadway, is spoiled society girl Tracy Lord, on the verge of getting married again. Grant is ex-husband C.K. Dexter Haven and Stewart, who won the Oscar for Best Actor, is Macaulay "Mike" Connor, a tabloid reporter who goes to interview Tracy and ends up falling in love with her. Donald Ogden Stewart won the Oscar for Best Adapted Screenplay based on the stage play by Phillip Barry. Hepburn and close friend Howard Hughes purchased the screen rights to the play.

It was an important film for Hepburn who had endured several bombs and been labeled "box-office poison," a moniker given her by theater managers. A lot of moviegoers saw the actress as priggish, aloof, and intolerant, very much like Tracy Lord. Kate's characterization of Tracy, however, helped break her image because the rich girl from Philadelphia turns out to be vulnerable and likeable and, like most folks, just seeking true love.

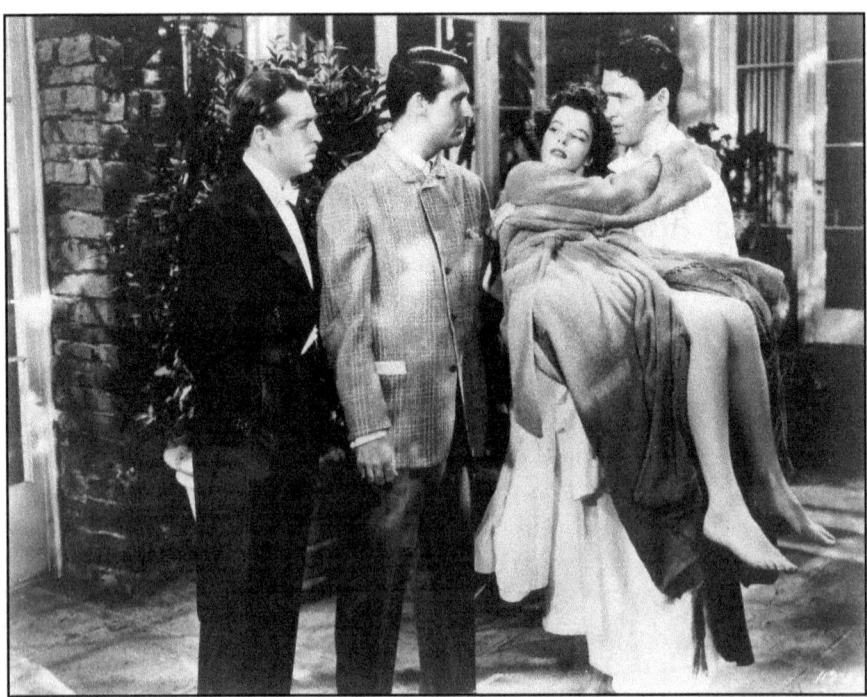

John Howard, Cary Grant, Katharine Hepburn and James Stewart in *The Philadelphia Story*.

Hussey plays Elizabeth Imbrie, Connor's accompanying photographer. Howard is George Kittredge, Tracy's fiancé. Halliday and Nash play Tracy's parents. Young is Uncle Willie. Weidler is Tracy's precocious little sister, Dinah.

- It was remade as a musical, *High Society* (1956), with Bing Crosby, Frank Sinatra, and Grace Kelly.
- The relationship between Hepburn and Howard Hughes is explored in Martin Scorsese's *The Aviator* (2004).
- Grant donated his entire salary, over $100,000, to the British War Relief Fund.
- Years later, Stewart said in an interview that his friend Henry Fonda should have won the Oscar that year for *The Grapes of Wrath*.

The Quiet Man

1952, USA, Republic, 129 minutes, Color
Producer: Merian C. Cooper, Director: John Ford
Cast: John Wayne, Maureen O'Hara, Victor McLaglen, Barry Fitzgerald, Ward Bond

> "One of John Ford's most entertaining and enjoyable pictures."
> —Joel W. Finler, *All-Time Movie Favorites*

Ford won the Oscar for Best Director for this beautiful and passionate film shot on location in Ireland. The picture also won for its outstanding color photography (Winton Hoch, Archie Stout). The charming and romantic cult-classic, the best film ever released by Republic Pictures, was also nominated for Best Picture. Adding to the artistry is Victor Young's fine score, with touches of familiar Irish melodies.

Wayne and O'Hara, one of Hollywood's most popular romantic couples (they made five movies together), have one of the screen's most memorable romantic scenes—a confrontational embrace...he arrives at his new place on a windy afternoon to find her cleaning his cottage. Frightened, she runs out the door but he catches her arm, pulls her back inside and kisses her (Spielberg used the clip as a TV shot in *E.T.: The Extraterrestrial*).

Maureen O'Hara, John Wayne and supporting players on the set of *The Quiet Man*.

Wayne is Sean Thornton, a former prizefighter who returns to live in his home in the village of Innisfree. Taxi driver, matchmaker, bookie, and boozer Michaeleen Flynn (Fitzgerald) describes Thornton as "a nice, quiet, peace loving man, come home to forget his troubles" (Sean killed a man in the ring then gave up fighting). Flynn sets out to match Thornton with lovely redhead Mary Kate Danaher (O'Hara) but her big bruiser of a brother, Red Will Danaher (McLaglen), doesn't like Thornton and intends to derail the wedding. The conflict over Will not wanting to turn over her dowry leads to one helluva donnybrook. Bond is Father Peter Lonergan, the scrappy local priest who loves to fish, almost as much as he loves to see a good Irish brawl.

- It was shot in the village of Cong in County Mayo and in the surrounding area; a few scenes were also filmed in County Galway and County Clare.
- Cong had no electricity before the movie company arrived.
- Except for the Hollywood principals, including Mildred Natwick, the rest of the cast were either locals or "Irish Players" from the Abbey Theatre.

- The Rev. Cyril Playfair was Arthur Shields, Fitzgerald's younger brother.
- That was real rain in the windy cottage scene when she runs across the stream and meadow. It was the only day it rained during the shoot. They had to use rain machines for other rainy scenes.

Rebel Without a Cause

1955, USA, Warner Bros., 111 minutes, Color
Producer: David Weisbart, Director: Nicholas Ray
Cast: James Dean, Natalie Wood, Sal Mineo, Jim Backus, Ann Doran

> "...consolidated Dean's stature as the country's most important new young actor since Brando, as well as affirming his status as a cult hero."
> —Clive Hirschhorn, *The Warner Bros. Story*

One of the all-time cult favorites, a timeless romantic-melodrama about misunderstood teens—young people looking for life's meaning.

Nicholas Ray with Natalie Wood and James Dean on the set of *Rebel Without a Cause*.

Dean plays Jim Stark, the new kid at school; Wood is Judy, who becomes his girlfriend. Mineo plays their mixed-up friend, Plato. Wood got an Oscar nomination for Best Supporting Actress. Dean received a nomination for Best Actor but not for this film—for *East of Eden*.

More pointedly, the story concerns young love, the growing pangs of the postwar youth, and conflict with their parents. Backus plays Jim's father and Doran is his mother.

There's an ironic scene in the film in which Dean engages in a "chicken run" with him leaping to safety before the car goes over the cliff, symbolic of the rebellious teen maturing before it's too late. In real life, Dean died in a car wreck. In fact, all three stars had tragic deaths. Wood drowned, Mineo was stabbed to death.

- Dennis Hopper, who appears as Goon, says Dean had bad eyesight—so bad that he couldn't see four feet in front of himself without his glasses.
- Griffith Park Observatory was used for both inside and outside shots.
- The swimming pool was the same one in *Sunset Boulevard* (1950) at the Getty Mansion at Wilshire and Irving, now torn down.
- There's an "inside joke" when Dean ad libs an impression of the cartoon character Mr. Magoo, whose voice in the cartoons belonged to Backus.
- Backus: "This (*Rebel Without a Cause*) is the first time in the history of motion pictures that a 24-year-old boy, with only one movie to his credit, was practically the co-director."

Wuthering Heights

1939, USA, United Artists, 102 minutes, B&W
Producer: Samuel Goldwyn, Director: William Wyler
Cast: Laurence Olivier, Merle Oberon, David Niven, Flora Robson, Geraldine Fitzgerald, Leo G. Carroll, Donald Crisp, Hugh Williams, Cecil Kellaway

> "…there's no denying that Oberon and Olivier are a wonderful couple, and their scene in the make-believe castle on Peniston Crag…is one of the most romantic bits in cinema history."
> —Danny Peary

Merle Oberon and Laurence Olivier in *Wuthering Heights*.

Goldwyn saw this as his *Gone With the Wind*. While the Selznick classic won Best Picture, *Wuthering Heights* was nominated for best film and won the Oscar for Best Cinematography (black-and-white) by Gregg Toland (who, the following year, would photograph *Citizen Kane*).

In order for you to get the most out of the film version of Emily Bronte's novel, you must suspend disbelief for 100 minutes, for the story is about ghosts, spirits of the after-life, phantoms of the night, and passion so strong that death itself cannot keep the lovers apart.

The picture opens thusly: "On the barren Yorkshire moors in England, a hundred years ago, stood a house as bleak and desolate as the wastes around it. Only a stranger lost in a storm would have dared to knock at the door of Wuthering Heights."

And so it begins with a lost stranger entering the house—and the story, as soon told by the housekeeper, Ellen (Robson). Olivier is the petulant and peculiar Heathcliff and Oberon is his beautiful lost love, Cathy, who has died—though her spirit lives on and wanders the moors in search of the man she loved in life. Prior to her death, Cathy, wanting more than Heathcliff had to offer, married the wealthy Edgar Linton (Niven, minus his mustache); forcing the tortured Heathcliff into a loveless marriage with Linton's sister, Isabella (Fitzgerald). And so the doomed love simmers to the fiery boiling point.

Williams is Cathy's brother, the abusive and alcoholic Hindley. Kellaway, in a short role, plays their father, Earnshaw. Crisp is Dr. Kenneth. Carroll plays the servant, Joseph.

- The love scenes were not easy for Olivier and Oberon because Olivier had wanted Vivien Leigh to play opposite him, but Goldwyn and Wyler had already signed Oberon for the part. As it turns out, it was great for Leigh who then nailed down the role of the century: Scarlett O'Hara. Oberon wasn't happy either because she had wanted her friend Douglas Fairbanks, Jr. for the role of Heathcliff.
- Olivier and Wyler didn't get along at first because Olivier was over-acting due to his stage experience. Later, Olivier admitted that it was Wyler who taught him screen acting.
- The Yorkshire moors were 500 acres in Chatsworth, Calif.
- It was Goldwyn who insisted on the heavenly ending; though doubles were used in the longshot since the stars had gone home for the day.

Comedy-Drama

All About Eve

1950, 20th Century-Fox, 138 minutes, B&W.
Producer: Darryl F. Zanuck. Director: Joseph L. Mankiewicz.
Cast: Bette Davis, Anne Baxter, George Sanders, Gary Merrill, Celeste Holm, Hugh Marlowe, Thelma Ritter, Gregory Ratoff, Marilyn Monroe.

> "The definitive thea-tah movie still holds the record for (Oscar) nominations."
> —Mike Clark, *USA Today*

Famous for Davis' role as aging and impassioned Broadway star Margo Channing and her line: "Fasten your seatbelts, it's going to be a bumpy night!" And it's famous for Monroe's small part as an ingénue, Miss Caswell.

The comedy-drama won Best Picture and Mankiewicz won two Oscars, for directing and screenplay. Both Davis and Baxter received Academy Award nominations for Best Actress. Baxter plays the insidious Eve Harrington, Margo's secretary and aspiring actress, worming her way to the top at the expense of Margo. Sanders, as newspaper critic Addison DeWitt, Eve's mentor, won Best Supporting Actor.

Holm plays Margo's friend Karen Richards, wife of playwright Lloyd Richards (Marlowe). Ritter is Birdie, Margo's dressing room guru. Merrill is director Bill Sampson and Ratoff is producer Max Fabian.

- It was finally tied for most Oscar nominations, 14, by *Titanic* in 1997.
- The theatre scenes were shot at San Francisco's Curran Theatre.

Gary Merrill, Bette Davis, George Sanders, Anne Baxter, Hugh Marlowe and Celeste Holm, in a publicity photo for *All About Eve*.

- Davis and Merrill fell in love during the film and got married; they divorced 10 years later.
- Davis' career was on the slide until she got the part—which she said "resurrected me from the dead."
- Claudette Colbert was originally picked to play Margo but suffered a back injury before shooting and had to drop out; Jeanne Crain was set to play Eve but got pregnant.
- It was turned into a Broadway musical in 1970 called *Applause* with Lauren Bacall.

It's A Wonderful Life

1946, Liberty Films/RKO Radio, 129 minutes, B&W.
Producer/Director: Frank Capra.
Cast: James Stewart, Donna Reed, Lionel Barrymore, Thomas Mitchell, Henry Travers, Gloria Grahame, H.B. Warner, Ward Bond.

"Frank Capra's personal favorite and one of the enduring achievements of the studio era."

—*The RKO Story.*

It was also Jimmy Stewart's personal favorite in a 50-year movie career. The most-famous family film, about love, sacrifice, and hope, has become a Christmas standard on television. Based on Philip Van Doren Stern's short story, it's a flashback-fantasy about a man who runs into financial troubles and, on the verge of possibly going to jail, decides to commit suicide—until a very unorthodox angel named Clarence Oddbody (Travers) intervenes. George Bailey (Stewart), in a state of depression, feels his life has been useless and wishes he'd never been born. Clarence, like no other guardian angel you'll ever meet, shows George that he's really had a great deal of good influence on a lot of people and that, in actuality, he's had a wonderful life.

The film, produced by Capra's Liberty Films, received an Academy Award nomination for Best Picture and Capra was nominated for Best Director. Stewart, as the troubled Bedford Falls Savings and Loan businessman, also got nominated for Best Actor.

Thomas Mitchell, Donna Reed, James Stewart and friends in *It's a Wonderful Life.*

There's a fine supporting cast: Reed is perfect as Bailey's wife, Mary; Barrymore, as Mr. Potter, becomes one of the screen's most despicable villains; Mitchell is George's Uncle Billy, the one who accidentally loses the bank deposit and pushes the business to the brink of bankruptcy; Grahame plays the town flirt, Violet Bick; Warner is Mr. Gower, the pharmacist; Bond is Bert the policeman.

- The scene in the saloon where Bailey says a prayer was filmed with a 16mm camera; Capra said it was only supposed to be a test shot before they brought in the 35mm camera, but the scene was so good that Capra decided it couldn't possibly be any better, so he had the film blown up to the larger size and that's what we see in the final product.
- The dance sequence, with the gym floor that opens over a swimming pool, was filmed at Beverly Hills High School.
- Beulah Bondi, Stewart's mother in Capra's *Mr. Smith Goes to Washington,* is also his mother in this film.
- Reed retired from the screen in 1958 to do *The Donna Reed Show* on TV; the show ran for eight seasons.
- During WWII, Stewart flew 20 missions over Germany as a bomber pilot; he ended his tour of duty as a colonel. Upon returning to Hollywood, he insisted to Capra and other producers that his military service not be mentioned in studio publicity releases.

Made For Each Other

1939, Selznick International, 93 minutes, B&W.
Producer: David O. Selznick. Director: John Cromwell.
Cast: James Stewart, Carole Lombard, Lucille Watson, Charles Coburn, Eddie Quillan.

> "First-rate soaper…Fine acting makes this all work."
> —*Leonard Maltin's Movie & Video Guide.*

One of the best of the comedy-dramas of the 30s featuring two major stars (it was a good year for Stewart who got a Best Actor nomination for *Mr. Smith Goes to Washington*). The very effective screenplay is by Jo Swerling.

Comedy-Drama 195

James Stewart and Carole Lombard embrace on the sofa as director John Cromwell and cameraman Leon Shamroy shoot a scene for *Made for Each Other*.

Stewart plays a young lawyer, John Mason, who meets Jane (Lombard), the girl of his dreams, while he was obtaining a deposition in Boston. It was love at first sight and, after knowing each other for just a day, they get married! Back in New York, things go awry from the start: their honeymoon is canceled because of the workload at the office; a dinner at John's home for his boss, Judge Doolittle (Coburn), gets fouled up; John's meddling mother (Watson) is allowed to live with them; within two months Jane gets pregnant; and, with Jane not working after the birth of their baby boy, they get behind on their bills. Jane sees that John is a pretty good lawyer and insists that he ask for a raise. But Judge Doolittle, a hard-of-hearing, no-nonsense boss, not only refuses but says the firm must make cuts and reduces John's salary. To top it all off, this struggling family must endure a new crisis: a sick baby. But Doolittle, at the end, puts his hard-nosed ways aside and helps John and Jane when the child gets seriously ill.

The film has some very funny moments but also very sad ones. It's both interesting and heartwarming to watch this nice young couple fall in love, start a new life together, face trials and yet, somehow, overcome and remain dedicated to one another, even though at times they doubted themselves and their decision to get married. It's a picture of life that so many face at first; a realization of what parents went through. The story not only shows the changes that take place with the couple but also with those who come in contact with them. The mother, the elder Mrs. Mason, reveals she is the way she is, too cranky and too hands-on, because she's lonely; Doolittle comes to the reality that work and making money is not all there is to life; and there's a brave pilot named Conway (Quillan) who risks his life to fly a plane through a storm to get serum to a dying child. The film's title eventually comes more clearly into focus—John and Jane are not the only ones made for each other; we are all made for the good of every other person.

- Lombard (1908-1942) died in a plane crash in Nevada following her appearance at a war bond rally. FDR paid tribute to her.
- Swerling is a man though he spelled his first name "Jo" for Joseph. He was born in Russia and wrote the screenplay for Capra's *It's a Wonderful Life* starring Stewart.
- Selznick had his hands full during production—he was also finishing his classic *Gone With the Wind*.

Meet John Doe

1941, Warner Bros., 135 minutes, B&W.
Producer/Director: Frank Capra.
Cast: Gary Cooper, Barbara Stanwyck, Walter Brennan, James Gleason, Edward Arnold, Gene Lockhart, Spring Byington.

> "Gary Cooper's 55th film…was also one of his very best."
> —Clive Hirschhorn, *The Warner Bros. Story*

Following on the heels of *Mr. Smith Goes to Washington* (1938), Capra continues his theme of corruption in the screen's darkest socio-comedy/drama. Ironically, it was the same year that Orson Welles produced *Citizen Kane*, about the establishment gone wrong.

As good as Cooper is in this part, Stanwyck is even better—probably her best acting, deserving of a Best Actress nod (and she did get nominated but for *Ball of Fire*). There is also excellent character support from

Frank Capra, Barbara Stanwyck and Gary Cooper share a joke on the set of *Meet John Doe*.

five screen veterans: Brennan, Gleason, Arnold, Lockhart, and Byington (both Brennan and Gleason received supporting Oscar nominations but for other films).

Cooper plays an allegedly suicidal hobo the press dubs "John Doe." He is so discouraged with the world that he threatens to jump off City Hall Tower on Christmas Eve. But it's all a hoax. Stanwyck is Ann Mitchell, a reporter who manufactures the story then blows it out of proportion. Connell the Editor (Gleason) reluctantly embraces the scheme to build circulation. Unscrupulous publisher D.B. Norton (Arnold) has bigger ideas: he plans to ride the symbol of the average American into the White House. Long John Willoughby (Cooper), an unemployed bush-league baseball pitcher, is chosen by Mitchell and Connell to be the phony John Doe who supposedly wrote the letter of despair to the newspaper. He takes the job only because he's hungry. His pal from the railroad cars is The Colonel (Brennan), constantly urging him not to get involved. The distraught Mayor is played by Lockhart. Ann's mother is played by Byington.

- It was Capra's first independent film after 10 years at Columbia; WB released it. By 1946 he would have his own company, Liberty Films, the banner under which he would produce his classic *It's a Wonderful Life*.
- The City Hall Tower scene was shot in an ice house to get the frosty-breath effect.
- The convention scene was shot at Chicago's Wrigley Field with rain-making machines.
- As far as the ending is concerned, Capra and writer Robert Riskin essentially wrote themselves into a corner. They added Norton and the crowd of concerned citizens because they didn't think Ann's lone appeal to stop John from killing himself would be strong enough.

Mister Roberts

1955, Warner Bros., 123 minutes, Color.
Producer: Leland Hayward. Directors: John Ford, Mervyn LeRoy.
Cast: Henry Fonda, James Cagney, William Powell, Jack Lemmon, Betsy Palmer.

> "**** Superb comedy-drama…"
> —*Leonard Maltin's Movie & Video Guide.*

Fonda had taken a hiatus from Hollywood for seven years to do this play on Broadway and then on a national tour. After its huge success, producer Hayward took it to the screen and got an Academy Award nomination for Best Picture. Lemmon also won the Oscar for Best Supporting Actor.

Comedy-Drama ○ 199

Jack Lemmon, James Cagney, Henry Fonda and William Powell pose for a publicity photo on the set of *Mister Roberts*.

The film is based on the hit play by Joshua Logan and Thomas Heggen, from Heggen's novel; the screenplay is by Frank Nugent. It happens during WWII; a war story without a war. The characters are in the South Pacific on a cargo ship appropriately named The *USS Reluctant*. Fonda plays Lt. Doug Roberts, a nonconformist cargo officer who hates his job—and the captain—and is constantly trying to get transferred, not just because he's bored but because he really wants sea action before the war ends. Cagney is the inept but ambitious captain of the ship. Lemmon plays a lazy and oblivious laundry and morale officer, Ensign Pulver. He was on board for 14 months before ever meeting the captain, and when they finally did meet, the captain wasn't savvy enough to find out where Pulver had been keeping himself (mostly sleeping in his bunk). Powell is the ship surgeon, Doc, a calm and experienced naval veteran who shares his wisdom of the ages whenever necessary, and it's often necessary.

One of the highlights is the giant explosion in the laundry room with a ton of soap suds rushing through the corridor, all caused by Pulver experimenting with making a giant firecracker to set off under the captain's cabin. Another humorous scene is when Doc and Doug help Pulver in his quest to lure navy nurses on-board by offering a bottle of Scotch. They create the liquor from a bottle of Coke, a half-bottle of ship hospital alcohol, and a little squirt of iodine. Palmer plays the head nurse.

Several regulars from the Ford rep company play sailors, including Ward Bond, Ken Curtis, Harry Carey, Jr., Pat Wayne, and Jack Pennick.

- Nugent was a former film critic; he wrote the screenplay for Ford's *The Searchers.*
- Powell (*The Thin Man*) came out of retirement to play the part.
- Fonda disagreed with Ford on some changes the director was making—and Ford didn't take kindly to the suggestions…he slugged the actor, but later apologized, though Ford eventually removed himself from the project.
- LeRoy (producer, *The Wizard of Oz*) replaced Ford more than halfway through production. The publicity release said Ford had become ill. The directing change didn't really hurt the picture, since the script was complete, all the cast and characterizations had been set, and the veteran film crew (led by Winton Hoch, *The Quiet Man*) knew how to resolve problems without "Pappy" Ford on-set.

Mr. Smith Goes to Washington

1939, Columbia, 127 minutes, B&W.
Producer/Director: Frank Capra.
Cast: James Stewart, Jean Arthur, Claude Rains, Edward Arnold, Thomas Mitchell, Harry Carey, Eugene Pallette, Guy Kibbee, Astrid Allwyn, Beulah Bondi, H.B. Warner.

> "It says all the things about America that have been crying out to be said again, and says them beautifully."
> —*The Los Angeles Times.*

Many critics liked to refer to Capra's films as "Capra-corn" but the public had a far different attitude toward his movies: they thought of them as mainstream America. This popular Capra comedy-drama with a social conscience was nominated for Best Picture and won the Oscar for Best

Original Story (Lewis R. Foster). Stewart, as a young, naïve, idealistic, small-town U.S. Senator, received a Best Actor nomination.

Jefferson Smith (Stewart) locks horns with a crooked politician, Sen. Joseph Paine (Rains), who is part of a greedy political machine run by Jim Taylor, played by Arnold (who would later play a similar role in Capra's *Meet John Doe*). Carey is perfect as the upright U.S. Vice-President/Senate President. Arthur plays Clarissa Saunders, Sen. Smith's tough, shrewd administrative aide who inspires the freshman lawmaker to follow his heart and do the right thing—even though it may cost him his job.

The highlight of the film is Smith's dramatic filibuster speech on the floor of the senate in his fight to get a boy's camp established where cor-

Veteran movie star James Stewart portrays Sen. Jefferson Smith in Frank Capra's *Mr. Smith Goes to Washington*.

rupt wheeler-dealers want to build a dam. Stewart delivers a long, stirring address to the point of hoarseness and physical collapse.

The cast is filled with veteran character actors: Mitchell as news-bureau chief Diz Moore, Allwyn as Susan Paine, Pallette as Taylor henchman Chick McGann, Kibbee as Gov. Hopper, Warner as Sen. Agnew, and Bondi as Ma Smith.

Also there are several notable (though uncredited) but easy-to-spot bit-players: Russell Simpson (Pa in *The Grapes of Wrath*) as political party mouthpiece Ken Allen, Dub "Cannonball" Taylor (a well-known B-Western sidekick) as a reporter, Jack Carson as a newsman, and Dickie Jones (*Pinocchio*) as a senate pageboy named Richard Jones.

- Many in Congress criticized the film for showing Washington corruption; and members of the D.C. press corps didn't like the way it portrayed them.
- The script was based on the novel *The Gentleman From Montana*; during the picture's premiere, the Senator from Montana walked out.
- An exact replica of the senate floor was created on a Hollywood soundstage.
- The Park Service denied the movie company official permission to film at monuments, so Capra took matters into his own hands; he, Stewart and cinematographer Joe Walker secretly shot the scenes (including the one at the Lincoln Memorial) with a hidden camera.
- Famous radio news commentator H.V. Kaltenborn appears as himself.
- To make his voice hoarse, Stewart dried out his throat with bicarbonate of soda.

One Flew Over the Cuckoo's Nest

1975, United Artists/Fantasy Films, 133 minutes, Color.
Producers: Michael Douglas, Saul Zaentz; Director: Milos Forman.
Cast: Jack Nicholson, Louise Fletcher, Will Sampson, Brad Dourif, Danny DeVito, William Redfield, Christopher Lloyd, Scatman Crothers, Dean Brooks.

Jack Nicholson is supported by Josip Elic as Will Sampson looks on in the basketball scene from *One Flew Over the Cuckoo's Nest*.

"Extraordinarily powerful...exhilarating...Jack Nicholson is superb."
—*The Wall Street Journal.*

Based on Ken Kesey's novel and Dale Wasserman's play, this chilling drama, about the world inside hospitals for the mentally ill, was the first film to win all five major Oscars since Capra's *It Happened One Night* in 1934. Nicholson won the Oscar for his role as Randle P. McMurphy who faked insanity at a prison farm to get out of work; Fletcher won as Nurse Ratched, a calculating and controlling ward supervisor who, day by day, appears crazier than the inmates she watches over. The film also won Best

Picture, Best Director and Best Screenplay (Bo Goldman, Lawrence Hauben). The movie was the top grossing picture of 1976.

All the characters are perfectly cast, making the audience wonder who was a real inmate and who was an actor. A standout is Sampson, a 6'7" American Indian, as Chief. McMurphy and Chief Bromden become pals but Randle's simple plan hits a serious roadblock when he's confronted by the deceptive nurse who demands strict obedience from the inmates. She has no actual interest in the humanistic welfare and mental improvement of the male patients, though she outwardly gives the impression that she's simply a good nurse and an efficient manager. The story is a marvelous depiction of establishment politics and lip-service. The film is also an example of heartless power and an indictment of the hideousness of electric-shock treatment. In the end, Chief is the one who flew over—or out of—the cuckoo's nest while McMurphy is the silly cuckoo bird.

While a few of the background people are actual inmates, the speaking cast consists entirely of professional actors, with the exception of Sampson (who had been a ranger at a nearby Oregon park) and Dean Brooks as Dr. Spivey. Dr. Brooks was the actual supervisor at the Oregon State Mental Hospital in Salem where the movie was made. A lot of the interview scene between Brooks and Nicholson was improvised. The fine cast includes: Dourif as Billy Bibbit, DeVito as Martini, Redfield as Harding, Lloyd as Taber, Crothers as Orderly Turkle, Sydney Lassick as Cheswick, Delos V. Smith, Jr. as Scanlon, and Josip Elic as Bancini.

- Kirk Douglas owned the film rights but got too old to do the role and turned the project over to his son. Kirk had played McMurphy on Broadway in 1963.
- Marlon Brando and Jane Fonda were originally considered for the lead parts.
- Redfield died a few months after making the film.
- Zaentz appears in a bit part as the captain on shore.

A Star Is Born

1937, United Artists, 111 minutes, Color.
Producer: David O. Selznick. Director: William A. Wellman.
Cast: Janet Gaynor, Fredric March, Adolphe Menjou, Andy Devine, May Robson, Lionel Stander, Edgar Kennedy.

"Good entertainment by any standards."
—*The New York Times.*

This movie probably has the most famous closing line in cinema history: "This is…Mrs. Norman Maine!" It's delivered after the star receives the Academy Award for Best Actress and, speaking to the radio audience, she wants the world to know she is not embarrassed by her husband's ill-fated demise.

Nominated for Best Picture, the film is about a star-struck young woman from the wintry upper Midwest, Esther Blodgett (Gaynor), who wants to become a movie star, though her mother and father discourage her ambition. However, all-knowing Grandmother Lettie (Robson) has faith in Esther and gives her the money to take the train to Hollywood. There, she quickly learns just how hard it is to survive while looking for work in a profession overcrowded with applicants. Nevertheless, she finds work—albeit not in the movie business. But while working as a waitress at a party, she meets well-known actor Norman Maine (March) who takes a liking to her and even gets her a screen test.

Janet Gaynor, Fredric March and Adolphe Menjou in *A Star is Born*.

As the plot evolves, Esther gets a studio contract and has her name changed to Vicki Lester—and marries Maine, while Norman's career takes a nosedive, partly due to his heavy drinking. Wellman and Robert Carson won Oscars for Best Original Story.

Shot in the early Technicolor process, the film begins with neon-like credits and opens on a shooting script of the movie we're about to see, and the film concludes in a similar fashion on the final dialogue and camera directions.

Menjou plays producer Oliver Niles and Stander is publicity man Matt Libby. Devine is Esther's first friend in Hollywood, assistant director Danny McGuire. Kennedy, a former comic in silent pictures, plays Esther's landlord "Pop" Randall.

- Lana Turner and Carole Landis are extras in the Santa Anita sequence.
- The story is based on episodes in the lives of actors John Barrymore, John Gilbert, John McCormick, and John Bowers who drowned off Malibu.
- The actual Oscar Janet receives was her own, won in 1927 for *Seventh Heaven*.
- The story was remade twice: Judy Garland in 1954 and Barbra Streisand in 1976.

The Sting

1973, Universal, 129 minutes, Color.
Producers: Tony Bill, Michael and Julia Phillips; Director: George Roy Hill.
Cast: Paul Newman, Robert Redford, Robert Shaw, Charles Durning, Ray Walston, Eileen Brennan, Harold Gould, Robert Earl Jones, Dimitra Arliss, Dana Elcar.

> "The teaming of Paul Newman and Robert Redford again proved to be box-office dynamite in *The Sting*, one of the year's big grossers, as well as blockbuster entertainment..."
> —Clive Hirschhorn, *The Universal Story*

Newman and Redford had already proved that their affable chemistry worked in *Butch Cassidy and the Sundance Kid* (1969), also directed

Robert Redford and Paul Newman in *The Sting*.

by Hill. Now they go from being Western bank robbers to con men in the 30s in the crime-riddled Midwest. And, in a delightful surprise ending, they even con the audience!

The comedy-drama, filled with twists and turns, won seven Oscars including Best Picture, Best Director, and Best Score (Marvin Hamlisch, using some of Scott Joplin's piano ragtime music). David S. Ward won the Oscar for his screenplay, based on the book *The Big Con* by David W. Maurer. The film was the #1 box-office hit of 1974.

Newman plays veteran con-man Henry Gondorff (alias Shaw) and Redford is up-and-comer Johnny Hooker (alias Kelly) in Depression-era Chicago. They set up a phony race-track betting operation to "sting" New York racketeer Doyle Lonnegan (Shaw) who had Hooker's mentor, Luther Coleman (Jones), killed. The scam is worth half-a-million dollars.

The terrific cast of characters includes: Durning as corrupt police lieutenant Snyder; Walston as J.J. Singleton, the race announcer; Brennan as Billie, the brothel madam/pickpocket; Gould as Kid Twist, Arliss as Loretta, Elcar as FBI agent Polk. Billy Benedict, Whitey from The Bowery Boys, is the roulette dealer.

- Famous magician John Scarne did 99% of the card manipulations and taught Newman one very good move: watch for one that we can see Paul does himself, as the camera moves from the cards in his hands to his face—without an edit.
- Redford didn't think the movie would be a hit and turned it down at first; then Jack Nicholson was offered the part and *he* turned it down; then Redford reconsidered.
- Richard Boone, Oliver Reed, and Stephen Boyd were all considered for the role of Lonnegan.
- Why did Shaw's character limp? Simply because Shaw had actually injured his ankle just prior to production.
- Most of the film was shot at Universal though a few exteriors were done in old parts of Chicago and Los Angeles.
- It was the first Universal film to win Best Picture since *All Quiet on the Western Front* in 1930.

Costume Drama

All That Money Can Buy

1941, RKO, 87 minutes, B&W.
Producer/Director: William Dieterle.
Cast: James Craig, Edward Arnold, Walter Huston, Anne Shirley, Simone Simon, Jane Darwell, Gene Lockhart, John Qualen, H.B. Warner.

> "Visually the film was a feast, with Joseph August's chiaroscuro camerawork and Vernon L. Walker's stunning special effects…"
>
> —*The RKO Story.*

One of the best black-and-white movies ever made with Bernard Herrmann winning the Oscar for his excellent score and Huston, as the Devil in disguise, nominated for Best Actor. Arnold, as Daniel Webster, also deserved but didn't get a nomination for his extraordinary three-minute closing summation to the "jury of the damned."

The screenplay is by Stephen Vincent Benet and Dan Totheroh from the story by Benet. It's one of the most spiritual and patriotic films ever produced, a modern viewpoint of an old Greek morality play. Which is best to acquire: money and power or a family, respect of others and doing good for the community?

The setting is New Hampshire in 1840. Jabez Stone (Craig) has nothing but trouble on his farm. His wife, Mary (Shirley), urges him to keep the faith. But Jabez feels that life can just "go to the Devil!" You called? Enter the Devil in the person of Mr. Scratch (Huston). In return for a pot of gold coins, Jabez sells his soul to the Devil with the due date carved on a tree seven years hence. Jabez pays off Miser Stevens (Qualen), already under

the sway of Scratch, for the land. But Jabez finds, with all his wealth, he is not happy. When he complains to the Devil, the central core of the plot emerges: Jabez wasn't promised happiness but "all that money can buy."

Darwell is Ma who teaches Jabez that "love is stronger than death." Lockhart plays Squire Slossum. Warner is Justice Hawthorne. And Simon is Belle the seductress.

- Arnold replaced Thomas Mitchell who broke his leg early in production.

- The blizzard consisted of 1200 lbs. of white onions and 2500 lbs. of mothballs.
- The film's original title was *The Devil and Daniel Webster* and was released as such but when the film was ready to open in the Bible belt, the studio decided to change the title out of fear that Southern patrons might object and not attend.

Barry Lyndon

1975, Warner Bros., 185 minutes, Color.
Producer/Director: Stanley Kubrick
Cast: Ryan O'Neal, Marisa Berenson, Patrick Magee, Hardy Kruger, Marie Kean, Leon Vitali, Murray Melvin, Michael Hordern.

> "Exquisite, meticulously detailed period piece…Long, deliberately paced but never boring."
> —*Leonard Maltin's Movie & Video Guide.*

It might be the finest costume drama ever made; after all, many of the eighteenth century costumes were real! It's a stylish and lavish film capturing the sweeping, lush landscapes of Ireland and England. The mood is a series of elegant portraits—come to life. The film won Oscars for cinematography (John Alcott), costumes, art direction/sets, and scoring—and it was nominated for Best Picture.

Based on the work of English novelist William Makepeace Thackeray, the story is one of innocence, first-love, seduction, self-indulgence, irresponsibility, fortune, and misfortune. The film has numerous morals, not the least of which are these two: life can never be totally fair, for injustice respects no legal bounds; assumption can lead to poverty—and death. (The protagonist decides not to kill his foe during a duel and it costs him dearly.)

O'Neal portrays the Irish lad, Redmond Barry, destined to become a wanderer—his life pock-marked by highwaymen, duels, gamblers, opportunists, battlefields—and beautiful women.

Berenson plays Lady Lyndon, stunning in a partial nude scene in a bath. Magee is the eye-patched Chevalier, a crooked gambler who embraces Redmond as a father and takes him into his world of aristocrats. Kruger is Captain Potzdorf, saved by Barry in battle. Kean is Barry's

Ryan O'Neal, with hands held high, as *Barry Lyndon*.

Mother. Vitali is Lord Bullingdon, Barry's stepson whose hatred of Redmond ends in a duel. Melvin plays cold, calculating Reverend Runt, Lady Lyndon's chaplain. The narrator is British actor Michael Hordern.

- Warner Bros. refused to finance the project unless a Top 10 star had the lead. O'Neal made the list that year due to *Love Story*. The studio had wanted Robert Redford, also a box-office leader, but he turned it down.
- Most of the film was shot without artificial lighting—only natural light and candlelight.
- Many of the costumes were authentic, bought at auction.
- There were numerous locations in England, Ireland, and Germany. A lot of outdoor scenes were filmed in County Dublin and County Kilkenny, Ireland. Sets included Dublin Castle and Castle Howard in North Yorkshire, England.

David And Bathsheba

1951, 20th Century-Fox, 116 minutes, Color.
Producer: Darryl F. Zanuck. Director: Henry King.
Cast: Gregory Peck, Susan Hayward, Raymond Massey, Jayne Meadows,

Kieron Moore, James Robertson Justice, Francis X. Bushman, Leo Pessin, Walter Talun.

"The film is among the very best of all the biblical epics."
—Tony Thomas and Aubrey Solomon,
The Films of 20th Century-Fox.

The #1 box-office hit of 1951 may lack the flash and special effects of a DeMille Bible movie but this marvelous script, by Philip Dunne, is not lacking in drama and emotion. Both stars are well-suited for the leads: Peck as King David of Israel and Hayward as Bathsheba, the beautiful but married woman he loves at first sight.

Gregory Peck and Susan Hayward co-star as *David and Bathsheba*.

Massey is perfect as the prophet Nathan who reveals David's sins as reasons that drought and famine have come upon the land of Israel. David committed adultery with Bathsheba and had her soldier-husband, Uriah (Moore), killed by placing him at the forefront of the battle.

Dunne's intelligent study of one of history's most famous love stories brings tears to the eyes on several occasions, notably when David goes into the tabernacle to ask God to forgive him and not allow Bathsheba to die and when, as a shepherd boy (Pessin), he slays the giant Goliath (Talun) with but a stone from his slingshot.

Meadows is Michal, David's bitter wife who accuses him of having an affair with Bathsheba. Justice is Abishai, David's devoted aide. Bushman plays King Saul.

The music is by Alfred Newman, photography by Leon Shamroy, and art direction by Lyle Wheeler.

- Outdoor scenes were shot at Nogales, Arizona.
- The Ark of the Covenant prop, made of acacia wood, was purchased later by Hayward at a studio auction.
- Goliath, according to scripture, was about nine feet tall.

David Copperfield

1935, MGM, 133 minutes, B&W.
Producer: David O. Selznick. Director: George Cukor.
Cast: Freddie Bartholomew, Frank Lawton, Madge Evans, Maureen O'Sullivan, Edna Mae Oliver, W.C. Fields, Elizabeth Allan, Jessie Ralph, Basil Rathbone, Lionel Barrymore, Roland Young, Lewis Stone, Lennox Pawle.

> "The most profoundly satisfying screen manipulation of a great novel that the camera has ever given us."
> —*The New York Times.*

Nominated for Best Picture, this Charles Dickens classic features one of the best large casts ever assembled for a motion picture—and Fields, comic actor by trade, surprisingly good as the optimistic though debt-ridden Micawber, nearly steals the show. Bartholomew plays David as a child, Lawton plays him as an adult.

W.C. Fields plays Micawber in *David Copperfield*.

David is raised by a widowed mother, Mrs. Copperfield (Allan), and a gentle helper, Nurse Peggotty (Ralph). His young world becomes complicated when his confused mother weds a cruel man, the autocratic and uncaring Mr. Murdstone (Rathbone). When life with his stepfather becomes unbearable, David runs away from home and goes to live with his eccentric aunt, Betsey (Oliver). David's subsequent adventures include marriage to a pretty but empty-headed young woman named Dora (O'Sullivan) and confrontation with a creepy and crooked accountant named Uriah Heep (Young).

Barrymore plays Dan Peggotty, Pawle is the dim-witted but lovable Mr. Dick, Stone is Mr. Wickfield, and Evans is Agnes Wickfield, the girl David grew up with—and the woman he finally realizes he has always loved.

- Cukor said Fields "was born to play the part." Fields stuck to the script without his usual ad-libs because he greatly admired the Dickens novel.
- Freddie was only 10 years old and got the role because he was one of the very few boys in Hollywood with talent and an English accent. It was his first American film. L.B. Mayer had wanted MGM contract player Jackie Cooper who, unfortunately, could not speak with a British accent.
- The actual title of the book is *The Personal History, Adventures, Experience, and Observation by David Copperfield the Younger of Blunderstone Rookery*.

The Hunchback of Notre Dame

1939, RKO, 114 minutes, B&W.
Producer: Pandro S. Berman. Director: William Dieterle.
Cast: Charles Laughton, Maureen O'Hara, Cedric Hardwicke, Thomas Mitchell, Edmond O'Brien, Harry Davenport, Walter Hampden.

> "The studio's last release of the decade was also one of the biggest and best films in RKO history."
> —*The RKO Story*.

Victor Hugo's immortal story about a deformed bell-ringer in the Cathedral of Notre Dame in fifteenth century Paris has been brought to the screen numerous times, most notably as a silent film in 1923 starring Lon Chaney. Anthony Quinn repeated the characterization in 1957 and Anthony Hopkins did so in 1982; Disney even produced an animated version in 1996.

While the Chaney classic is most famous, the Laughton sound remake 16 years later was able to bring more technical expertise to the production, enhancing the story on several levels. It is certainly arguable whether Chaney or Laughton gave the better interpretation of Quasimodo. But there is no doubt that RKO poured more craftsmanship into their film. Van Nest Polglase (*Citizen Kane*) was in charge of art direction, Darrell Silvera (*The Body Snatcher*) built the sets; Walter Plunkett (*Gone With the Wind*) designed the costumes, Joseph H. August (*Gunga Din*) handled photography, and Perc Westmore (*Treasure of the Sierra Madre*) did the terrific make-up.

O'Hara, in her U.S. debut, plays Esmeralda, the gypsy dancing girl with whom Quasimodo falls in love after she offers him water during a public flogging. The hunchback saves her from execution for a crime she didn't commit then hides her in the bell tower. O'Brien plays the poet, Pierre, who also loves her. Mitchell is the beggar king, Davenport plays King Louis XI, Hampden is the archbishop, and Hardwicke is the archbishop's evil brother.

- The Paris set was built in the San Fernando Valley.
- 3,000 extras were employed.
- There is no evidence that there really was a man like Quasimodo at Notre Dame.

Charles Laughton as *The Hunchback of Notre Dame*.

- Polglase spent a year in Cuba designing the Presidential Palace in Havana.
- Berman was instrumental in the careers of Astaire and Rogers and Katharine Hepburn.
- Dieterle, of German descent, always directed wearing white gloves.

Jane Eyre

1944, 20th Century-Fox, 96 minutes, B&W.
Producers: William Goetz, Kenneth Macgowan; Director: Robert Stevenson.
Cast: Joan Fontaine, Orson Welles, Henry Daniell, Agnes Moorehead, Peggy Ann Garner, Elizabeth Taylor, Margaret O'Brien, John Sutton, Sara Allgood.

> "The contributions of so many fine artists make this a classic item of gothic cinema."
> —Tony Thomas and Aubrey Solomon, *The Films of 20th Century-Fox*

Based on Charlotte Bronte's 1847 novel, *Jane Eyre* is a Victorian-era tale done as a misty and brooding film with familiar Wellesian overtones. Even though Welles did not direct, his influence for doom and foreboding is evident everywhere. For example, Bernard Herrmann, who composed and conducted the music for Welles' *Citizen Kane* and *The Magnificent Ambersons*, created this tormenting score. John Houseman, Welles' former associate producer, contributed to the screenplay, and Moorehead, as Mrs. Reed, came to Hollywood as a member of Welles' Mercury Theatre Company.

Welles, in make-up that builds up the bridge of his nose, plays Edward Rochester, master of ominous Thornfield Manor, a mansion filled with mad laughter and cries from a tortured soul hidden somewhere within the stone walls. Jane (Fontaine) answers Rochester's advertisement for a governess, meeting her employer at night—he, on a black stallion, emerging in the fog like the headless horseman.

O'Brien plays Adele, Rochester's only child. Garner plays Jane as a child. Taylor is Helen, Jane's childhood friend. Daniell is the sadistic Mr. Brocklehurst, headmaster at Lowood Institution. Sutton portrays Dr. Rivers and Allgood is Bessie.

Joan Fontaine, sister of Olivia de Havilland, stars as *Jane Eyre*.

- Moorehead attested to the fact that Welles had his hand in virtually every aspect of the production.
- Stevenson was a member of England's Bronte Society.
- Charlotte was the sister of Emily Bronte who wrote *Wuthering Heights*.
- Some film historians have wondered why the film received no Oscar nominations and the best guess is that newspaper mogul William Randolph Heast's influence on the Academy and media was still exceptionally strong in 1944, only three years after the controversy over *Citizen Kane*.

Jezebel

1938, Warner Bros., 104 minutes, B&W.
Producer: Jack L. Warner. Director: William Wyler
Cast: Bette Davis, Henry Fonda, George Brent, Margaret Lindsay, Fay Bainter.

> "**** Davis is sensational in this excellent melodrama…"
> —Jay A. Brown & Consumer Guide, *Rating the Movies*

Davis desperately wanted to play Scarlett O'Hara in *Gone With the Wind* and when she lost the part to Vivien Leigh, she demanded that WB (which held her studio contract) find her a role to upstage *GWTW*, to be

Bette Davis wearing the scandalous red dress in *Jezebel*.

released the next year. They did just that. Based on a play by Owen Davis, it turned out to be a good investment: Davis, in the lead, won the Oscar for Best Actress and the film got nominated for Best Picture.

The plot is about a manipulative Southern belle in 1850s New Orleans: Julie Marsden (Davis) is a tempestuous "belle of the ball," but she is also symbolic of the Bible's spoiled and selfish Jezebel—which is how Aunt Belle (Bainter) describes Julie. Bainter won the Oscar for Best Supporting Actress.

Julie shows her true colors at the Mardi Gras when she humiliates her fiancé, Preston Dillard (Fonda), by wearing a scandalous red dress at the Olympus Ball, an event reserved for white gowns for single young ladies. Buck Cantrell (Brent, Davis' frequent leading man) is a chivalrous suitor who duels for Julie. Preston leaves Julie to marry Northerner Amy Bradford (Lindsay). The dramatic conclusion, played against the background of a yellow fever epidemic, is a scene of redemption and survival.

The music is by Max Steiner who also did the music for *Gone With the Wind*. While *GWTW* is the South from the Confederate point-of-view, *Jezebel* sees the South from the Yankee perspective. Adding to that viewpoint is the picture of black slaves as naïve and uneducated with a song in their heart to relieve their misery.

- Many genuine antiques were used on the sets.
- John Huston was one of four contributors to the screenplay.
- Ernie Haller, Davis' favorite cameraman, got an Oscar nomination for cinematography.
- Ruth Elizabeth Davis took "Bette" from Balzac's "Cousin Bette."
- History records that more than 8,000 people died in the yellow fever epidemic of 1853.

Moulin Rouge

1952, Romulus Films/United Artists, 123 minutes, Color.
Producers: John Woolf, James Woolf; Director: John Huston.
Cast: Jose Ferrer, Colette Marchand, Suzanne Flon, Zsa Zsa Gabor, Katherine Kath.

> "John Huston's masterly portrait of the life and times of Toulouse-Lautrec (1864-1901)."
>
> —*TV Guide.*

Nominated for eight Academy Awards, including Best Picture, this luxuriant film stars Ferrer as nineteenth century painter Henri de Toulouse-Lautrec, and Ferrer received an Oscar nomination for Best Actor for his superb performance. (He also doubles as Henri's father.) The picture won Oscars for its sets and costumes. Oswald Morris was nominated for his outstanding photography that somehow resembled the paintings of the great artist; even the opening titles are done the way Henri might have painted them.

The overall work is a sensitive portrayal of the dwarf-like Frenchman whose broken legs never mended from childhood, though the rest of his body developed fully. The film emphasizes Henri's addiction to cognac, his tragic love-life and his favorite haunt: Montmartre and the café that Toulouse made famous—the Moulin Rouge.

Gabor plays Jane Avril, the lovely but superficial singer at the Moulin Rouge. Kath is spirited dancer La Goulue. Marchand plays Marie Charlet, the prostitute who finds it impossible to adjust to Henri's passion for her. Flon is Myriamme, the model who understands Henri (she didn't care about his legs) and falls in love with him. The Can-Can sequence is a highlight and Henri's hallucinations in the finale are extremely touching. Music: Georges Auric. "The Theme From Moulin Rouge (Where Is Your Heart?)" (performed by Percy Faith) became a hit recording.

Colette Marchand and Jose Ferrer in *Moulin Rouge.*

Lautrec, son of a wealthy nobleman, became famous in his own lifetime for his art of seedy Parisian nightlife and colorful posters of his work by lithographer Pere Cotelle. His paintings today are worth multiple millions.

- A music hall bearing the name "Moulin Rouge" exists today in Paris.
- There are several close-ups of Henri sketching and painting. It's the hand of Marcel Vertes who did the costume design.
- For full-body long-shots, a dwarf was used and photographed from the back; he would disappear behind some large object and Jose would be filmed, from the waist up, emerging from the other side.

Samson and Delilah

1950, Paramount, 131 minutes, Color.
Producer/Director: Cecil B. DeMille.
Cast: Victor Mature, Hedy Lamarr, George Sanders, Angela Lansbury.

> "With expected DeMille touches, this remains a tremendously entertaining film."
> —Leonard Maltin.

What the *Motion Picture Herald* called "a king-size attraction" was the top moneymaker of 1950. The spectacle won Academy Awards for costumes, art direction, and sets. The last spectacular scene, with the pagan temple toppling, took a year in preparation. The excellent score is by Victor Young.

The Biblical story is from the book of Judges, chapters 13-16, about Samson (Mature), a Danite strongman, and the beautiful and inexorable Delilah (Lamarr). When Samson chooses her sister (Lansbury) instead of her, Delilah, in a moment of revenge, lures Samson into her tent and gets him to reveal the secret of his great strength…strength enough to kill a lion with his bare-hands, to lift and throw a warrior a great distance, and to destroy hundreds of Philistines with the jawbone of an ass.

And what was the secret of Samson's fantastic strength? His long hair! Putting him to sleep with wine, Delilah cuts his long locks and renders

Victor Mature in costume, Cecil B. DeMille (holding a spear) and Angela Lansbury on the set of *Samson and Delilah*.

him as normal as any other man, normal enough for his enemies to take him away in chains and tie him to the grinding wheel so people can mock him. But there is one aspect Delilah didn't count on: the evil Saran (Sanders) also blinds him, which meant Samson could no longer gaze upon her beauty. In the end, their love grows for each other and when the city has a feast and brings in Samson to be further ridiculed, Delilah helps Samson find a way of escape. Samson's destruction of the temple is one of the most memorable climaxes in cinema history.

- There are movie miniatures of all sizes, but models for this film are extraordinary: the temple itself was nearly 40 feet high and the model of the idol's statue in the temple was almost 20 feet high.

- The screenplay is by Jesse Lasky, Jr. and Fred Frank from a treatment by Vladimir Jabotinsky whose research found that pillars of some ancient temples narrowed at the base, making it practical for Samson to push the pillars apart.
- Mature played Samson's father in a movie-made-for-TV remake in 1984.
- Lamarr became famous for a nude-swim scene in the 1933 Czech film *Ecstasy*. Upon arriving in Hollywood, publicists billed her as "the world's most beautiful woman."

The Scarlet Empress

1934, Paramount, 110 minutes, B&W.
Producer; Adolph Zukor. Director: Josef von Sternberg.
Cast: Marlene Dietrich, John Lodge, Sam Jaffe, Louise Dresser, Ruthelma Stevens.

> "Visually, the film is dazzling, the most imaginative American film of the sound era prior to *Citizen Kane*."
> —Danny Peary, *Guide for the Film Fanatic*

The sixth of the seven Dietrich/Sternberg collaborations is one of the most peculiar yet mesmerizing films ever made. Created around odd images and gigantic sets, the story is about a woman's rise to power through sexual activity. The stunning finale, accompanied by resounding music and clamorous bells ("The 1812 Overture"), has the star riding a stallion up the palace steps to assume power.

Dietrich plays a nymphomaniac, Catherine the Great of Russia, and Lodge plays one of her many lovers, Count Alexei. Jaffe portrays Grand Duke Peter, the idiotic leader that she—as a young girl—is forced to marry, though they never consummate the marriage. A son, the heir, is born to her but it is not the Grand Duke's child. Stevens plays Peter's strange mistress. Dresser is Empress Elisabeth, whom Peter replaces on the throne when she dies. But Catherine quickly realizes that if she is to survive, if Russia is to survive, she must step in and control the situation since her husband is a total fool. Catherine, who dresses in military uniforms, sets out to make "friends" (in whatever way necessary) with all the military and political leaders in the land.

Marlene Dietrich as *The Scarlet Empress*.

The baroque and gargoyle-laden sets are by Hans Dreier, costumes by Travis Banton (who designed Dietrich's costumes in all her Paramount films), and photography in the capable hands of Bert Glennon. The music is that of Mendelssohn and Tchaikovsky.

- The screenplay is allegedly taken from the diary of Catherine.
- Catherine has been played on-screen eight times, first by Pola Negri in 1924.
- It is generally believed that, at times, Catherine *did* wear military garb in real life.
- Dietrich's eight-year-old daughter, Maria, plays Catherine as a child.
- Lodge, grandson of Sen. Henry Cabot Lodge, served as a congressman and governor of Connecticut in the 40s and 50s.

Spartacus

1960, Universal, 197 minutes, Color.
Producer: Edward Lewis. Director: Stanley Kubrick.
Cast: Kirk Douglas, Jean Simmons, Tony Curtis, Peter Ustinov, Laurence Olivier, Charles Laughton, John Gavin, John Ireland, Woody Strode, Nina Foch.

> "It took $12 million and two years of intensive planning.... the end results justified the enormous expense...aided by Douglas' granite-strong performance..."
> —Clive Hirschhorn, *The Universal Story*

Kirk Douglas as *Spartacus*.

Winner of five Academy Awards, the picture (after a slow build and then playing in some theaters for months) became the box-office hit of 1962. The film depicts the unsuccessful slave revolt, led by Spartacus (Douglas), against Imperial Rome between 73-71 B.C., with an outstanding interpretation of gladiators in the Coliseum. The memorable conclusion shows hundreds of martyred slaves crucified along the Appian Way from Capua to Rome.

The screenplay by formerly blacklisted writer Dalton Trumbo is taken from the novel by Howard Fast. There were Oscars for photography, art direction, sets, costumes, and Ustinov, as slave-trader Batiatus, for Best Supporting Actor.

Simmons is Varinia, a beautiful slave-girl working at the school of gladiators; she falls in love with Spartacus and becomes his wife. Olivier plays the mean and ambitious Roman general, Marcus Crassus. Curtis is Antoninus, friend of Spartacus but personal slave to Crassus. Laughton is Gracchus, political enemy of Crassus. Gavin portrays Julius Caesar; Foch is Helena, a Roman noblewoman; Ireland and Strode play slave/gladiators Crixus and Draba.

- Anthony Mann (uncredited) began as director and was replaced by Kubrick. Mann shot the salt mine sequence.
- Ingrid Bergman and Jeanne Moreau turned down the part of Varinia.
- It was shot outside Madrid with 8,000 Spanish extras portraying the slave army of 60,000.
- More than 180 stunt people were used, most from Hollywood.
- The most famous line from the film: "*I* am Spartacus!"

A Tale of Two Cities

1936, MGM, 121 minutes, B&W.
Producer: David O. Selznick. Director: Jack Conway.
Cast: Ronald Colman, Elizabeth Allan, Donald Woods, Edna May Oliver, Blanche Yurka, Basil Rathbone, Henry B. Walthall, Reginald Owen, H.B. Warner.

"...a screen classic."
—Frank N. Magill, *Magill's Survey of Cinema*

Nominated for Best Picture, Selznick's expensive production of the Charles Dickens novel is one of Hollywood's best efforts at bringing great books to the screen. Colman is Sydney Carton, a smart but alcoholic English lawyer during the French Revolution; he drinks so he "can stand his fellow man better." In the end, his compassion for his fellow man leads him to the ultimate sacrifice…he gives his life for the husband of the woman he loves: "It's a far, far better thing I do now than I have ever done; it is a far, far better rest I go to than I have ever known."

The story concerns London and Paris at the time of "The Reign of Terror." The English look on in horror from afar as the 1789 revolt of the masses puts the heads of hundreds of French aristocrats under the guillotine. Charles Darnay (Woods) is one of those falsely accused; his new wife, Lucie Manette (Allan), has, unbeknown to her, overcome the heart of Carton.

Ronald Colman as Sydney Carton in *A Tale of Two Cities*.

Rathbone plays the pompous and tyrannical Marquis St. Evremonde. Yurka plays the mean and hateful Madame DeFarge. Oliver is Miss Pross, tough defender of the innocent, who personally fights DeFarge to the death. Walthall is Dr. Manette (father of Lucie), Warner is Gabelle, and Owen is Stryver.

- Colman shaved off his famous mustache for the role.
- Val Lewton and Jacques Tourneur (*Cat People, I Walked With a Zombie*) directed the Fall of Bastille sequence using hundreds of extras.
- Lucille LaVerne, the cackling revolutionary, was the voice of the Old Witch in *Snow White and the Seven Dwarfs*.

Drama

The Best Years Of Our Lives

1946, Goldwyn/RKO, 170 minutes, B&W.
Producer: Sam Goldwyn. Director: William Wyler.
Cast: Fredric March, Dana Andrews, Myrna Loy, Teresa Wright, Harold Russell, Virginia Mayo, Cathy O'Donnell, Hoagy Carmichael.

> "Superlative!"
> —*The New York Times.*

Winner of the Academy Award for Best Picture, the romantic drama is about the problems war veterans had to endure after WWII as they tried to pick up the pieces and return to private life. The film, whose three leads represent the Army, Navy, and Air Force, won seven Oscars including Best Director.

Russell, who lost his own hands in a dynamite blast during war maneuvers, won two Oscars for his portrayal of Homer Parrish, an armless sailor. In the film's most dramatic moment, a frustrated Homer crashes his hooks-for-hands through a glass window.

Wyler discovered Russell while searching hospitals and military film footage for handicapped veterans; he wanted someone without acting experience. Russell ended up surprising everybody by winning *two* Oscars, the only person ever to win two Oscars for the same role. What happened was—the Academy wanted to make sure that Russell got acknowledged and arranged before the ceremony to give Russell a Special Oscar; then he also won the Oscar for Best Supporting Actor.

March plays Sgt. Al Stephenson who returns to his job as a loan officer at a bank and encounters troubles making readjustment to civilian life.

Dana Andrews at the airplane graveyard in *The Best Years of Our Lives*.

Andrews is Fred Derry, a decorated Air Force pilot, who can only muster a job as a sales clerk. The title, *The Best Years of Our Lives*, refers not to the time just after the war—when the story takes place—but to the actual war years. Mayo, as Marie, Fred's good-looking, fun-loving wife, puts it in perspective when she angrily tells her down-on-his-luck husband, "I gave up the best years of my life—and what have you done?"

Loy plays Al's compassionate wife, Milly. Wright is their daughter, Peggy; she soon falls in love with Fred, who suffers battlefield nightmares. O'Donnell is Wilma, Homer's girlfriend. Carmichael is Butch, bar-owner and piano player at the local tavern where the veterans hang out.

- Homer asks Butch to play "Lazy River," and says, "Remember that?" Carmichael composed it.
- Russell was an ex-paratrooper.
- Wyler chose only WWII veterans as members of the film crew.
- The airplane graveyard was real; Wyler found it in Ontario, Calif.
- During WWII, Wyler served in the Air Force and was assigned the job of producing war documentaries; he did two during bombing missions over Germany: *The Memphis Belle* and *Thunderbolt*. Wyler rose to the rank of Lt. Colonel.

Citizen Kane

1941, RKO Radio, 119 minutes, B&W.
Producer/Director: Orson Welles.
Cast: Orson Welles, Joseph Cotten, Dorothy Comingore, Ruth Warrick, Ray Collins, Everett Sloane, William Alland, Agnes Moorehead, George Coulouris.

> "Often acclaimed as the best film of all time: certainly none has used the medium with more vigour and enthusiasm... there isn't a dull scene in the film's 119 minutes."
> —Leslie Halliwell, *Halliwell's Filmgoer's Companion*

A masterpiece of filmmaking, a true *tour de force*. What makes it even more remarkable is the fact that Welles was only 25 years old when he made the movie! And it was his first film! How did he even get the chance to make a motion picture? Welles had been a success in New York with his Mercury Theatre on the Air, the highlight of which was the *War*

Orson Welles and cinematographer Gregg Toland (lower right) shooting the warehouse scene for *Citizen Kane*.

of the Worlds broadcast on October 30, 1938. The radio program, about alien spaceships invading America, was so real to many listeners that it caused a national sensation. RKO thought Welles might bring some of that artistry to movies. They were right.

Citizen Kane got nine Oscar nominations, including Best Picture, Best Director and Best Actor (Welles), but won only one: Best Original Screenplay, shared by Welles and Herman J. Mankiewicz. There is only one reason the film didn't win Best Picture and didn't make a lot of money on its original release: publisher William Randolph Hearst. Suspicious that the drama was about him, Hearst used all of his influence to keep the picture out of theaters and to keep votes off the Academy of Arts and Sciences ballots. Obviously, to prevent being sued, Welles insisted the movie was not about Hearst and his protégée, actress Marion Davies. In truth, Hearst *was* the pattern for wealthy and egomaniacal publisher/politician Charles Foster Kane, played by Welles. John Houseman, a producer and long-time Welles associate, later said the Kane character was a lot like Orson himself. The story is also about lost childhood. Part of the secret of the film is Welles' background and talent as a magician. He made the movie illusionary, leading the audience to believe they were about to be let in on some hidden knowledge, thus his use of the device that gives us the mysterious word "Rosebud."

How did Welles learn movie technique so quickly? He said he studied the masters, John Ford, John Ford, and John Ford. Orson said he watched *Stagecoach* 40 times! Besides Mankiewicz, two other men helped Welles immensely: composer Bernard Herrmann, who produced a marvelous score, and cameraman Gregg Toland, famous for deep-focus photography and low-angle compositions (note how the film shows ceilings, rare in those days).

- Many members of the cast had been Mercury actors: Cotten (Jedediah Leland), Sloane (Bernstein), Moorehead (Kane's mother), Collins (Gettys), Coulouris (Thatcher), Alland (Thompson). Only Comingore (Susan Alexander, Kane's mistress) and Warrick (Kane's wife) had not worked with Orson before.
- Xanadu, Kane's hideaway, is a reference to Hearst Castle at San Simeon, Calif. The exterior of Xanadu was artwork, done by former Disney artists on the order of the castle in *Snow White and the Seven Dwarfs*.

- Two later directors, Robert Wise and Mark Robson, edited; two famous cuts are the skylight introduction of Susan and the rising shot in the opera house.

East Of Eden

1955, Warner Bros., 115 minutes, Color.
Producer/Director: Elia Kazan.
Cast: James Dean, Julie Harris, Raymond Massey, Jo Van Fleet, Richard Davalos.

> "**** A superb film!"
> —Steven H. Scheuer, *Movies on TV*

The legend of James Dean is phenomenal: no one in the history of motion pictures has gained such fame on such a short career. Dean made three movies in one year, this was his first, and observers knew they were watching history being made. Director Elia Kazan said, "At the very end of shooting, the last few days, you felt a star was going to be born. Everybody smelled it; all the publicity people began to hang around him." After *East of Eden, Rebel Without a Cause*, and *Giant*, it all ended and then it all began with Dean's death in an automobile accident. He was just 24 years old.

Based on John Steinbeck's novel, *East of Eden* is set in 1917 in Salinas/Monterey, California. Cal (Dean) and Aron (Davalos) are two sons vying for the love of their self-righteous father, Adam Trask (Massey). Abra (Harris), girlfriend of the favorite son, Aron, eventually comes to know and love melancholy Cal.

Van Fleet received the Oscar for Best Supporting Actress as the mother who refused to allow her husband to control her and now runs an out-of-the-way brothel. Dean got a Best Actor Nomination and Kazan was nominated for Best Director.

- At 5:45 PM, Friday, Sept. 30, 1955, Dean was roaring his Porsche Spyder westbound on state highway 466 in central California heading to a sports-car race in Salinas. Nearing the village of Cholame (population 65), intersected by highway 41, a 1950 Ford sedan starts a left turn in front of Dean's on-coming car; Dean tried to swerve away but they collide. Dean died in an ambulance rushing

James Dean in a costume test for *East of Eden*.

his broken body to nearby Paso Robles. The college student driving the sedan survived to re-live the nightmare of that tragic afternoon.
- Steinbeck's title comes from the Book of Genesis: "Therefore the LORD God sent him forth from the Garden of Eden…And Cain went out from the presence of the LORD, and dwelt in the land of Nod, on the east of Eden."
- Kazan on Dean (from an interview with the author): "He wasn't much of an actor when I got him." Comparing Dean and Brando, Kazan said Dean "was a far, far sicker kid, and Brando's

not sick, he's just troubled." Brando on Dean: "No, when I finally met Dean it was at a party, where he was throwing himself around, acting the madman. So I spoke to him…He listened to me. He knew he was sick. I gave him the name of an analyst, and he went. At least his work improved."

Elmer Gantry

1960, United Artists, 146 minutes, Color.
Producer: Bernard Smith. Director: Richard Brooks.
Cast: Burt Lancaster, Jean Simmons, Arthur Kennedy, Shirley Jones, Dean Jagger, Patti Page.

> "A landmark film…absolutely extraordinary."
> —Professor Richard Brown.

Sinclair Lewis wrote the novel in 1927 and now, decades later, the subject remains as up-to-date as ever, due to the success of television evangelism. The story is loosely based on real-life radio evangelist Aimee Semple McPherson who founded Angelus Temple in Los Angeles; her flamboyant style included flowing, white-chiffon robes.

The film, centering on exploitation and misconduct within "Old Time Religion" fundamentalism, received an Academy Award nomination for Best Picture. Lancaster as a sawdust-trail tent-preacher, won the Oscar for Best Actor. Jones, a musical star playing against type, won the Best Supporting Oscar for her role as a sexy prostitute, Lulu Baines.

Simmons, wife of director Brooks, is perfect as Sister Sharon Falconer, who yields to the flesh and becomes mistress to rogue revivalist Gantry. Kennedy plays the inquiring but admiring reporter, Jim Lefferts. Jagger is the evangelical group's manager and Page, a pop music recording star in the 50s, plays the choir director and soloist.

- The most astonishing part of the film is the climax in which a fire engulfs Falconer's huge church. The fire is real. Brooks asked a battalion fire chief how to start a fire and, reluctantly, he advised loading the banners throughout the hall with film stock, which the crew did. But the fire was completely managed with a stuntman assigned next to each person in the crowd.

Burt Lancaster as evangelist *Elmer Gantry*.

- Lancaster, commenting on his role, said, "Some parts you fall into like an old glove. Elmer really wasn't acting—that was me!"
- In one of his sermons, Gantry condemns liberal writer Sinclair Lewis. And in another sermon, Gantry condemns "Russellism," the teachings of Charles Russell, head of the Watchtower Bible and Tract Society, publishing arm of Jehovah's Witnesses.

The Grapes of Wrath

1940, 20th Century-Fox, 128 minutes, B&W.
Producer: Darryl F. Zanuck. Director: John Ford.
Cast: Henry Fonda, Jane Darwell, John Carradine, Russell Simpson, Charley Grapewin, John Qualen.

> "The performance of Fonda…is among the most indelible impressions ever made on the screen."
> —Tony Thomas and Aubrey Solomon,
> *The Films of 20th Century-Fox*

The great drama about the Great Depression, based on John Steinbeck's illustrious book. The film received an Academy Award nomination for Best Picture but was chosen as Best Film by the New York Film Critics. Ford won the Oscar for Best Director and Fonda got nominated for Best Actor. (Jimmy Stewart who *did* win for *The Philadelphia Story* said his friend, Henry, should have won.) Darwell, as the dauntless and magnanimous Ma Joad, a metaphor for Mother Earth, won the Oscar for Best Supporting Actress. Inextricably, the Academy overlooked the marvelous contribution of four character actors, each of whom deserved a supporting nomination: Carradine as Casey, the one-time rural preacher who inspires Tom; Simpson as Pa Joad, Grapewin as Grampa Joad; and Qualen as Muley, one of the forlorn farmers who becomes a self-appointed watchman in the night for the deserted landscape.

Fonda in the role of a lifetime as Tom Joad is tremendously inspirational, an honest beacon of truth in an indifferent world, a pensive man trying to make sense of a nonsensical society—with the words of screenwriter Nunnally Johnson: "…a fellow ain't got a soul of his own, just a piece of a big soul, the big soul that belongs to everybody…I'll be around in the dark, I'll be everywhere, wherever you can look; wherever there's a fight so hungry people can eat, I'll be there. Wherever there's a cop beatin'

A cast photo, with Henry Fonda (far right), for *The Grapes of Wrath*.

up a guy, I'll be there. I'll be in the way guys yell when they're mad. I'll be in the way kids laugh when they're hungry and they know supper's ready. And when the people are eatin' the stuff they raise and livin' in the houses they build. I'll be there, too."

The Joads are "Okies" from Oklahoma, tenant farmers uprooted by the "dust bowl" and onerous landlords. Forced like nomads to the road, the ne'er-do-well Joads pile on a dilapidated truck bound for California. Nondescript handbills from "the promised land" say that 800 fruit-pickers are wanted.

The photographer is Gregg Toland who did *Citizen Kane*. He captures mood and poignancy with unforgettable visual images: candlelight shadows, windshield reflections, desert silhouettes at night. The score is by Alfred Newman (*Gunga Din, How Green Was My Valley*); he used "The Red River Valley" as the theme.

- It was filmed at Needles and near Pomona, Calif.
- The memorable farewell scene between Fonda and Darwell was done in one take: "I had to light a match," said Fonda, "and then the cameraman, Gregg Toland, rigged a light in the palm of my hand with wires going up my arm. The light, which was supposed to be the glow from the match, had to light Ma's face just right. It took half-an-hour to set up that piece of business."
- Fonda on acting: "My goal is that the audience must never see the wheels go around, not see the work that goes into this. It must seem effortless and real."

How Green Was My Valley

1941, 20th Century-Fox, 118 minutes, B&W.
Producer: Darryl F. Zanuck. Director: John Ford.
Cast: Walter Pidgeon, Maureen O'Hara, Donald Crisp, Sara Allgood, Roddy McDowall, Anna Lee, Patric Knowles, Barry Fitzgerald, Arthur Shields, Ann Todd, John Loder, Rhys Williams, The Welsh Singers.

"Possesses great beauty, great charm and character."
—*The New York Times.*

For a while, film buffs only remembered this sentimental drama as the movie that beat out *Citizen Kane*. Yet, despite its controversial place in film history, it deserves all the accolades it's received. The film not only won Best Picture but also won an Oscar for director Ford plus a Best Supporting Oscar for Crisp as a strong-minded, coal-mining father, Gwilym Morgan, in a Welsh mining village. And there were three other technical Academy Awards.

The Philip Dunne screenplay is based on Richard Llewellyn's prize-winning novel about the crises of the close-knit Morgan family. The family breaks apart over a union/labor dispute, a strike, and subsequent unemployment. The plot depicts a life of songs (The Welsh Singers), respect for parental authority, and daily Bible readings, revolving around a local protestant church as strict overseer. The story is told by 60-year-old Huw Morgan (narration by Irving Pichel), reminiscing about his life as a boy (McDowall). Pidgeon is perfectly cast as the village minister, Mr. Gruffydd, who must decide whether to give up his love, Angharad Morgan (O'Hara), because of his poverty as a poor preacher.

The full cast couldn't be better: Allgood as the devoted mother, Beth Morgan; Knowles as Ivor, the older brother; Shields as the unbending

A cast photo of the Morgan family for John Ford's *How Green Was My Valley*.

deacon, Mr. Parry. Also with: Lee (Bronwyn), Fitzgerald (Cyfartha), Todd (Cienwen), Loder (Ianto), Williams (the boxer).

- In the wedding scene, as O'Hara leaves the church, what appears to be a perfectly placed gust of wind sends her veil up above her head; O'Hara says that was no accident: Ford used a wind machine and they did the scene several times to get it just right.
- Zanuck and Ford wanted to shoot in Wales but were prevented by the war.
- An 80-acre set was constructed in the Ventura Hills in the Santa Monica Mountains.
- Tons of coal was brought in for the tunnel collapse scene but, due to a coal shortage because of the war, they had to use 20 gallons of black paint to cover the hills with what looked like coal slag.
- Fitzgerald and Shields are brothers and were steady members of the Ford stock company.
- The film premiered successfully at a theater in Wilkes-Barre, Pa., a coal-mining region.

The Magnificent Ambersons

1942, RKO, 88 minutes, B&W.
Producer: Bryan Foy. Director: Orson Welles.
Cast: Joseph Cotten, Tim Holt, Agnes Moorehead, Dolores Costello, Anne Baxter, Ray Collins, Richard Bennett. Narrated by Orson Welles.

> "A magnificent movie!"
>
> —*TIME.*

Nominated for Best Picture, Welles' second of three films for RKO (*Citizen Kane, Journey Into Fear*) is a marred masterpiece about America in the 1870s, at the outset of industrialization; but the fault lies not with Welles (who flew off to South America to produce a documentary requested by the government) but with RKO boss George Schaefer who—fearing WWII audiences wouldn't accept a somber story—ordered 50 minutes cut and the plot changed to an upbeat ending. Nevertheless, even

Agnes Moorehead and Tim Holt in *The Magnificent Ambersons*.

with the changes, it's an outstanding adaptation of the Booth Tarkington novel, portraying the swiftness of a passing, crumbling generation.

Holt, an RKO contract cowboy, shows that even B-players, under the guidance of Welles, could produce top-notch acting. Surprisingly, Holt is perfect as George Minafer, spoiled son of the only daughter of the prominent Amberson family of Indianapolis. Costello is Isabel Amberson Minafer, George's mother. Cotten plays automobile entrepreneur Eugene Morgan, who always loved Isabel. Baxter is the widowed Morgan's daughter, Lucy; George wants Lucy to marry him; but she wants the smug young man to make better plans for his future instead of just wanting to become a yachtsman. And a lot of folks around town would very much like to see brash and selfish George get his comeuppance. Collins plays Isabel's father, Jack Amberson, and Bennett is Jack's increasingly senile dad, Major Amberson. But it is Moorehead in her finest role, and who nearly steals the show, as Aunt Fanny—secretly in love with Eugene. One of the most memorable moments has George stuffing his mouth while devouring Fanny's strawberry shortcake. Here, so much is said of youth taking advantage of the moment, taking advantage of their elders.

With the excellent camera-work of Stanley Cortez, the film is a cinematic wonderland. The snow scene is one of the screen's most classic sequences, with horseless carriage versus horse-drawn sleigh, emphasizing progress and a break in society. There are exquisite light and dark shadings, silhouettes, reflection shots, POV shots, circular shots, and traveling shots (notably up the huge staircase).

- The snow scene was shot in a Los Angeles ice house.
- Part of the lost footage includes a POV sequence by Cortez (with a camera strapped to his chest) walking eerily through the empty Amberson mansion.
- Welles, whose full name is George Orson Welles, suspected that Tarkington, a friend of the Welles family, based George Minafer on Welles, a spoiled child growing up.

The Misfits

1961, United Artists, 124 minutes, B&W.
Producer: Frank E. Taylor. Director: John Huston.
Cast: Marilyn Monroe, Clark Gable, Montgomery Clift, Eli Wallach, Thelma Ritter, Kevin McCarthy.

> "…it presented both her (Monroe) and Clark Gable with splendid roles, their performances alone being sufficient to raise the picture to the level of a modern 'classic'."
> —Joel W. Finler, *All-Time Movie Favorites*

For those who believed Marilyn Monroe was only an untalented sex goddess, this film proves them wrong; she *is* a sex goddess but also a fine actress. And it demonstrates just why MM has now become Hollywood's most legendary female star. She has, in effect, become the Queen of Hollywood, just as Gable was always thought of as the King of Hollywood. And here they are—together for the only time, and in the last film each would make. That, in itself, makes this a full-blown classic.

Marilyn Monroe, Eli Wallach and Clark Gable in *The Misfits*.

With script by Arthur Miller, Monroe's husband, Marilyn plays Roslyn Taber, a woman-child, fragile and disillusioned, in Reno, Nevada to get a divorce from husband Raymond (McCarthy). There she meets Gay Langland (Gable), an aging, bewildered cowboy, now earning a living catching wild horses for sale to dog food makers. Their pals are Perce Howland (Clift), a broken-down rodeo-rider helping out "because anything's better than wages"; Guido (Wallach), Gay's plane-flying partner; and Isabelle Steers (Ritter), Roslyn's landlady.

The story is a clash of femininity and masculinity, and conflict over changing times, a modern world most of us have little or no hand in creating. Roslyn loves her new friends but can't stand the idea of destroying wild animals. In the end, Gay sees it her way. Referring to her radiance, Gay says, "Honey, when you smile it's like the sun comin' up."

- A shot of Marilyn Monroe's naked breasts in the bedroom was cut.
- Robert Mitchum turned down the role of Gay.
- Gable died of a heart attack ten days after shooting ended.
- Monroe died of mysterious circumstances the following year.
- Monroe and Miller divorced after making the film.

Of Human Bondage

1934, RKO, 83 minutes, B&W.
Producer: Pandro S. Berman. Director: John Cromwell.
Cast: Bette Davis, Leslie Howard, Frances Dee, Kay Johnson.

> "…she lays waste his apartment, destroying his paintings and books, and burning the bonds that sustain him. In this one scene, it is possible to watch the baptism of a great actress and a major star."
>
> —*The RKO Story*.

Based on W. Somerset Maugham's searing novel, the melodrama caused a stir in Hollywood when Davis' electrifying performance didn't even get an Oscar nomination. As a result, a write-in campaign ensued—without success. Nevertheless, the episode caused the Motion Picture Academy to, in the future, assign tallying ballots to the accounting firm of Price-Waterhouse.

As to the story itself, one wonders if Maugham might not have had such an experience himself, getting involved with a person who rejects his love and attention, only to find oneself inextricably drawn to helping that individual to the end of life.

Davis, a WB contract player loaned out to RKO, stars as a coarse cockney waitress named Mildred Rogers who becomes a drug addict and prostitute—and who becomes the obsession of Philip Carey (Howard), a medical student with a clubfoot; Philip, to forget his misery, dabbles in art. Sally (Dee) and Norah (Johnson) are other women in Philip's troubled life.

Bette Davis and Leslie Howard in *Of Human Bondage*.

Here is part of Davis' dialogue excoriating Carey from screenwriter Lester Cohen's script: "Yew cad, yew dirty swine. I never cared for yew—not once. I was always making a fool of yuh. Yuh bored me stiff. I hated you. It made me sick when I had to let yuh kiss me. I only did it because yuh begged me. Yuh hounded me, yuh drove me crazy, and, after yuh kissed me, I always used to wipe my mouth. Wipe my mouth!"

- Davis was one of Hollywood's most honored actresses, nominated 10 times for an Oscar and winning twice (*Dangerous, Jezebel*).
- Davis believed it was she who gave the golden statuette its name; once when accepting the award, she announced, it looked like her husband, Oscar Nelson.

- Davis had a cockney-speaking Englishwoman live in her house for two months prior to filming so she could learn the accent.
- Howard was killed during WWII, shot down in a plane by Nazis while flying from Lisbon to London.

On The Waterfront

1954, Horizon/Columbia, 108 minutes, B&W.
Producer: Sam Spiegel. Director: Elia Kazan.
Cast: Marlon Brando, Karl Malden, Eva Marie Saint, Rod Steiger, Lee J. Cobb.

Marlon Brando in *On the Waterfront*.

"…brilliantly directed by Kazan. Working with such heavyweight Actors Studio alumnae as Brando, Steiger and Malden, Kazan was very much in his element; and on turf suited his own crusading temperament."
—Clive Hirschhorn, *The Columbia Story*

One of the great social consciousness-raising dramas of all time, this powerful film, about corrupt union bosses on New York City's waterfront, won eight Oscars including Best Picture. Kazan won for Best Director and Brando, in a stunning performance as Terry Malloy, an ex-prizefighter turned longshoreman, won for Best Actor. (Brando had been passed over three years earlier for his impressive performance in Kazan's *A Streetcar Named Desire*.) Saint, in her film debut, won for Best Supporting Actress. She plays Edie Doyle, a longshoreman's daughter, who falls in love with Terry and supports his struggle against the local mob.

Steiger plays Terry's gangster-bruised older brother, Charley. Their famous scene together in the back of a taxicab is worth the price of admission: "That skunk we got you for a manager, he brought you along too fast." "It wasn't him, Charley—it was you. Remember that night in the Garden? You came down to my dressing room and said, 'Kid, this ain't your night. We're going for the price on Wilson.' You remember that? *This ain't your night!* I could've taken Wilson apart! So what happens? He gets the title shot outdoors in a ballpark and what do I get? A one-way ticket to Palookaville. You was my brother, Charley—you should've taken care of me just a little bit, so I wouldn't have to take them dives for the short-end money."

Budd Schulberg won the Oscar for his screenplay. Malden is Father Barry, urging Malloy to stand up and fight on. Cobb is Johnny Friendly, the crooked union leader.

- It was shot in Hoboken, New Jersey.
- Steiger said on the first day of shooting there were "guys dressed like me trying to intimidate the movie company and shutdown production."
- Many longshoremen were used as extras.
- Frank Sinatra was originally considered for the role of Terry.
- Grace Kelly turned down the role of Edie.

A Place In The Sun

1951, Paramount, 122 minutes, B&W.
Producer/Director: George Stevens.
Cast: Elizabeth Taylor, Montgomery Clift, Shelley Winters, Raymond Burr, Anne Revere, Fred Clark.

> "The company's prestige picture of the year...proved to be also a highly profitable one."
> —John Douglas Eames, *The Paramount Story*

Nominated for nine Oscars, including Best Picture (it won six), the drama's big scene is when Clift tells Liz softly and fearfully that he loves her and she, in extreme close-up, says, "Tell Mama, tell Mama all." Both stars, Taylor and Clift, received Oscar nominations and Stevens won for Best Director.

Based on Theodore Dreiser's novel, *An American Tragedy*, the story concerns a young man, brought up poor, who seeks his place in society, his place in the sun, and meets a beautiful and rich young woman

Elizabeth Taylor and Montgomery Clift in *A Place in the Sun*.

who totally possesses every fiber of his being. Clift plays the man, George Eastman, who has absolutely no will power over his desire for sexy and wealthy Angela Vickers, perfectly played by Taylor.

The trouble in all of this is that Eastman has already impregnated a frumpy, manipulating woman named Alice Tripp (Winters) who insists that he marry her; all of which pushes George to the breaking point; he has murder, not marriage, on his mind.

Two memorable moments occur when George is invited to a party at the mansion of his uncle and rich boss. In the crowded foyer, he, momentarily, thinks he's welcomed by the lady of the house though she passes by him to shake hands with others; and the first meeting with Liz in the billiard parlor is unforgettable as she peeks in just as he, alone, sinks a trick shot.

The fine cast includes Burr (he later became TV's "Perry Mason") as D.A. Frank Marlowe, Clark as defense attorney Bellows, and Revere as Hannah Eastman, George's mother. (Revere was a descendant of Paul Revere.)

- Stevens did it in black-and-white to match the dark tone of the story.
- A lot of it was shot at Lake Tahoe, Calif.`
- Winters, known at the time as a sex symbol, convinced Stevens to use her as Alice by meeting the director dressed in some of her sister's plain clothes.
- To get in the mood for the film's climax, Clift was allowed by San Quentin Prison to spend the night on death row.

Raging Bull

1980, United Artists, 129 minutes, B&W.
Producers: Robert Chartoff, Irwin Winkler; Director: Martin Scorsese.
Cast: Robert De Niro, Cathy Moriarty, Joe Pesci.

> "The best film of the 80s."
>
> —*Premiere.*

Nominated for Best Picture, this highly stylized drama about the "Bronx Bull," middleweight boxer Jake LaMotta, is intense, brutal, violent, sexually explicit, and profane. However, while it is a bleak film it is also a

Robert DeNiro in *Raging Bull*.

great film—demonstrating the very depths of the carnality of man; as it steps through the mire of the prizefighter's self-destructive and paranoid lifestyle. De Niro, who put on 50lbs. to look like a bloated has-been at the end of the film, won the Academy Award for Best Actor as the high-strung, emotionally-charged LaMotta. The film also won the Oscar for Best Editing (Thelma Schoonmaker).

The screenplay is by Paul Schrader and Mardik Martin, based on LaMotta's book. The film not only covers highlights of LaMotta's boxing career, his brief championship, but dwells on his private crises: his marriage to a pretty teenager, Vickie (Moriarty); his stint as a Florida nightclub owner, time in prison (on a charge of serving a drink to a minor), and his drunken decline as a stand-up act in second-rate nightspots. Pesci plays his brother, Joey.

The black-and-white photography (by Michael Chapman) and the sound (by Frank Warner) mix realistically and creatively with the plot. For example, in a nightclub when De Niro sees Moriarty across the room, the effect is that time, and presumably his heart, stand still; to produce the scene, Moriarty and friends are shot in slow-motion while the reaction shots of De Niro are at normal speed. The sound mix, too, is highly effective—from the crunch of powerful punches in the ring to snippets of background music from the era (Benny Goodman, Artie Shaw, Bob Crosby, Ted Weems, Gene Krupa, Harry James, The Ink Spots) to portions of original recordings of blow-by-blow accounts of LaMotta fights (Ted Husing announcing the actual LaMotta/Sugar Ray Robinson bout of Feb. 14, 1951).

- Though a B&W film, for contrast the opening credits have color underneath and color is used again in a home-movie sequence.
- Scorsese didn't want to do the film because he didn't like sports movies; he had to be talked into it by De Niro and LaMotta.
- De Niro worked out with several real boxers, including LaMotta, to learn some of the finer points of the sport.

The Razor's Edge

1946, 20th Century-Fox, 146 minutes, B&W.
Producer: Darryl F. Zanuck. Director: Edmund Goulding.
Cast: Tyrone Power, Gene Tierney, Anne Baxter, Herbert Marshall, Clifton Webb.

> "A dramatic triumph in every sense of the word."
> —*Variety.*

Seldom has Hollywood embarked on a film project which encourages a search for spiritual truth but that's exactly what this unusual film does. Based on the novel by W. Somerset Maugham, the drama was nominated for Best Picture and Baxter won the Oscar for Best Supporting Actress.

Power plays Larry Darrell, a young man searching for truth and the meaning of life in 1919...a search that would take him from Chicago to Europe, India, and the Orient. His search for knowledge and understanding begins in Paris after a fellow soldier in WWI gave his life to save Larry.

Darrell's quest is played out against the backdrop of the wild parties of the Twenties. The title of the story comes from a Holy Man (Cecil Humpreys) who warns Larry that the road to peace and wisdom is as difficult as the sharp edge of a razor.

Baxter is Sophie Nelson who becomes an alcoholic after a car wreck takes the lives of her husband and baby. Tierney is Isabel Bradley, rich and alluring but selfish, though she desperately loves Larry. Isabel frowns upon Larry's Spartan existence, his lack of interest in making money. Webb plays Isabel's uncle, Elliott Templeton, an outspoken but lovable snob. Marshall portrays Somerset Maugham. A memorable moment is Maugham extolling how exquisite Isabel is and only getting a kiss on the

Herbert Marshall portrays novelist Somerset Maugham in *The Razor's Edge*.

cheek, prompting his desire for a better kiss on the mouth—which he gets. Maugham's conclusion about Darrell? "Goodness is the greatest force in the world, and he's got it."

- Marshall had only one leg; he lost his right leg in WWI.
- The costumes were designed by Oleg Cassini, Tierney's husband at the time.
- Baxter was the granddaughter of famous architect Frank Lloyd Wright.
- Zanuck went all out for the film having famous artist Norman Rockwell do the poster art.

Schindler's List

1993, Universal, 197 minutes, B&W w/Color segments.
Producers: Steven Spielberg, Branko Lustig; Director: Steven Spielberg.
Cast: Liam Neeson, Ben Kingsley, Ralph Fiennes, Caroline Goodall.

> "A passionate cry, a towering drama, a masterwork in its field."
> —Gene Shalit, *The Today Show.*

The most powerful feature film ever about the Holocaust won seven Academy Awards, including Best Picture and Best Director. Steven Zaillian won for his adapted screenplay from the novel by Thomas Keneally.

Based on a true story, a Czech businessman, Oskar Schindler (Neeson), saves 1,100 Jews from Nazi concentration camps and certain death in the gas chambers at Auschwitz. Schindler sets up a production plant in Poland making cooking utensils, and eventually munitions, for German troops using Jewish slave labor. But along the way he has a conversion after watching the evil that the Nazis are bringing on the people. In one very telling moment, Schindler—while high on a bluff overlooking the town—tearfully watches a little girl in a red dress trying to escape the Nazis; later he sees her dead on a cart of corpses.

The most vicious of the local Nazis is camp commandant Amon Goeth (Fiennes) whom Schindler must convince to deal with him. Schindler uses his profits to pay off the Nazi officer to let him put over a thousand Jews, including women and children, on a special list of workers, workers

Steven Spielberg directs Liam Neeson on the set of *Schindler's List*.

Schindler claims he must have to do the job at the plant. In fact, most of the workers are not skilled at all; Schindler, with the help of Jewish accountant Itzhak Stern (Kingsley), continually ingratiates himself with the Nazis in order to protect and save condemned Jews.

Schindler is an enigma: at first he seeks big profits, likes to party, and is a womanizer though he has a wife, Emilie (Goodall). But by the end, he is torn apart by having not spent more of what he has had to save others.

- The little girl in red is symbolic of all the bloodshed and horror all around them. Her dress is the only color in the film with the exception of the epilogue in which hundreds of 6,000 descendants of the Schindler Jews lay stones on Schindler's grave, a Jewish tradition when one visits a gravesite. Mrs. Schindler, in a wheelchair, participates in the ceremony.
- Neeson, whose face is not shown, is the one who places the flower on the grave at the end.
- Spielberg, without glasses, portrays one of the liberated Schindler Jews crossing the field.
- Spielberg did the film for free. His salary and royalties went to the Shoah Foundation.
- Co-producer Lustig is an Auschwitz survivor. He also produced *Sophie's Choice* and *Shoah*.

- The film was shot in Poland using 20,000 extras but the filmmakers had to construct a death camp set outside the walls of Auschwitz because authorities wouldn't give permission to shoot on the real site.
- The actual list was found in Schindler's Frankfurt, Germany apartment after his death in 1974.

A Streetcar Named Desire

1951, Warner Bros., 122 minutes, B&W.
Producer: Charles K. Feldman. Director: Elia Kazan.
Cast: Vivien Leigh, Marlon Brando, Kim Hunter, Karl Malden.

> "...Vivien Leigh, playing opposite Marlon Brando, gave a screen performance of consummate greatness as Blanche Dubois..."
>
> —Clive Hirschhorn, *The Warner Bros. Story*

Marlon Brando and Elia Kazan on the set of *A Streetcar Named Desire*.

One of only a handful of films that have received a dozen or more Oscar nominations. Based on the Tennessee Williams Broadway hit, which won the Pulitzer Prize, the drama's 12 Academy Award nominations included Best Picture and Best Director (Kazan also directed the New York stage production). Brando, outstanding as T-shirted Stanley Kowalski, got nominated for Best Actor and Leigh, as mentally fragile Blanche, won the Oscar for Best Actress. Both of the Academy's Supporting Oscars were also won for this film: Hunter as Stella, Blanche's sister and Stanley's wife, and Malden as Harold "Mitch" Mitchell, Stanley's poker-playing buddy who makes a play for Blanche. This was the first film to win three of the Academy's four acting awards.

The plot shows the Old South coming into conflict with the new, more obscene South. The film opens with Blanche, an aging Southern Belle on the edge of madness, arriving in New Orleans to stay with her sister and brother-in-law; she catches a streetcar named "Desire" to reach her destination. The once vivacious Blanche, whose past life inclined toward nymphomania and prostitution, is emotionally pushed over the line—away from reality—by the brutish Stanley.

Jessica Tandy played Blanche on Broadway but she didn't have the star quality to carry the film; similarly, Brando was unknown at the time. Leigh had never seen the Tandy production, but before doing the movie, Vivien played Blanche in a London production directed by her husband, Laurence Olivier. Except for Scarlett O'Hara, Leigh had never wanted to play a role more than she did that of Blanche Dubois. When making the film, which took three months to shoot, Vivien was eager to get to the studio every day and was the last to leave.

- Williams fought with the censors, and won, to keep the pivotal rape scene in.
- Vivien adored Hunter but there was tension between Leigh and Brando at first; they eventually became friends.
- Leigh, a manic-depressive, was sent into a state of melancholy, like Blanche, soon after completing the picture.
- Kazan, Brando, and Malden would work together again, three years later, in *On the Waterfront*. Brando and Malden appeared together once more in *One-Eyed Jacks*.

To Kill A Mockingbird

1962, Universal, 129 minutes, B&W.
Producer: Alan J. Pakula. Director: Robert Mulligan.
Cast: Gregory Peck, Mary Badham, Phillip Alford, Robert Duvall, Brock Peters, John Megna.

> "**** Topnotch. In its own quiet way this is one of the best movies dealing with race relations that the American film industry has ever made."
> —Steven H. Scheuer, *Movies on TV*

Based on the Harper Lee novel, this inspiring drama, nominated for Best Picture, is about racial injustice but it is also a good scenario of children growing into the reality of life. Peck won the Academy Award for Best Actor as Atticus Finch, an Alabama attorney defending a black man against the false charge of raping a "white trash" woman.

Set during the Great Depression, Finch is a widowed father of two small children: a six-year-old little girl they call Scout (Badham) and her 10-year-old brother Jem (Alford). Dill (Megna) is their playmate. Duvall,

Phillip Alford, Mary Badham and Gregory Peck in *To Kill a Mockingbird*.

in his screen debut, plays a mysterious neighbor who never comes out during the day—a developmentally disabled man named Boo Radley. The black defendant, Tom Robinson, is played by Peters.

The film also won Oscars for screenplay (Horton Foote), art direction (Alexander Golitzen, Henry Bumstead) and sets (Oliver Emert); the trio built a small Southern town with courthouse on the back-lot at Universal.

- The narrator is Kim Stanley.
- Peck's nine-minute summation speech was done in one take.
- The courtroom was an exact reproduction of the courthouse in Lee's hometown of Monroeville, Alabama, which is now a tourist site.
- Peck's watch was a prop but after the movie was made, Lee gave him her father's watch and chain as a gift; Peck was wearing it the night he accepted the Oscar.
- Badham and Peck continued to correspond with each other long after the movie finished; he always referred to her as Scout.
- Peters delivered the eulogy at Peck's funeral in 2003.

The Treasure of the Sierra Madre

1948, Warner Bros., 126 minutes, B&W.
Producer: Henry Blanke. Director: John Huston.
Cast: Humphrey Bogart, Tim Holt, Walter Huston, Bruce Bennett, Alfonso Bedoya, Barton MacLane.

> "A magnificent and unconventional piece of screen entertainment."
>
> —*TIME.*

Not since the 1923 silent classic *Greed* has the subject been so thoroughly explored on-screen: how money, gold in this case, changes a man's soul. Based on the novel by the mysterious B. Traven, the adventure-drama is about three men prospecting for gold in the Mexican mountains outside Tampico in the 1920s. We get inside their minds as they combat jungle, winds, bandits, and each other in their quest for the precious metal.

The film was nominated for Best Picture and both Hustons won Oscars: John, two, for screenplay and directing, and his father for Best Sup-

Humphrey Bogart, Walter Huston and Tim Holt in the train scene in *Treasure of the Sierra Madre*.

porting Actor. And in a bewildering oversight by the Academy, Bogart—in one of his finest performances—wasn't even nominated.

Bogie's greedy Fred C. Dobbs is classic. The elder Huston is also right-on-the-mark as Howard, a wonderfully likeable old timer, experienced at prospecting. He joins Dobbs and another greenhorn, Curtin, well-played by Tim Holt (who also did a good job for Orson Welles in *The Magnificent Ambersons*). But it's Bedoya as Gold Hat, a Mexican bandit, who delivers the film's most famous line: "I don't have to show you any stinkin' badges!"

MacLane plays the crooked oil rig foreman; Bennett plays the outsider who follows the trio into the mountains.

The story's moral is impressive: There is a seeming unknown force at work, overseeing good and evil, balancing righteousness and wickedness, through acts of nature—and, though life is not fair, justice will surreptitiously prevail—if not *by* man's hand then without it.

- Who was B. Traven? Some say he was Traven Toravan, a Communist revolutionary deported in the 20s from England to Mexico.

- A highlight is Walter's little dance when they first find gold; the jig was Walter's idea.
- That's John, of course, as the American tourist in the white suit repeatedly hit upon by Dobbs for a handout.
- Robert Blake plays the Mexican boy who sells Bogart a lottery ticket.
- The film was shot at Tampico, Acapulco, Jungapeo, and San Jose Purma, Mexico; and in the Mojave Desert of Calif., and Kernville, Calif., at Kelly's Rainbow Mine.
- Originally, Dobbs was decapitated—but the censors cut the scene.

The Verdict

1982, 20th Century-Fox, 122 minutes, Color.
Producers: Richard D. Zanuck, David Brown; Director: Sidney Lumet.
Cast: Paul Newman, Jack Warden, James Mason, Charlotte Rampling, Lindsay Crouse.

> "**** Paul Newman is brilliant…"
>
> —*TV Guide.*

Newman conducts an acting clinic in this emotional courtroom drama. And he got cheated out of an Oscar, though he did get nominated. Director Lumet also got an Academy Award nomination and the film got nominated for Best Picture.

Newman is Frank Galvin, a broken-down, alcoholic Boston lawyer, an ambulance chaser. His hands are so shaky he has to sip a shot of booze off the table without touching the glass. His breakfast is a raw egg in a glass of beer in a bar.

Based on Barry Reed's novel with screenplay by David Mamet, the story is about fighting the establishment and incompetent doctors. A young woman who was about to deliver went into a hospital and was given the wrong anesthetic which sent her into a coma; she's turned into a vegetable, tied to a machine. Galvin, who has lost four cases in three years, turns down a $210,000 settlement and decides to let the jury determine the matter.

Crouse plays the nurse who knows the truth. On the defense team are Mike (Warden) and Laura (Rampling). Mason plays the rich and pow-

Paul Newman and director Sidney Lumet on the set of *The Verdict*.

erful opposing attorney with an unlimited legal staff. Galvin's chances of getting the verdict in his favor are slim and none.

- Crouse is the daughter of playwright Russell Crouse and the wife of screenwriter Mamet. She's also with Newman in *Slap Shot*.
- English actress Rampling is a former model; you can catch her in Woody Allen's *Stardust Memories*.
- The music is by Johnny Mandel, a former trumpeter and trombonist with Count Basie. Mandel also did the score for *M*A*S*H*.

Epic

Ben-Hur

1959, MGM, 212 minutes, Color.
Producer: Sam Zimbalist. Director: William Wyler.
Cast: Charlton Heston, Stephen Boyd, Haya Harareet, Jack Hawkins, Hugh Griffith, Martha Scott, Cathy O'Donnell, Sam Jaffe, Frank Thring.

> "The most tasteful and visually exciting film spectacle yet produced by an American company."
> —*The Film Quarterly*.

The epic was all alone in winning the most Oscars, 11, until 1997 when *Titanic* tied it. But it's also a fact that there are more Academy Award categories now. *Ben-Hur* won for Best Picture, Wyler for Best Director, and Heston for Best Actor.

Based on the 1880 bestseller by Civil War Gen. Lew Wallace, the story concerns a first century galley slave, Judah Ben-Hur (Heston), who becomes the adopted son of a Roman commander (Hawkins), after Judah saved the Roman in a sea-battle. Judah's conversion to Christianity leads to a confrontation with his former boyhood friend, Messala (Boyd), who is now a Roman warrior.

The film is famous for its elaborate chariot race that runs nine minutes on-screen. The race took six months to prepare and Heston had to learn to drive his own chariot for the close-ups. In 1899, *Ben-Hur* was a Broadway stage production featuring chariots on treadmills. The story was also done as a silent picture in 1926 starring Ramon Novarro and Francis X. Bushman.

Charlton Heston, Stephen Boyd and director William Wyler on the set of *Ben-Hur*.

The fictional tale includes Esther, played by Harareet, a slave girl given her freedom by the formerly well-to do Ben-Hur; to complicate matters, she has fallen in love with her former slave-owner. (In real-life, Harareet, born in Haifa, served two years in Israel's armed forces before becoming an actress.) Griffith (who won the Oscar for Best Supporting Actor) is a peripatetic sheik who gets Ben-Hur to race his chariot against the Romans in the Jerusalem games. Thring plays Pontius Pilate, Jaffe portrays an astute slave, O'Donnell is Judah's sister, and Scott is Heston's mother again; she played his mother in *The Ten Commandments*.

- The chariot-race unit was under the direction of former B-Western stuntman Yakima Canutt. Heston tells the story that

he told Canutt that he was worried about racing his chariot against all the more experienced drivers and Yakima responded: "Chuck, you just stay in the chariot—I guarantee you'll win the race."
- The production, using 300 sets and nine soundstages, was filmed at the vast Cinecitta Studios a few miles from Rome.
- A high-speed restaurant was constructed to feed the cast and crew of 5,000 in half-an-hour.
- During the long hours of shooting in the hot sun, two-dozen waterboys in costume moved among the actors to keep everybody refreshed.
- In 1966, Boyd starred opposite Raquel Welch in the sci-fi hit *Fantastic Voyage*.
- Zimbalist never saw his masterpiece finished—he died a week before the production wrapped.

Cleopatra

1963, 20th Century-Fox, 243 minutes, Color.
Producer: Walter Wanger. Director: Joseph L. Mankiewicz.
Cast: Elizabeth Taylor, Rex Harrison, Richard Burton, Roddy McDowall, Hume Cronyn, Cesare Danova.

> "The most costly-to-date-film ever made, and a splendid telling of the celebrated Queen and her doomed love for Marc Antony."
> —Tony Thomas and Aubrey Solomon,
> *The Films of 20th Century-Fox*

Not every classic film is a *really* great film; D.W. Griffith's *Birth of a Nation* fits into that category, as does this picture. The costumes, photography, special effects, sets, and art direction are outstanding, and, in fact, all of those things won Academy Awards; the film itself was nominated for Best Picture. But the movie—at over four hours—is too long and badly needed more editing. The trouble is, when you spend that much money on a film, the studio heads want to see it all up there on the screen. In this case, they would have been better off leaving half of it on the cutting-room floor, which is what most critics preferred.

Elizabeth Taylor and Roddy McDowall in *Cleopatra*.

The film cost over $31 million (budgeted for $5 million) though compared to today's movie budgets, that doesn't sound like a lot, but if the same movie were made today it would cost ten times that amount. Taylor as Cleopatra was paid a whopping million dollars, the first star to demand that kind of money. Liz was at the top of her game and her extraordinary beauty is one of the reasons this film should be seen.

Another reason to see this film is to witness one of the most spectacular scenes ever filmed—Cleopatra's processional entrance into Rome on a 65-ft.-long sphinx.

Harrison stars as Julius Caesar, Burton is Marc Antony, McDowall portrays the evil Octavian; Cronyn is the Queen's advisor, Sosigenes; and Danova is her personal slave, Apollodorus.

- The film was riddled with blockages and slowdowns, including strikes and bad weather; adding to the complications, Taylor and Burton fell in love and weren't always on time to the set, partly due to the fact that the press was constantly dogging them.
- It was shot in Italy and at Pinewood Studios, London.

- The story of Cleopatra (69-30 BC) had been played four other times, by Helen Gardner (1911), Theda Bara (1917), Claudette Colbert (1934), and Rhonda Fleming (1953).

Dances With Wolves

1990, Orion/TIG Productions, 181 minutes, Color.
Producers: Jim Wilson, Kevin Costner; Director: Kevin Costner.
Cast: Kevin Costner, Mary McDonnell, Graham Greene, Rodney A. Grant, Robert Pastorelli, Floyd Red Crow Westerman.

Kevin Costner in *Dances With Wolves*.

"Four stars: Kevin Costner's epic tribute to Native Americans."

—TV Guide.

Winner of seven Oscars, including Best Picture and Best Director, Costner stars as Army Lt. John Dunbar who chooses, after the Civil War, to be assigned to an abandoned fort in the Dakota Territory. Dunbar said he wanted to see the frontier before it disappeared. Once there, he becomes a trusted friend of his Sioux neighbors—and falls in love with a white woman, Stands With a Fist (McDonnell), who had been reared by the tribe. The Indians give Dunbar the name "Dances With Wolves" because he befriends a lonely wolf who visits his fort.

Michael Blake won an Academy Award for his screenplay that takes us step-by-step through Dunbar's adventure as he learns the ways of the Indians and sees their travails and miseries in a daily effort to survive invasion of their homeland. Dean Semler won an Oscar for his beautiful photography of the wide-open spaces of South Dakota. John Barry also won for his exciting score.

Greene plays Kicking Bird, Westerman is Ten Bears, Pastorelli is Timmons, and Grant is Wind In His Hair—all speaking the real Lakota dialect, taught by a team of Indian language experts.

- The film was shot in sequence in order to be consistent with the weather.
- The buffalo herd consisted of 2,000 head.
- The buffalo stampede had to be done in one take because of the difficulty of rounding up the animals; nine cameras were used.
- The buffalo Costner kills up close is mechanical; none of the buffaloes was actually killed during the hunt.

Doctor Zhivago

1965, MGM, 197 minutes, Color, UK.
Producer: Carlo Ponti. Director: David Lean.
Cast: Omar Sharif, Julie Christie, Geraldine Chaplin, Rod Steiger, Alec Guinness, Tom Courtenay, Siobhan McKenna, Ralph Richardson, Rita Tushingham.

A cast photo for *Doctor Zhivago*.

"Excellent acting and brilliant production."
—*The Chicago Tribune.*

Probably the greatest romantic-epic of all time and the only sweeping film of its kind to dramatically show the evils of Communism. Based on Boris Pasternak's Nobel Prize-winning novel, the spectacle about the 1917 Russian Revolution won five Academy Awards and was nominated for Best Picture (*The Sound of Music* won).

Dr. Yuri Zhivago (Sharif), a physician/poet/humanitarian, is forced by the government into service as an army doctor. But his personal dilemma is as great as his physical crisis: Yuri loves two women—his lovely and delicate wife Tonya (Chaplin) and the beautiful and passionate Lara (Christie), who at 17 learned the secrets of sex from her tutor, Komarovsky (Steiger). The story of Yuri, Lara, and Tonya is told by Zhivago's brother (Guinness) to a girl (Tushingham) whom he suspects is the lost daughter of Yuri and Lara. McKenna and Richardson portray Anna and Alexander in whose household Yuri grew up.

The inspired production provides some of the finest technical achievements ever seen on film, and was so rewarded: veteran cameraman Freddie Young won the Oscar for his cinematography, Robert Bolt won for Best Screenplay, Maurice Jarre for Best Score (including "Lara's Theme"), John Box for Best Art Direction, and Phyllis Dalton for Best Costumes.

- Like the before-and-after of Tara in *GWTW*, we see the land as it was before the war and what it has become.
- Note Yuri and Lara, before they knew each other, passing on a streetcar; they repeat the scene at the end.
- Sharif's son, Tarek, plays Yuri at age eight.
- The battle reflected in the glasses of Pasha the revolutionary (Courtenay), knocked to the ground, recalls Eisenstein's pince-nez shot in *Battleship Potemkin*.
- Sharif, who also stars in Lean's *Lawrence of Arabia*, is an expert bridge player.
- It was filmed, not in Russia, but in Finland and Spain.

Giant

1956, Warner Bros., 198 minutes, Color.
Producer/Director: George Stevens.
Cast: Elizabeth Taylor, Rock Hudson, James Dean, Mercedes McCambridge, Chill Wills, Dennis Hopper, Carroll Baker, Earl Holliman, Sal Mineo.

> "…something the film colony often claims but seldom achieves: an epic."
> —*TIME.*

A box-office hit, based on the novel by Edna Ferber, *Giant* spans 25 years in the life of a big Texas family during the era when oil wells were replacing beef cattle. The film received 10 Academy Award nominations including Best Picture. Stevens won as Best Director. The legendary Dean, in his last role and explosive as Jett Rink, was nominated for Best Actor. The famous theme is by Dimitri Tiomkin.

The story, which begins in the early 1920s, is about power and prejudice, developed through a scenario of family values and tradition. Texas cattle king Bick Benedict (Hudson) goes to Maryland to buy a prize stal-

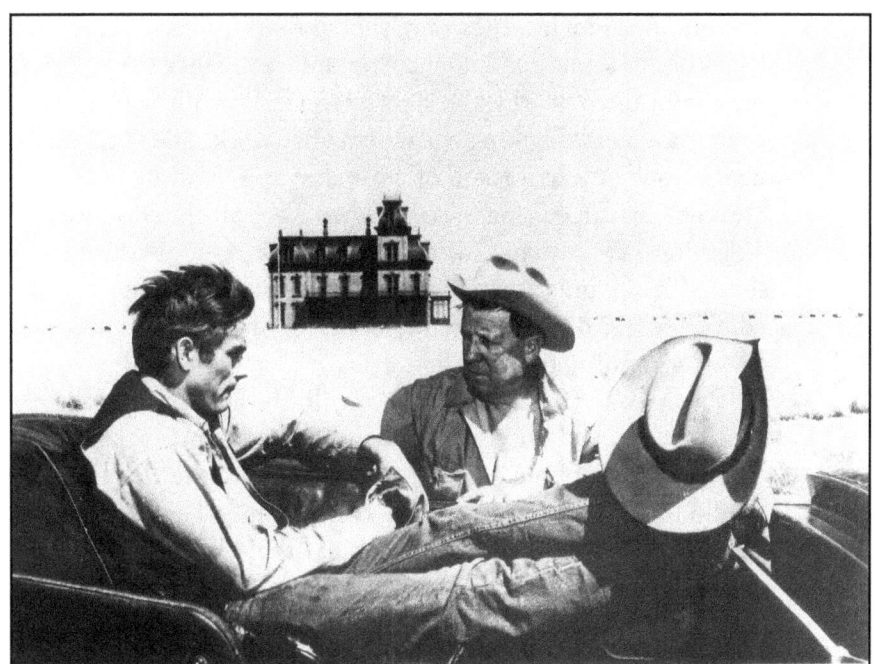

James Dean and director George Stevens planning a scene for *Giant*.

lion and meets Leslie Lynnton (Taylor), a beautiful and independent-minded young woman. It's love at first sight. They immediately marry and Bick brings her back to Reata, his 595,000-acre Texas ranch. But Bick's sister, Luz (McCambridge), the matriarch, feels intimidated by Leslie's arrival and there's friction from the start. Rink is a moody Reata ranch-hand who also falls in love with Leslie. She likes Jett and his head-strong manner but remains faithful to Bick. Jett ends up with a tiny strip of land that strikes it rich with oil; it grows into giant real estate; unfortunately, Jett doesn't grow with it.

Highlights: Dean's initial appearance and meeting with Liz; Dean's rope twirl in Bick's office; Jett marking off his land; Rink's oil strike that leaves him covered with the black stuff and then slugging Bick afterwards; Jett and Leslie's tea party at his place; Rink's drunken speech to an empty ballroom; Hudson's fist-fight with a café proprietor as "The Yellow Rose Of Texas" plays on the jukebox; Mineo's funeral.

Hopper and Baker play the son and daughter of Bick and Leslie. Holliman plays the young rancher who marries Baker. Wills is the organ-playing uncle. Mineo plays a neighbor, a patriotic Mexican-American, who joins the army.

- The outdoor ranch scenes were shot at Marfa, Texas, where the locals got to know and like the cast and crew. Since there was no big city or town nearby, the stars often visited with the locals, even eating and drinking with them after work. The ranch is nearly gone now as a result of fans taking pieces away.
- Stevens was still editing the film when 24-year-old Dean was killed in a car crash in California two weeks later. Because of the sudden popularity of the star, Stevens went back and found edited footage of Dean and put it back in, which accounts for the long running time.
- Baker on Dean (from an interview with the author): "Jimmy was very odd and I don't pretend that I knew him, even though we spent a lot of time together, and we went to the Actors Studio together, we used to go to concerts together—within groups, of course—but I can't really say that I knew Jimmy that well. He was desperate to be the top. I saw him one day in the commissary actually get down on his knees in front of (columnist) Hedda Hopper; he did it in a funny gesture, he would ignore small people on the film, he did it as a joke but he was also paying court to her."

The Godfather

1972, Paramount, 175 minutes, Color.
Producer: Albert S. Ruddy. Director: Francis Ford Coppola.
Cast: Marlon Brando, Al Pacino, James Caan, Robert Duvall, Diane Keaton, Richard Castellano, John Cazale, Abe Vigoda, Talia Shire, Richard Conte, Sterling Hayden.

> "*The Godfather* contains startling effects. Coppola and his cameraman Gordon Willis created nostalgia scenes of the 1940s in which shadow and light symbolize guilt and happiness, death, and innocence. The director's use of cinematic chiaroscuro reaches a climax in the baptismal sequence."
> —*An Introduction to American Movies.*

The epic film, about the saga of the changing dynasty of a crime family in New York City, is both a great dramatic and technical achievement.

Marlon Brando in *The Godfather*.

It's really the modern monster movie and the creatures live amongst us, appearing in the guise of a religious family and respectable leaders of the community, when, in fact, they are evil personified. The personification richly arrives toward the end of the picture when Don Vito Corleone (Brando), playing chase with his grandson in the family garden, inserts an orange peel over his teeth and feigns—what else?—the boogyman!

Based on the popular novel by Mario Puzo, the film received 10 Oscar nominations and won the Academy Award for Best Picture. Puzo and Coppola won Oscars for co-writing the screenplay and Brando, in a remarkable performance, won Best Actor.

What did the underworld think of the film? Apparently, they liked it, and had been willing to see the production go forward providing the words "Mafia" and "Cosa Nostra" would be deleted from the script. Producer Ruddy got that word during a meeting of the Italian-American Civil Rights League.

The powerful but violent drama has a multitude of memorable scenes: the wedding party, the horsehead in the bed, the attack at the fruit-stand, Michael (Pacino) protecting his wounded father at the hospital, Michael plotting the murder of family enemies and its execution in a restaurant, the brutal beating at the fire hydrant by Sonny (Caan), the attack on Sonny at the toll plaza, the courtship and wedding in Sicily, the meeting of the Mafia heads, Brando and Pacino in the garden, Brando and the flit-gun, the brilliantly edited massacre juxtaposed against an infant baptism (the birth of a new Godfather?), and the closing consolation of the sister (Shire) and the wife (Keaton).

The excellent supporting cast includes: Duvall as the family lawyer, Tom Hagen; Castellano as the overweight hit-man, Clemenza; Cazale as the dumb son, Fredo; Vigoda as Tessio, another henchman; Conte as Barzini, the rival boss; Hayden as McCluskey, the corrupt cop; John Marley as the producer; and Al Martino as Johnny Fontaine, the singer-actor indebted to the Don for getting him work in Hollywood.

- Brando auditioned for the role by stuffing Kleenex tissues in his cheeks to give the aging effect of sagging jowls.
- The part of Fontaine (suggestive of Sinatra's early days) was first offered to singer Vic Damone who turned it down. Damone later fired his agent for the bad decision.
- Lenny Montana (Luca Brassi), an ex-wrestler, was picked from a location crowd.
- The horsehead in the bed was real!

The Godfather Part II

1974, Paramount, 200 minutes, Color.
Producer/Director: Francis Ford Coppola.
Cast: Al Pacino, Robert De Niro, Robert Duvall, Diane Keaton, John Cazale, Lee Strasberg, Michael V. Gazzo, Abe Vigoda, Talia Shire, G.D. Spradin, Bruno Kirby.

> "The complete work is an epic vision of the corruption of America."
> —*The New Yorker*

The crime classic sequel, nominated for 12 Oscars, shows how the mob boss became so powerful. De Niro, who won the Oscar for Best Supporting Actor, plays the young Vito Corleone, protector of immigrants in New York's Little Italy. The drama, originally from the Mario Puzo book, won six Oscars including Best Picture and Best Director.

Robert DeNiro in *The Godfather Part II*.

Told through the flashback process, the more subdued follow-up has several memorable scenes; one in particular with Strasberg as Hyman Roth, head of the Jewish Mafia, meeting with all the crime bosses on a hotel patio in Havana, cutting up a birthday cake—symbolic of cutting up the pieces of the underworld wealth.

Pacino stars as Don Michael Corleone, recipient of the family business after the death of his father. But Michael goes far beyond his forebear, in ambition and deceit. And in the end, Michael becomes a cruel, cold, and lonely man.

Keaton is Michael's wife, Kay. Duvall also returns as the family lawyer, Tom Hagen. Cazale is back as the weak brother, Fredo. Shire, again, is sister Connie. Vigoda reprises his role as henchman Tessio. Gazzo plays stoolie Frankie Pentangeli, Spradin is Sen. Pat Geary, and Kirby is the

Young Clemenza.

- This was the first sequel to win an Academy Award for Best Picture.
- Roth is based on gangster Meyer Lansky who lived in Miami.
- James Caan, Sonny in the original, appears in a cameo flashback.
- There are 16 deaths in the film.
- The Havana hotel sequence was shot in Santo Domingo.
- Merle Johnson, Connie's boyfriend, is played by 50s heartthrob Troy Donahue, whose real name is Merle Johnson.

Gone With the Wind

1939, MGM/Selznick International, 219 minutes, Color.
Producer: David O. Selznick. Director: Victor Fleming.
Cast: Vivien Leigh, Clark Gable, Leslie Howard, Olivia de Havilland, Thomas Mitchell, Hattie McDaniel, Butterfly McQueen.

> "*Gone With the Wind* has brought pleasure to everyone in the world with the possible exception of the people who made it...Yet out of all this ferment and torment emerged the most beloved motion picture of all time."
> —*Pictorial History of "Gone With the Wind."*

This famous epic, based on the bestseller by Margaret Mitchell, won nine Oscars, including Best Picture. Leigh, as exquisite child/woman Scarlett O'Hara, won for Best Actress and McDaniel, as Mammy, won for Best Supporting Actress—the first black person to win an Oscar. Sidney Howard won for Best Screenplay but it was Ben Hecht who penned the opening title: "There was a land of Cavaliers and Cotton Fields called the Old South...Here in this pretty world Gallantry took its last bow...Here was the last ever to be seen of Knights and their Ladies Fair, of Master and of Slave...Look for it only in books, for it is no more than a dream remembered, a Civilization gone with the wind."

There was a controversy in Hollywood when Gable, perfect as the dashing Rhett Butler, was passed over for Best Actor: Robert Donat won as the teacher in *Goodbye, Mr. Chips*. Another oversight was Max Steiner not

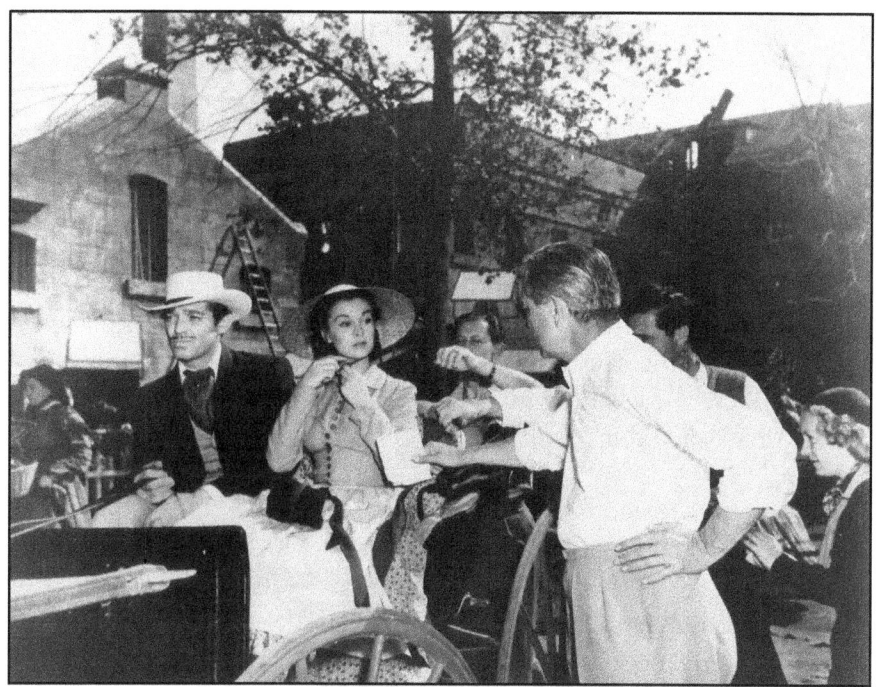

Clark Gable, Vivien Leigh and director Victor Fleming on the set of *Gone With the Wind*.

winning for Best Score which included the incomparable "Tara's Theme." Fleming won for Best Director though several uncredited directors worked on the film, including Sam Wood, George Cukor, B. Reeves Eason, and William Cameron Menzies. MGM's Louis B. Mayer called Fleming off the set of *The Wizard of Oz* after Cukor was fired. Toward the end of filming *GWTW*, Fleming fell ill and Wood finished the picture.

The talented cast included Howard as weak dreamer Ashley Wilkes, de Havilland as good-hearted Melanie Hamilton, Mitchell as Gerald O'Hara, Scarlett's father; and McQueen as Prissy ("I don't know nothin' about birthin' babies"). The MGM publicity department claimed they had looked at 1,400 actresses to find Scarlett and tested 90, among them Katharine Hepburn, Bette Davis, Joan Crawford, Paulette Goddard, Susan Hayward, Lana Turner, and Lucille Ball. On set, Vivien was poised and a quick study, but her profanity shocked both cast and crew, though men admired her and women envied her ability to learn lines fast and to quickly jump into character.

- Adjusted for inflation, the film has made $2 billion worldwide!

- It was the first movie with an intermission.
- It previewed with great success in Riverside, California; the premiere was in Atlanta in a gala event on December 15, 1939.
- *GWTW* used 90 sets.
- The first scene filmed was the burning of Atlanta with stunt-doubles for Gable and Leigh; in fact, Vivien was chosen for the lead the night of the fire shoot.
- The extraordinary scene in which a crane-camera rises above the 2,000 dead and wounded in the streets of Atlanta was actually shot by Menzies. Half were live extras, the rest were dummies.
- There was a battle with the censors over Rhett's last line, "Frankly, my dear, I don't give a damn." Obviously, Selznick won out.

Lawrence Of Arabia

1962, Horizon/Columbia, 216 minutes, Color, UK.
Producer: Sam Spiegel. Director: David Lean.
Cast: Peter O'Toole, Omar Sharif, Alec Guinness, Anthony Quinn, Jack Hawkins, Jose Ferrer, Arthur Kennedy, Claude Rains.

> "**** Blockbuster biography of enigmatic adventurer T.E. Lawrence is that rarity, an epic film that is also literate."
> —*Leonard Maltin's Movie and Video Guide.*

Surrounded by an outstanding cast and beautiful panoramic photography (by Freddie Young, *Doctor Zhivago*), the screen version of the life of the man the media dubbed "Lawrence of Arabia" is magnificent. O'Toole, in golden hair and white flowing robes, is an irresistible figure to watch. As Lawrence, a British officer assigned to Arabia during World War I, O'Toole shows us the capriciousness of this legendary character as he tries to unite warring Arab factions. His dichotomy? Must he be more like an Arab or an Englishman in the midday sun? Unfortunately, Lawrence begins to think of himself as neither but more as a god who can do anything: "Nothing is written!" He soon learns, however, that he *is* only a man after the Turks capture him and subject him to torture. The film begins with the death of Lawrence in a motorcycle accident in England in 1935, then flashes back to his episodic life in the wind, dust, heat, and sand sinkholes of the Arabian desert.

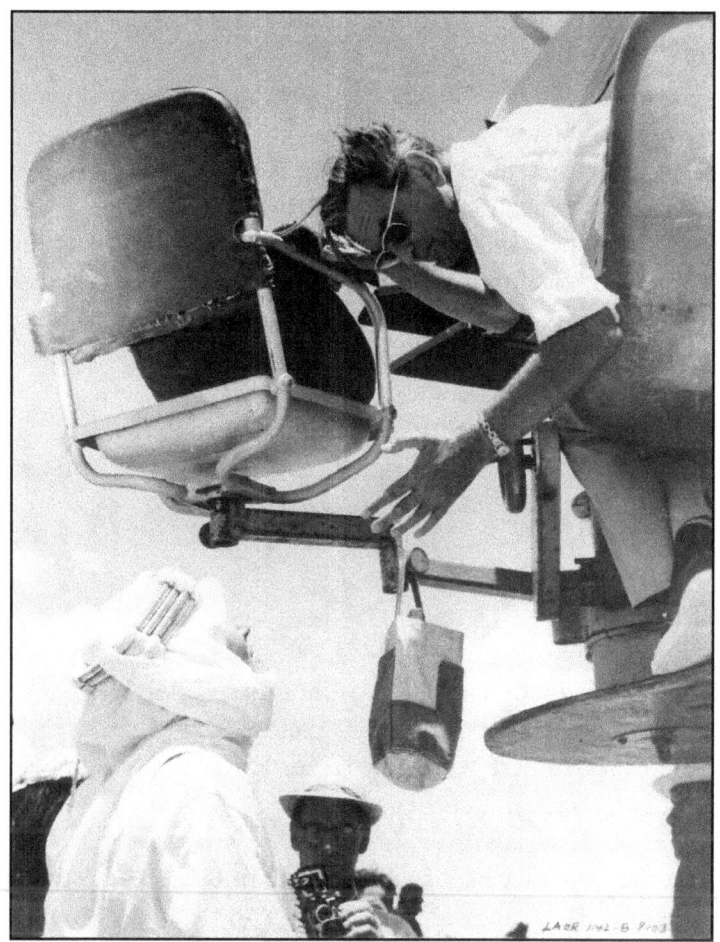

Peter O'Toole taking instructions from director David Lean on the set of *Lawrence of Arabia*.

The biopic won seven Oscars including Best Picture, Best Director, and Best Cinematography. This was O'Toole's best chance of ever winning an Oscar, but he lost to Gregory Peck for *To Kill a Mockingbird*. (O'Toole was nominated seven times but never won though he did receive a Special Honorary Oscar.)

Kennedy plays Jackson Bentley, the correspondent who goes to the desert and reports on the incomparable Lawrence. (The reporter's name in real-life was Lowell Thomas; it was he who invented the term "Lawrence of Arabia.") Sharif plays Ali, Lawrence's friend; Guinness is Prince Feisal (Guinness studied Sharif's accent, since Omar is Egyptian, to give an Arabian flair to his speech); Quinn is a rebel sheik, Ferrer is the evil

Turkish general, Rains is a diplomat, Hawkins portrays Gen. Allenby.

- It was shot in Jordan, Morocco, and Spain; the train wreck was filmed in Spain.
- Much of the budget was spent on paying for use of the Jordanian army, including military hardware and camels.
- O'Toole spent many days learning to ride a camel and finally used a layer of sponge rubber under the saddle to get through it.
- The film has no women in speaking roles.
- There was a crew constantly keeping the desert sand natural-looking and pristine for each exterior shot.
- The cut from Lawrence's blown-out match to the desert sunrise is part of Robert Bolt's original script. Bolt was Oscar-nominated for Best Original Screenplay.

Ryan's Daughter

1970, Faraway Productions/MGM, 196 minutes, Color, UK.
Producer: Anthony Havelock-Allan. Director: David Lean.
Cast: Sarah Miles, Robert Mitchum, Trevor Howard, Christopher Jones, John Mills, Leo McKern, Barry Foster.

> "…a superbly played, visually striking, moving and exciting motion picture."
> —Jerry Vermilye, *The Great British Films*

Lean on the film: "It is a love story about a girl becoming a woman. It is also about temptation, about the animal just beneath the skin of us all, which can be very exciting but very dangerous."

Miles received an Oscar nomination for Best Actress. Mills as Michael, the village idiot, won the Academy Award for Best Supporting Actor. His performance provides one of the most touching, amazing transformations of actor to character in the history of cinema.

Set in the small village of Kirrary, Ireland in 1916, the romantic-drama concerns a tavern owner's daughter who marries a middle-aged schoolteacher and promptly has an affair with a handsome, young British officer, an affair that stuns the locals. Miles is the girl, Rosy Ryan, and McKern is her red-nosed father, barkeep Tom Ryan. Mitchum plays Rosy's impotent

Sarah Miles as *Ryan's Daughter*.

husband, Charles Shaughnessy. Jones is war-crippled, shell-shocked Major Randolph Doryan. Howard plays the tough but kindly priest, Father Hugh Collins. Foster is Irish Republican Army leader Tim O'Leary.

The photography is by Freddie Young, the screenplay by Robert Bolt, and the score by Maurice Jarre; all three had worked for Lean on *Lawrence of Arabia* and *Doctor Zhivago*. Young won his third Oscar for this film.

- Bolt and Miles were married at the time.
- Production designer Stephen Grimes took six months building the village set.
- The film was mostly shot on the Dingle Peninsula in Ireland's County Kerry where beach scenes were also filmed, but some beach sequences had to be done on the beach at Cape Town, South Africa. The storm scene was done at County Clare, Ireland.
- When Lean asked Mitchum to take the part, Bob told him, "I'm sure there's some out-of-work actor who would deeply appreciate the role." Lean said, "We want you. Unless you have other

plans." Mitchum said, "I was planning suicide." "I see," said Lean. "Well, if you do the film first, *then* do yourself in, I'd happily stand the expense of the burial."

The Ten Commandments

1956, Paramount, 219 minutes, Color.
Producer/Director: Cecil B. DeMille.
Cast: Charlton Heston, Yul Brynner, Anne Baxter, Edward G. Robinson, Cedric Hardwicke, Yvonne De Carlo, Debra Paget, John Derek, Nina Foch, Marsha Scott, Judith Anderson, Vincent Price, John Carradine.

"Undeniably impressive…"
—John Douglas Eames, *The Paramount Story*

DeMille's last film is his masterpiece: the greatest Biblical epic ever made. It is also one of the biggest moneymakers of all time: #4 on the list

Charlton Heston as Moses receiving direction from Cecil B. DeMille for *The Ten Commandments*.

of top grossing films (adjusted for inflation) behind *Gone With the Wind, Star Wars,* and *E.T.*

The remake of DeMille's 1923 silent version of the story of Moses received an Academy Award nomination for Best Picture. And John P. Fulton won the Oscar for Best Special Effects: parting the Red Sea, recreating God's plagues on Egypt, producing a pillar of fire to hold back Pharaoh's army, writing the commandments in stone with the finger of God—plus the burning bush, Moses' staff changing into a serpent, the deadly mist from the Angel of Death, the earthquake in the desert destroying the riotous Israelites, and the ever-changing red clouds above Mt. Sinai.

Heston is unforgettable in his most famous role as Moses. Brynner is his nemesis, Rameses II. Hardwicke is the old Pharaoh. Foch is the Egyptian princess who removes Moses from the bulrushes and gives him his name. Anderson is Memnet, the evil handmaiden who knows the secret. Scott is Yochabel, Moses' real mother.

The plot is filled with drama, intrigue, action, and romance. Baxter plays Nefretiri, the Egyptian who loves Moses though she is promised to Rameses. De Carlo plays Sephora, the one who finally marries Moses. Derek plays Joshua and Paget is the Hebrew water-girl who falls in love with Joshua. Carradine is Aaron, Price is Baka, and Robinson is the villainous Dathan who stirs up the Israelites to worship the golden calf.

- Utilizing 12,000 lead players and extras and 15,000 animals, DeMille's Exodus might appear as spectacular as the actual Exodus.
- The Egyptians in pursuit, 300 chariots strong, are driven by modern Egyptian soldiers (trained in the carriages for four months).
- The infant Moses is Charlton's son, Fraser.

Titanic

1997, Paramount/20th Century-Fox, 194 minutes, Color.
Producer/Director: James Cameron.
Cast: Leonardo DiCaprio, Kate Winslet, Billy Zane, Gloria Stuart, Frances Fisher, Kathy Bates, Bill Paxton, Bernard Hill, Victor Garber.

> "It's the movie event of the year. Jaw-dropping! It'll get to you."
> —Peter Travers, *Rolling Stone.*

Gloria Stuart, 87, wore make-up to make her look even older for *Titanic*.

At $200 million, the most expensive movie ever made, but it took in more than three times what it cost! In actual fact, the film cost more than the *Titanic* itself cost to build! The disaster movie stayed atop the box-office charts for a record 15 straight weeks! From writing to post-production, the film took five years to make.

The epic, based on the true story, tied *Ben-Hur* for winning the most Oscars: 11. It had already tied *All About Eve* for receiving the most Academy Award nominations. Among the Oscars were Best Picture, Best Director, Best Visual Effects, and Best Original Song: "My Heart Will Go On" (sung by Celine Dion). 87-year-old Stuart, a star of the 30s, was nominated for Best Supporting Oscar as old Rose, the 101-year-old survivor of the tragedy who narrates the story.

Jack Dawson (DiCaprio) and Rose DeWitt Bukater (Winslet), he an artist from steerage and she engaged to a rich snob (Zane), become lovers just before the "unsinkable" liner strikes an iceberg in the North Atlantic. There were only 20 lifeboats on the doomed ship, barely enough for half those on-board; several lifeboats floated off only partially full. Of the 2,200 passengers and crew, 1,523 men, women, and children drowned.

Bates plays Molly Brown. Fisher is Rose's mother. Hill is Capt. Edward J. Smith. Garber is Thomas Andrews, the ship's designer. Paxton is the submersible commander.

- Cameron shot real footage of the sunken Titanic using Panavision's newly-developed deep-sea camera. But they had to do 12 dives because the camera could hold only 12 minutes' worth of film. Cameron made several dives himself.
- The model ship in the giant water tank is 1/20th to scale.
- The ship exterior set was constructed in a tank on a beach near Rosarito, Baja California, Mexico. The entire set was mounted on hydraulic jacks so it could be tilted.
- The ocean into which the 1,000 extras and 100 stunt people are jumping was only about three feet deep.
- The scene on board where a young boy plays with a top, as his father looks on, is based on an old photo taken on the Titanic by a photographer who left the ship when it docked briefly in Ireland.
- Cameron, while accepting his Oscar, asked for a moment of silence in memory of those who died on the Titanic in 1912.
- A first-class suite on the ship cost $4,350—$75,000 by today's standards.

Family Films

The Alamo

1960, United Artists, 190 minutes, Color.
Producer/Director: John Wayne.
Cast: John Wayne, Richard Widmark, Laurence Harvey, Linda Cristal, Chill Wills, Richard Boone, Ken Curtis.

> "A diamond-hard, 'rough-hewn' masterpiece…emotionally and dramatically potent enough to make all hearts beat with pride."
> —*Chicago Daily News*.

A story that all school-kids need to see, an inspirational and patriotic adventure based on a true event in American history: 185 brave volunteers defending a tiny Texas mission for 13 days against oppressors in the form of an army of 4,000-7,000 Mexican soldiers. The mission, called The Alamo, is under the command of Col. William Travis (Harvey) and among his men are former Tennessee congressman and Indian fighter Davy Crockett (Wayne) and buckskinned Jim Bowie (Widmark), famous for his Bowie-knife.

The film received seven Academy Award nominations including Best Picture. It's a stirring movie with excellent battle sequences. Dimitri Tiomkin's score is memorable. The theme "The Green Leaves of Summer" was often heard on radio during the days of the picture's release.

It was a difficult film to make for Wayne, who put every dollar he had into the production, a story he had wanted to do for many years. His roles as producer, director, and actor took a toll on the star who lost weight and lots of sleep during production. Considering the stress and pressure he was on, Wayne did an admirable job though it would be years before the movie turned a profit.

John Wayne, Richard Widmark and Laurence Harvey, up front for the cast photo for *The Alamo*.

Cristal portrays Crockett's romantic interest; Wills plays one of Davy's volunteers; Boone is Sam Houston; Curtis is Lt. Dickenson.

- The film was shot on 20,000 acres at Bracketville, Texas where Wayne constructed the little church based on historical documents. The set remains as "Happy Shahan's Alamo Village."
- More than 2,000 horses were used with riders in authentic uniforms.
- When Harvey lights the fuse of the cannon on top of the mission, it fires and recoils on his foot, breaking it, but he hardly grimaces and continues the scene.

A Christmas Carol (Scrooge)

1951, Renown Pictures/United Artists, 86 minutes, B&W, UK.
Producer/Director: Brian Desmond Hurst.
Cast: Alastair Sim, Mervyn Johns, Glyn Dearman, Hermione Baddeley, Michael Hordern, George Cole, Brian Worth, Roddy Hughes.

"The most literal translation of the story to date as well as the best at re-creating the mood and feel of the original."
—Frank N. Magill, *Magill's Survey of Cinema*

The resume of Charles Dickens is one of the most extensive in fiction, and this classic has probably been read and seen on-stage and on-screen by more people than any of his famous works. Yet the Dickens world, in nineteenth century England, is not all sweetness and light; it's mostly a dark time of poverty and misery, crooks and thieves, sickness and hard-times, whether it's *Oliver Twist, David Copperfield, Nicholas Nickleby, Great Expectations,* or *A Tale of Two Cities;* the story of *A Christmas Carol* is no different— though, at the end, there is a total transformation of the beleaguered protagonist.

Ebenezer Scrooge (Sim), who hates Christmas (he calls it "a humbug"), has become so well known that anyone we see today who is an old, mean-spirited, penny-pincher is called "Scrooge." What makes the story so endearing is that we get to see how Scrooge became so embittered and we are relieved, in the end, to see him change and, in doing so, be an influence for good for all who come in contact with him. But the change is not something effected by Scrooge alone; he has help, lots of it, from

Mervyn Johns and Alastair Sim in *A Christmas Carol*.

spirit visits: his dead business partner, Jacob Marley (Hordern), and the Spirits of Christmas Past, Present and Future. In flashback, we learn about Scrooge as a young man (Cole).

The other most indelible characters in the story are Bob Cratchit (Johns), Scrooge's overworked and underpaid employee; Bob's wife (Baddeley), and their crippled son, Tiny Tim (Dearman)—famous for his line "God bless us everyone"; also Fred (Worth), Scrooge's nephew, an optimistic young man who invites Uncle Ebenezer to his home for Christmas; and there's idyllic Fezziwig (Hughes), Scrooge's former employee. But it is Mr. Sim in the lead who wonderfully brings this formidable story to life, no doubt for many generations to come.

- Patrick Macnee (TV's *The Avengers*) plays a young Marley.
- Johns is the father of actress Glynis Johns (Mrs. Banks in *Mary Poppins*).
- Hurst learned his craft as an assistant to John Ford; he then returned to England and made a number of British films.
- Dickens was married with 10 children; he became infatuated with a pretty young actress, Ellen Ternan, and left his wife of 22 years.

E.T. The Extra-Terrestrial

1982, Universal, 115 minutes, Color.
Producers: Steven Spielberg, Kathleen Kennedy; Director: Steven Spielberg.
Cast: Henry Thomas, Dee Wallace, Robert McNaughton, Drew Barrymore, Peter Coyote.

> "The film touched the critics' hearts as much as those of the general audiences and they praised it as an instant classic of children's movies."
>
> —Peter Van Gelder.

One of the Top Ten greatest grossing films of all time and the greatest challenge to *The Wizard of Oz* as the best family-fantasy film ever made. It was also a winner at the Academy Awards, landing four Oscars: score (John Williams), sound, sound effects, visual effects. The enchanting movie was nominated for Best Picture and Spielberg was nominated for Best Director.

Henry Thomas, as Elliott, gets direction from Steven Spielberg for *E.T. The Extra-Terrestrial*.

Thomas plays a 10-year-old boy named Elliott who finds and befriends a little space creature that the boy calls "E.T." The lovable alien gets lost and left behind when his spaceship is detected in suburban woods and has to leave quickly. Elliott takes E.T. in and teaches the visitor about the things and ways of planet Earth.

One of the best scenes in the movie is a display of E.T.'s special powers of telepathy and telekinesis. While E.T. is home watching *The Quiet Man* on TV, his thoughts transfer to Elliott at school and Elliott, with a pretty girl in the classroom, suddenly recreates a romantic scene between John Wayne and Maureen O'Hara.

Wallace plays Elliott's single-parent mom; McNaughton is Michael, Elliott's older brother; 6-year-old Barrymore is their cute little sister, Gertie; Coyote is the government UFO researcher tracking E.T. and the spaceship.

- The makers of Reese's Pieces, the candy Elliott uses to lure E.T. into the family garage, saw sales skyrocket 85%.
- Carlo Rambaldi, who did the space-monster for *Alien*, created the hand-operated, radio-controlled creature.
- E.T. cost $1.5 million to build.

- Whenever E.T. walks, it's one of several tiny actors in an E.T. suit.
- The boys on the bikes taking flight against the moon were little models produced in the studios of Industrial Light and Magic. The scene became the logo for Spielberg's Amblin Productions.

Houdini

1953, Paramount, 106 minutes, Color.
Producer: George Pal. Director: George Marshall.
Cast: Tony Curtis, Janet Leigh, Angela Clarke, Torin Thatcher.

> "…spectacular highlights of Houdini's colorful story…"
> —Arthur Winsten, *The New York Times*.

Millions of kids became magic enthusiasts in the Fifties, and made a run on local magic stores after seeing this well-produced biopic of the famous magician/escape artist. Curtis stars as Harry Houdini and Leigh, Tony's wife in real-life, plays Bess, Houdini's wife. The film was one of Paramount's biggest box-office hits of the decade.

In this romanticized version of magic's most famous performer, screenplay by Philip Yordan, Houdini begins by playing a wild man in gorilla costume in a Coney Island sideshow, where he meets his bride-to-be who visits as a patron. After a whirlwind romance, they marry and Harry becomes an apparatus-magic performer with Bess as stage assistant, but they quit for lack of work. He takes a job as an assistant locksmith where he learns the art of picking locks, which leads to his expertise as an escape artist. Re-starting his career by mixing escapes with stage illusions, Houdini becomes a sensation in Europe and America, achieving headlines for his underwater and straitjacket escapes—and his boasting that no jail can hold him.

The latter part of the film deals with Houdini's expose of fake mediums, a crusade that began in his effort to contact his beloved mother (Clarke) from beyond the grave, after her death left him depressed. Thatcher plays Otto, Houdini's backstage assistant.

- Curtis actually performs a number of real magic illusions and, in fact, became quite accomplished for an amateur.
- Houdini's real name was Eric Weiss. He chose the name "Hou-

Tony Curtis and Janet Leigh in *Houdini*.

dini" as a tribute to the French magician Robert Houdin, by simply adding an "i" to the name.
- Houdini did die on Halloween, as indicated in the movie, but not on-stage; he had a ruptured appendix and died in the hospital.
- In the film, it appears Houdini died from trying to do the Chinese Water Torture escape. In truth, he often performed that feat without incident.
- Bess Houdini, for years after Harry's death, held séances on Halloween in an effort to contact her husband from the dead, obviously without success.

The Little Princess

1939, 20th Century-Fox, 91 minutes, Color.
Producer: Darryl F. Zanuck. Director: Walter Lang.
Cast: Shirley Temple, Arthur Treacher, Ian Hunter, Mary Nash, Richard Greene, Tina Louise, Cesar Romero, Beryl Mercer.

> "Probably her best film."
> —Steven H. Scheuer, *Movies on TV*

So many adults, from two generations, have grown up with Shirley Temple it is almost an impossibility to pick her best film—we all like her for different reasons. (My own pleasure is watching her dance with the great Bill "Bojangles" Robinson in *The Little Colonel*, *The Littlest Rebel* and *Rebecca of Sunnybrook Farm*.) She was a box-office star for years and has given us many memorable moments, via the movie screen, TV, and video.

The Little Princess certainly qualifies as one of her best, partly because it was her only color film (surprise, Shirley is a redhead). She was nearly 11 when she made the movie and her maturity is on display; there are several scenes in which she shows off her dramatic ability, though the best scene is a dream sequence in which she imagines herself as a little princess.

The story takes place in 1899 in England, Queen Victoria (Mercer) is on the throne. The British Empire is fighting on two fronts, the India frontier and South Africa. Shirley is Sara Crewe whose father, Captain Crewe (Hunter), is called to fight in South Africa. Since Sara's mother has already passed away, she is left at a boarding school run by Amanda Minchin (Nash) who turns out to be a rather harsh and unforgiving woman. And when it is reported that the Captain has died in battle with no available bank account to support Sara, the young girl is left to be a servant in the school, much to the delight of the other kids. In due course, we learn that the Captain has been missing-in-action and is left shell-shocked, a truth which Sara herself stumbles upon when she visits a hospital for the returning wounded.

There is fine support for Temple, notably from Treacher who plays the brother of Miss Minchin and who sings and dances with Shirley. Romero plays a mysterious neighbor, Ram Dass, who does nice things to give solace to Sara. Greene and Louise are Geoffrey and Rose Hamilton, also Sara's friends.

- The film has such extraordinary color because at that time the base of the film stock was made with silver. *Gone With the Wind* also used the process.
- The daughter of a bank teller, Temple took dancing lessons at three and made it into one-reelers by the age of four.
- After just one year in movies, Shirley received a Special Academy Award.
- Temple was the #1 Box-Office star from 1935-1938 and remained in the Top 10 in 1939.
- In the 60s and 70s, Temple served as U.S. representative to the U.N. and U.S. ambassador to Ghana.

Mary Poppins

1964, Buena Vista, 140 minutes, Color.
Producer: Walt Disney. Director: Robert Stevenson.
Cast: Julie Andrews, Dick Van Dyke, David Tomlinson, Glynis Johns, Karen Dotrice, Matthew Garber, Ed Wynn.

> "**** There's charm, wit, and movie magic to spare…"
> —Leonard Maltin.

This could well be the second greatest musical-fantasy film ever made, behind *The Wizard of Oz*. The film received 13 Academy Award nominations, including Best Picture, and won five Oscars—including Best Actress (Andrews), Special Visual Effects (for the live-action/animation process), and Best Song: "Chim Chim Cheree."

Based on the book by P.L. Travers, Mary Poppins, played by Andrews, is a magical nanny who visits the Banks family of London's Cherry Tree Lane and turns the house upside-down as she teaches that life can be fun, even when it comes to doing chores or taking medicine. Tomlinson and

Julie Andrews as *Mary Poppins*. © The Walt Disney Company.

Johns play Mr. And Mrs. Banks and Dotrice and Garber are their delightful children. Wynn is funny Uncle Albert who rises to the ceiling whenever he laughs. Van Dyke is Bert, a cockney street minstrel and chimney sweep, who knows the secret of who Mary really is.

The songs (by Richard and Robert Sherman) have become part of our children's' lexicon: "A Spoonful of Sugar," "Jolly Holiday," "Supercalifragilisticexpialidocious," "Step In Time," "Let Go Fly A Kite," "I Love To Laugh," and more.

- Several veteran character players have bit parts: Elsa Lanchester as Katie Nanna, Reginald Owen as Admiral Boom, Arthur Treacher as Constable Jones, and Jane Darwell, in her last screen appearance, as the Bird Lady.
- When Andrews won the Oscar, she thanked Jack Warner because he had passed her over in favor of Audrey Hepburn to play Eliza Doolittle in *My Fair Lady*, the part Julie had made famous on Broadway.
- Disney won more Oscars, 30, than anyone; this was Walt's last big film before his unexpected death two years later.

Miracle on 34th Street

1947, 20th Century-Fox, 96 minutes, B&W.
Producer: William Perlberg. Director: George Seaton.
Cast: Maureen O'Hara, John Payne, Edmund Gwenn, Natalie Wood, Gene Lockhart, William Frawley.

> "(M)arvelous adaptation of Valentine Davies' fantasy…offbeat humor, sharp satire, tremendous warmth, and scenes that will have you choking up."
> —Danny Peary.

This annual TV holiday favorite was nominated for Best Picture and won three Oscars: original story (Davies), screenplay (Seaton), and Gwenn for Best Supporting Actor in the role of Santa Claus.

Doris Walker (O'Hara), a divorced single mom, is coordinator of special events for Macy's Department Store on 34th street in Manhattan. And one of those special events is Macy's Thanksgiving Day Parade that

Edmund Gwenn and Natalie Wood in *The Miracle on 34th Street*.

features Santa Claus. Doris hires a kindly old fellow to play Santa; he's perfect but he thinks he really *is* Kris Kringle (Gwenn)! Naturally, Doris doesn't believe him, but her seven-year-old daughter, Susan (Wood), also doesn't believe in Santa—any Santa Claus.

In the course of the story, the old man is taken to court to prove he is who he says he is. Fred Gailey (Payne) is St. Nick's defense attorney and Lockhart plays the judge who must decide the matter. Frawley is terrific as political party hack Charlie Halloran who reminds the judge about his quandary: if he rules that Santa doesn't exist, there'll be a whole lot of mothers and fathers who'll remember that decision come election day.

- The movie was actually filmed at Macy's in New York. Short of electrical outlets, the crew had to set up a mini power station in the basement to handle the lights and camera load.
- Studio boss Darryl Zanuck didn't have much confidence in the film and tried to bury it by releasing it during the summer of 1947. It was a big hit and was still running at Christmas.
- The film created a controversy in 1985 when it became the first black-and-white movie to be colorized by computer.

- Both Macy's and Gimbels had to approve use of their names but only after the film was completed. Had they not liked the film there would have had to be extensive re-shooting and editing.
- The scenes of the Thanksgiving Day Parade are real, shot in 1946.
- Most parade-watchers were unaware that the man playing Santa on the parade float was actually the movie Santa—Mr. Gwenn!

The Pride of The Yankees

1942, RKO, 128 minutes, B&W.
Producer: Samuel Goldwyn. Director: Sam Wood.
Cast: Gary Cooper, Teresa Wright, Walter Brennan, Dan Duryea.

> "**** An exceptional film biography."
> —Jay A. Brown & Consumer Guide, *Rating the Movies*

The best of the baseball movies received an Academy Award nomination for Best Picture and its star, Gary Cooper, got nominated for Best Actor in his role as Lou Gehrig, slugging first baseman of the New York Yankees. Wright, as Gehrig's wife Eleanor, also got nominated for Best Actress.

The story (by Jo Swerling and Herman Mankiewicz) is not only about success on the baseball diamond, it's also about love and romance and personal tragedy—and how to deal with it. Gehrig died of a rare muscle disease which now bears his name. He was only 37 at the time. Gehrig is remembered fondly for his inspirational remarks at Yankee Stadium during a tribute to him shortly before his death: "People all say I've had a bad break. But today—today I consider myself the luckiest man on the face of the earth."

There's an outstanding supporting cast, including several ballplayers as themselves: Babe Ruth, Bill Dickey, Mark Koenig, Bob Meusel. Sportswriter Bill Stern plays himself. Brennan is sportswriter Sam Blake, Duryea is Hank Hanneman.

- The film was released 17 months after Gehrig's death and was a major box-office success.
- Cooper was right-handed and Gehrig left-handed. To look natural at the plate, Coop batted right and film editor Dan Mandell reversed the shot to make him look left-handed. Mandell won the Oscar for Best Editing.

Babe Ruth and Gary Cooper (as Lou Gehrig) in *The Pride of the Yankees*.

- Major leaguer Lefty O'Doul coached Gary on batting and fielding.
- Gehrig, a lifetime .340 hitter, earned the title "Iron Man of Baseball" by virtue of the fact that he played in 2,130 consecutive games, a record finally broken in modern times by Cal Ripken, Jr.

The Wizard of Oz

1939, MGM, 101 minutes, Color w/B&W segments.
Producer: Mervyn LeRoy. Director: Victor Fleming.
Cast: Judy Garland, Frank Morgan, Ray Bolger, Bert Lahr, Jack Haley, Margaret Hamilton, Billie Burke, Charley Grapewin, Clara Blandick.

> "There's an audience for it wherever there's a projection machine and a screen."
>
> —*Variety*.

Panned by critics at the outset, *The Wizard of Oz* is now considered by film historians to be the greatest family-fantasy film ever made. And it's a musical, too. The movie was nominated for Best Picture and won the Oscar for Best Song: "Over The Rainbow," which became Garland's signature tune. Judy, 17 at the time, received a Special Oscar for her role as Dorothy. In retrospect, she was a marvelous choice though the studio had sought to use Shirley Temple at first.

Based on L. Frank Baum's book, the film immortalizes the ruby slippers and the line: "There's no place like home;" and features some of the most famous characters: the Wizard/Professor Marvel (Morgan), the Scarecrow (Bolger), the Cowardly Lion (Lahr), the Tin Man (Haley), the Wicked Witch (Hamilton), Glinda the Good Witch (Burke), Uncle Henry (Grapewin), and Auntie Em (Blandick). And don't forget Toto the dog, Winged Monkeys, and the Munchkins (played by about 125 midgets).

The movie begins in black-and-white on a farm in Kansas where a tornado tosses Dorothy and her house into the Land of Oz. When she opens the door, the film turns to color. Dorothy spends the rest of the film trying to get home.

Jack Haley, Ray Bolger, Judy Garland and Bert Lahr in *The Wizard of Oz*.

The songs, by E.Y. Harburg and Harold Arlen, are now part of the American musical lexicon: "Follow The Yellow Brick Road," "If I Only Had A Brain" (Bolger), "If I Only Had A Heart" (Haley), "If I Were King Of The Forest" (Lahr), "Courage" (Lahr), "We're Off To See The Wizard," "Merry Old Land Of Oz," "Ding Dong The Witch Is Dead."

Fleming was one of six directors on the film. He was pulled off the project after four months so he could take over *Gone With the Wind*. Others directing were King Vidor (who shot "Over The Rainbow" and the cyclone sequence), George Cukor, Lewis Milestone, Richard Thorpe, and LeRoy himself. The project took over five months.

- A. Arnold "Buddy" Gillespie made the tornado (he created the earthquake in *San Francisco*). The twister was a 35-ft. muslin wind-sock, moved about by a crew in the distance, on a miniature set fed by air hoses.
- Incredibly, "Over The Rainbow" was nearly cut due to the length of the film, but preview audiences loved it and so did LeRoy who fought successfully to keep it in. The dance number "Jitterbug" was cut instead.
- Hamilton was burned in the smoke scene when she vanishes in the Emerald City; she spent several days in the hospital.
- Buddy Ebsen was originally cast as the Tin Man but dropped out due to an allergic reaction to aluminum dust in the silver make-up.
- Bolger's make-up took nearly two hours to apply each day, one hour just to glue the rubber bag, simulating burlap, to his head.
- The "horse of a different color" was done by applications of colored Jello, which the animal kept licking off.

Film Noir

Chinatown

1974, Paramount, 131 minutes, Color.
Producer: Robert Evans. Director: Roman Polanski.
Cast: Jack Nicholson, Faye Dunaway, John Huston, Perry Lopez, John Hillerman, Burt Young, Darrell Zwerling, Roman Polanski, Diane Ladd, Roy Jenson.

> "…the whole movie is a tour-de-force."
> —Roger Ebert, *Roger Ebert's Movie Home Companion*

Set in the late 30s in Los Angeles, in the style of Raymond Chandler and Dashiell Hammett, this exciting *film noir* mystery/thriller was nominated for Best Picture and won the Oscar for Best Original Screenplay (Robert Towne). Nicholson is excellent as private-eye Jake "J.J." Gittes, a former cop whose beat was Chinatown, where corruption abounds and where anything is possible. Gittes finds that the immorality of Chinatown has spread its tentacles into the rest of society. Jake gets caught up in the web of lies and deceit when he's hired by Evelyn Cross Mulwray (Dunaway) to investigate her husband's alleged extramarital affairs.

> Evelyn to Jake: "What did you do in Chinatown?"
> Jake: "As little as possible."

The intrigue involves a land and water scheme. Power-mad multimillionaire Noah Cross (Huston), Evelyn's father, is secretly diverting water during a drought, causing desert-land prices to drop for a quick buy-up, and then he'll get the land incorporated into the city for a big profit.

Jack Nicholson as Jake Gittes in *Chinatown*.

> Jake to Cross: "Why are you doing it? How much better can you eat? What can you buy that you can't already afford?"
>
> Cross bellows back: "The future, Mr. Gittes, the future!"

Zwerling plays Evelyn's husband, water boss Hollis Mulwray. Hillerman is city hall crony Russ Yelburton. Young is Curly, one of Jake's clients. Ladd is unlucky Ida Sessions. Jenson is Claude Mulvihill the goon. Polanski plays "the midget" with the knife. Lopez is Lt. Lou Escobar.

Many film historians have picked John Huston's *The Maltese Falcon* as the best detective-mystery ever made. This newer classic of the genre challenges that claim and, ironically, Huston himself appears in this film in a strong supporting role.

- Mulwray is a take-off on former water czar William Mulholland after whom the Mulholland Dam was named in 1925. Mulholland brought the Owens River to L.A. turning Owens Valley into a desert.

- Nicholson actually slaps Dunaway—hard.
- The prop knife Polanski uses to cut Jack's nose releases what looks like blood but the edge *was* actually semi-sharp, which made Jack very nervous.
- Evans wanted Jane Fonda but Roman insisted on Dunaway.
- The outstanding score is by Jerry Goldsmith; the trumpet solos are by Uan Rasey.
- It was the first of a planned trilogy; the sequel, *The Two Jakes* (directed by Nicholson), was poorly received which caused the studio to cancel part three, *Cloverleaf*, about the building of the Los Angeles interchange.

Double Indemnity

1944, Paramount, 107 minutes, B&W.
Producer: Joseph Sistrom. Director: Billy Wilder.
Cast: Fred MacMurray, Barbara Stanwyck, Edward G. Robinson.

> "…a bona-fide cinema masterpiece…"
>
> —Danny Peary.

If not the first *film noir*, certainly the first great *film noir*. Nominated for Best Picture, Wilder's classic, taken from a magazine novella by James M. Cain, has one of Hollywood's best opening scenes: Stanwyck, as calculating slut-wife Phyllis Dietrichson, appearing at the top of the stairs covered only by a bath towel, deciding, in that moment, that it will be Walter Neff (MacMurray) who will extricate her from her personal hell.

The script is based on a real case: in 1927, in Queens, New York, Albert Snyder was killed for his life insurance money by wife Ruth and her lover Judd Gray. Similarly, Walter, an insurance salesman, and Phyllis plot to murder her husband for the dough. Naturally, they plan to make the murder look like an accident. One of the film's many highlights: claims investigator Barton Keyes (Robinson), who eats and drinks the insurance business, unleashing an array of statistics on suicidal possibilities.

Incredibly, Robinson didn't get an Oscar nomination. In fact, in his whole 50 years in Hollywood, he never got nominated—despite numerous fine performances! Both Wilder and Stanwyck got nominated as did cinematographer John Seitz.

Barbara Stanwyck and Fred MacMurray in *Double Indemnity*.

Wilder and Raymond Chandler (*The Big Sleep*) wrote the screenplay. Wilder had wanted Cain but he was working on *Western Union* (1941). Producer Sistrom recommended Chandler because his style resembled Cain. But Chandler, an alcoholic, had never written a screenplay and didn't like working with Wilder. After five weeks, Chandler finished his script and turned it over to Wilder who hated it. Wilder insisted on Chandler collaborating with him; he agreed, reluctantly. The result, after six months, was this movie.

- Wilder used several exteriors around L.A. The secret meetings between Walter and Phyllis were shot in Jerry's Market on Melrose Ave. They used the Southern Pacific Railroad Station at 400 West Cerritos Ave. in Glendale. Phyllis' California Spanish house still stands at 6301 Quebec St. in the Hollywood Hills.
- The bad blonde wig was Wilder's idea and he eventually realized the mistake but they had shot too much footage by then to change it.
- George Raft turned down the role of Neff. Dick Powell wanted it but his studio wouldn't release him.

- Goof: the film is set in 1938 but the radio in Phyllis' house is playing "Tangerine" which wasn't written until 1942.
- Originally, Wilder and Chandler wrote Neff going to the gas chamber in the final scene; they even filmed it—but Wilder soon opted for the better ending.

Gilda

1946, Columbia, 110 minutes, B&W
Producer: Virginia Van Upp. Director: Charles Vidor
Cast: Rita Hayworth, Glenn Ford, George Macready, Joseph Calleia, Steven Geray

> "Most of all, Hayworth's Gilda is neither the *femme fatale* Dietrich personified nor the beautiful clotheshorse Fifties films were to make fashionable, but a living personality, provocative, intelligent, unforgettable."
> —John Baxter, *Sixty Years of Hollywood*

Rita Hayworth and George Macready in *Gilda*.

In the Forties, with her face painted on the Bikini Atoll atom bomb and thousands of pin-up photos mailed to GIs overseas, Rita Hayworth became one of Hollywood's greatest sex goddesses. In *Gilda*, the unsurpassed beauty, glamour and eroticism of this famous sex symbol is on display more than in any of her films. (Remember the prison inmates lusting for her in *The Shawshank Redemption*?) Her nightclub dance, "Put The Blame On Mame," a limited striptease as she peels off long black gloves, is the highlight of the film and her career.

Some see *Gilda* as having undertones of some sort of perverse sexuality, but that's only in the mind of the beholder; there is no dialogue or plot motivation to suggest such affectation. Nonetheless, the story is filled with tension, but naturally so. Johnny Farrell (Ford) is a down-and-out crooked gambler who somehow finds himself being mugged on the backstreets of Buenos Aires. Ballin Mundson (Macready), owner of an illegal gambling casino, saves him and offers Johnny a job running his establishment. Mundson walks around with a hidden cane-sword, which adds an element of danger. Things get very risky when Mundson goes away and finds a wife—who turns out to be Gilda. But what Mundson doesn't know is that Farrell and Gilda once had an affair. And to make matters worse, Mundson assigns Farrell the task of watching over Gilda, to make sure she doesn't get into any trouble. Yeah, sure.

Almost overlooked is another fine dance number by Rita, "Amado Mio." Calleia plays the suspicious detective Oregon. Geray is a strange little man called Uncle Pio.

- Choreographer Jack Cole, who worked with Marilyn Monroe on *Let's Make Love,* wrote the "Mame" number but gave Rita the credit for making it work.
- Vidor, Hungarian by birth, made four films with Hayworth.
- Hayworth's real name was Margarita Carmen Cansino. As a teenager she danced with her father, a Spanish dancer, in nightclubs in New York where she was born.
- When Rita moved from Fox to Columbia, Harry Cohn named her Rita Haworth and then added "y" because he was afraid her name might not be properly pronounced.

The Lady From Shanghai

1947, Columbia, 86 minutes, B&W.
Producer/Director: Orson Welles.
Cast: Orson Welles, Rita Hayworth, Everett Sloane, Glenn Anders.

> "The range of focus in the film astonishes, and no other Welles film has explored his own country with such precision, such ruthlessness."
> —Charles Higham, *The Films of Orson Welles*

Only Welles, the magician, could think up such illusionary locations as backdrops: an aquarium for a love scene in front of the shark tank, a Chinese Theatre for plot resolution, a courthouse filled with incompetents, and a crazy-house with a mirror maze. A cult favorite for Welles fans, the film is paradoxical: full of intrigue and plot twists, noxious characters like Bannister's very strange business partner (Anders), and a beautiful but deadly blonde with short hair (Orson's wife at the time) who pulls the protagonist into her spider's web of deceit and murder.

Orson Welles and Rita Hayworth in the mirror maze in *The Lady From Shanghai*.

Hayworth is the sexy yet cold Elsa Bannister, the China-born wife of crippled and hateful defense attorney Arthur Bannister (Sloane). Welles, with a brogue, plays Michael O'Hara, an Irish sailor/writer—drawn like a moth to the flame by dangerous Elsa (glowingly photographed by Charles Lawton, Jr. who also photographed Rita in *Miss Sadie Thompson*). The screenplay is loosely based on the paperback mystery *If I Die Before I Wake* by Sherwood King.

The best scene is the climax in a fun-house with Orson falling down a 125-ft. zigzag slide coming out of the mouth of a 30-ft. high dragon into a mirror maze of 80 seven-ft. mirrors. The set included 24 distorted mirrors and some two-way mirrors for cameramen; quite a production that sent the film over budget.

- The exterior of the fun-house was San Francisco's Playland-at-the Beach, now torn down; the rest was shot on a soundstage.
- Shooting was done on Errol Flynn's yacht at Acapulco and Sausalito on San Francisco Bay.
- Welles wrote the screenplay. He had thumbed-through King's book but hadn't planned to use it until Columbia boss Harry Cohn called and pressured Orson to give him the title and outline of his next film to fulfill a contract. Orson invented the title off the top of his head and adjusted the book to fit his vision. Cohn, by the way, was not happy with Welles for cutting Rita's hair and coloring the redhead to blonde. She was, after all, the studio's biggest star. Cohn held up release of the film for a year.

Mildred Pierce

1945, Warner Bros., 112 minutes, B&W.
Producer: Jerry Wald. Director: Michael Curtiz.
Cast: Joan Crawford, Ann Blyth, Zachary Scott, Jack Carson, Eve Arden, Bruce Bennett, Butterfly McQueen, Jo Ann Marlowe.

> "One of the great soap operas of the forties."
> —Clive Hirschhorn, *The Warner Bros. Story*

Crawford's comeback film, which earned her a Best Actress Oscar, was also nominated for Best Picture. Crawford plays Mildred Pierce, a

Joan Crawford and Ann Blyth in *Mildred Pierce*.

struggling divorced mother who works her way up from waitress to head of a chain of restaurants. She works hard for her daughters, Veda (Blyth) and Kay (Marlowe), but a happy home-life it is not. Young Kay falls ill and dies and Veda is a selfish, ungrateful brat. The melodrama, from James M. Cain's novel, is also a murder-mystery.

The film opens at night with the sound of gunfire: inside a beach-house a man falls to the floor and utters one last word, "Mildred." We soon learn, in flashback, the man is Monte Beragon (Scott), a social gigolo and Pierce's former lover. Did she kill him? Out on the pier, Mildred contemplates suicide when an old associate happens by. She detracts Wally Fay (Carson) to the house where he gets mysteriously locked in and where both he and the body are soon found by police.

Cinematographer Ernest Haller shoots Crawford with a shadow across one eye, leaving the impression that she's hiding something. Bennett is Bert Pierce, Mildred's ex-husband. Arden plays Ida, Mildred's friend. McQueen is Mildred's maid, Lottie.

- Bette Davis turned down the role and later knew she'd made one of the biggest mistakes of her life.

- Shirley Temple was originally considered for the role of Veda but she felt the part would hurt her image.
- The beach-house was real and owned by Curtiz.
- Curtiz didn't want to work with Crawford, though by the end of the shoot he was won over by her talent and hard work; she was always on time and prepared.
- Cain, after seeing the film, sent Crawford a personal note thanking her for "bringing Mildred to life."
- Crawford had a real-life Veda of sorts: her adopted daughter Christina wrote "Mommie Dearest" (which became a movie), describing Joan as a rather horrid person. But Joan's friends called it fantasy. Douglas Fairbanks, Jr., who was married to Crawford for four years, said he never saw any of what was described in the book.

Nightmare Alley

1947, 20th Century-Fox, 111 minutes, B&W.
Producer: George Jessel. Director: Edmund Goulding.
Cast: Tyrone Power, Joan Blondell, Coleen Gray, Helen Walker, Mike Mazurki, Ian Keith, Taylor Holmes.

> "(A) fine gothic horror film…an excellent performance from Power."
>
> —Tony Thomas and Aubrey Solomon,
> *The Films of 20th Century-Fox*

A cult classic, Power—in his best film—plays Stan Carlisle, a mind-reading sensation known as "The Great Stanton" who goes from the heights to the gutter as a lowly and sickening carnival act.

Handsome Ty Power was haunted by the realization that most people, particularly critics, saw him only as a pretty face. This *film noir*-horror film is his legacy and proves them all wrong: he's a fine actor and the film is one of the best black-and-whites ever made. The photography by Lee Garmes gives the effect of our being enclosed, as in an alleyway, and Cyril Mockridge's eerie music provides the feeling of entrapment in a nightmare. It's an A-picture in the B-movie style. Screenwriter Jules Furthman adapted William Lindsay Gresham's novel.

Tyrone Power plays stage mind-reader Stan Carlisle in *Nightmare Alley*.

Zeena (Blondell) is Stan's mentor who teaches the secrets for his phony act. Molly (Gray) is Stan's girlfriend, "The Electric Girl." Walker is Lilith Ritter, a corrupt psychologist. Holmes is Ezra Grindle, Mazurki is Bruno the strong man, and Keith plays a carnival-midway alcoholic named Pete.

- It was Power's personal favorite of all his films, which included 10 films with director Henry King.
- Power visited carnivals to get the atmosphere for his role as a sleazy opportunist.
- Stan hits bottom and becomes a geek, a carnival freak who bites the head off a live chicken.

- Jessel worked in vaudeville before becoming a movie producer. But his forte, among the Hollywood in-crowd, was appearing as master-of-ceremonies at film industry events and as eulogist at funerals for film personalities. Eddie Cantor once said of him: "Did you ever catch him at a funeral? It's wonderful! All through the years he makes notes on his friends. He wants to be ready."

Out Of The Past

1947, RKO, 97 minutes, B&W.
Producer: Warren Duff. Director: Jacques Tourneur.
Cast: Robert Mitchum, Jane Greer, Kirk Douglas, Rhonda Fleming, Dickie Moore, Virginia Huston, Steve Brodie, Richard Webb.

> "A film still largely unappreciated…The picture was a major victory for director Tourneur, whose rich visual style added a crucial dimension to the story, and long-time RKO employee Nicholas Musuraca whose hypnotic cinematography was always in sync with the psychological zigzags inherent in the plot."
> —*The RKO Story.*

Film noir is a French term meaning "dark film" and film historians feel this is one of the best of the genre ever made; in fact, this writer believes it's *the* best. The genre came to signify moody, fatalistic post-WWII black-and-white melodramas, made up of cynical, menacing characters; sexy, double-crossing *femme fatales* in a story of impending doom; all against a backdrop of bleak, gloomy urban landscapes. The screenplay is by Daniel Mainwaring who wrote it, for some reason, under the pseudonym Geoffrey Homes, based on his novel *Build My Gallows High*—a line Mitchum uses late in the film.

Mitchum is former private-eye Jeff Markham who has changed his name to Jeff Bailey and moved away from the nastiness of the big city to the country; his new friends are a teenage boy, a deaf mute (Moore), who works at Jeff's gas station, and Ann, the new woman in his life, though she is also being suited by the local peace officer, Jim (Webb). But from out of the past comes one last job, one he must take from gangster Whit Sterling (Douglas) who sends errand-boy Jack Fisher (Brodie) to threateningly lure Jeff back to the dirty business.

Robert Mitchum and Jane Greer in *Out of the Past*.

And the job? Find Whit's old girlfriend; she's run away and Jeff must find her and bring her back. She's beautiful Kathie Moffat (Greer). When Jeff catches up with her in Mexico he can't get her out of his memory. His first sight of her remains forever fresh: "Then I saw her, coming out of the sun, and I know why Whit didn't care about that forty grand." To Jeff's great disadvantage, he falls in love with her—and maybe, just maybe she's in love with him. But alas, as he puts it to her: "You're like a leaf, you blow from gutter to gutter." Whit's ally in his double-dealings? Another lovely creature named Meta (Fleming). So the stage is set.

- Warner Bros. wanted Bogie to do it but he didn't like its similarity to *The Maltese Falcon* and *The Big Sleep* and rejected it. RKO picked it up.
- Both John Garfield and Dick Powell turned down the Mitchum role.
- Greer's career was cut short by Howard Hughes who had acquired controlling interest in RKO in 1948. After he tried to date Jane, she repeatedly turned him down and Hughes stymied her career.

- Richard Webb was TV's "Captain Midnight."
- The script was remade in 1984 as *Against All Odds;* its only saving grace was a great title song by Phil Collins. Greer does a cameo.

The Postman Always Rings Twice

1946, MGM, 113 minutes, B&W.
Producer: Carey Wilson. Director: Tay Garnett.
Cast: Lana Turner, John Garfield, Cecil Kellaway, Leon Ames, Hume Cronyn.

> "Exciting adaptation of the James M. Cain novel about a perfect crime and how the criminals are ironically punished."
> —Steven H. Scheuer, *Movies on TV*

John Garfield and Lana Turner in *The Postman Always Rings Twice.*

A perfect *film noir* and one of the best about the hand of fate invisibly metering out justice where man's law has failed. It was this film with Lana as a white-clad vixen, in white shorts, halter top and turban, that established the star's persona as an icy and aloof *femme fatale*, untouchable yet available—for a price.

Turner is Cora Smith, a beautiful young woman married to a much older man, Rick (Kellaway), owner of a California roadside café/gas station. Frank Chambers (Garfield), a drifter, goes to work for the Smiths as a handyman but falls madly in love with Cora—and falls for the murder plot she hatches against her husband. Ames is Kyle Sackett, the dogged district attorney. Cronyn is Keats, the mitigating defense attorney.

The title metaphorically relates to a postman trying to deliver a package. It's a good idea to rush to the door at the end of the first ring because it's a warning that the deliverer will vanish after the second ring. When the principals in the story botch a murder attempt, they should have heard the bell and heeded.

- Lana was a student at Hollywood High School when, as the legend goes, she skipped school one day and was discovered by a talent scout as she sipped a soda, while wearing a tight sweater, seated at the fountain counter of Schwab's Drug Store on Sunset Boulevard. In pictures she was billed as "The Sweater Girl."
- It took 12 years to produce a screenplay that the censors would accept. "It was a real chore to do *Postman* under the Hays Office," said Garnett, "but I think I managed to get the sex across."
- Jack Nicholson and Jessica Lange did a 1981 remake that emphasized erotica.
- Cain also wrote *Double Indemnity* and *Mildred Pierce*.

Scarlet Street

1945, Universal, 106 minutes, B&W.
Producers: Walter Wanger, Fritz Lang; Director: Fritz Lang.
Cast: Edward G. Robinson, Joan Bennett, Dan Duryea, Rosalind Ivan, Margaret Lindsay.

> "A dark, brooding, beautifully realized *film noir* of illicit desire…"
> —Jay A. Brown & Consumer Guide, *Rating the Movies*

Joan Bennett and Edward G. Robinson in *Scarlet Street*.

Andrew Sarris, critic for *The Village Voice*, has mused that Lang's films are the stuff of nightmares, and this one is every bit that. Robinson plays a sad, henpecked New York husband, Chris Cross, who works as a cashier but dabbles in painting. One night in Greenwich Village, after receiving a gold watch at a testimonial dinner for his long service, he stops a mugging at a street corner. After the alleged thief runs away, the very pretty Kitty (Bennett) goes into a café for a drink with Chris. This chance encounter turns into a life of trouble and misery for Chris as Kitty, who is really a prostitute, leads him on. And as it turns out, the assailant Chris frightened off was actually Kitty's boyfriend, Johnny (Duryea), a smooth-talking opportunist. Once the *femme fatale* learns that Chris is an amateur artist, she takes advantage of his talent by selling his art as her own. Surprisingly, critics find the art extremely inventive and worth a lot of money. All of this is going on without the knowledge of Chris' hateful and selfish wife, Adele (Ivan).

This is a most unusual film, centered on guilt and conscience. It's about an older man who wonders what it would be like to be loved by an attractive young woman, undoubtedly a situation that exists to a certain extent in every society. Chris tries to take advantage of the opportunity to secretly have an affair while, in fact, she is taking advantage of him.

The stars had already worked together in Lang's *The Woman in the Window*, a 1944 *film noir*. This screenplay, by Dudley Nichols, is a remake of Jean Renoir's *La Chienne*. The song "My Melancholy Baby" is a running theme. Lindsay plays a model, Kitty's roommate.

- Robinson (1893-1973), real name Emmanuel Goldenberg, for a long time had Hollywood's finest art collection.
- Ivan, who often played this kind of mean woman, was known on the set as "Ivan the Terrible."
- Bennett and Wanger, at the time of this film, had been married for five years. In 1952, Wanger went to prison for less than a year in a shooting incident involving Bennett and her agent Jennings Lang over an alleged affair. Bennett and Wanger eventually divorced 10 years later..

Sunset Boulevard

1950, Paramount, 111 minutes, B&W.
Producer: Charles Brackett. Director: Billy Wilder.
Cast: Gloria Swanson, William Holden, Erich von Stroheim, Nancy Olson, Cecil B. DeMille, Jack Webb.

> "For sheer audacity, *Sunset Boulevard* has rarely been equaled."
> —*The Paramount Story.*

Hollywood's most cynical film about itself (written by Wilder and Brackett with D.M. Marshman, Jr.) won the Oscar for Best Screenplay; and the film noir got nominated for Best Picture. Wilder also got nominated for Best Director.

The final scene is one of the most memorable ever created: a mad former silent screen star, Norma Desmond (Swanson), immersed in what she thinks is her comeback, descending her staircase as Salome, surrounded by cops and press photographers—finishing with the line, "I'm ready for my close-up, Mr. DeMille."

The skillful but grim drama has an equally memorable opening: a dead man, screenwriter Joe Gillis (Holden), tells the story—as the movie begins—with himself, the murdered narrator, floating facedown in the

Gloria Swanson in the final scene of *Sunset Boulevard*.

swimming pool at the eerie mansion of the aging actress; she driven to madness since the advent of sound.

Swanson is stunning as the faded film legend and von Stroheim is haunting as Norma's butler and chauffeur at 10086 Sunset Boulevard. His Max von Mayerling is ironic: like his character, von Stroheim (*Greed*) was once a great director before studio bosses swept him under the rug because of his temperament and production excesses. All four leading players received Oscar nominations: Swanson for Best Actress, Holden for Best Actor, von Stroheim and Olson for supporting Oscars. The film also won Academy Awards for score, photography, sets and art direction.

DeMille plays himself. He is seen at Paramount directing a scene from *Samson and Delilah* which he was actually producing at the time. It is rather strange, indeed, that DeMille, who starred Swanson in six of his erotic films of the 1920s, films that helped set the stage for a censor in the 1930s, appears in the movie. Olson is a script-reader, Betty Schaefer. Her boyfriend, Artie Green, is played by Webb (Sgt. Joe Friday in TV's "Dragnet").

- Famous dialogue: "You're Norma Desmond," says Joe. "You used to be in silent pictures. You used to be big." "I am big," replies Norma, "it's the pictures that got small."

- The Desmond mansion, now torn down, was really a vacant mansion, owned by the former wife of multimillionaire J.Paul Getty, though it was not on Sunset but at Wilshire and Irving. It had no swimming pool, so the movie company put one in, but without plumbing.
- There are cameos by gossip columnist Hedda Hopper, silent comedian Buster Keaton, H.B. Warner (Christ in DeMille's *The King of Kings*), and Anna Q. Nilsson (a silent star from Sweden), the latter three playing bridge with Norma.
- Both Mae West and Mary Pickford turned down the Desmond role.

Witness for The Prosecution

1957, United Artists, 114 minutes, B&W.
Producer: Arthur Hornblow. Director: Billy Wilder.
Cast: Charles Laughton, Tyrone Power, Marlene Dietrich, Elsa Lanchester

> "One of the most successful adaptations of an Agatha Christie original, the courtroom melodrama benefited from a witty script by Billy Wilder, who also directed."
> —Leslie Halliwell

A leading candidate for the best courtroom movie ever made, the polished cast couldn't be better. It may also be Laughton's finest performance in a career spanning 50 films in both England and Hollywood. It is reported that he often stayed late on the set, after everyone else had left, offering suggestions to Wilder about the next day's work. He was, after all, an outstanding director—though he only directed one film, but what a good one (*The Night of the Hunter*).

Laughton, as esteemed British barrister Sir Wilfrid Robarts, received an Oscar nomination for Best Actor; Lanchester (Laughton's wife in real life) was nominated for Best Supporting Actress, Wilder got nominated for Best Director, and the film itself nominated for Best Picture.

Wilder co-wrote the Christie stage play with Harry Kurnitz. The London story, with twists and turns and a surprise ending, is about a handsome young gigolo, Leonard Vole (Power), on trial for the murder

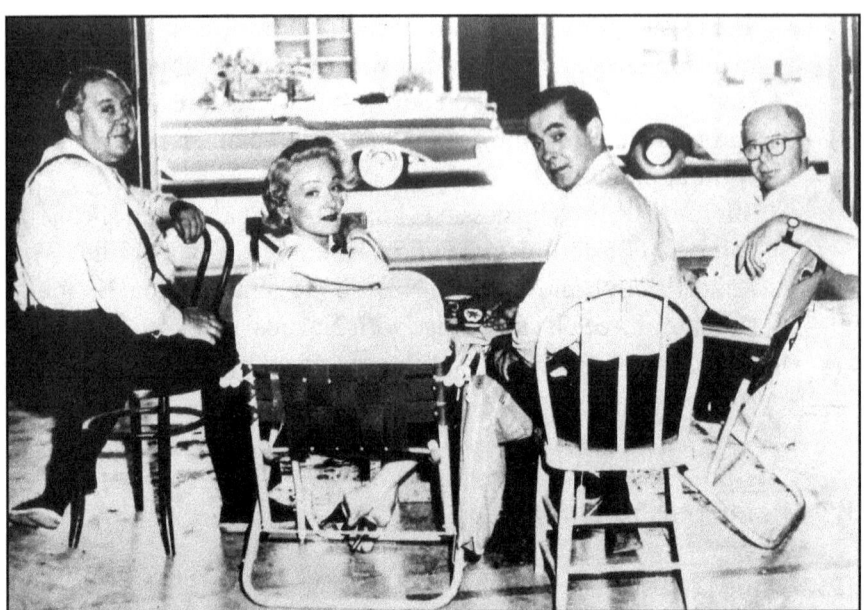
Charles Laughton, Marlene Dietrich, Tyrone Power and Billy Wilder in a coffee-break while shooting *Witness for the Prosecution*.

of a wealthy woman after receiving money from her will. He insists on his innocence, as does his wife, Christine Vole (Dietrich). But there are devastating secrets yet to be revealed during the course of the trial, things that cast a dark shadow over both Vole and his bride. Sir Robarts is Vole's defense attorney and Miss Plimsoll (Lanchster) is the great lawyer's nurse, always out to protect his questionable health as Sir Wilfrid secretly seeks consolation in borrowed cigars.

- Both the trailer and film introduction urge the audience not to reveal the ending to their friends.
- The scene where Dietrich reveals one of her famously lovely legs was especially written for that purpose at a further cost of $90,000 for an additional set and extras.
- It was Power's last film. He died of a heart attack while making *Solomon and Sheba* (Yul Brynner took over the role).
- Kurnitz: "Billy Wilder at work is two people: Mr. Hyde and Mr. Hyde."

Mystery-Thrillers

And Then There Were None

1945, 20th Century-Fox, 98 minutes, B&W.
Producer/Director: Rene Clair.
Cast: Louis Hayward, June Duprez, Barry Fitzgerald, Walter Huston, Judith Anderson, Roland Young, C. Aubrey Smith, Richard Haydn. Mischa Auer, Queenie Leonard, Harry Thurston.

> "Rich in the elements which have made mystery melodramas popular…"
>
> —*The Hollywood Reporter*

Based on the book and play, *Ten Little Indians*, by Agatha Christie, the sinister plot concerns a secret person who has decided to impose belated justice on a group of ten people. Unaware of the real purpose of their invitation, they are taken by boat to an island, Indian Island (shaped in the form of an Indian head), where they are to spend a weekend ostensibly for rest and relaxation. But the adventure turns out to be much more than they could ever have imagined. One by one they will be murdered by various means. The murders occur according to the nursery rhyme "Ten Little Indian Boys" which begins "Ten little Indian boys going out to dine, one choked his little self, and then there were nine." Indeed, the first victim—poisoned—dies coughing. After each death, an Indian figure in a China centerpiece turns up broken. Is the killer hiding somewhere on the island or is the murderer amongst them?

The characters are an engrossing cross-section of society: Judge Quinncannon (Fitzgerald), Dr. Armstrong (Huston), Detective Blore (Young), General Mandrake (Smith), a professional house guest named

Nikki Starloff (Auer), a spinster by the name of Emily (Anderson); the butler and cook, Tom and Ethel Rogers (Haydn, Leonard), Fred the boatman (Thurston), and a young man and woman, Philip and Vera, drawn romantically to one another (Hayward, Duprez)

- Christie (1891-1976) was England's foremost writer of mystery plays and novels; her two most famous detectives are Hercule Poirot and Jane Marple.
- Hayward was a Marine in World War II and was awarded the Bronze Star.
- Dublin-born Fitzgerald is the brother of actor Arthur Shields.

The Big Sleep

1946, Warner Bros., 111 minutes, B&W.
Producer/Director: Howard Hawks.
Cast: Humphrey Bogart, Lauren Bacall, Martha Vickers, Dorothy Malone, Elisha Cook, Jr., John Ridgley, Charles Waldron, Regis Toomey, Bob Steele.

"...crackerjack detective classic...film contains the sharpest, toughest, wittiest, sexiest dialogue ever written for a detective film."
—Danny Peary, *Guide for the Film Fanatic*

Bogart, the best actor in detective roles there ever was, is Raymond Chandler's wisecracking private-eye Philip Marlowe. Bogie is drawn into a web of deceit and danger in a hypnotizing but convoluted script (by William Faulkner, Leigh Brackett, and Jules Furthman) about blackmail, pornography, drug deals—and murder.

Complicating the complications are a pretty but immature flirt named Carmen (Vickers), a bookstore nymph (Malone), a sexy but spoiled socialite named Vivien (Bacall), and a steely-eyed killer (Steele). Somehow the cynical but incorruptible Marlowe survives it all. Carmen and Vivien are the wealthy daughters of millionaire General Sternwood (Waldron) who survives, paralyzed in a hothouse, vicariously savoring the cigarettes and booze of other people.

The film gets its title from an episode in the frivolous life of drug-dazed Carmen who winds up with a dead man at her feet; she and he obviously *sleeping* through a maze of malfeasance.

Howard Hawks (left) leads a script conference on the set of *The Big Sleep*.

Cook, Wilmer from *The Maltese Falcon*, is back, still mixing with bad company as Harry Jones. Ridgley plays porno-dealer Eddie Mars. Toomey is Bernie the cop.

- Marlowe has also been played by Robert Mitchum, Dick Powell, Robert Montgomery, Elliott Gould, and James Garner.
- Steele is a former B-Western star from the 30s and 40s.
- Screenwriter Brackett is a woman, despite the spelling of her first name; she also worked with Hawks on three John Wayne Westerns: *Rio Bravo, El Dorado, Rio Lobo*.
- This is the second of four films Bogart and Bacall made together: *To Have and Have Not, Dark Passage, Key Largo*. They fell in love during the making of *The Big Sleep*.

Charade

1963, Universal, 113 minutes, Color.
Producer/Director: Stanley Donen.
Cast: Cary Grant, Audrey Hepburn, Walter Matthau, James Coburn, George Kennedy, Jacques Marin, Ned Glass.

> "An absolute delight."
>
> —*Newsweek*.

A crisp, Hitchcockian romantic-thriller, dazzlingly set in Paris, is the perfect vehicle for Grant and Hepburn, even though there's a 25 year difference between them. Grant even worried about that but screenwriter Peter Stone fixed it by letting Hepburn come onto him.

Just who is Grant? Is he Peter Joshua, Carson Dyle, Adam Canfield, or a guy named Crookshank? In any event, he comes to the aid of widow Regina Lampert (Hepburn) whose husband just got murdered and tossed from a moving train. But maybe Cary's character had something to do with it? Added to the plot, just to make things even more confusing, is a government agent named Bartholemew (Matthau) and a trio of strange guys in search of $250,000—formerly in the hands of Regina's husband who she obviously didn't know every well. Coburn plays Tex, Kennedy is Scobie, and Glass is Gideon. Also, in the shadows, trying to unravel the mystery is a French police inspector (Marin).

Cary Grant and Audrey Hepburn in *Charade*.

The British Academy named Hepburn Best Actress for the film. There are two funny scenes: Cary takes a shower in his suit and he and Audrey play an orange-under-the-chin game at a nightclub. The music is by Henry Mancini; the *Charade* theme was a hit recording. The ending in a theatre is perfect for the concept of the principal characters "acting" a charade.

- The film has played quite often on TV because of its public domain status due to the fact that Universal did not properly list the copyright notice.
- There's an inside joke: getting off the elevator, Grant says to Audrey, "Here we are, on the street where you live." A reference to her role in *My Fair Lady*.
- Some critics questioned Donen and Stone doing a film so very much in the Hitchcock style but Donen said while he greatly admired Hitch, "Mr. Hitchcock didn't own the rights" to such suspense-thrillers.

Foreign Correspondent

1940, United Artists, 119 minutes, B&W.
Producer: Walter Wanger. Director: Alfred Hitchcock.
Cast: Joel McCrea, Laraine Day, Herbert Marshall, George Sanders, Albert Basserman, Robert Benchley, Edmund Gwenn.

> "Hitchcock's first American thriller, a welcome return to his best form apart from the final message: 'Don't let the lights go out all over Europe!' Splendid moments in a Dutch windmill, a crashing aeroplane, and Westminster Cathedral."
> —Leslie Halliwell, *Halliwell's Filmgoer's Companion*

A prewar spy-thriller, nominated for Best Picture, that served as a great propaganda tool for the Allies at the start of WWII. A New York

Joel McCrea plays a reporter caught up in political intrigue in *Foreign Correspondent*.

City newspaper assigns its crime reporter, Johnny Jones, to go to Europe to check out the war clouds. McCrea is the foreign correspondent who changes his name to Huntley Haverstock to get more respect.

In Holland, Haverstock stumbles upon a big story, the assassination of a peace-seeking Dutch diplomat in daylight in a rainstorm. The murder occurs in Amsterdam Square as the gunman flees under cover of dozens of umbrellas, wonderfully photographed from above by Rudy Mate. Haverstock chases the killer into a cluster of windmills; the newsman hides inside a windmill to eavesdrop on the Nazi conspirators.

Basserman, nominated for Best Supporting Actor, plays diplomat Van Meer. Marshall is an alleged peace advocate, Stephen Fisher, who has a secret agenda. His beautiful daughter, Carol (Day), gets emotionally involved with Haverstock. Sanders is Scotty, an eccentric British reporter and Benchley is Stebbins, a jaded American journalist. Gwenn is Rowley, not the nice guy he appears to be: he's an assassin who takes Haverstock to the top of Westminster Cathedral for some malfeasance.

The climax includes a dramatic plane crash in the Atlantic Ocean followed by Haverstock's plea to America to help the British in their time of greatest need.

- Basserman was a German refugee to America.
- Amsterdam Square was a 10-acre facsimile.
- The water-filled tank and airplane with a wingspan half a football field was one of the biggest sets of its day.
- Hitchcock quoted in *The Celluloid Muse*: "The windmill episode in *Foreign Correspondent* was a notion of mine based on a particular approach I have to settings. I'm a great believer in that; if you have a setting, it should be dramatized, and be indigenous to the whole picture, not just a background...So in *Foreign Correspondent*, set in Holland, I asked myself, 'Now what is there in Holland that I can dramatize?' Tulips? There was no color in those days, so no tulips. Windmills? Naturally. And how did I use them? I had one mill going the wrong way while Joel McCrea's hat blew the other way; then he realized it was a sign for an airplane to land."

Gaslight

1944, MGM, 114 minutes, B&W.
Producer: Arthur Hornblow, Jr. Director: George Cukor.
Cast: Ingrid Bergman, Charles Boyer, Joseph Cotten, Angela Lansbury.

> "A top cast turns in stylish performances to bring out the chills."
> —Jay A. Brown & Consumer Guide, *Rating the Movies*

Bergman won her first Oscar for Best Actress (and later for *Anastasia*, 1956) as Paula Alquist, being driven mad by her malevolent husband, Gregory Anton (Boyer). The film gets its name from the flickering house lights, secretly produced by Anton, that cause Paula to drift toward insanity.

Why is Anton trying to destroy his own wife? Money. He didn't really love her when he married her. Anton had learned that there were very expensive jewels hidden in their London home, probably in the attic, a house once owned by Paula's aunt. Anton wants Paula out of the way: hopefully in an insane asylum, so he can find the stuff. Meanwhile,

Joseph Cotten, Ingrid Bergman and Charles Boyer star in *Gaslight*.

the pretty maid, Nancy Oliver (Lansbury), has a flirtatious eye for Anton. Scotland Yard's venerable inspector Brian Cameron (Cotten) sets out to uncover the mystery of the wavering gaslights, and in the process finds he's falling in love with the beautiful victim.

The Victorian mystery-thriller won Oscars for art direction (Cedric Gibbons) and sets (Edwin Willis). The original Broadway play ran successfully as *Angel Street*.

- Terry Moore, billed as Judy Ford, plays Paula at 14.
- Bergman visited a mental institution to study patients who had suffered emotional breakdowns.
- This was Lansbury's film debut; she was 17.
- Irene Dunne and Hedy Lamarr both turned down the role of Paula.
- Boyer committed suicide two days after the death of his wife, actress Pat Patterson, after they had been married 44 years.
- Orson Welles, in the early days, told his friend Cotten, who had worked on radio with Orson's Mercury Theatre: "You're very lucky to be tall and thin and have curly hair. You can also move about the stage without running into the furniture. But these are fringe assets, and I'm afraid you'll never make it as an actor…But as a star…but as a star, I think you well might hit the jackpot."

Laura

1944, 20th Century-Fox, 88 minutes, B&W.
Producer/Director: Otto Preminger.
Cast: Gene Tierney, Dana Andrews, Clifton Webb, Vincent Price, Judith Anderson.

> "Everybody's favorite chic murder mystery."
> —*The New Yorker.*

"I shall never forget the weekend Laura died…"—and so the psychological *film noir* begins, as narrated by Webb as Waldo Lydecker, one of many who had fallen in love with this mysterious woman who has been murdered at the very outset. The story is based on the novel by Vera Caspary.

Lovely Gene Tierney stars as the mysterious *Laura*.

Tierney stars as lovely advertising executive Laura Hunt. Laura's social mentor is Lydecker, a sarcastic critic: "I don't use a pen. I write with a goose quill dipped in venom." Price is Laura's fiancé, Shelby Carpenter. Anderson is Laura's aunt, Ann Treadwell, who is actually in love with Shelby. And Andrews plays Det. Lt. Mark McPherson, the policeman investigating the strange death of Laura…along the way, sniffing her perfume and reading her love letters…thus, in due course, Mark, like so many others, also falls in love with Laura, even though she's dead.

Joseph LaShelle won the Oscar for Best Cinematography (black-and-white). Preminger received an Academy Award nomination for Best Director and Webb got nominated for Best Supporting Actor. The haunting theme, "Laura," which became a hit standard, was written by David Raksin with lyrics added later by Johnny Mercer.

- Rouben Mamoulian began production and shot quite a lot of footage until Darryl Zanuck replaced him with producer Preminger who was able to provide a more darker tone.
- Originally, the ending was supposed to be a dream but Preminger changed it.
- Jennifer Jones turned down the role of Laura and, later, Hedy Lamarr rejected it.
- Raksin wrote the theme in one weekend, the weekend that his wife left him.
- The portrait of Laura was an enlarged photograph of the actress that was carefully brushed over with oil paints.

The Maltese Falcon

1941, Warner Bros., 101 minutes, B&W.
Producer: Hal B. Wallis. Director: John Huston.
Cast: Humphrey Bogart, Mary Astor, Sydney Greenstreet, Peter Lorre, Elisha Cook, Jr., Lee Patrick, Gladys George, Barton MacLane, Ward Bond, Jerome Cowan.

> "It set new standards in crime thrillers and turned Bogart into a major star."
>
> —Clive Hirschhorn,
> *The Warner Bros. Story*

One of the three greatest detective-mysteries ever made (*Chinatown, The Big Sleep*) was nominated for Best Picture with Huston making his directorial debut. Based on Dashiell Hammett's novel, Bogart is San Francisco private-eye Sam Spade whose partner, Miles Archer (Cowan), gets mysteriously shot and killed. The trail leads to a cadre of crooks led by "the fat man," Kasper Gutman (Greenstreet), in quest of "the black bird," the Maltese Falcon, a bejeweled statuette with its wealth hidden by heavy layers of black paint.

As the legend goes, the Falcon was delivered by the Knights of Rhodes to Emperor Charles V of Spain in 1539 in gratitude for his giving them the isle of Malta. The elusive bird has been secreted about for centuries and the undaunted Gutman, all 357 lbs. of him, believes he's traced it to San Francisco, and is willing to kill for it.

Humphrey Bogart, Peter Lorre, Mary Astor and Sydney Greenstreet in *The Maltese Falcon*.

Gutman's nomads in search of the Falcon, what Spade calls "the stuff that dreams are made of," are gardenia-scented Joel Cairo (Lorre) and Wilmer the Gunsel (Cook). Also tagging along in the search for riches is a lovely *femme fatale*, Brigid O'Shaughnessy (Astor), who would do anything (that, too) to get a piece of the action; naturally, she makes a move on Sam to solicit his help.

Patrick is Effie, Sam's secretary. George is Iva Archer, Miles' widow. MacLane is Det. Lt. Dundy and Bond plays Det. Tom Polhaus.

- The working title was *The Gent From Frisco*.
- George Raft turned down the role of Spade.
- This was Greenstreet's first film; he was 60 years old.
- Floyd Thursby, talked about in the plot, never appears.
- Walter Huston, John's father, shows up, uncredited, as the dying ship captain who drops off the Falcon at Spade's office.
- The true existence of such an artifact is doubtful though there was a seventeenth century hawk encrusted with precious stones owned by the Count of the Holy Roman Empire.

The Manchurian Candidate

1962, United Artists, 126 minutes, B&W.
Producers: George Axelrod, John Frankenheimer; Director: John Frankenheimer.
Cast: Frank Sinatra, Laurence Harvey, Angela Lansbury, Janet Leigh, James Gregory, Leslie Parrish, Henry Silva.

> "Although it's a thriller, it may be the most sophisticated political satire ever to come out of Hollywood."
> —Pauline Kael.

The aim of the political thriller, said Frankenheimer, was "to expose the idiocy of political fanaticism both of the extreme Right and the extreme Left." The film managed that and a lot more with great success. In 1998, the American Film Institute put it at #67 on its list of America's 100 Greatest Movies.

Harvey plays Lt. Raymond Shaw, a spurious Medal of Honor winner during the Korean War; he was captured, drugged and brainwashed by the North Koreans and Chinese Communists and turned into a political

Frank Sinatra and Laurence Harvey in a lunch-break during filming of *The Manchurian Candidate*.

assassin. Shaw is hypnotically controlled by the appearance of a playing card, the Queen of Diamonds. One of his compatriots during the capture was Capt. Ben Marco (Sinatra), now in Army Intelligence. Marco has had nightmares about his POW ordeal and, now encountering Shaw, Ben is determined to discover the truth about what actually happened. Leigh plays Rosie, a beautiful young woman who meets Marco by happenstance, immediately falls in love with him and sets out to help him… first by preventing his suicide.

Lansbury as the ruthless and scheming Mrs. Iselin received an Oscar nomination for Best Supporting Actress. Lansbury is unforgettable as Raymond's vile mother, suggesting—with a kiss on her son's lips—an Oedipus complex. Gregory plays her manipulated husband and Shaw's stepfather, Sen. John Iselin, being groomed as a vice-presidential nominee. Parrish is Jocelyn, Shaw's fiancé. Silva is Shaw's valet, in reality a Communist agent.

The excellent screenplay is by Axelrod and Frankenheimer, based on the book by Richard Condon. The material made good use of the cold-war hysteria following the "McCarthyism" of the 50s.

- Harvey was only three years younger than Lansbury who plays his mother.
- Sinatra broke a finger hitting the table during the Karate fight with Silva. The hand healed incorrectly and Frank's injury pained him all his life.
- The political convention scenes were shot at the old Madison Square Garden.
- Oops! There are 50 stars in the U.S. flag in the Korean bar but there were only 48 states.
- The film was not shown in theaters after the assassination of President Kennedy in 1963 but reappeared on CBS-TV in 1965.

Marathon Man

1976, Paramount, 125 minutes, Color.
Producers: Robert Evans, Sidney Beckerman; Director: John Schlesinger. Cast: Dustin Hoffman, Roy Scheider, Laurence Olivier, William Devane, Marthe Keller.

"A commercial bonanza with the Nazi-hunt thriller."
—*The Film Encyclopedia.*

The most fantastic espionage-thriller of the seventies with one of the most famous lines in all cinema: "Is it safe?"

With screenplay by William Goldman from his bestselling novel, Hoffman plays Thomas "Babe" Levy, a Columbia graduate student training for a 26-mile marathon. His mysterious brother, Doc (Scheider), is not what he seems: he doesn't work in the oil business in Washington, as his brother thinks; he is actually a member of a secret organization called The Division that does what the FBI and CIA won't do. Babe gets drawn into Doc's shenanigans because the bad guys broke the rules that say personal families are off-limits.

Dustin Hoffman discusses a scene with director John Schlesinger for *Marathon Man.*

At the center of this complex plot is Dr. Christian Szell (Olivier), a Nazi dentist hiding out in South America. Szell, who carries a devastating wrist-dagger up his sleeve, had extracted gold from the mouths of concentration camp victims. His brother in New York exchanged the gold for diamonds and placed it in a safe deposit box, but the brother accidentally dies in a car crash. So Szell goes to New York to get the treasure. But he suspects that Doc and his associates, possibly even his brother, plan to rob him after he leaves the bank. Babe is kidnapped and Szell and his henchmen tie Babe up to find out if it's safe to go to the bank. To discover the truth, Szell, in a horrendous display of torture, drills one of Babe's teeth.

Olivier received a Best Supporting Actor nomination for his powerful performance as the evil Nazi. Devane is Peter Janeway, a double-dealing super-secret agent. Keller is Elsa, a German undercover pawn.

- As an indicator of Olivier's incredible range as an actor, his character is just the opposite in *Boys From Brazil* (1978) when he plays an aging Jewish Nazi-hunter.
- The drilling scene was cut short because at the preview, a few members of the audience got sick and ran from the theater.
- Szell is based on Dr. Josef Mengele, the notorious Nazi doctor of Auschwitz. Rumor had it that Mengele was still alive and living in South America at the time the movie was made.
- Julie Christie turned down the role of Elsa.

Marnie

1964, Universal, 130 minutes, Color.
Producer: Albert Whitlock. Director: Alfred Hitchcock.
Cast: Tippi Hedren, Sean Connery, Diane Baker, Louise Latham, Martin Gabel.

> "...the master of suspense again revealing himself to be a supreme craftsman, capable of extracting the most from the least, and of investing the commonplace with a sense of the macabre."
> —Clive Hirschhorn, *The Universal Story*

Alfred Hitchcock giving ideas to Tippi Hedren for *Marnie*.

In this psychological thriller, ex-model Hedren follows *The Birds* with another good performance, this time about the angst of a female thief, Margaret "Marnie" Edgar, a compulsive liar who gets secretarial jobs at up-scale businesses and then steals them blind. Marnie is a depressed woman suffering anxiety and panic attacks and excruciating nightmares. Connery (in the same year he became James Bond) plays industrialist Mark Rutland who hires Marnie and becomes infatuated with her, even though he knows she's a crook. Mark keeps her on just to study her, hoping to find out what makes this beautiful but mixed-up woman tick. It's psycho-drama at its best, based on the novel by Winston Graham. (There's even a non-graphic rape scene, delicately written by screenwriter Jay Presson Allen.)

Latham plays Marnie's equally-confused and disturbed mother, the big reason Marnie is the way she is. Baker is Lil Mainwaring who has more than a passing interest in Mark; she's the sister of Mark's dead wife. Gabel is Sidney Strutt, one of the wealthy businessmen who was victimized by Marnie.

There are some interesting impressionistic sets by Robert Boyle and another outstanding score by Bernard Herrmann, famous for his work on *Psycho* and *Citizen Kane*.

- Hitchcock makes his usual brief appearance, this time for a moment in a hallway.
- The role of Marnie was offered to Grace Kelly but she turned it down; others considered were Eva Marie Saint, Vera Miles, and Lee Remick.
- Hedren (the mother of actress Melanie Griffith) rides a mechanical horse from the Disney studios.
- Catherine Deneuve said she wished she had played Marnie.

Murder, My Sweet

1945, RKO, 95 minutes, B&W.
Producer: Adrian Scott. Director: Edward Dmytryk.
Cast: Dick Powell, Claire Trevor, Anne Shirley, Mike Mazurki, Otto Kruger.

> "Pulse-quickening entertainment."
> —*The New York Times*.

If you think you're watching another version of *The Big Sleep*, that would be understandable. It's based on Raymond Chandler's *Farewell, My Lovely* from which Howard Hawks took *The Big Sleep*. Powell as Philip Marlowe is no Bogart but, nevertheless, he does a very good job as the famous private detective. Powell wanted this role badly so he could break out of his persona as a musical star. He succeeded. Chandler himself liked Powell in the part and, in fact, he felt this was the best screen version of all his works. John Paxton (*Crossfire*) did the screenplay.

All the criminal elements are on display for Marlowe to figure out: murder, blackmail, thievery (they're looking for a jade necklace), and a two-faced, double-crossing dame: Trevor, looking a lot like Lana Turner, plays the mysterious Velma. Mazurki is the big goon, Moose Malloy,

Dick Powell and Claire Trevor in *Murder, My Sweet*.

looking for Velma. Kruger plays his rather traditional role as the inscrutable bad guy. And Miss Shirley is Ann Grayle, trying to protect her father while protecting her romantic interest in Mr. Marlowe.

One of the best scenes is when Kruger's men kidnap Marlowe and drug him, in the belief that Marlowe has the stolen jewels or knows where they are. Special effects artist Vernon Walker provides an inventive sequence to give us some idea of what Marlowe sees and feels while under the influence of drugs.

- If Mazurki looks like a wrestler that's because he was—before getting into pictures.
- The film was remade in 1975 using the original title, *Farewell, My Lovely*, starring Robert Mitchum.
- Dmytryk was blacklisted but cleared in 1951 by the House Committee on Un-American Activities when he named names, including the producer of this film.

North By Northwest

1959, MGM, 136 minutes, Color.
Producer/Director: Alfred Hitchcock.
Cast: Cary Grant, Eva Marie Saint, James Mason, Leo G. Carroll, Jessie Royce Landis, Martin Landau.

> "This Alfred Hitchcock masterpiece, one of his most enjoyable pictures...has outstanding performances, technical brilliance, a great deal of humor, terrific locations for suspense scenes..."
>
> —Danny Peary.

James Mason, Eva Marie Saint and Cary Grant pause in front of Mount Rushmore while filming *North By Northwest*.

A great espionage thriller in the Hitchcock tradition of *The 39 Steps* and *The Lady Vanishes*, a literal cliffhanger climaxing atop a national monument: Mount Rushmore. And, again, there's the familiar Hitchcock gimmick of having a regular person become the victim of mistaken identity, leading to flight from the law, narrow escapes from death, and sexy scenes with a dazzling blonde (also one of Hitch's hallmarks).

The film is particularly famous for two scenes: Grant being chased in a lonely, wide-open farmland by a crop-dusting biplane that explodes into a tanker truck—and for his and Saint's fight for life on Mount Rushmore.

Grant is Manhattan executive Roger O. Thornhill, an adman, who gets mistaken as a CIA agent by a spy ring. (Don't miss the beginning in the Plaza Hotel Oak Bar—when he beckons to the bellboy—or you'll miss the reason he was wrongly picked by the villains.) Saint plays a cool, good-looking and mysterious blonde, Eve Kendall.

Mason is the head of the ring, Phillip Vandamm. Landau is Vandamm's strong-arm "secretary." Carroll is "the Professor," the government man who, along the way, unveils the plot. Landis is comedy relief as Grant's mother (even though he was 10 months older than her).

Other memorable scenes, from Ernest Lehman's excellent screenplay, include: the murder at the U.N., the shooting in the Rushmore cafeteria, the escape engineered at the auction gallery, the faked drunk-drive down a mountain road, and the sexual encounter aboard the 20th Century Limited.

The technical crew was absolutely ingenious: cinematographer Robert Burks (*Vertigo, Marnie*), art director Robert Boyle (*Saboteur, The Birds*), composer Bernard Herrmann (*Psycho, Citizen Kane*).

- The climactic chase was not shot on Mount Rushmore; they couldn't get permission so a replica of the monument was built in a studio.
- The plane sequence was shot near Bakersfield, Calif. There was no cornfield, they had to truck it in. The exact moment of the plane crash into the truck is done with models and, for live-action, a stunt-double fills in for Grant.
- Hitch, as usual, makes a quick appearance—this time during the opening credits as he just misses catching a bus.
- Before Eve shoots the gun in the cafeteria, a little boy covers his ears too early.
- Hitchcock originally thought of calling the film *The Man in Lincoln's Nose.*

- The title is a play on words: Thornhill takes Northwest Airlines to his destination, North-Northwest to South Dakota; and it was Hamlet who said, "I am but mad North-Northwest."

Notorious

1946, RKO, 103 minutes, B&W.
Producer/Director: Alfred Hitchcock.
Cast: Cary Grant, Ingrid Bergman, Claude Rains, Louis Calhern.

> "One of those rare cinematic masterpieces that casts a spell over audiences."
> —*The RKO Story.*

This espionage-thriller is famous for two things: a kiss and a crane-shot. In those days, a kiss on-screen wasn't supposed to be longer than

Ingrid Bergman filming the key-in-the-hand scene for *Notorious*, directed by Alfred Hitchcock.

three seconds (according to the censor, the Hayes Code) but Bergman said they couldn't cut it because she and Grant never kissed for more than three seconds at any point: "We did other things; we nibbled on each other's ears, and kissed a cheek, so that it looked endless, and became sensational in Hollywood." And look for a famous slow crane-shot (by cameraman Ted Tetzlaff), a zoom from the top of a grand staircase to a tight close-up of a key in Ingrid's fist at Rains' party.

Grant is T.R. Devlin, a U.S. agent, and Bergman is Alicia Huberman, refugee-daughter of a convicted Nazi traitor, embarking on a dangerous secret assignment in Rio de Janeiro. To show her loyalty to the American government, Alicia agrees to marry her father's co-conspirator: Alexander Sebastian (Rains). Things get complicated when Devlin, Alicia's boss, falls in love with her.

Calhern plays Capt. Prescott. Rains got Oscar-nominated for Best Supporting Actor. Ben Hecht received an Academy Award nomination for Best Original Screenplay.

- Hitchcock originally wanted Clifton Webb for the part of Sebastian but was very pleased with Rains' performance and critical notices.
- Rains did scenes with the very tall Bergman while standing on a box.
- Hitchcock liked to say that FBI men visited the set because Hecht used uranium as a plot device at the time of the first A-bomb and that made the government curious about how much Hecht really knew about the making of atomic weapons. Some film historians claim the story is a myth or that the FBI never showed up on set.
- Hitch, who always liked to make an almost-undetected appearance in his films, gets a glass of champagne from the bartender at the party in Sebastian's mansion.

Rebecca

1940, Selznick/United Artists, 130 minutes, B&W.
Producer: David O. Selznick. Director: Alfred Hitchcock.
Cast: Laurence Olivier, Joan Fontaine, Judith Anderson, George Sanders.

Alfred Hitchcock, Joan Fontaine and Laurence Olivier on the set of *Rebecca*.

"A splendid example of the cinema as a popular storyteller."
—Leslie Halliwell

The film has the most famous opening line in the history of movies: "Last night, I dreamt I went to Manderly again."

Based on Daphne du Maurier's novel, the gothic mystery-thriller received eight Academy Award nominations and two Oscars: for Best Picture and Best Cinematography (George Barnes). Hitchcock, for his first American film, got nominated for Best Director. *Rebecca* made it two straight for Selznick following his legendary *Gone With the Wind* in 1939.

Strangely atmospheric with a sinister mood enveloping throughout the proceedings, the film features a narrator/heroine, a shy, dowdy young woman without a name (Fontaine) who is quickly taken in marriage by a wealthy widower, Maxim de Winter (Olivier); he is the aristocratic landowner of a Cornish estate called Manderly. Rebecca, de Winter's drowned wife, is never shown on the screen, even in flashback, but her influence, who she was and how she lived, dominates the story. Anderson, in one of the screen's best villainous roles, plays Mrs. Danvers, Rebecca's obsessive and pathological housekeeper. Sanders is Rebecca's flip cousin, Jack Favell, who strongly suspects that Rebecca was murdered.

There is an outstanding veteran supporting cast: Florence Bates plays Fontaine's former peevish employer, Mrs. Van Hopper. C. Aubrey Smith is de Winter's friend and influential community leader, Col. Julyan. Nigel Bruce is the brother-in-law, Maj. Lacy. Gladys Cooper is de Winter's sister, Beatrice. Leo G. Carroll plays Dr. Baker.

And Reginald Denny is Frank Crawley.

- The only Hitchcock film to win the Oscar for Best Picture.
- Olivier wanted Vivian Leigh for the Fontaine part; he and Vivian were dating at the time.
- Maureen O'Hara, Loretta Young, and Anne Baxter were all considered for the lead.
- Ronald Colman was the first choice over Olivier but he turned it down.
- Manderly was a miniature.

Shadow of A Doubt

1943, Universal, 107 minutes, B&W.
Producer: Jack H. Skirball. Director: Alfred Hitchcock.
Cast: Joseph Cotten, Teresa Wright, Macdonald Carey, Patricia Collinge, Henry Travers, Hume Cronyn, Edna Mae Wonacutt.

> "A gripping character study of a murderer."
> — *The Universal Story*

While Hitchcock's fame is linked by *Psycho, North By Northwest* and *Vertigo,* this little film is just as good, at least Hitch thought so; it was his favorite of all his American films. He liked the idea of showing a killer as a nice guy on the surface. It was the famous director's view that murderers might just as easily be embodied in everyday, well-liked, small-town individuals as in urban criminals. The man in this story, by Gordon McDonell, is a pathological killer. Hitchcock's wife, Alma, worked on the screenplay along with Thornton Wilder.

Cotten, as usual, is superb as Uncle Charlie Oakley who comes from Philadelphia to visit his sister and her family in the little town of Santa

Joseph Cotten plays a sinister uncle in *Shadow of a Doubt*.

Rosa, Calif. (where the film was actually shot). But Oakley isn't just visiting…he is, in fact, on the run from the police: he's the "Merry Widow Murderer" who marries and murders rich widows.

Wright is niece "Charlie"—nicknamed for Uncle Charlie—and Collinge is Oakley's unsuspecting sister, Emma Newton. Wonacutt is the youngest daughter, Ann. Carey plays Jack Graham, the detective on the trail of the cross-country killer. The father is Joseph Newton (Travers) a reader of dime murder mysteries and Cronyn is his friend, Herbie Hawkins, an amateur sleuth.

Hitchcock builds on the concept of the two Charlies, innocence vs. evil, big city set against small community, two double-brandies at the Til 2 Bar by a waitress who has worked there for two weeks.

- Wonacutt, who plays Wright's little sister, was a local, the daughter of a grocer; Hitch found her and thought she'd be perfect for the part.
- While filming the funeral scene in Santa Rosa, men on the street, citizens not hired as extras, took their hats off as the coffin passed by.
- Hitch had wanted Joan Fontaine, with whom he had worked in *Rebecca*, but she was not available. He also wanted William Powell to play Uncle Charlie but MGM wouldn't release him.
- The house chosen as the Newton home was painted by the owner just prior to the crew arriving, much to Hitchcock's dismay; he had wanted the older, worn look, so he had the crew repaint it to make it look like it did when Hitchcock picked it.

Touch of Evil

1958, Universal, 108 minutes, B&W.
Producer: Albert Zugsmith. Director: Orson Welles.
Cast: Charlton Heston, Janet Leigh, Orson Welles, Marlene Dietrich, Joseph Calleia, Akim Tamiroff, Dennis Weaver.

> "…a stylistic triumph…an unqualified winner…"
> —Clive Hirschhorn

From its ingenious three minute-20 second opening shot to its closing scene of an obese Welles floating like a dead whale in the water, *Touch of Evil* is an hour-long course in moviemaking. Welles here teaches young filmmakers how to take a simple story, dress it up with curious characters, and design scenes so unique no one would dare go out for popcorn lest they miss a moment of pure excitement.

Welles not only brings his own rich talent to the job, but he also enlists the help of several personal friends, which is another reason why Orson could produce such an epoch. He talked Dietrich into showing up and, because he wrote the screenplay, gave her enough lines to force the studio to give her billing and increase her wages. Joseph Cotten, Zsa Zsa Gabor, Ray Collins, and Mercedes McCambridge all do cameos.

Based on Whit Masterson's pulp novel, *Badge of Evil*, the story is about a murder and narcotics investigation along the Mexican-U.S. bor-

Orson Welles as a bigoted and unscrupulous policeman in *Touch of Evil*.

der. Welles plays a vile, corrupt cop, putty-nosed, bloated police Capt. Hank Quinlan. Heston, with dyed black hair and mustache, is a Mexican narcotics agent, Mike Vargas. His new American bride is Susie—captured and terrorized by a gang of thugs led by McCambridge.

Dietrich is Tanya, gypsyesque Madame of a Mexican bordello. Gabor is owner of a striptease joint. Tamiroff is Uncle Joe Grandi, overseer of the town's vice. Calleia plays police Sgt. Pete Menzies who falsifies evidence for Quinlan. Collins is D.A. Adair and Cotten is the coroner. Weaver plays a nutty night manager at a rural motel where Susie is injected with drugs to discredit Vargas' attempt to nail Quinlan. Russell Metty did the photography, Henry Mancini wrote the Latin-beat music.

- When Heston was hired, Zugsmith still hadn't decided on a director, though he had signed Welles to act. Heston said, "Why not ask Orson to also direct? He's a damned good director you know."
- Zugsmith was also producing *The Incredible Shrinking Man* at the time. To provide a little extra money for Welles, he got Orson to do the voice-over for the trailer for his sci-fi film.
- It was shot in Venice, Calif.
- Leigh had a broken arm and filmed with the cast covered or with the cast off.

Vertigo

1958, Paramount, 128 minutes, Color.
Producer/Director: Alfred Hitchcock.
Cast: James Stewart, Kim Novak, Barbara Bel Geddes, Tom Helmore.

> "Many a Hitchcock buff will tell you that the master's masterpiece is *Vertigo*."
> —John Douglas Eames, *The Paramount Story*

James Stewart and Kim Novak between shots in the mission stables in *Vertigo*.

The best psychological mystery-thriller ever made, and the first major feature film in which the protagonist loses (he probably goes crazy), the heroine dies, and the villain gets away scot-free. David Thomson calls it, "the darkest of American movies."

Stewart is John "Scottie" Ferguson, a retired detective afraid of heights in a city with the steepest hills: San Francisco. He is obsessed by another man's wife, the mysterious and elusive Madeleine—played perfectly by the elegantly blonde Novak. In fact, she plays a dual role as Judy Barton, Madeleine's counterpart, a red-haired shop girl.

Madeleine apparently thinks she has been reincarnated; that many years ago she was a local madwoman named Carlotta Valdez. But Madeleine also dies, and Stewart's character can't get her out of his head. Hitchcock summed up the plot this way: "To put it plainly, the man wants to go to bed with a woman who's dead; he is indulging in a form of necrophilia."

Three technical elements add greatly to the film: Bernard Herrmann's haunting music, the photography of Robert Burks (both also worked on Hitch's other thriller classic *North By Northwest*), and John P. Fulton's special effects (he parted the Red Sea for DeMille's *The Ten Commandments*).

Helmore plays Gavin Elster, the husband who hires Ferguson to follow his wife. Bel Geddes is Midge, Ferguson's very concerned ex-girlfriend.

- Vera Miles was the original choice for the Novak roles but she got pregnant. Hitch signed her a year later for *Psycho.*
- Artist John Ferren did the "Nightmare Sequence" and Carlotta's portrait.
- Brian De Palma, the noted Hitchcock imitator, did a somewhat similar thriller in 1976 called *Obsession.*

Horror

The Birds

1963, Universal, 119 minutes, Color.
Producer/Director: Alfred Hitchcock.
Cast: Tippi Hedren, Rod Taylor, Jessica Tandy, Suzanne Pleshette, Veronica Cartwright, Ethel Griffies.

> "Now it's justifiably regarded as one of Hitchcock's true gems, an exciting, complex picture that is technically dazzling, extremely well written, and ideal for viewers who enjoy digging for themes."
> —Danny Peary, *Guide for the Film Fanatic*

Here's a horror film, sci-fi movie, and mystery-thriller all rolled into one—and, oddly, done without music but loaded with special effects. It is truly a cult film, just ask the people of the little town of Bodega Bay, Calif. where it was shot. People come there from all around the world to see the location where birds went crazy and attacked every human in sight; and they particularly want to see the little schoolhouse where dozens of children were terrorized—and, luckily, the building is still there. And so is The Tides restaurant where scenes were filmed.

The idea is from a short story by Daphne du Maurier with screenplay by mystery writer Evan Hunter. Why *do* the birds attack? Figuring out the motive is part of the fun of the film. Are the fates trying to teach mankind a lesson?—but what lesson? To be kinder to our feathered friends? Or is this the beginning of the end of the world?

Part of the mystery revolves around pretty playgirl Melanie Daniels (Hedren) who makes a car trip up the coast to a little village to drop off some caged lovebirds, a surprise gift for Mitch Brenner (Taylor), a man she met in a San Francisco bird shop. Birds suddenly seem to have it in for Melanie and attack her first. By the end of the film, they nearly kill her.

Tandy is Mitch's doting mother, Lydia. Cartwright is Cathy, the little sister. Pleshette plays Mitch's former girlfriend, Annie Hayworth. Griffies is Mrs. Bundy, the bird expert.

- Thousands of real birds were used along with bird hand puppets and about 400 trick photographic shots, some supervised by Disney artist Ub Iwerks (who helped create Mickey Mouse). The bird trainer was Ray Berwick.
- One of the most famous scenes is the high overhead shot of the exploding gas station pump; but there was no service station there—it was done in-studio. Now, however, a service station *has* been built at that site.
- Hedren got cut, scratched, and pecked during the attic attack scene in which a few birds were attached by nylon threads to her clothes. Hedren had to be hospitalized for several days due to exhaustion after shooting that scene.

Tippi Hedren and Rod Taylor in Hitchcock's *The Birds*.

- Tippi had nightmares about bird attacks for months after making the film.
- The Potter Schoolhouse was built in 1873 and remained a school until the 1960s; it was turned into a restaurant in the 70s, then an art gallery and more recently a private residence.
- Why do seagulls stand around without flying away? The crew fed them wheat mixed with whiskey!
- The originally planned ending was to have the Golden Gate Bridge lined with birds but the studio thought that was too shocking and nixed it.

The Bride of Frankenstein

1935, Universal, 75 minutes, B&W.
Producer: Carl Laemmle, Jr. Director: James Whale.
Cast: Boris Karloff, Colin Clive, Elsa Lanchester, Ernest Thesiger, Valerie Hobson, O.P. Heggie, Dwight Frye.

> "At once the best of the horror films and a gentle mockery of them, this elegant Gothic piece with its 18th century prologue is full of wry humor and pictorial delights."
> —Leslie Halliwell, *Halliwell's Filmgoer's Companion*

Frankenstein, the 1931 smash-hit, made millions—with the cost only a fraction of the gross profits, so the studio was eager for a sequel with Clive back as Dr. Henry Frankenstein and Karloff returning as the Monster. Two additional cast-members gave the script its singularity: Lanchester as the Monster's Bride and Thesiger as Dr. Pretorius, Henry's former tutor.

Pretorius reveals his own brand of created life forms, in miniature, kept in glass bottles. This skeletal madman very nearly steals the show, until bandaged Lanchester arrives—hissing and screeching with her hair slant-bundled on the back of her head, its white streaks on the sides suggestive of the wavy lightning charges that sparked her herky-jerky being to life.

Heggie plays a blind hermit who befriends the Monster and teaches him to talk. Hobson is Elizabeth, Mrs. Frankenstein (Mae Clarke played her in the original). Frye is Karl, the hunchback assistant. John Carradine has a bit part as a hunter. Jack Pierce did the famous make-up.

Elsa Lanchester and Boris Karloff in *The Bride of Frankenstein*.

- Lanchester has a dual role: in the prologue she plays the author of *Frankenstein,* Mary Wollstonecraft Shelley, wife of poet Percy Shelley (played by Douglas Walton). Lord Byron, also in the scene, is played by Gavin Gordon.
- To make the title work even better, screenwriters John Balderston and William Hurlbut considered letting Elizabeth get killed and having her brain put in the Monster's Bride, but they decided against it.
- Worried about typecasting, Clive, an alcoholic actor, wanted his character to die in this film and was upset that the studio changed its mind and re-shot footage allowing Henry to escape for the next sequel; though in the scene where the lab explodes, he can still be seen in the lower left of the frame.

Cat People

1942, RKO, 72 minutes, B&W.
Producer: Val Lewton. Director: Jacques Tourneur.
Cast: Simone Simon, Kent Smith, Jane Randolph, Tom Conway.

> "A classic."
> —Danny Peary, *Guide for the Film Fanatic*

Lewton wasn't big on horror films filled with shock scenes. When he saw a screenplay by DeWitt Bodeen that emphasized atmospherics over monsters, he knew he had a winner. RKO, a financially stressed studio, had authorized Lewton to make a horror flick but on a very strict budget. Lewton chose this psychological drama about a young Serbian woman who believes in a legend from the old country that some women are cursed to become a cat, actually a black panther, if their sexuality is aroused by the man she loves.

Lewton and director Tourneur brought in cinematographer Nicholas Musuraca to create foreboding and suspense by shadows, aided by the

excellent score of Roy Webb. Some of the RKO brass wanted more shots of creeping panthers but Lewton fought them; Tourneur was even fired at one point but Lewton had him reinstated.

Consequently, panther images are at a minimum. The result is one of the most imaginative horror films ever made, a film void of the usual blood and gore within the genre. The scary swimming pool scene in which the cat girl stalks a woman who leaps into the water for safety is one of the eeriest and most memorable in cinema history.

Simon stars as the doomed girl, Irena Dubrovna. Her new husband, Manhattan ship designer Oliver Reed, is played by Smith. Irena's rival is Alice Moore (Randolph), Oliver's attractive co-worker. Conway plays psychiatrist Dr. Judd who is drawn to Irena and decides fatefully to test the theory. The very cat-like woman in the café is Elizabeth Russell.

- The film was a surprise box-office hit and stayed in the theaters for several weeks. The picture made over $180,000.
- The staircase was the same one used in Orson Welles' *The Magnificent Ambersons*.
- Simon and Smith also starred in Lewton's sequel, *The Curse of the Cat People* (1944).

Dracula

1931, Universal, 84 minutes, B&W.
Producer: Carl Laemmle, Jr. Director: Tod Browning.
Cast: Bela Lugosi, Helen Chandler, Dwight Frye, David Manners, Edward Van Sloan.

> "Of its kind, of its folkloric popularity, the Hollywood *Dracula* is a classic. But Lugosi said that nobody on the set of its production was aware that they were making a kind of history."
> —*Horrors: A History of Horror Movies.*

Universal's biggest moneymaker of the year did so well that the studio decided to launch a whole series of horror films; probably the best decision Universal ever made. Memorabilia from the Universal monster series (*Dracula, Frankenstein, The Wolf Man, The Mummy*) still makes big bucks at the Universal amusement park.

Director Tod Browning (left) with Bela Lugosi and others on the set of *Dracula*.

Few actors have been so indelibly identified with one character: Lugosi is among that select group. For the role of the notorious vampire Count Dracula, which he played on Broadway, Lugosi's thick Hungarian accent actually helped rather than hurt. It added just the right erotic tone for lines like, "I am Dracula," "I never drink—wine," "Wolves—children of the night—what music they make."

Frye plays Renfield, the English real-estate man who becomes a prisoner in the Count's castle in Transylvania. Chandler is Minna Seward, the vampire's lovely victim. Manners is John Harker, Minna's lover. Van Sloan portrays Professor Van Helsing, the one who finally drives the stake through the vampire's heart.

The film's limited background music includes slight doses of Tchaikovsky's "Swan Lake." The photography is by Czech-born Karl Freund (*Metropolis*, *The Mummy*).

- Bram Stoker's *Dracula* was published as a gothic novel in 1897 and was first filmed as a German silent, *Nosferatu*, in 1922.
- Bela Blasko was born in Lugos, Hungary and created his stage name by adding an "i" to his birthplace.
- Lugosi, a drug addict, at the end appeared in several cheap horror films produced by Ed Wood; Johnny Depp stars in a film about those days—*Ed Wood* features Martin Landau as Lugosi.
- Lugosi left instructions that he be buried in his Dracula cape—and he was.

The Exorcist

1973, Warner Bros., 121 minutes, Color.
Producer: William Peter Blatty. Director: William Friedkin.
Cast: Ellen Burstyn, Linda Blair, Max Von Sydow, Jason Miller, Lee J. Cobb.

> "The scariest movie of all time."
> —*Entertainment Weekly.*

Not a film for the faint of heart, this horror classic, about demon possession of a young girl named Regan MacNeil (Blair), received an Academy Award nomination for Best Picture and won an Oscar for William Peter Blatty for Best Adapted Screenplay, based on his bestselling novel. Blatty said the script was based on a true story that he had heard and read about when he was a university student in 1949. A real exorcism had occurred in Mt. Rainer, Maryland involving a 13-year-old boy. There's a clue early in the film that Regan had been playing around with a Ouija Board and may have accidentally summoned up the evil spirit.

The film includes foul language and numerous scenes in which the demon causes an assortment of shocking scenes including masturbation, the girl's head turning completely around (done with a dummy face on a stick), bed shaking and levitation, and vomiting (actually green pea soup) into the face of a priest (Miller). The special effects all artfully under the control of sfx expert Marcel Vercoutere.

Burstyn plays the girl's mother, Von Sydow is the exorcist, and Cobb is a detective. Eileen Dietz, uncredited, is the stunt-double for Blair.

Swedish actor Max von Sydow portrays *The Exorcist*, William Friedkin's horror classic.

- Veteran actress Mercedes McCambridge was the voice of the demon.
- Father Dyer is played by Rev. William O'Malley, an actual priest who still teaches at Fordham University.
- The archaeological digs at the beginning of the film are the actual sites of Nineveh and the Tower of Babel in Iraq.
- The refrigerated bedroom, to show frosted breath, would drop to 40 below zero.
- Strangely, nine people working on the film died during production; there was also a major fire on one set that was never explained.

Frankenstein

1931, Universal, 71 minutes, B&W.
Producer: Carl Laemmle, Jr. Director: James Whale.
Cast: Boris Karloff, Colin Clive, Mae Clarke, John Boles, Dwight Frye, Edward Van Sloan, Marilyn Harris.

> "One of the most famous horror films and one which brought well-deserved fame to Boris Karloff as the monster (a role he was to play three times)."
> —Georges Sadoul, *Dictionary of Films*.

Hollywood's most popular monster made an international star of Karloff who deserved, but didn't get, an Oscar nomination for Best Ac-

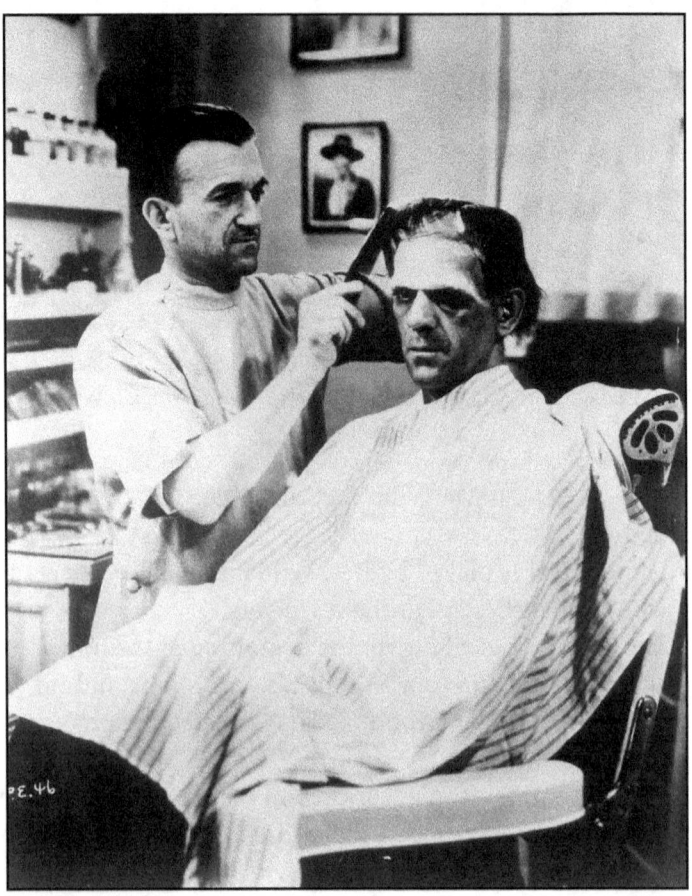

Jack Pierce applying make-up to Boris Karloff for *Frankenstein*.

tor; his heavy facial make-up and cumbersome costume forced him to act with his eyes and limited his head and body movements. (Ironically, Fredric March won the Oscar in 1931 for another horror hit: *Dr. Jekyll and Mr. Hyde*.) Bela Lugosi had turned down the monster role precisely because he felt the make-up and non-speaking role would inhibit his ability to act. Whale actually wanted Karloff anyway because of Boris' gaunt features.

Clive plays Baron Henry Frankenstein who, with the help of his assistant Fritz (Frye), built the creature from pieces of exhumed corpses. The man-made experiment is then energized by lightning. When the monster shows signs of life, Clive utters one of cinema's most famous lines: "It's alive!" Clarke is Elizabeth, Dr. Henry's horrified fiancé. Boles is their friend, Victor. Van Sloan is Dr. Waldman; Van Sloan, as himself, makes an appearance in the prologue warning the audience about what they're about to see.

The most controversial scene was cut in early releases, and then restored in edited form. It shows the monster meeting a little girl named Maria (Harris) alongside a pond. Oddly, the girl is not frightened by the creature and plays a game with him, tossing flowers into the water. He, too, likes her but gets excited when the flowers run out and, to continue the game, throws her into the water. Her death is an unintended accident but the villagers don't see it that way and pursue the monster into the hillside.

The monster's make-up took three hours for Jack Pierce to apply and nearly two hours to remove. The padded clothes, with legs stiffened by steel rods, added 60 lbs. to his weight. Karloff's footwear lifted him four inches off the ground and each boot weighed 18 lbs. His half-closed eyelids were weighted down with mortician's wax. There were also wire clamps in his mouth. His trousers were purposely cut short to make him look taller. The flat head was to give the impression that the skull had been sawed off at the top. Bolts, electrodes, in the neck were the finishing touch in one of the most amazing and familiar make-up jobs in movie history.

- In 1909, Edison made the first film version of the novel by Mary Wollstonecraft Shelley who was only 19 when she wrote the gothic classic about man's attempt to play God.
- Ken Strickfaden's fantastic laboratory equipment, producing profound electrical effects, was used again in Mel Brooks' comedy, *Young Frankenstein* (1974).

- Karloff reprised the role in 1935 with *The Bride of Frankenstein* and in 1939 with *Son of Frankenstein.*

King Kong

1933, RKO, 103 minutes, B&W.
Producers/Directors: Merian C. Cooper, Ernest B. Schoedsack.
Cast: Fay Wray, Robert Armstrong, Bruce Cabot.

> "...the greatest monster film of its time—or all time?"
> —*Horror Films.*

It was RKO's most important film because, without it, *Citizen Kane* wouldn't have been made; the studio was near bankruptcy until the lovable ape emerged to save the company; attendance records were broken at New York's Radio City Music Hall and at Grauman's Chinese Theater in Hollywood.

Willis O'Brien's marvelous stop-motion photography—using a bendable gorilla model—was responsible for making this cult classic. The film's finale, with Kong atop the Empire State Building defending himself against attacking biplanes, remains one of cinema's most enduring screen moments.

Carl Denham (Armstrong) hires a ship and crew and an out-of-work actress, Ann Darrow (Wray), to go to a far-off island, Skull Island, that Denham heard about where it was said a giant 50-ft. gorilla hides among frightened natives. But when Kong spots beautiful Ann, the creature falls in love with her and snatches her away from the intruders. First-mate Jack Driscoll (Cabot), who has also fallen for Ann, races after her in the jungle; a strange place, it turns out, that also is home to over-grown dinosaurs. The opportunity soon exists for Kong to battle these incongruous creatures to protect the girl. Using gas bombs, Denham and his men are able to save Ann and capture Kong. They take him back to New York to put him on display but chains don't hold him and he tears the place apart.

In the final death scene, Denham sums it up with one of the screen's most famous closing lines: "It was beauty killed the beast."

- Kong was made of rubber and wire, a model easy to bend; it was only 18 inches high.

- The hand that holds Wray was eight feet long with a steel bar inside operated up-and-down like a crane.
- Cooper and Schoedsack are the pilots in the main biplane.
- RKO stands for Radio-Keith-Orpheum.

The Night of The Hunter

1955, United Artists, 94 minutes, B&W.
Producer: Paul Gregory. Director: Charles Laughton.
Cast: Robert Mitchum, Lillian Gish, Shelley Winters, Billy Chapin, Sally Jane Bruce.

> "...one of the most frightening movies ever made."
> —Pauline Kael.

This haunting film was the only movie directed by the fine British actor Charles Laughton. It has been reported that he didn't do more because *The Night of the Hunter* was not well-received upon its original release.

Now film historians see it for what it is: a horror classic. So, we have only ourselves to blame; it's truly our loss, because this film is extraordinary on several levels: the plot (the script is by film critic James Agee), the cinematography (by Stanley Cortez who did *The Magnificent Ambersons*), the acting, and brilliant casting.

Mitchum, as the psychopathic preacher, is playing against type, since the main thrust of his career was as a he-man, good-guy lead (*Cape Fear*, in which he again dons the evil mask, was made after this film). But the casting of Gish as Rachel is a stroke of pure genius. Certainly, producer Gregory deserves accolades in all this. Rachel is a Bible-thumping, gun-toting Ohio River Valley farm woman who shelters and protects Depression-era homeless children. It's the appearance of Gish that supplies the key element—the clash of Good vs. Evil. And it is Gish, with her ties to D.W. Griffith and the silent-film morality plays, who gives the film its gripping fairy-tale atmo-

Robert Mitchum and Shelley Winters rehearsing a scene for *The Night of the Hunter*.

sphere. Harry Powell (Mitchum) is the embodiment of evil, even though he's a preacher. His mental instability most apparent by the words printed on his fingers, on one hand L-O-V-E, and on the other H-A-T-E. Powell had spent time in prison for car theft. While there, an inmate—just before his execution—told Powell about money he had stolen and left at the wife's house. Powell is determined to get it; even by marrying the widow, Willa Harper (Winters), just to find the stash. But it's Willa's children, John (Chapin), and Pearl (Bruce), who accidentally end up with the loot. Alone and forced to flee, the children escape into the night—hunted by a madman, eerily singing a hymn, "Leaning On The Everlasting Arms."

There are many memorable shots by Cortez, such as the time-lapses of the moon-crest as viewed through the barn window, the nature journey down the river under a starry sky, and most striking of all—the body in the old car in the bottom of the lake with the sun streaking through the water against fluttering sea-weed.

- A midget on a pony was used in place of the larger Mitchum on horseback in the long silhouette-shot across the meadow, because it was done in-studio and required more distance.
- Mitchum said it was his favorite of all the movies he acted in.
- Peter Graves, in a brief role, plays the inmate/father of the children. Graves was in *Airplane!* He was the brother of James Arness, star of TV's *Gunsmoke*.

Night of The Living Dead

1968, Image Ten, 96 minutes, B&W.
Producers: Russell Streiner, Karl Hardman. Director: George A. Romero.
Cast: Judith O'Dea, Duane Jones, Karl Hardman, Marilyn Eastman, Keith Wayne, Judith Ridley, Kyra Schon.

> "...the total effect of the film is of such a strip cartoon brought to life, but invested with a ferocious poetry."
> —*Horrors: A History of Horror Movies.*

The best low-budget movie ever made, now a cult horror classic. It cost $114,000 and grossed $12 million in the U.S. and $30 million worldwide! And several video producers took advantage of its public domain

A scene from the cult classic *Night of the Living Dead*.

status and made more money on it. Romero and company had failed to put a copyright notice at the start of the film and it fell into public domain.

Romero and co-writer John Russo started with a simple plot: recently deceased people re-energized due to a NASA rocket satellite emitting radiation toward the cemetery, somehow turning the dead into human flesh-eating zombies. So this isn't just another zombie movie; these grave-dwellers are cannibals seeking the flesh of living people to survive. In the search for victims, seven terrified people barricade themselves in a vacant country farmhouse. Two aspects make the film work: the appearance of the ghouls themselves and the gruesomeness of several scenes.

Adding to the uniqueness of the film is a black lead actor (Jones as Ben) playing opposite a white woman (O'Dea as Barbara). Others of the unknown cast are: Eastman (Helen), Wayne (Tom), Ridley (Judy), Schon (Karen), and Hardman, who also produced, as Harry.

- Chocolate syrup was used as blood.
- The zombie actors are eating cooked ham covered with chocolate syrup when pretending to devour bodies.

- The house used was about to be demolished anyway so the owner didn't care what the filmmakers did to the structure.
- The film was shot at Pittsburgh.
- Romero said he was greatly influenced by horror comics as a kid.
- Romero made two color sequels: *Dawn of the Dead* (1978) and *Day of the Dead* (1985).

Psycho

1960, Paramount, 109 minutes, B&W.
Producer/Director: Alfred Hitchcock.
Cast: Anthony Perkins, Janet Leigh, Vera Miles, Martin Balsam, John Gavin.

> "Scenes of the ferocious stabbing in a shower…and the later killing of an investigator…are still regarded as classics in the genre."
> —John Douglas Eames, *The Paramount Story*

For some moviegoers, it's their most memorable film and among that group it may be the one film that they'd like to forget. After release of the horror-thriller, Hitchcock said he received many letters from angry viewers saying they had not slept in weeks, victimized by nightmares and even fear of the shower. It truly is one of cinema's most shocking sequences: a pretty woman knifed to death in a motel shower by a shadowy figure whose blade even slashes through the shower curtain. It is particularly shocking since the victim is the film's female star (Leigh) who dies within the first 45 minutes of the movie, something that just wasn't done in those days. Soon the audience settles down and puts its faith in an impregnable detective, Milton Arbogast (Balsam), who—we feel—will surely get to the bottom of this horrible crime. But Hitch shocks us again when the insurance investigator is stabbed to death by a mysterious woman (viewed in a dramatic overhead shot) followed by a close-up of the male victim stumbling backward down a flight of stairs inside a foreboding old house. Nowadays, such scenes are the usual fare in modern "slasher movies" but that's just the point: *Psycho* was first and is the most copied horror-thriller of all time.

The ominous old house on the hill and the silhouette of Anthony Perkins in *Psycho*.

For a lot of us, *Psycho* was our introduction to screen violence, psychopaths, schizophrenia, the Oedipus complex, and even taxidermy.

The story is from Robert Bloch's novel. Hitchcock received an Academy Award nomination for Best Director and Leigh, as Marion Crane, got nominated for Best Supporting Actress. Miles plays her sister, Lila. Gavin is Marion's lover, Sam Loomis. And Perkins has one of the choicest roles in film history as mentally-warped Norman Bates, manager of the Bates Motel.

- The shower scene, while just 45 seconds long, uses 78 pieces of film. No stab wounds are visible. The sequence took a week to shoot.
- Leigh said she did 71 takes. She wore a flesh-colored molding that began to wash away at about the 68th take. Hitchcock asked her if she wanted to stop to reapply the make-up; tired, she said "Go ahead." Janet was nude by the final shot.
- Hitchcock, host of his popular "Alfred Hitchcock Presents" TV program, used his television crew at a cost of just $800,000. The film made a profit of $15 million.

- No one was allowed to be seated in the theater after the film started. Ads also urged people who had seen the film not to divulge the story to their friends.

Son of Frankenstein

1939, Universal, 94 minutes, B&W.
Producer/Director: Rowland V. Lee.
Cast: Basil Rathbone, Boris Karloff, Bela Lugosi, Lionel Atwill, Josephine Hutchinson, Donnie Dunagan.

> "Well mounted…Universal has given 'A' production layout to the thriller in all departments."
>
> —*Variety.*

Karloff's third and final feature portrayal of the Frankenstein Monster. While there are fine performances all-around, there are two stand-outs: Lugosi and Atwill. You have to look closely to realize it's Lugosi—excellent

Boris Karloff, Bela Lugosi and Basil Rathbone in *Son of Frankenstein*.

as Ygor, the hunchback assistant; and Atwill, as police inspector Krogh, is memorable for his lost arm "torn out by the roots" by the Monster.

It's been 25 years since the infamous Dr. Frankenstein has died. Now his son, Baron Wolf von Frankenstein (Rathbone), returns to the family castle with his wife, Elsa (Hutchinson), and young son (Dunagan).

Ygor, a mad shepherd, has found the Monster half-alive and brings him to the Baron for strengthening. The Baron is fascinated by the possibility of restoring the Monster to clear his father's name, to show the world that his father wasn't really crazy.

- Jack Pierce took four hours each day to turn Karloff into the Monster.
- Claude Rains was considered for the role of Wolf.
- Lee kept increasing Lugosi's part so Bela could make more money but studio reps didn't buy it, and knowing Lugosi badly needed money, only paid the horror star $600 a week.
- In 1940, Karloff appeared as the Monster at a celebrity baseball game in Hollywood—as the umpire!

The Wolf Man

1941, Universal, 70 minutes, B&W.
Producer/Director: George Waggner.
Cast: Lon Chaney, Jr., Claude Rains, Evelyn Ankers, Warren William, Ralph Bellamy, Bela Lugosi, Maria Ouspenskaya, Patric Knowles.

> "One of the finest horror films ever made."
> —Leonard Maltin.

While this was not the first werewolf movie at the studio (*Werewolf of London* with Henry Hull was the first in 1935), this film is the beginning of one of the more popular horror film characters of Universal: The Wolf Man, played by Chaney, son of the great silent screen star, would reappear in four more films: *Frankenstein Meets the Wolf Man, House of Frankenstein, House of Dracula, Abbott and Costello Meet Frankenstein.*

Larry Talbot, after 18 years, returns to Talbot Castle to help his father run the estate, but becomes cursed when he is bitten by a werewolf. Gwen (Ankers), a pretty shop girl, meets Talbot and is overcome about

Lon Chaney, Jr. as *The Wolf Man*.

his dilemma and tries to help him. Rains (Universal's *The Invisible Man*) plays Larry's father, Sir John Talbot. Bellamy portrays police investigator Montford, William is psychiatrist Dr. Lloyd, and Knowles is Gwen's fiancé Frank Andrews.

A man who will become a werewolf has a pentagram (a five-pointed star in a circle) in the palm of his hand and can only be killed by a silver wolfhead cane, a silver knife, or a silver bullet. Lugosi, another of Universal's horror stars, plays a fortune teller and werewolf/son of Maleva (Ouspenskaya), the old gypsy woman who is well aware of the werewolf curse. "Even a man who is pure at heart and says his prayers by night, may become a wolf when the wolfbane blooms and the autumn moon is bright."

- Jack Pierce took six hours to apply Chaney's make-up.
- In the face transformation, there are 17 face shots in a continuous dissolve.

- This was not an old gypsy folk legend; screenwriter Curt Siodmak admitted he made it all up.
- The music, by Charles Previn, Frank Skinner and Hans Salter, was used in other Universal horror films.
- It was one of Universal's top grossing films of 1942.
- Chaney was very proud of his Wolf Man character which he felt was the highlight of his career.

Science Fiction

Blade Runner

1982, Ladd Co./Warner Bros., 118 minutes, Color.
Producer: Michael Deeley. Director: Ridley Scott.
Cast: Harrison Ford, Rutger Hauer, Sean Young, Edward James Olmos, Darryl Hannah, William Sanderson, Joe Turkel, Joanna Cassidy, M. Emmet Walsh, Brion James.

> "…the world of *Blade Runner* has undeniably become one of the visual touchstones of modern movies."
> —Roger Ebert, *Roger Ebert's Video Companion*

A chilling cult classic that's a throwback to *Metropolis* and Raymond Chandler detective movies. Based on Philip K. Dick's *Do Androids Dream of Electric Sheep?* Scott's futuristic sci-fi thriller shows a decayed world of aging, unhealthy people in dilapidated Los Angeles in 2019. It's an environment of acid rain, crowded and ethnically dense streets, deserted retrofitted buildings, neon signs, and flying police cruisers that spin off into gloomy skies; the rich have already fled to Earth's "off-worlds."

Ford is Deckard, a blade runner, a burned-out bounty hunter who chases outlaw replicants—near-human androids, illegal slave labor that have gone astray. Turkel is Tyrell, the master robot-builder; Young is Rachael, the most perfect replicant of all and so beautiful that Deckard falls in love with her. Dutch actor Hauer is Roy Batty, a lead replicant who has returned to find his maker to convince Tyrell to allow him to extend his life. Batty and Deckard engage in an unforgettable man vs. machine finale. Hannah plays Pris, also a replicant and Roy's somersaulting girlfriend.

Daryl Hannah and Rutger Hauer as replicants in *Blade Runner*.

Also with Olmos as Gaff, a secret police tracker; Walsh as Bryant, the blade runner boss; Sanderson as Sebastian, a genetic scientist; James as Leon, and Cassidy as Zhora, a violent snake-charming replicant.

The music is by Vangelis. Photography by Jordan Cronenweth. The special effects are in the capable hands of Douglas Trumbull and Richard Yurevich, model-maker Mark Stetson, conceptual artist Syd Mead, and set designer Laurence G. Paull; they stacked together bits and pieces from several previous films to create a new and horrific future world.

- Debbie Harry was the original choice to play Pris.
- Several stars were considered for the lead, including Dustin Hoffman, Sean Connery, Jack Nicholson, Clint Eastwood, and Arnold Schwarzenegger.

- A male gymnast served as a stunt double for Hannah's attack on Deckard.
- Stunt double Lee Pulford, not Cassidy, is really the one crashing through the glass.
- Joanna's snake is real, in fact, it belonged to her!
- It was shot mostly on the old New York set at Burbank Studios.

Close Encounters of The Third Kind

1977, Columbia, 135 minutes, Color.
Producers: Julia Phillips, Michael Phillips; Director: Steven Spielberg.
Cast: Richard Dreyfuss, Melinda Dillon, Francois Truffaut, Teri Garr, Cary Guffey, Bob Balaban.

> "The last 40 minutes of *Close Encounters* give it a historic place in cinema history. The screen lights up with stunning visual and aural sensations. The night skies, blinking lights, and colored shapes offer an extraordinary psychedelic light show. It is a breathtaking sequence..."
> —*An Introduction to American Movies.*

The movie for UFO buffs, about the possibility of life elsewhere in the universe, is a dazzling examination of the UFO phenomena. The science-fiction extravaganza, with a thrilling score by John Williams, received eight Academy Award nominations and won two Oscars: Best Cinematography (Vilmos Zsigmond) and Best Sound Effects Editing; the excellent special effects are by Douglas Trumbull (*2001: A Space Odyssey*).

Roy Neary (Dreyfuss), a utility worker in Indiana, sees a flying saucer in the night sky and his life is changed forever. His wife, Ronnie (Garr), is confused and not able to understand the change taking place in her husband. Roy, however, finds solace with Jillian Guiler (Dillon) who also experienced the strange craft. In fact, her adorable little boy, Barry (Guffey), was abducted by the aliens in the UFO.

The film is also a study in government cover-up, misinformation, and diversion. Once scientists get word that the aliens are trying to meet with humans at Devil's Tower, Wyoming, Washington develops a plan to keep the public away from the site. However, Roy and Jilian are inexorably drawn to the area beyond their will and break through the military bar-

A scene from the finale of *Close Encounters of the Third Kind*.

rier to finally make contact with the outer-space visitors.

Truffaut portrays French UFO investigator Lacombe, based on a real ufologist, Jacques Vallee. Balaban is Lacombe's assistant.

- UFO investigator J. Allen Hynek (who appears in a shot at the end—he's the one with the pipe and goatee) coined the phrase that became the title of the movie. A close encounter of the first kind is a UFO sighting, the second kind is a sighting that leaves physical evidence, and the third kind is a confrontation with or abduction by aliens.
- It was partly shot in an abandoned dirigible hanger in Mobile, Alabama because they couldn't find a soundstage big enough.
- The alien children are really kids, girls, in rubber suits. Spielberg also wanted them on roller skates for a gliding effect but they kept falling down.

The Day the Earth Stood Still

1951, 20th Century-Fox, 92 minutes, B&W.
Producer: Julian Blaustein. Director: Robert Wise.
Cast: Michael Rennie, Patricia Neal, Sam Jaffe, Lock Martin, Billy Gray.

"One of the finest science-fiction movies ever made...The score by Bernard Herrmann has become a classic and even theologians have studied the peculiar Jesus Christ symbolism and Biblical analogy that permeate the film."
—*John Stanley's Creature Features Movie Guide.*

A flying saucer is spotted by numerous countries as the craft flies around the world, soon coming to rest in a baseball field on the Washington Mall. Stepping outside is a space-suited being with a human-like body. With him is a menacing giant in what appears to be chrome-plated attire. What do they want? Are they friend or foe?

The alien visitor eventually explains to a scientist, Professor Dr. Barnhardt (Jaffe), that he has traveled 250 million miles to warn the Earth

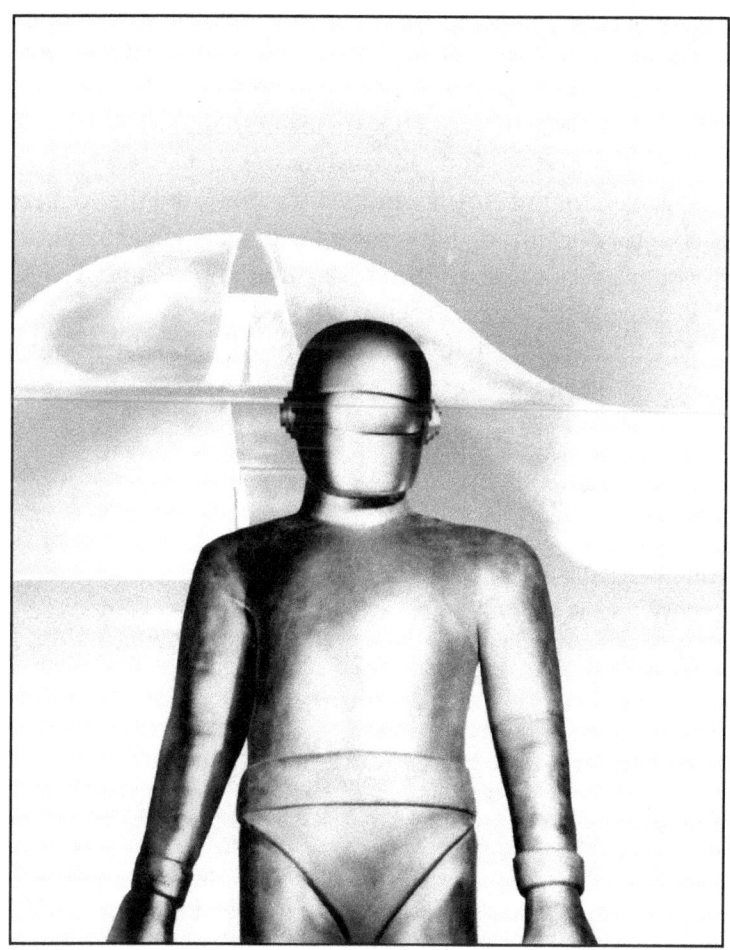

The alien robot Gort in *The Day the Earth Stood Still.*

that they must cease wars and extinguish all nuclear weapons—or he will allow his powerful 7-foot-7 robot, Gort (Martin), to destroy this planet… out of fear that our destructive ways will spread beyond our galaxy.

The alien, named Klaatu (Rennie), decides to secretly mingle among people to learn more about Earth. He uses the name Carpenter to rent a place in a rooming house and is befriended by a single mom, Helen Benson (Neal), and her young son, Bobby (Gray). Klaatu, in the end, lets the people of Earth think about their situation as he and his craft leave in peace.

While the plot may seem rather simplistic and unbelievable, it worked extremely well in its day because of the flying saucer scare (the Roswell case had happened in 1947), the beginning of the cold war, and the advent of atomic weapons (1945). Lending an air of credibility to the story were the appearance of several noted news broadcasters: H.V. Kaltenborn, Drew Pearson, Elmer Davis and Gabriel Heatter. Fred Sersen created the special effects including Gort's laser-beam attacks on the military's weapons.

- J. Lockard Martin was a doorman at Grauman's Chinese Theater in Hollywood when discovered for the part.
- Writer Edmund North admitted that he based the concept on the story of Christ, though Wise and Blaustein apparently were not aware of the connection. North used the name "Carpenter" because Jesus was a carpenter.
- Klaatu! Barada! Nikto! Those are the three operative words Neal utters to halt the advancing robot.

Invasion of The Body Snatchers

1956, Allied Artists, 80 minutes, B&W.
Producer: Walter Wanger. Director: Don Siegel.
Cast: Kevin McCarthy, Dana Wynter, King Donovan, Carolyn Jones, Larry Gates.

> "One of the all-time great science-fiction films."
> —Roger Ebert

Is the town of Santa Mira going nuts? Or as its psychiatrist, Dr. Dan Kaufman (Gates), suggests, "It's an epidemic of mass hysteria." Is that really the case? Or have aliens from another planet secretly arrived, via space pods, and begun to take over the bodies of residents in the little California community? General practitioner Dr. Miles Bennel (McCarthy) didn't think so at first but every day he's finding evidence that an invasion *is* taking place.

Once the invaders take over a person, the real body is destroyed and replaced by a new body, even though something is missing—character, love, feelings—a soul? Bennel and his girlfriend, Becky Driscoll (Wynter), become terribly frightened to see people are changing all around them; a person they knew 24 hours earlier is now acting differently, void of personality, though the body looks the same. The screenplay for this box-office hit is by Dan Mainwaring, based on Jack Finney's magazine story "The Body Snatchers."

Donovan and Jones play Jack and Theodora, friends of the protagonists. Sam Peckinpah, who went on to direct *The Wild Bunch,* has a bit part as Charlie, the gas-meter reader. Three other elements come together to make this the cult classic that it is: Carmen Dragon's music, Milt Rice's simple but effective special effects, and the photography of Ellsworth Fredericks.

Dana Wynter, King Donovan, Carolyn Jones and Kevin McCarthy in *Invasion of the Body Snatchers.*

- Made after the 1954 Army-McCarthy anti-Communist hearings, some critics saw the film as an allegory of brainwashing from within society. Ironically, the lead actor's name is McCarthy.
- The studio changed the ending to be more upbeat. Originally, Miles was running down the highway yelling at cars, "You're next! You're next!" McCarthy does that, in a cameo, in Philip Kaufman's 1978 remake, which changes the setting from Santa Mira to San Francisco.
- The center of Santa Mira is really the intersection of Beachwood and Belden near the famous Hollywood sign.
- The tunnel scene was filmed at Bronson Canyon Cave in Griffith Park.

Jurassic Park

1993, Universal, 127 minutes, Color.
Producers: Kathleen Kennedy, Gerald R. Molen; Director: Steven Spielberg.
Cast: Sam Neill, Laura Dern, Jeff Goldblum, Richard Attenborough, Ariana Richards, Joseph Mazzello.

> "The dinosaurs of *Jurassic Park* live and breathe. They will astonish you—and scare the heck out of you."
> —Jack Garner, *Gannett News Service*.

One of the best sci-fi films and one of the biggest blockbusters of all time: $51 million to make, grossing $850 million by the end of 1993. Spielberg said he didn't want to take on the project unless he could be assured that the dinosaurs would look real; they do—*very* real. The Oscar folks thought so, too, and gave the creative team the Academy Award for Best Visual Effects plus the Oscars for Best Sound and Sound Effects Editing. The dinosaurs are a combination of computer-generated models and animatronics.

Based on the book by Michael Crichton, it's all about a rich eccentric, John Hammond (Attenborough), who builds a theme park on an island off Costa Rica with live dinosaurs—created by DNA research scientists. How? The DNA was found in the blood contained in fossilized mosqui-

toes. But, as fate would have it, the high-tech security system fails and the formerly-extinct creatures run amok.

The little group that ends up battling the T-rexes and other dinos are: paleontologist Dr. Alan Grant (Neill), his girlfriend and botanist Dr. Ellie Sattler (Dern), and scientist Ian Malcolm (Goldberg). Adding to the anxiety are Hammond's grandkids: 12-year-old Lex (Richards) and her little brother Tim (Mazzello).

- George Lucas' Industrial Light and Magic pieced all the sfx together; and though the film runs over two hours, the dinosaurs are on-screen for only 15 minutes: nine minutes of Stan Winston's animatronics and six minutes of ILM's CGI.
- Universal paid Crichton $2 million for rights to the novel.
- The film was shot in Kauai, Hawaii.

Planet of The Apes

1968, 20th Century-Fox, 112 minutes, Color.
Producer: Arthur P. Jacobs. Director: Franklin J. Schaffner.
Cast: Charlton Heston, Linda Harrison, Roddy McDowall, Kim Hunter, Maurice Evans, James Whitmore.

> "The year 1968 was an important year in Sf (sci-fi) history. The final preparations for America's moon landing stepped up Hollywood's interest in Sf movies...Early in the year, 20th Century-Fox premiered the extremely popular *Planet of the Apes*."
> —*Great Science Fiction Films.*

Make-up artist John Chambers won a Special Academy Award for his ingenuously conceived ape creations for this cult film, based on the novel "Monkey Planet" by Pierre Boulle. Rod Serling (TV's *Twilight Zone*) and Michael Wilson (*Lawrence of Arabia*) wrote the screenplay for this box-office hit. Utilizing the time-warp concept, the story shows how fear of knowledge and racial discrimination can destroy a society.

"Take your stinking paws off me, you damned dirty ape!" That's the now memorable line spoken by Heston as astronaut George Taylor, who crash-lands his spaceship on an unknown planet and is taken prisoner by apes, creatures who have evolved to such an extent that they can talk—and rule! Harrison plays Nova, a beautiful girl on this strange planet: Is she the last of humans who may have once governed this world?

Cornelius, the main chimpanzee scientist, is played by McDowall. Hunter is Dr. Zira, Evans portrays Dr. Zaius, and Whitmore is the President of the Assembly.

- It took three hours to apply the ape make-up and some actors got sick because the suits were so hot. Meals were liquid, like soups and sodas, drunk through straws because they had to keep the make-up on. Chambers had a make-up team of 80 people.
- Edward G. Robinson did a test as Zaius but eventually turned down the part for health reasons. But the test was very helpful for the producer and director to see how the ape get-up would look with a talented actor inside.

Charlton Heston, Linda Harrison and captors in *Planet of the Apes*.

- Ingrid Bergman turned down the role of Zira and later regretted doing so.
- Famous "little people" Billy Curtis and Jerry Maren were child apes.
- Hollywood reporters James Bacon and Army Archerd donned ape suits and appeared in the film as extras.
- Serling wrote the famous last scene, shot on Malibu with the Statue of Liberty as a matte painting.
- This was the first of five *Apes* movies.

Star Wars

1977, 20th Century-Fox/Lucasfilm, 121 minutes, Color.
Producer: Gary Kurtz. Director: George Lucas.
Cast: Mark Hamill, Harrison Ford, Carrie Fisher, Alec Guinness, Peter Cushing, David Prowse, Anthony Daniels, Kenny Baker, Peter Mayhew, James Earl Jones.

> "A great work of popular art, fully deserving the riches it has reaped."
> —*TIME*.

Lucas, inspired by the *Flash Gordon* movie serial and comic book future-hero Buck Rogers, created a super-colossal space-fantasy/adventure series that set a whole new standard for blockbusters. Like the old serials of the 30s and 40s, the film begins with an explanation—with the words crawling up into the stratosphere: *A long time ago in a galaxy far, far away...*

This was the first of a six-part series of films though it is really Episode Four; the next five in the series also made big bucks at the box-office and in video/DVD sales. Furthermore, memorabilia connected with the series is among the most sought-after collectibles. And it was the first sci-fi film to clean-up at the Academy Awards—winning eight Oscars, plus a Special Technical Oscar for John Dykstra's computerized camera. Among the Oscars: John Williams for his now very familiar and popular score and Ben Burtt for Special Effects. The film was also nominated for Best Picture.

Hamill stars as Luke Skywalker, a farmer's son-turned-warrior, gathering forces (and "The Force") to fight the evil ruler of the Imperial Galactic Empire: Grand Moff Tarkin (Cushing) and his henchman, iron-masked Lord Darth Vader (Prowse with the voice of Jones). On Luke's team are Princess Leia Organa (Fisher) and mercenary Han Solo (Ford), captain of the Millennium Falcon. Their helpers are a shaggy dog-like creature named Chewbacca (Mayhew) and a pair of funny robotic companions, R2-D2 (Daniels) and C-3PO (Baker). Guinness plays the mysterious Obi-Wan "Ben" Kenobi.

Subsequent entries in the series: *The Empire Strikes Back, Return of the Jedi, The Phantom Menace, Attack of the Clones, Revenge of the Sith.*

- The nearly $10 million spent to make the movie was recovered at the box-office on the first day of release.
- Mayhew is 7'2" tall.
- There are 365 sfx shots in the film.
- The film was later given a second part of the title to distinguish it from the two sequels and three prequels: *A New Hope*.
- Dogfights from *The Battle of Britain* were used as guides for the spacecraft battles.

Mark Hamill, Carrie Fisher, Peter Mayhew (Chewbacca) and Harrison Ford in a publicity pose for *Star Wars*. © Lucasfilm LTD.

The Thing (From Another World)

1951, RKO, 81 minutes, B&W.
Producer: Howard Hawks. Director: Christian Nyby.
Cast: Kenneth Tobey, Margaret Sheridan, James Arness, Robert Cornthwaite, Douglas Spencer, George Fenneman, James Young.

> "In America, at least, *The Thing* is the only science-fiction film that *every* serious sf fan—including today's sf filmmakers—loves and agrees is a masterpiece, the first masterpiece of the fifties sci-fi cycle. In fact, to qualify as a true fan of the genre, one must see this film many times."
>
> —Danny Peary.

This great sci-fi cult film had its enormous opening success due to the fact that it was released at the crest of the flying saucer craze. In 1947, pilot Kenneth Arnold coined the term "flying saucer" when he reported seeing nine shiny spacecraft looking like upside-down saucers in the skies over the Pacific Northwest. That incident was followed that year with the

report of a spacecraft down near Roswell, New Mexico. Numerous other reports followed. John W. Campbell's story "Who Goes There?" became the perfect fodder for a movie and Hawks, normally a maker of Westerns, ran with the idea and it paid off. Hawks' Winchester Pictures, with film editor Nyby directing, gave the film a sort of documentary flavor, giving the audience reason to take such a story very seriously.

A military-scientific team, led by Capt. Pat Hendry (Tobey), a prototype of James Kirk, is assigned to investigate a crashed craft near a polar outpost in the Arctic Circle. Arriving, they can see the outline buried under the ice—and when they mark it off, it's circular! Embedded next to the craft is the figure of a man-sized creature. The expedition team cuts out a large chunk of ice surrounding the frozen being and transports it to their camp—and here's where the fun begins. The vegetable-like spaceman comes alive and sets about making life miserable for the explorers. Composer Dmitri Tiomkin uses a therein for the uncanny sounds embellishing the appearance of the eight-foot alien (Arness).

Among those trying to solve the mystery of "the thing" is a lovely scientific investigator named Nikki (Sheridan), and Dr. Carrington (Cornthwaite), Dr. Redding (Fenneman), Lt. Eddie Dykes (Young), and a newspaperman they call Scotty (Spencer).

- There was a long debate after release of the film as to whether Hawks or Nyby actually directed. Arness, in a more recent interview, said while Hawks was often on the set, Nyby did direct the movie.
- Portions were filmed in Glacier National Park and at an ice house in Los Angeles.
- Make-up man Lee Greenway worked on creature design for nearly six months prior to shooting. A frustrated Hawks finally told him to make the head somewhat like the Frankenstein monster, and they did.
- Veteran stuntman Tom Steele (who starred in the serial *The Masked Marvel*) stood in for Arness in the fire scene; Steele wore an asbestos suit.
- Arness later starred as Matt Dillon in TV's *Gunsmoke* and Fenneman was the announcer-foil on Groucho Marx's TV quiz show *You Bet Your Life*.

The Time Machine

1960, MGM, 103 minutes, Color.
Producer/Director: George Pal.
Cast: Rod Taylor, Yvette Mimieux, Alan Young.

> "An inventive, exciting, fanciful thriller."
> —*The New York Times*.

Before the film begins, ahead of the titles/credits, clocks of all sorts are seen floating through space. The story begins in 1899 and is told in flashback as George, an English inventor, informs a group of stunned associates that he had just experienced time travel.

Based on the H.G. Wells novel, George (Taylor) sits in his time machine, built like a large sled but with porcelain dials, colored lights, and a large spinning disc resembling a computer/satellite dish situated behind the padded seat. Pushing all the right buttons and levers, he travels through the fourth dimension into the future, past World War I, World War II and a nuclear war and subsequent volcanic eruption, coming to rest thousands of years into the future.

Rod Taylor in *The Time Machine*.

George finds a disturbing scene, a distant civilization of the unfeeling, uneducated Elois serving the underground mutants, the cannibalistic Morlocks. But he also finds love among the Eloi in the form of a beautiful young woman named Weena (Mimieux). He eventually goes back to his former home where he tells his friends about his amazing excursion, but also finds his relationship with Weena was too strong and thus returns to the future; but before leaving he removes three books off his shelf to take with him—which ones we don't know. (As Filby comments, which ones would *you* take?)

The film won the Oscar for Best Visual Effects (Gene Warren, Tim Baer). Young has a dual role as George's doubting friend David Filby and Filby's son James.

- The lava in the volcano scene was oatmeal mixed with red and orange food coloring.
- If you look closely at the plaque on the control panel you'll find it reads, "Manufactured by H. George Wells."
- Pal made puppet-animated featurettes in the 40s called Puppetoons. He also made three other sci-fi films: *Destination Moon, When Worlds Collide,* and *The War of the Worlds.*

2001: A Space Odyssey

1968, MGM, 139 minutes, Color, US/UK.
Producer/Director: Stanley Kubrick.
Cast: Keir Dullea, Gary Lockwood, Douglas Rain, William Sylvester.

> "A uniquely poetic piece of science-fiction, hypnotically entertaining; technically and imaginatively it is staggering."
> —*The New Yorker.*

Probably the most thought-provoking sci-fi film ever made. *2001,* in an oblique sort of way, probes the meaning of life and causes the audience to evoke answers for the universe. The script is by Kubrick and Arthur C. Clarke from whose short story, "The Sentinel" the movie is based.

The film won the Oscar for Best Special Visual Effects (Douglas Trumbull) and deserved, but didn't get, a nomination for Best Picture. Originally produced in Cinerama (later in CinemaScope/35mm), with

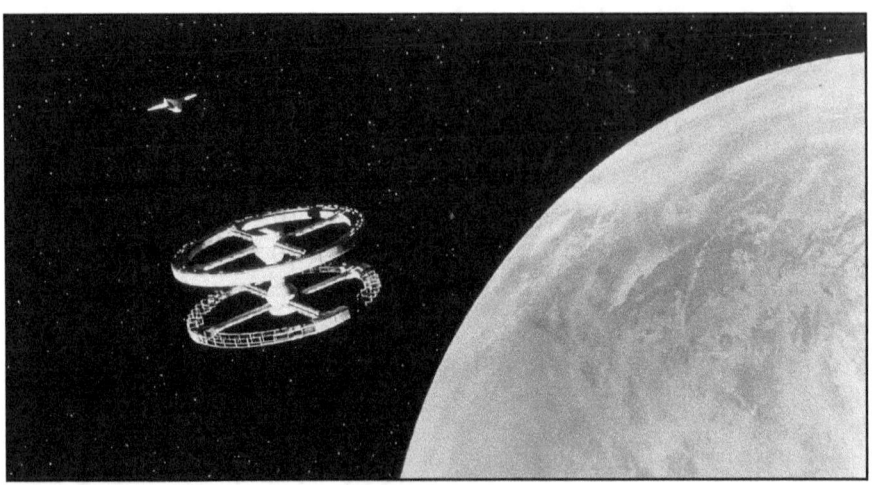

Space Shuttle Five orbiting 200 miles above the Earth in *2001: A Space Odyssey*.

photography by Geoffrey Unsworth, the film introduces a mysterious black monolith and concludes with a light show—then a Star Child—in the blackness of outer space. Kubrick very effectively uses "Also Sprach Zarathustra" and Strauss' "Blue Danube Waltz" as music background. The movie became a favorite of the 60s "flower children" because of its Stargate sequence: billed as "the ultimate trip."

What's the secret of the floating monolith? Clarke said, "If you understand *2001* completely, we failed. We wanted to raise far more questions than we answered." Nonetheless, much speculation saw the monolith as an envoy, hidden away on the moon, waiting for man's expansiveness—and once achieved, it became the open door for humans to go beyond the realm to finally make contact with the Creative Spirit. Beyond that, your guess is as good as anybody's.

Heading up the *Discovery* spacecraft's investigative journey to Jupiter are Dave Bowman (Dullea) and Frank Poole (Lockwood). Sylvester is Dr. Heywood Floyd. Rain, a Canadian actor, is the voice of the HAL 9000 computer that thinks it can think for itself. Dave's unhooking of the computer's brain, with HAL singing "Daisy, I'm Half Crazy," is one of the screen's eeriest moments.

- The first dialogue we hear is spoken by a stewardess over 25 minutes into the picture and there is no dialogue in the last 23 minutes of the film.
- Kubrick himself supplied the breathing in the spacesuits.

- The little girl playing the daughter of Dr. Floyd on the videophone is Vivian, Kubrick's daughter.
- The title was chosen because it was the first year of the new century and the beginning of the next millennium.

War of The Worlds

1953, Paramount, 85 minutes, Color.
Producer: George Pal. Director: Byron Haskin.
Cast: Gene Barry, Ann Robinson, Les Tremayne, Robert Cornthwaite, Lewis Martin, Paul Frees, Cedric Hardwicke.

> "(E)xceptional visual and aural effects."
> —John Douglas Eames, *The Paramount Story*

In 1938, Orson Welles gained international fame when he electrified the vast radio audience with his dramatization of H.G. Wells' "The War of the Worlds," which a lot of listeners were convinced was the real thing—

The invasion of the Earth by Martian spaceships in *The War of the Worlds*.

an invasion by aliens from the planet Mars! Fifteen years later, filmmaker George Pal decided to turn the work into a movie and approached Orson to get involved, but Welles was overseas making a series of pictures in Italy, France, and England. So he was unavailable (which is too bad, his voice as narrator would have been the perfect added punch). Consequently, Pal turned that task over to Sir Cedric Hardwicke, who also did an admirable job.

Oddly, it was Cecil B. DeMille, the Paramount giant, who had pressed for the studio to do the film but he was too busy with *The Greatest Show On Earth* plus making preparations for *The Ten Commandments*. So he suggested Pal who already had two sci-fi hits under his belt, *Destination Moon* and *When Worlds Collide*.

Pal had wanted part of the film shot in 3-D but the studio thought it would be too costly. Most of the budget was already targeted for special effects so the stars wouldn't see big salaries. (The film would go on to win the Oscar for special visual effects/editing.) Pal searched about for an inexpensive lead actor with a fair amount of audience recognition and found him in TV, as "Bat Masterson." Gene Barry was cast as Dr. Clayton Forrester, the handsome scientist who confronts the invaders.

Robinson is Forrester's new female companion, Sylvia Van Buren. Tremayne plays Major-General Mann. Cornthwaite (who played a scientist in *The Thing*) is Dr. Pryor. Martin is Pastor Matthew Collins who tries to reason with the aliens and loses his life in the process. Frees, a broadcaster by trade, plays the radio announcer.

- As a tribute from Pal to DeMille, C.B.'s *Samson and Delilah* is on the theater marquee.
- Robinson hated the hair-do; it was a wig.
- The H.G. Wells estate was so happy with the film that they gave permission for Pal to do *The Time Machine*.

War Films

All Quiet on The Western Front

1930, Universal, 140 minutes, B&W.
Producer: Carl Laemmle, Jr. Director: Lewis Milestone.
Cast: Lew Ayres, Louis Wolheim, John Wray, Arnold Lucy, Ben Alexander, Raymond Griffith, Beryl Mercer.

> "No film, before or since, has managed to capture the futility of war with such quiet simplicity, and it remains one of the masterpieces of the American cinema."
> —Clive Hirschhorn, *The Universal Story*

The greatest anti-war film ever made won the Oscar for Best Picture and Milestone won for Best Director. Based on Erich Maria Remarque's bestseller, the film was planned as a silent picture but cooler heads prevailed and, fortunately, it was made a talkie. The story is about a group of seven young German soldiers on the battlefields along the Western Front of World War I, the so-called "Great War." The road from youthful patriots to disillusioned veterans is paved with heartbreak and horror, as each man becomes a war victim one-by-one, either wounded or killed in action.

The film's most famous scene is the very end when Paul Baumer (Ayres), in a respite from battle, reaches out to catch a butterfly and takes a bullet from a French sniper's rifle. But the most inspirational scene is when Baumer finds a Frenchman (Griffith) in a trench, stabs him, and then repents in tears.

Mercer plays Baumer's mother. Alexander is Paul's friend, Kemmerick. Wolheim plays the tried-and-tested Sergeant Katczinsky. Wray is Himmelstoss, the town postman who becomes a hard-bitten corporal in

Lew Ayres and Louis Wolheim in *All Quiet on the Western Front*.

training camp. Lucy portrays Professor Kantorek, the schoolmaster who exhorts his pupils to enlist.

- The film was banned in Germany; the Nazis felt it hurt their recruitment efforts.
- ZaSu Pitts, well known in comedic parts, began as Baumer's mother but was replaced after a preview audience laughed at Pitts; her scenes were cut and re-shot with Mercer.
- Milestone improvised the butterfly ending but that is not Ayres' hand; it belongs to Milestone—Ayres had already left the set for the day.
- In real life, Ayres vicariously lived his character by becoming a conscientious objector during WWII serving in the medical corps.

Battleground

1949, MGM, 119 minutes, B&W.
Producer: Dore Schary. Director: William Wellman.
Cast: Van Johnson, George Murphy, John Hodiak, Ricardo Montalban, James Whitmore, Douglas Fowley, Leon Ames.

> "(A) truly extraordinary celluloid achievement."
> —*Variety*.

MGM boss Louis B. Mayer didn't want to do this film because he felt the public wouldn't go to see a picture about the long war that had only ended in 1945. He was wrong. The film was a major hit and it propelled producer Schary into the top job at MGM replacing Mayer. The movie, one of the best war films ever made, got nominated for six Oscars, including Best Picture, and won Academy Awards for screenplay (Robert Pirosh) and photography (Paul Vogel); Whitmore as top sergeant Kinnie was nominated for Best Supporting Actor.

The story is about "The Battle of the Bulge" and the aptly named "Battered Bastards of Bastogne" and their determined fight to hold back the Nazis in the Belgian Ardennes forest in the icy-cold winter of December 1944 through January 1945. This attack was the last German offensive on the Western Front. The Nazis had surprised the Americans creating a bulge in the Allied lines. The Germans, sensing victory, called for the Americans to surrender but the U.S. commander replied simply "Nuts!"—as he and his men continued to fight on, eventually defeating the German army.

Among the GIs: Johnson as Holley, Murphy as "Pop", Montalban as Roderiguez, Hodiak as Jarvess, a former small-town reporter; Fowley as false-teeth-clicking "Kipp", and Ames as the Lutheran chaplain. Others: Marshall Thompson (Layton), Jerome Courtland (Abner), Don Taylor (Standiferd), Richard Jaeckel (Bettis).

- Screenwriter Pirosh based the story on his experiences as a foot soldier in the battle. He was not with the 101st Airborne though he gathered information from members of the division.
- 20 veterans of the 101st who served in the battle provided insight for the actors and also served as extras in the film.
- Whitmore wasn't in the 101st; he was in the Marine Corps during WWII.

Van Johnson in *Battleground*.

- When Wellman (nicknamed "Wild Bill") saw how effectively Fowley could click his teeth, he worked the bit in several more times for comedy relief.

The Bridge on The River Kwai

1957, Horizon/Columbia, 161 minutes, Color, US/UK.
Producer: Sam Spiegel. Director: David Lean.
Cast: William Holden, Alec Guinness, Sessue Hayakawa, Jack Hawkins, James Donald, Geoffrey Horne.

> "**** A superb war drama..."
> —Jay A. Brown & Consumer Guide, *Rating the Movies*

Based on Pierre Boulle's novel, taken from a true incident on the Kwai River during WWII, Lean's exciting production won seven Academy Awards, including Best Picture, Best Director, and Best Actor (Guinness). Sir Alec is outstanding as the officious Col. Nicholson, a spit-and-polish British officer in charge of POWs held by the Japanese in the jungles of Burma.

Not stopping to think about the consequences of his action, Col. Nicholson's misguided pride helps the enemy build a strategic railroad bridge over a key river, much to the despair of Shears, an American officer (Holden), and Maj. Clipton, the British medical officer (Donald), both of whom see the whole project for what it really is: madness. Hayakawa, who received a nomination for Best Supporting Actor, is perfect as Col. Saito, the truculent Japanese camp commander. Hawkins plays Maj. Warden, the emotionally-charged British commando bent on rescuing his comrades. Horne is Lt. Joyce.

Alec Guinness as Col. Nicholson in *The Bridge on the River Kwai*.

And who's the hero in all of it? As it turns out, appearances are deceiving…the indifferent one, the crude, undisciplined, and reluctant Shears, becomes the bravest of the lot.

- Laurence Olivier turned down the role of Nicholson. Charles Laughton took it but withdrew after considering he couldn't stand the heat.
- It was photographed, by Jack Hildyard (who won the Oscar), in Ceylon.
- Michael Wilson and Carl Foreman, victims of the Hollywood blacklist, were uncredited screenwriters.
- The movie company, with 500 workers, took eight months to build the bridge: 425 ft. long, 50 ft. above water.
- The catchy theme, "The Colonel Bogey March," became a hit single, and also inspired a famed childhood playground tune affectionately entitled "Comet."
- In real-life, the English officer in charge of building the bridge, Lt. Col. Philip Toosey, did all he could to undermine the project. The real Saito was actually respectful of the POWs, so much so that Toosey spoke up on his behalf at the war-crimes tribunal after the war. Saito, 10 years after Toosey's 1975 death, visited Toosey's grave in England.

The Caine Mutiny

1954, Columbia, 125 minutes, Color.
Producer: Stanley Kramer. Director: Edward Dmytryk.
Cast: Humphrey Bogart, Jose Ferrer, Van Johnson, Fred MacMurray, Robert Francis, Tom Tully, May Wynn.

> "Humphrey Bogart gave his last notable performance as the paranoic Captain Queeg in this solid film version by Edward Dmytryk of Herman Wouk's bestseller…"
> —Leslie Halliwell, *Halliwell's Filmgoer's Companion*

The film, set in 1944, received an Academy Award nomination for Best Picture and Bogart, as Lt. Commander Philip Francis Queeg, got nominated for Best Actor. Queeg takes over a beaten old minesweeper named *The Caine* from a crusty naval veteran, Commander DeVriess, memorably played by Tully, who received a supporting Oscar nomination.

Queeg, obviously too long at sea, has become mentally disturbed, rolling steel balls in his hand when his condition becomes acute. And, sure enough, he makes one bad decision too many causing two officers to take control of the ship during a dangerous typhoon. The two brought before a court-martial are Executive Officer Lt. Steve Maryk (Johnson) and young Ensign Willie Keith (Francis). A third officer, Lt. Tom Keefer (MacMurray), should also be on trial—but he cowardly skipped out of the mutiny even though it was he who originally encouraged it.

It is one of the best courtroom dramas ever made, particularly so since there has actually never been a mutiny in the U.S. Navy (a fact brought out at the beginning of the picture, at the insistence of the Defense Department).

Ferrer is excellent as the defense attorney, Lt. Barney Greenwald, and Marshall is very good as the prosecutor; Wynn plays Keith's girlfriend, a San Francisco nightclub singer.

Fred MacMurray, Robert Francis, Van Johnson and Humphrey Bogart in *The Caine Mutiny*.

- Wynn's real name was Donna Lee Hickey but she oddly took the name of the character, May Wynn, as her own stage name even though it was also the name of the girl in Wouk's novel. She went on to make several more pictures using that name.
- *The Caine* was actually the minesweeper *USS Thompson*.
- Lee Marvin has a bit part as a sailor named Meatball. Because of Marvin's naval experience, Dmytryk asked him to also serve as a technical advisor, which he did.
- Dmytryk was one of the blacklisted "Hollywood Ten" and went to prison for six months.
- The typhoon sequence, using a *Caine* model, was created in a studio tank by special effects man Lawrence Butler.

The Dirty Dozen

1967, MGM, 149 minutes, Color.
Producer: Kenneth Hyman. Director: Robert Aldrich.
Cast: Lee Marvin, Charles Bronson, Donald Sutherland, Telly Savalas, John Cassavetes, Jim Brown, Richard Jaeckel, Ernest Borgnine, George Kennedy, Robert Ryan, Clint Walker, George Meeker, Trini Lopez

> "Violent action, spine-tingling suspense, earthy humor and thrilling excitement."
> —*The Los Angeles Herald Examiner.*

The #1 grossing film of 1967, based on the novel by E.M. Nathanson, won the Oscar for Sound Effects (John Poyner). The film was released at the height of the Vietnam War and drew people from both sides: anti-war activists saw the film as showing the madness of war. With an all-star cast, the story takes place in 1944 just ahead of D-Day. A group of men in military prison are given the chance for pardons and freedom if they take on a suicide mission: find and destroy a hideout for German officers in occupied France.

Army Major John Reisman (Marvin) is given the task of whipping the convicted GIs into shape and to lead the perilous attack on a chateau used as a retreat by the Nazis. The team of mostly psychotic misfits includes: Joe Wladislaw (Bronson), a murderer; Pinkley (Sutherland), an idiot; Maggott (Savalas), a sex maniac; Franko (Cassavetes), a psychopath; Jefferson (Brown), a black bigot; Posey (Walker), a brute; Jimenez (Lopez), a stupid man-child.

The officers are: Gen. Worden (Borgnine), Major Armbruster (Kennedy), Capt. Kinder (Meeker), and Col. Breed (Ryan). Sgt. Bowen (Jaeckel) is the top sergeant. It's Jaeckel's character who gives the team its name, "the dirty dozen."

- It was filmed in Britain.
- The French chateau set was one of the largest ever built—240 feet across and 50 feet high.
- A scene at the end became controversial because Brown drops hand grenades into a bomb shelter filled with German officers and their female friends. Aldrich left in the scene because he said he wanted to show that war is hell.
- Jack Palance turned down the Savalas role.

Robert Aldrich, director of *The Dirty Dozen*.

- John Wayne rejected the Reisman role because he was planning his own war film, *The Green Berets*.
- Aldrich on Marvin: "Look, this feller is a pretty good boozer, he's got a short fuse, but he can be handled okay."
- Marvin on Aldrich: "I loved Aldrich. Very saddened by his passing. Richard Jaeckel was a good friend of his. He went to see him on his last stretch in the hospital. He was in a coma much of the time. And Jaeckel asks if there is anything he can get him. And Aldrich says, 'Yeah, a good script.'"

From Here To Eternity

1953, Columbia, 118 minutes, B&W.
Producer: Buddy Adler. Director: Fred Zinnemann.
Cast: Burt Lancaster, Montgomery Clift, Deborah Kerr, Donna Reed, Frank Sinatra, Ernest Borgnine.

> "**** One of the best American films made in the fifties."
> —Steven H. Scheuer, *Movies on TV*

Winner of eight Academy Awards, including Best Picture and Best Director, the romantic-war film is most famous for a beach love-scene between Lancaster and Kerr. The plot, from the James Jones novel, is about American soldiers stationed at Schofield Barracks in Hawaii just before the Japanese attack on Pearl Harbor. Sinatra, making a screen comeback in a non-singing role, won the Oscar for Best Supporting Actor. Reed also won a supporting Oscar as a prostitute, Alma/Lorene.

Sinatra plays Pvt. Maggio, the tough, outspoken pal of fellow hardhead Pvt. Robert E. Lee Prewitt (Clift), a loner, camp bugler, and former boxer. Prewitt gets into trouble with his platoon for refusing to enter the battalion boxing competition. Lancaster plays Milton Warden, a smart, respected headquarters sergeant, a "lifer." Warden has a torrid affair with the captain's wife, Karen Holmes (Kerr). Borgnine is "Fatso" Judson, the villainous stockade sergeant.

One of the best sequences is a building barroom brawl between Maggio and Judson, stopped by Warden by challenging "Fatso" with a broken beer bottle; followed by a deadly back alley knife fight between "Fatso" and Prewitt.

Author James Jones with Mongomery Clift and Frank Sinatra on the set of *From Here to Eternity*.

- It was shot on location at the actual barracks on Oahu.
- The beach scene took three days to shoot because they had to get the waves to float in just right.
- Sinatra wanted the role so badly that he told Columbia boss Harry Cohn he'd take the part for just $8,000. Cohn accepted.
- Joan Fontaine turned down the role of Karen for personal reasons and later regretted it.
- Borgnine and Sinatra stayed in touch after making the movie and Ernest always signed his notes "Fatso."

The Great Escape

1963, United Artists, 168 minutes, Color.
Producer/Director: John Sturges.
Cast: Steve McQueen, Richard Attenborough, James Garner, Donald Pleasence, Charles Bronson, James Coburn, David McCallum, James Donald, Robert Desmond.

> "Classic cinema of action…simply great escapism."
> —*TIME*.

Most of what you see in this exceptional war film actually happened. It's based on a true story from the book by Paul Brickhill. *The Great Escape* was a big box-office hit, featuring three stars of a previous 1960 hit, *The Magnificent Seven*: McQueen, Bronson and Coburn, and with the same director.

Shot in Germany, the film is about the largest mass escape of POWs from a Nazi prison camp. McQueen stars as American loner "Cooler King" Hilts, always bent on escape and who seems to spend more time in solitary confinement (the cooler box) than in the barracks. McQueen's expertise as a motorcyclist is highlighted in the film; in fact, something he insisted on before accepting the role.

Attenborough is Bartlett, the British officer who heads up the escape plan. Garner plays Hendley "The Scrounger," with the ability to acquire just about anything. Pleasence is Blythe "The Forger." Bronson portrays Velinski "The Tunnel-Digger" and, ironically, he is claustrophobic. Coburn is Sedgwick "The Manufacturer." Desmond is Griffith "The Tailor." McCallum is Ashley-Pitt and Donald plays Senior Officer Ramsey.

- Brickhill was a Spitfire pilot who was shot down and taken to Stalag Luft 111 in Germany; he helped plan the escape.
- Attenborough and Pleasence were RAF pilots during the war and Pleasance was shot down and taken prisoner.
- The movie camp was built near Munich.
- McQueen did his own motorcycle riding, though stuntman Bud Ekins doubles for him for the dangerous 60-ft. leap over the barbed wire fence.
- The barbed-wire fence was made up of little black rubber stars, twisted into place by cast and crew in their free time.

Steve McQueen, James Garner and director John Sturges on the set of *The Great Escape*.

- In real-life, 600 men prepared for the escape for a year; the escape occurred on the night of March 24, 1944.

The Guns of Navarone

1961, Columbia, 159 minutes, Color.
Producer: Carl Foreman. Director: J. Lee Thompson.
Cast: Gregory Peck, David Niven, Anthony Quinn, Anthony Quayle, Stanley Baker, James Darren, Irene Papas, Gia Scala, James Robertson Justice, Richard Harris.

> "One of the best World War II adventure films...Don't miss this marvelous movie."
> —Steven H. Scheuer.

Based on the novel by Alistair Maclean, the war film was Oscar-nominated for Best Picture and Thompson received a nomination for Best Director. The film won for Best Special Effects and was the box-office hit of 1961.

Allied commandoes, soldiers, and guerrilla forces team up for an against-the-clock mission: destroy a mighty Nazi fortress housing massive, newly-designed, radar-controlled guns atop the island of Navarone in the Aegean Sea.

Scaling a sheer mountain in the middle of a stormy night are: American mountaineer Keith Mallory (Peck), explosives expert Miller (Niven), Greek resistance fighter Andrea Stavros (Quinn), British Major Franklin (Quayle), knife expert "Butcher" Brown (Baker), and Pvt. Spyros Pappadimos (Darren). Helping them on the island are two women—Maria (Papas) and Anna (Scala). Harris is RAF squadron leader Barnsby and Justice is Commander Jensen; Justice also does the opening narration. (Oh, by the way, one of the above is a traitor.)

Producer Foreman also wrote the screenplay, which is fiction. The photography is by Oswald Morris, the score is by Dimitri Tiomkin.

- The outdoor scenes were shot on the island of Rhodes, Greece.
- The shipwreck in a storm sequence was shot in a water tank at London's Shepperton and Elstree Studios.

A behind-the-scenes view of the camera crew on the set of *The Guns of Navarone*.

- The rock face they climbed was actually scenery laid on the studio floor so the actors could crawl on it. When the footage was turned, it appeared they were climbing up.
- Foreman, one of the blacklisted Hollywood Ten, moved to England where he continued to write.

(READ THE FOLLOWING AT YOUR OWN RISK: IT MIGHT RUIN THE MOVIE FOR YOU.)

- The exploding fortress at the end is a miniature.
- There never were any guns at Navarone; in fact, there is no Navarone!

Hell's Angels

1930, Caddo Co., United Artists, 119 minutes, B&W.
Producer/Director: Howard Hughes.
Cast: Ben Lyon, James Hall, Jean Harlow.

> "A brilliant aviation film in which the producer-director, millionaire Howard Hughes, introduced platinum blonde Jean Harlow."
> —Georges Sadoul, *Dictionary of Films.*

Remarkably, the mysterious Mr. Hughes, with absolutely no training in moviemaking, turned out a pretty good picture. True, it took three years to make—and, at $4 million (a lot of money following the stock market crash), it was the most expensive film up to that time. It was a box-office hit but still didn't turn a profit until its re-release.

It's about British flying aces in WWI and the adventures of two brothers, Monte and Roy Rutledge (Lyon, Hall). The film began as a silent movie but when sound came in, and was a success, Hughes immediately started re-shooting it as a talkie; though there are some titles, like those used in silent films; silent aerial footage was retained with sound added. The aerial photography, by Harry Perry and 27 other cameramen, is an amazing accomplishment in cinematic history. There were 50 planes and 100 pilots and Hughes, an aviation buff, flew one of the planes himself.

Multi-millionaire aviator-filmmaker Howard Hughes, producer-director of *Hell's Angels*.

The film is famous for its aerial sequences but also for Harlow's debut and her sexy line when, already in a seductive gown, she says to one of the guys, "Do you mind if I slip into something more comfortable?"

Most stunning of all is the zeppelin raid on London: the black airship appearing ever-so-silently through white clouds. Seeking speed and altitude as British airmen target the blimp, German crewmembers jump overboard to rid the ship of weight. In a spectacular climax to the sequence, a British pilot commits suicide by flying his plane into the zeppelin creating a massive fireball.

- The flying locations included Iverson Ranch in Chatsworth, Hughes' Caddo Field, which is now Van Nuys Airport, and the skies over Oakland.
- Hughes hired a number of pilots who actually flew in WWI.

- Three pilots died during production.
- James Whale and Lewis Milestone were assistant directors.
- All the prints were tinted and hand-colored.
- The two-strip Technicolor ball scene of Harlow is the only color footage of the star. The footage was found in John Wayne's vault in 1989. The scene was added by the UCLA Film Archives for the picture's restored version.
- The 2004 film, *The Aviator,* about Howard Hughes, includes some scenes from *Hell's Angels.*

The Longest Day

1962, 20th Century-Fox, 180 minutes, B&W.
Producer: Darryl F. Zanuck. Directors: Ken Annakin, Andrew Marton, Bernhard Wicki, Elmo Williams.
Cast: John Wayne, Robert Mitchum, Henry Fonda, Richard Burton, Robert Ryan, Red Buttons, Peter Lawford, Sean Connery, Kenneth More, Richard Todd, Edmond O'Brien, Wolfgang Preiss, Werner Hinz, Curt Jurgens, Eddie Albert, Arletty, Hans Christian Blech, Mel Ferrer, Gert Frobe, Leo Genn, Paul Anka.

> "A solid and stunning war epic."
> —*Variety.*

Even Zanuck himself did some of the directing (uncredited) on this all-star production about the Allied invasion of Nazi-occupied France on D-Day, June 6, 1944, the last phase of WWII. Shot in CinemaScope in France and Corsica, the film was nominated for Best Picture and won Oscars for photography and special effects.

The screenplay was by Cornelius Ryan based on his book about D-Day. The actual Normandy invasion was awesome: 4,000 ships, 3 million men, 11,000 planes. And the re-creation looks very much like the real thing. The U.S. Defense Department provided troops, along with the governments of England and France—over 23,000 in all. There are more than 150 speaking parts including three-dozen well-known actors. (German and French dialogue is subtitled.)

Buttons has one of the more memorable roles playing paratrooper John Steele who parachutes into Ste. Mere-Eglise only to have his chute caught on a church steeple; he dangles and watches in horror as fellow soldiers are shot by Germans below him.

Wayne is Lt. Col. Benjamin Vandervoort, Mitchum plays Brig. Gen. Norman Cota, Fonda portrays Brig. Gen. Teddy Roosevelt, Jr. Others in the cast: Burton (Flight Officer David Campbell), Ryan (Brig. Gen. James Gavin), Lawford (Lord Lovat), Connery (Pvt. Flanagan), More (Capt. Colin Maud), Todd (Maj. John Howard), O'Brien (Gen. Raymond Barton), Preiss (Maj. Gen. Max Pemsel), Hinz (Field Marshal Rommel), Jurgens (Maj. Gen. Blumentritt), Albert (Col. Thompson), Arletty (Madame Barrault), Blech (Maj. Werner Pluskat), Ferrer (Maj. Gen. Robert Haines), Frobe (Sgt. Kaffekanne), Genn (Brig. Gen. Edwin Parker), Anka (U.S. Army Ranger).

John Wayne as Lt. Col. Benjamin Vandervoort in *The Longest Day*.

- Anka wrote the theme music.
- Todd was actually a participant on D-Day; Capt. Todd parachuted into Normandy.
- At a cost of $10 million, this was the most expensive black-and-white film up to that time; *Schindler's List* topped it in 1993.
- Wayne was the highest-paid at $250,000; all the other stars got $25,000 each.
- While clearing a section of the Normandy beach near Ponte Du Hoc, the film's crew unearthed a British tank; they cleaned it up and used it in the film.

Patton

1970, 20th Century-Fox, 170 minutes, Color.
Producer: Frank McCarthy. Director: Franklin J. Schaffner.
Cast: George C. Scott, Karl Malden, Michael Bates, Karl Michael Vogler, Edward Binns, James Edwards.

> "****It is not about war but about Patton at war, and it is one of the best screen biographies ever made."
> —Roger Ebert, *Roger Ebert's Video Companion*

It has one of the best openings ever filmed, with Scott as Gen. George S. Patton standing in front of a giant American flag giving a speech to his men: "I want you to remember that no bastard ever won a war by dying for his country. He won it by making the other poor dumb bastard die for his country."

Photographed in Spain, Morocco, Crete, England, and in the U.S., the battlefield drama is based on two books: *Patton: Ordeal and Triumph* by Ladislas Farago and *A Soldier's Story* by Gen. Omar N. Bradley. Bradley is played in the movie by Malden.

Scott easily nailed down the Oscar for Best Actor, one of eight Academy Awards won by the film, including Best Picture, Best Director, and Best Screenplay (Francis Ford Coppola, Edmund H. North). Scott, however, refused to accept the Oscar at the Academy Awards ceremony, saying he didn't like the idea of comparing one actor's performance against another.

Patton, known by his men as "Old Blood and Guts," designed his own uniforms and wore ivory-handled six-guns. He believed in God, pre-

George C. Scott as Gen. George S. Patton and Karl Malden as Gen. Omar Bradley in *Patton*.

destination, and reincarnation. The strong-willed and hot-tempered U.S. Army commander led American forces in Europe and North Africa during World War II. As leader of the Third Army, he spearheaded the spectacular final drive of U.S. forces against the Germans. He was, as a Nazi officer comments in the film, "a pure warrior, a magnificent anachronism." Indeed, Patton hated the twentieth century with its atomic warfare and politicians who run the wars, leaving soldiers with more wars to fight.

Bates plays Field Marshal Montgomery, Vogler is Field Marshal Rommel, Binns is Maj. Gen. Walter Bedell Smith; Edwards is Sgt. George Meeks, Patton's aide.

- Robert Mitchum rejected the role because, he said, the part needed someone with the high energy to fight to maintain the

integrity of the character; he suggested Scott for the role.
- John Wayne wanted the role but was turned down by the producer.
- Coppola and North had never met each other until they accepted their trophies on the evening of the Oscar ceremony. They had submitted separate portions of the script without contact with one another.
- The opening speech is a compilation of quotes from several Patton speeches.
- McCarthy was a retired brigadier general who served on the staff of Gen. George C. Marshall and had wanted to make a film about Patton for 20 years.

Sergeant York

1941, Warner Bros., 134 minutes, B&W.
Producers: Jesse Lasky, Jr., Hal B. Wallis; Director: Howard Hawks.
Cast: Gary Cooper, Joan Leslie, Walter Brennan, Margaret Wycherly, Ward Bond, June Lockhart, Dickie Moore, George Tobias.

> "It has all the flavor of true Americana, the blunt and homely humor of backwoodsmen and the raw integrity peculiar to simple folk."
> —Bosley Crowther, *The New York Times.*

Nominated for 11 Academy Awards, including Best Picture, the film tells the story of the #1 hero of World War I: Alvin C. York who single-handedly killed 25 Germans and captured 132 prisoners even though he was a conscientious objector. Cooper, perfect as the Southern farmer who became a soldier, won the Oscar for Best Actor.

The film, one of the most touching and inspirational Hollywood ever made, takes York through his early life in the Tennessee Valley, his religious experience, conflict over his pacifism, battlefield experiences, his devotion to the girl back home, Gracie Williams (Leslie), and his inner battle with being a hero who must reject Madison Avenue's attempts to use him to endorse products.

Best Supporting Oscar nominations went to Brennan as Pastor Pile and Wycherly as Ma York. Bond is Alvin's friend, Ike. Moore and Lock-

Gary Cooper and the real Alvin York during the making of *Sergeant York*.

hart play York's younger brother and sister. Tobias plays York's fellow soldier "Pusher" Ross.

- The screenplay by Howard Koch (*Casablanca*) and John Huston (*The Red Badge of Courage*) is based on York's personal diary.
- The working title was *The Amazing Life of Sergeant York*.
- Leslie was only 16.
- Moore, a former *Our Gang* kid actor, gave Shirley Temple her first screen kiss in *Miss Annie Rooney* (1942).

Westerns

Butch Cassidy and the Sundance Kid

1969, 20th Century-Fox, 112 minutes, Color.
Producer: John Foreman. Director: George Roy Hill.
Cast: Paul Newman, Robert Redford, Katharine Ross, Strother Martin.

> "The film is a masterpiece of photographic inventiveness and deft direction, with appealing performances."
> —Tony Thomas and Aubrey Solomon,
> *The Films of 20th Century-Fox*

Who would have thought that a plot about a couple of real outlaws could become the most beloved comedy-Western of all time? But that's what happened. The Newman-Redford pairing was so popular that it spawned another classic with these superstars: *The Sting* (1973).

The man mostly responsible for the success of the movie is screenwriter William Goldman who won one of the four Oscars the film received; veteran cameraman Conrad Hall also got one of the golden statues. (Hall's dramatic freeze-frame ending, pulled back for an extreme long-shot, is now a classic piece of footage.) Goldman had long been fascinated by the true story of these end-of-an-era bank-and-train robbers and how they managed time after time to escape the law, and how they eventually ended up on the run all the way to Bolivia, where they apparently met their fate in a wild shootout. What made the story even more interesting is how a pretty young woman named Etta Place, either a teacher or a prostitute, tagged along with the men throughout most of their capricious ride into folklore.

While the film received an Academy Award nomination for Best Picture in America, the British Academy went one better and named it Best Picture.

Paul Newman and Robert Redford in the famous climactic shot of *Butch Cassidy and the Sundance Kid*.

The film also received Oscars for its score (Burt Bacharach) and for Best Song: "Raindrops Keep Fallin' On My Head" (Bacharach and Hal David).

Newman plays the likeable Butch and Redford is his mustachioed pal, Sundance, one of the West's fastest gunslingers. Ross plays Etta. Martin plays a tobacco-chewing bank courier in Bolivia who gives Butch and Sundance jobs as security guards in their effort to finally go straight.

- Dustin Hoffman was considered for the role of Butch and Steve McQueen and Warren Beatty were considered for the role of Sundance.
- The sister of Cassidy visited the set and told Newman and Redford stories about her brother's escapades.
- The actual name of Butch's gang was not "The Hole in the Wall Gang" but "The Wild Bunch". But because the film *The Wild Bunch* was released earlier in the year, Hill decided to change the name to avoid confusion.
- Butch's real name was George Leroy Parker. Sundance's name was Harry Longbaugh; he got his nickname after robbing a bank in Sundance, Nev.

Duel In The Sun

1946, Selznick, 138 minutes, Color.
Producer: David O. Selznick. Director: King Vidor.
Cast: Jennifer Jones, Gregory Peck, Joseph Cotten, Lionel Barrymore, Lillian Gish, Walter Huston, Herbert Marshall, Charles Bickford, Harry Carey, Butterfly McQueen.

> "…grandiose, passionate, spectacular…"
> —Georges Sadoul, *Dictionary of Films.*

In scope, it's Selznick's Western *Gone With the Wind*, except the film belongs just as much to Vidor as Selznick. The movie is alive with stunning set pieces, a style Vidor is known for: the single rider against the looming landscape, the red sky over the plains, the funeral silhouetted

A publicity photo for Jennifer Jones in *Duel in the Sun*.

against the daylight; and Vidor's big scenes are emotionally charged: the ride of the cowboys against the railroad joined by horse soldiers, the train crash and explosion, Gish's dying scene (crawling to Barrymore on her knees), and the closing "duel in the sun."

Jones, as hot-blooded half-breed Pearl Chavez, received a Best Actress nomination. Gish, as Laura Belle McCanles, got nominated for Best Supporting Actress; Barrymore plays Laura Belle's husband, Texas land baron Sen. McCanles. Pearl is in love with both of the Senator's sons—brash Lewt (Peck) and pragmatic Jesse (Cotten). Selznick wrote the screenplay based on the novel by Niven Busch.

The film opens gloriously...the sun across the desert with a rock-face framed in the left with one flower-blooming cactus in the valley below—and Orson Welles (uncredited) narrating this legend of the West.

The fine supporting cast includes Huston as The Sinkiller, Bickford as ranch boss Sam Pierce, Marshall is Pearl's father, Scott Chavez; Carey plays Lem Smoot, and McQueen (famous from Selznick's *GWTW*) is Vashti.

The cinematography is by Lee Garmes, Ray Rennahan, and Hal Rosson. Music by Dimitri Tiomkin.

- Josef von Sternberg, Marlene Dietrich's director, was an assistant director. Asked what he did, Vidor said, "He was just doing whatever I left him to do."
- It was shot in the desert near Tucson.
- It was originally 26 hours long!
- Selznick spent $2 million, unheard of in those days, to promote the film.
- Three years after the film, Jones married Selznick.

High Noon

1952, United Artists, 85 minutes, B&W.
Producer: Stanley Kramer. Director: Fred Zinnemann.
Cast: Gary Cooper, Grace Kelly, Lloyd Bridges, Katy Jurado, Thomas Mitchell, Lon Chaney, Jr., Ian MacDonald, Otto Kruger, Tom London.

> "...a big hit with public and critics alike."
> —Peter Van Gelder, *That's Hollywood*

One of the greatest Westerns ever made—some say, *the* greatest. The film was nominated for Best Picture and Cooper won his second Oscar (*Sergeant York*) as Marshal Will Kane, whose town turns its back on him when he needs them most. Blacklisted screenwriter Carl Foreman did the script based on John W. Cunningham's short story, *The Tin Star*. Both the score and title song, by Dimitri Tiomkin and Ned Washington, won Oscars; the song ("Do Not Forsake Me, Oh My Darlin'") is sung by B-Western star Tex Ritter.

One of the shortest major feature films ever made, the story is created around the ticking clock: all the action is seen within the bounds of 85 minutes from 10:40 AM to 12:05 PM. The most memorable shot in

Gary Cooper in *High Noon*.

the film is Floyd Crosby's high crane-camera view of Kane alone in the deserted streets.

Amy Kane (Kelly), Will's new Quaker bride, can't understand her husband's determination to stand up, alone if necessary, to Frank Miller (MacDonald) and his three killers. Miller has just been pardoned and released from prison and vowed to return to Hadleyville to kill Kane, the man who put him behind bars.

Bridges plays Harvey Pell, the young deputy who wants Will's job. Jurado is Kane's ex-lover, Helen Ramirez, who owns the saloon. London is Helen's right-hand man. Mitchell is Mayor Henderson, a double-talking politician. Chaney is Martin Howe, the former lawman Kane idolized. Kruger is the judge. The cast includes three character actors who've played badmen in many Westerns: Lee Van Cleef (Colby), Robert Wilke (Pierce), and Jack Elam, though this time he plays Charlie, the town drunk.

- Cooper was not well during the making of the film, suffering the effects of a bleeding ulcer. Coop, one of Hollywood's most likeable stars, died of cancer in 1961 at the age of 60.
- No stunt-double was used for Cooper in his fight sequence with Bridges.
- Gregory Peck was offered the Kane role first but turned it down because he felt it was too much like his film *The Gunfighter*.
- Director Howard Hawks didn't like the content of the film because he saw Kane as an unprofessional lawman by asking townspeople to help him out; Hawks made *Rio Bravo* (with John Wayne) to show, in his mind, how it should be done.
- Wayne accepted Cooper's Oscar because Gary was too ill to appear at the Academy Awards ceremony.
- London was in the first Western in 1903, *The Great Train Robbery*, as the engineer, a job he actually held once in real-life.

How The West Was Won

1963, MGM, 164 minutes, Color.
Producer: Bernard Smith. Directors: Henry Hathaway, John Ford, George Marshall.
Cast: Debbie Reynolds, Carroll Baker, George Peppard, Gregory Peck, James Stewart, Henry Fonda, John Wayne, Robert Preston, Karl Malden,

Richard Widmark, Lee J. Cobb, Eli Wallach, Thelma Ritter, Agnes Moorehead, Walter Brennan, Spencer Tracy.

> "Enough plot twists and spectacular climaxes to equip a dozen movies."
> —*The MGM Story*.

Nominated for eight Academy Awards, including Best Picture, the all-star Western epic, narrated by Spencer Tracy, connects stories of three generations of one family via three Cinerama cameras producing a widescreen classic. James Webb won the Oscar for his story and screenplay.

Sadly, those who did not see it in Cinerama, and that would be most people, truly missed a special three-dimensional movie-going experience (luckily, your author *did* enjoy it on the huge Cinerama screen). All that is left of the three-camera system for the modern viewer are the two lines that connected the trio of cameras. No single camera was used in the production, consequently the two white dividing lines are visible, sometimes only slightly other times quite intrusively. Nevertheless, it *is* a great film,

A family of pioneers attempt to keep their raft afloat in the Ohio River rapids in *How the West Was Won*. Carroll Baker, Agnes Moorehead and Debbie Reynolds at the oars, Karl Malden in the rear and young Bryan Russell in the foreground.

not unlike watching a silent classic, though we are aware that something is missing from the screen.

The plot follows one family in the building of America's West, the Prescotts from New England, fighting the Missouri rapids on a raft in their quest to start a new life for themselves and, along the way, helping create a whole new world for millions of Americans. Malden plays the father, Zebulon Prescott, Moorehead is his wife, Rebecca. Their daughters are Eve (Baker) and Lilith (Reynolds). And from the union of Eve and trapper Linus Rawlings (Stewart) comes son Zeb Rawlings (Peppard) who grows up to become a wild West lawman.

Key elements of the development of the West are touched on: the building of the railroad, wagon trains, Indian wars and treaties, the gold rush and the building of San Francisco, and more. Among the scenes: a buffalo stampede (with Cinerama cameras right in the middle), an Indian attack, the battle at the Alamo, a Civil War battlefield, and a shootout on a moving train.

Peck is Cleve, a riverboat gambler who wins Lilith's heart; Ritter is Lilith's traveling companion, Fonda is a mountain man who keeps moving away from civilization, Brennan portrays a wilderness con man, Cobb plays Marshal Ramsey, Carolyn Jones plays Zeb's wife, Julie; Preston plays Morgan, the wagonmaster; Widmark is the railroad boss, Wallach is outlaw Charlie Gant, and Wayne is Gen. Sherman.

- Doubling for Peppard, stuntman Robert Morgan, husband of actress Yvonne De Carlo, was very seriously injured in the moving train sequence involving rolling logs that came loose when a chain snapped.
- The Gold City sequence was shot at Parkinsville, Ariz. where the train station still stands.
- The opening and closing scenes, viewing modern America from the air, are from the 1952 film *This Is Cinerama*.

Jesse James

1939, 20th Century-Fox, 105 minutes, Color.
Producer: Darryl F. Zanuck, Director: Henry King.
Cast: Tyrone Power, Henry Fonda, Nancy Kelly, Randolph Scott, John Carradine, Henry Hull, Jane Darwell, Ernest Whitman.

"An authentic American panorama."
—*The New York Times.*

Excellent filmmaking about the legendary outlaw of the Old West, Jesse James (1847-1882), played by Ty Power whose performance sent him to #2 on the box-office Top 10 list; no easy task since it was probably the greatest year of great movies, including *Gone With the Wind*, *The Wizard of Oz* and *Stagecoach*.

The fine screenplay, though romanticized, is by Nunnally Johnson (*The Grapes of Wrath*). The script starts with Jesse as a farmer whose mother (Darwell) is swindled and murdered by crooked land-dealers on behalf of the railroad crossing its way through Missouri. Jesse and brother Frank (Fonda) track down the killers, which begins the James' life on the run. In revenge, they form the James Gang and rob trains but, in time, banks are also targets. Many regular folks in five states come to respect the James boys for challenging those that the people felt had cheated them out of their land and savings.

Highlights: the clever jailbreak; the Great Northfield Raid with Jesse and Frank on horseback crashing through a large storefront window

Henry Fonda and Tyrone Power, sitting on a train caboose in Missouri, signing autographs and chatting with fans on location for *Jesse James*.

when both ends of the street are protected by shooters; the posse chase and the James' plunge on horses off a cliff into water.

Kelly plays Jesse's wife, Zee. Hull is Zee's uncle, Major Cobb, a cantankerous newspaper publisher whose editorials defend Jesse as a Robin Hood of the West. Whitman is Pinky, the James' devoted black farm boss. Scott is Marshal Will Wright. Carradine is Bob Ford whose bullet in Jesse's back spawned the 1880s folk song: "The dirty little coward who shot Mr. Howard." In the end of his life, Jesse was hiding out under the name Tom Howard.

- The scene in which horses fall to their death from a cliff led to the American Humane Association's overseeing of future treatment of animals in movies.
- Screenwriter William Goldman said he was inspired by the posse chase and the cliff plunge to do similar scenes for *Butch Cassidy and the Sundance Kid*.
- After getting Johnson's script, King flew to Kearney, Missouri and drove a rented car out to the old James house. Robert James, Frank's son, was still living there and Jesse's tombstone was in the backyard.
- The film was shot at Pineville in the Missouri Ozarks.
- On location, after filming, Power and Fonda sat on a railroad car and signed autographs for local sightseers.
- The sequel is *The Return of Frank James* (1940) with Fonda.

The Magnificent Seven

1960, United Artists, 126 minutes, Color.
Producer/Director: John Sturges.
Cast: Yul Brynner, Steve McQueen, Charles Bronson, James Coburn, Eli Wallach, Robert Vaughn, Horst Buchholz, Brad Dexter.

> "A Western to rank along the very finest of the genre ever made!"
> —*The Los Angeles Times*.

A cult favorite and box-office hit, based on Akira Kurosawa's *Seven Samurai*. William Roberts' screenplay has Brynner as a bald-headed frontier gunfighter named Chris Adams, in place of Toshiro Mifune's strong-minded samurai warrior. In this Western update, Brynner is called upon by poor Mexican villagers to defend against rampaging outlaws led by a vicious bandit named Calvera (Wallach).

Chris seeks out some of the toughest gunmen in the territory: Vin, the top gun, stoically played by McQueen; Bronson, another out-of-work transient, is Bernardo O'Reilly; Coburn is Britt, whose knife is as dangerous as any handgun; Vaughn is Lee, starting to doubt his own abilities; Dexter, who thinks Chris is really doing it to find hidden gold, plays Harry Luck; and Buchholz is Chico, a young wannabe gunslinger.

A major highlight of the film is its music by Elmer Bernstein; it became one of the most recognizable themes in movie history. The cinematography is by Charles Lang who had already done the photography for two other Westerns: *Gunfight at the O.K. Corral* and *One-Eyed Jacks*.

Steve McQueen and Yul Brynner hitch a ride uphill on a lighting truck on the outdoor set of *The Magnificent Seven*.

- George Peppard was considered for the McQueen role because Steve was doing the TV series *Wanted: Dead Or Alive* and had trouble finding time for other projects.
- It was filmed in Mexico.
- The sequel, also with Brynner, is *Return of the Seven* (1966).
- Brynner reprised his character as a robot in *Westworld* (1973).

My Darling Clementine

1946, 20th Century-Fox, 97 minutes, B&W.
Producer: Samuel G. Engel. Director: John Ford.
Cast: Henry Fonda, Victor Mature, Linda Darnell, Walter Brennan, Cathy Downs, Ward Bond, Tim Holt, John Ireland, Grant Withers.

> "Shot after shot, this is truly a beautiful movie. Tombstone at night, with the streets half lit by light filtering from the buildings. The saloon, with thick smoke hovering in the air. The valley, with mountains in the distance and a hazy gray, panoramic sky overhead…"
>
> —*Cult Movies 2.*

Ford's version of the Earp-Clanton feud and "the gunfight at the O.K. Corral" is handsomely photographed by Joseph P. MacDonald who did *Viva Zapata* for Elia Kazan. Ford actually knew Wyatt Earp who visited frontier pals working as extras and stuntmen in the early days of Hollywood, and Ford used bits of Earp's stories in the making of this classic Western. But Ford generously added to the Earp legend, which was begun by John Clum, editor of the old *Tombstone Epitaph* newspaper.

Fonda plays Wyatt Earp, marshal of Tombstone, Ariz. in the early 1880s. Mature is gambling gunslinger Doc Holliday. Darnell is Chihuahua, a Mexican-Indian saloon prostitute in love with Doc. Downs is Clementine, the schoolmarm from the East, visiting Tombstone in hopes of rekindling a former affair with Holliday; instead, she fires up a romance at arm's length between her and Wyatt.

Brennan plays Old Man Clanton, Ireland is Billy Clanton, Withers is Ike Clanton, Bond is Morgan Earp, and Holt plays Virgil Earp.

Henry Fonda and Cathy Downs in *My Darling Clementine*.

- The real Holliday was a dentist and survived the shootout to die in a TB sanitarium in 1885.
- This was Fonda's first film after returning from the Navy during WWII.
- Jeanne Crain, an upcoming 20th Century-Fox starlet, was picked for the role of Clementine but Darryl Zanuck ruled against it because he thought the part was too small.
- After Darnell throws a pitcher of milk in Ward's face, Ford left it to Fonda to react any way he wanted. Henry, improvising, shuffled his feet on a saloon porch post while balancing in his chair.
- Highlights: Wyatt apprehending the drunken Indian gunman, the dance with Fonda and Downs, the showdown between Wyatt and Doc, and the gunfight at the O.K. Corral.

One-Eyed Jacks

1961, Pennebaker/Paramount, 141 minutes, Color.
Producer: Frank P. Rosenberg. Director: Marlon Brando.
Cast: Marlon Brando, Karl Malden, Pina Pellicer, Ben Johnson, Slim Pickens, Katy Jurado, Larry Duran.

> "The film remains one of Hollywood's most memorable Westerns. Brando showing substantial ability as a filmmaker in a story more pedestrian directors would have made merely routine...dazzling landscape-poems and light effects never bettered even in the best of Hollywood's outdoor films..."
> —John Baxter.

A psychological cult classic and the best of the off-beat Westerns, with Brando (directing his first and only film) as a gunslinger named Rio and Malden as his former outlaw-pal, Dad Longworth, who ostensibly withdraws from criminality to become a sheriff...but Rio doesn't buy it—he's seen the *true* side of Longworth: he's a one-eyed jack.

Marlon Brando and Karl Malden preparing the whipping post scene in
One-Eyed Jacks.

Based on a novel by Charles Neider, the plot takes place in 1880 in Monterey, California. The theme is revenge. Rio is left to fend for himself against the law after he and Dad rob a bank and Longworth runs away. Rio spends five years in a horrible prison and escapes with a fellow inmate named Modesto (Duran, Brando's long-time double). Rio sets out to find Longworth and kill him. He and Modesto join up with a gang of thieves run by brutal bank-robber Bob Emory (Johnson). Complications arise when Rio catches up with Dad only to find romance with Dad's daughter, Louisa (Pellicer). Jurado plays her mother, Maria. Pickens plays Dad's sadistic deputy, Lon.

Photography is by Charles Lang, Jr. (*The Magnificent Seven*), art direction by Hal Pereira (*Shane*), music by Hugo Friedhofer (*Vera Cruz*).

- Brando took over the directing job after Stanley Kubrick quit following disagreements with the producer.
- The stories are legend about Brando: waiting for hours on the beach to have the camera catch waves just right; inspection of every detail; morning script meetings in which he got input from actors and crew.
- The film was budgeted for $1.8 million but grew to $6 million.
- It was supposed to take six weeks but took six months.
- The final cut was four hours 42 minutes; two hours were cut.
- The whipping at the hitching post used a real bullwhip with Malden pulling up short by a foot, just missing Marlon's body. Brando's spitting into Malden's face was ad libbed.

Red River

1948, United Artists, 125 minutes, B&W.
Producer/Director: Howard Hawks.
Cast: John Wayne, Montgomery Clift, Walter Brennan, Joanne Dru, Harry Carey, John Ireland, Noah Beery, Jr., Coleen Gray, Harry Carey, Jr., Chief Yowlachie.

> "Monumental…sweeping…powerful…one of the screen's supreme examples of motion picture art and entertainment."
> —*Variety*.

Howard Hawks, John Ireland and Montgomery Clift on the set of *Red River*.

Hawks told John Ford that, indeed, *Stagecoach* made John Wayne a star, but *Red River* made him an actor. Allegedly, grand master Ford agreed.

Here, Wayne plays a man 20 years older, a brutal man, a single-minded cattle king named Tom Dunson. Dunson gets mean, really mean, after Indians kill his true love, a pretty young woman named Fen (Gray). And his meanness and hate reach full fury as he heads the first cattle drive on the Old Chisholm Trail from Laredo, Texas to Abilene, Kansas. Dunson seems to relish directing much of his anger at his adopted son, Matthew Garth (Clift), an escapee from the burning wagon train that took Fen's life. But Matt learns to stand up to the father who adopted him and is just about the only man around willing to challenge Tom—except for a toothless chuck-wagon cookie, Groot Nadine (Brennan), who's also not afraid to speak his mind: "You were wrong, Mr. Dunson!"

The film is based on a magazine story by Borden Chase who co-wrote the screenplay with Charles Schnee. One of the many highlights is the very end when Tom and Matt fight it out, only to be stopped by Tess Millay (Dru), wielding a wild six-shooter; Tess, you see, has fallen in love with Matt.

Ireland is memorable as gunslinger Cherry Valance. The fine supporting cast also includes Carey as Mr. Melville; Carey, Jr. as Dan; Beery as Buster, and Chief Yowlachie as Quo.

- This was Clift's first film, though it was released after *The Search*.
- Dru, sister of TV game-show host Peter Marshall, married Ireland not long after making the movie.
- Wayne and Clift, on opposite poles of the political spectrum, got along well during filming by agreeing early not to discuss politics.
- At the start of the stampede to move the herd, each cowboy yells while sitting on the same dummy horse.
- The first cattle drive on the Chisholm Trail was actually in 1867 not 1865.
- It was shot in Rain Valley, Arizona; so named because it never rains there. But it did rain and hard—and Hawks just kept right on shooting.

The Searchers

1956, Warner Bros., 119 minutes, Color.
Producer: Merian C. Cooper. Director: John Ford.
Cast: John Wayne, Jeffrey Hunter, Ward Bond, Vera Miles, Harry Carey, Jr., Ken Curtis, Natalie Wood, John Qualen, Henry Brandon, Pippa Scott, Hank Worden.

> "One of John Ford's best films…"
> —Clive Hirschhorn, *The Warner Bros. Story*

The collaboration of Ford and Wayne evolved through 12 films together: *The Searchers* is the apex of that relationship. With an economy of dialogue, this Western is a film of stark contrasts—the changing seasons and beautiful landscapes, warmth and savagery, despair and hatred, passion and terror. Its moods are swift, intermingled with comedy and color.

The film begins and ends with a shot through a cabin door, opening at the beginning, closing at the end—as if, for two hours, we are allowed the special privilege of a personal glimpse through a time-frame, into a watercolor West, romantically toned for our viewing; a homily of the real larger-than-life pioneers who risked everything to settle a strange new world.

Wayne, in his favorite role, is Ethan Edwards, an ex-Confederate soldier, bitter and alone, returned from the Civil War. And he's something else: *a racist*, an Indian-hater. As we learn in an early tombstone shot,

John Ford, director of *The Searchers*; undoubtedly his greatest work among dozens of Westerns.

Ethan's mother was killed by Commanches. He soon becomes obsessed in a five-year search for his kidnapped nine-year-old niece, Debbie (Wood), a captive of Commanche Indians. Ethan's dilemma? When he finally finds her, must he rescue her—or kill her? For Debbie is now a teenager and no doubt sexually aware and more than likely a sexual concubine.

Hunter plays Martin Pawley, Ethan's half-breed nephew and co-searcher; Miles is Laurie, Marty's longsuffering lady-friend. Curtis is Charlie McCorry, who tries to come between them. Carey and Qualen portray Laurie's Scandinavian parents. Carey, Jr. is Brad Jorgensen, Debbie's brother. Scott is Lucy, Debbie's older sister. Bond, a Ford regular, is Captain-the-Reverend Samuel Clayton. Worden is Mose. Brandon is Chief Scar.

- The last scene, with Wayne framed in the doorway, pays tribute to his friend, Harry Carey; Wayne, in a familiar Carey pose, reaches across his body and holds his other arm at the elbow. Olive Carey, Harry's widow, was looking on and very moved at the moment.
- Lana Wood, Natalie's younger sister, is Debbie as a child.
- It was filmed in Monument Valley, Utah, where Ford made nine pictures. Ford liked shooting there because of the marvelous landscape but also because it gave work to locals of the Navajo Indian tribe.
- Ethan's line, "That'll be the day!" used several times, inspired a song by that title from rock-and-roll artist Buddy Holly.
- In 1962, Wayne named one of his sons John Ethan Wayne; he goes by his middle name.

Shane

1953, Paramount, 118 minutes, Color.
Producer/Director: George Stevens.
Cast: Alan Ladd, Brandon De Wilde, Jean Arthur, Van Heflin, Jack Palance, Ben Johnson, Elisha Cook, Jr., Emile Meyer.

> "One of the small minority of Westerns with a valid claim to be works of art...meticulously directed....excellently performed...one of the most shocking murder scenes on film."
> —John Douglas Eames, *The Paramount Story*

The quintessential story of good vs. evil on the Western frontier with Ladd, in his best role, as Shane, a mysterious, buckskinned gunfighter who drifts into a Wyoming range war and is befriended by a family of homesteaders. Shane's antithesis is another gunfighter, Jack Wilson (Palance), a grinning, black-suited, cold-blooded killer hired by villainous cattlemen to drive the farmers off the land.

This serious candidate for the best Western ever made received Academy Award nominations for Best Picture and Best Director and Loyal Griggs, photographing under cloudy skies with the Grand Teton Mountains as backdrop, won the Oscar for Best Cinematography. The story, based on the book by Jack Schaefer, is seen through the eyes of an endear-

George Stevens, Emile Meyer and Alan Ladd on the set of *Shane*.

ing boy, Joey (De Wilde), whose cry at the end of the film has become a classic line: "Shane! Shane! Come back!"

Heflin and Arthur play Joey's parents, Joe and Marian Starrett. Meyer plays Rufus Ryker, the grizzled, hate-filled cattle baron. Cook is Torrey, the rambunctious farmer who gets shot down in the mud by Wilson. Johnson is Chris, who picks a fight with Shane in Grafton's Saloon: it's probably the most realistic fistfight ever filmed.

Also memorable are two more shooting scenes: the extra-loud gunfire when Shane demonstrates his shooting skill for Joey—and the quick-draw between Shane and Wilson in the saloon.

- Stuntman Rodd Redwing does Shane's fancy gun-twirl, in close-up, at the end.
- Cook wore a wire that pulled him backwards six feet into the mud when Palance shoots.
- Originally, Montgomery Clift was considered for the role of Shane and William Holden as Joe Starrett.
- Schaefer had never been west of Cleveland when he wrote his book.

- Stevens purposely over-modulated Shane's shooting exhibition. When the picture was released, Stevens was in the audience at a local theater and was horrified to find the volume of the gunfire lowered. He raced to the projectionist's booth and learned that the house manager had insisted the sound be dropped because it was extra loud. Stevens complained adamantly and said, "I'm standing here at the next showing and if you touch the volume, I'll break your damned hand!" The film played as the director intended.

The Shootist

1976, Paramount, 99 minutes, Color.
Producers: M.J. Frankovich, William Self; Director: Don Siegel.
Cast: John Wayne, Lauren Bacall, Ron Howard, James Stewart, Richard Boone, Hugh O'Brien, Bill McKinney, Harry Morgan, John Carradine, Sheree North, Richard Lenz, Scatman Crothers.

> "The cast is excellent…Don Siegel's direction reveals a sensitivity we didn't suspect after films like *Dirty Harry*."
> —Roger Ebert.

Duke's last film and a cult favorite, not only because it was Wayne's final work, but because it's a very good Western, about the last eight days in the life of an aging gunfighter, based on a novel by Glendon Swarthout. Wayne, in one of his finest screen portrayals, plays John Bernard Books who is dying of cancer; ironically, Wayne himself would succumb to the disease three years later. (There's a montage of some of Duke's Westerns at the start of the movie.)

Bacall plays Bond Rogers, the lady who runs a rooming house where Books stays just before his death. Her son, Gillom (Howard), admires Books much to the chagrin of his single mom. Stewart portrays the physician, Dr. Hostetler, who suggests Books not die the painfully slow death of a cancer victim; he, instead, infers that Books use his six-guns and his notoriety to speed up the inevitable.

Three despicable men in the town learn that Books is there and dying and each would like to be the one to kill him, for whatever fame and fortune. They are Sweeney (Boone), Cobb (McKinney), and Pulford

Ron Howard and John Wayne in *The Shootist*.

(O'Brien), a gambler/gunslinger. Books arranges to meet all three at the same time in the saloon—for the express purpose of being shot.

Carradine is perfect as the undertaker, Hezekiah Beckum. Lenz is the reporter who plans to write about Books. Morgan is Marshal Thibido. Crothers is funny as Moses, the livery stable operator. And North is Serepta, Books' old girlfriend who comes to pay him one last visit.

- Some may think this was the first pairing of Wayne and Bacall, but not so; they did *Blood Alley* in 1956.
- Duke wasn't diagnosed with stomach cancer until January 1979. He had beaten lung cancer years earlier. Wayne had not intended for this to be his final film.
- The Stewart role was really only a cameo for which he was paid $50,000. Duke had asked that Jimmy be given the part. They had worked together in 1961 in *The Man Who Shot Liberty Valance*.
- It was filmed at Carson City, Nevada.

Stagecoach

1939, United Artists, 97 minutes, B&W.
Producer: Walter Wanger. Director: John Ford.
Cast: John Wayne, Claire Trevor, Thomas Mitchell, John Carradine, Louise Platt, Andy Devine, George Bancroft, Berton Churchill, Donald Meek, Tom Tyler.

> "Before filming *Citizen Kane*, I studied the masters: John Ford, John Ford, and John Ford. I watched *Stagecoach* 40 times."
> —Orson Welles.

Nine people, two women and seven men, leave on a stagecoach for a little town in New Mexico and their adventuresome journey provides one of the most dynamic and interesting Westerns ever made, with a key element involving social prejudice. Based on Ernest Haycox's magazine story, "Stage to Lordsburg," the film was nominated for Best Picture and won two Oscars: Best Score (the work of four composers utilizing 17 American folk songs), and Best Supporting Actor (Mitchell).

Wayne, in his first major role (after a 10-year career in B-Westerns), plays The Ringo Kid, a jail escapee who had been doing time on a frame-up. In cameraman Bert Glennon's unique longshot-to-medium close-up of Wayne twirling his rifle, the stage stops for Ringo standing in the middle of the road. Ringo joins the six passengers, one of whom is a pretty woman named Dallas (Trevor) and he soon develops a strong affinity for her; what he doesn't know is that she's a prostitute who just got run of the last town.

The passengers are really a microcosm of society: besides Ringo the alleged outlaw and Dallas the prostitute, there's pregnant Lucy Mallory (Pratt) on her way to join her husband in the military; Hatfield the gambler (Carradine) who becomes Lucy's protector; Samuel Peacock (Meek), a whiskey salesman who loses his samples to Doc Boone (Mitchell), an alcoholic who must sober up to deliver Lucy's baby; Henry Gatewood (Churchill), the unscrupulous banker; Marshal Curly Wilcox (Bancroft), riding shotgun (he takes Ringo into custody), and Buck (Devine) the stage driver who represents the everyday working man.

Highlights: Ringo's shootout with the Plummers (with Tyler as Hank Plummer) and a nearly seven-minute Apache attack featuring stuntman Yakima Canutt's famous jump to the horses and his slide under the stagecoach.

John Wayne as "The Ringo Kid" in *Stagecoach*.

- This was Ford's first shoot in Monument Valley, Utah, where he would later do many classic Westerns. Ford said he liked filming there, not just because of the beautiful landscape, but because it gave work to the Navajos living in the area.
- It was trading post owner Harry Goulding who first thought it would be a great place to make movies and tipped off Ford to visit the site.
- The Indian chase was actually shot in the Mojave Desert near Victorville, Calif.
- When Ford first spoke to Wayne about the film, he baited Duke and asked him who he thought would be good in the role of Ringo and Wayne replied, "Lloyd Nolan." Ford and Wayne did 13 films together.

- Wayne was in the box-office Top 10 list for a quarter-century (1949-1974), missing only 1958—and he was first four times.

True Grit

1969, Paramount, 128 minutes, Color.
Producer: Hal B. Wallis. Director: Henry Hathaway.
Cast: John Wayne, Kim Darby, Glen Campbell, Robert Duvall, Jeff Corey, Strother Martin, Dennis Hopper.

> "Old Duke's never been better, and he's been damn good several times before."
>
> —Steven H. Scheuer

This was Wayne's first and only Best Actor Oscar in a career spanning 40 years and 250 films. Some critics said "Duke" won as a gesture of sentimentality by academy members. Nothing could be further from the truth. No major Hollywood star could have played the part but big John, who was overweight and 61 at the time, perfect for the role of a fat, old, gruff, drunken, one-eyed U.S. marshal with a checkered past. Wayne had played alongside all the great character actors of his day: George "Gabby" Hayes, Walter Brennan, Ward Bond, Edgar Buchanan, John Carradine, Andy Devine, Thomas Mitchell, Russell Simpson, Bruce Cabot, Jay C. Flippen, and more. And he put a little bit of all of them into his onerous but heartwarming character, Reuben J. "Rooster" Cogburn. No, Wayne's performance wasn't a sympathy win; he knew exactly what he was doing in a role he was born to play—and it was an Oscar that was well-deserved.

The script, about a veteran lawman with "true grit," is by Marguerite Roberts based on the book by Charles Portis. A young girl in her upper teens, Mattie Ross (Darby), hires Cogburn to go after the man who shot and killed her father. The villain on the run in Indian country near Fort Smith, Arkansas is Tom Chaney (Corey) who throws in with a gang of killers led by Ned Pepper (Duvall). Joining Cogburn and Mattie in the search is a Texas Ranger named La Boeuf (Campbell) who's also looking for Chaney for murdering a senator in Texas. Their many adventures conclude with "Rooster" alone facing down Pepper and three of his men in a showdown on horseback with guns blazing and Cogburn proving to Mattie he isn't just a big-mouth drunk but that he really does have "true grit."

John Wayne as Rooster Cogburn in *True Grit*.

H.W. Gim is Cogburn's roommate, Chen Lee; Martin plays horse-trader Col. Stonehill; Hopper is Moon, one of Ned's gang, and Hank Worden, a veteran of many John Wayne/John Ford films, plays the undertaker.

- Roberts added the last scene at the family cemetery that led to Wayne jumping his horse over a fence with the shot of "Duke" in flight frozen over the closing credits.
- Stuntman Chuck Hayward says Wayne actually did the jumping scene, riding Chuck's own horse named Twinkletoes.
- Campbell sings the title song.
- Elvis Presley was considered for the role of La Boeuf and Sally Field was considered for the part of Mattie.
- It was filmed in Colorado at Ouray and Ridgway.

The Wild Bunch

1969, Warner Bros./Seven Arts, 145 minutes, Color.
Producer: Phil Feldman. Director: Sam Peckinpah.
Cast: William Holden, Robert Ryan, Ernest Borgnine, Edmond O'Brien, Warren Oates, Ben Johnson, Jaime Sanchez, Emilio Fernandez, Strother Martin, L.Q. Jones, Albert Dekker, Bo Hopkins.

> "A towering achievement! A riveting, brilliant work of art."
> —Peter Travers, *Rolling Stone*

It *is* the most violent super-Western ever made, but somehow I'm not offended by its massive bloody violence; why wouldn't you expect to see a horrific ending for a gang of thieves and killers called "the wild bunch?"—especially since they take on what looks like the whole Mexican army at the end.

Thomas Jefferson once said that shedding the blood of tyrants from time to time, for the sake of liberty, is not a bad thing. And this bunch suddenly has an epiphany and do their bit to rid the landscape of oppressors.

Robert Ryan after the massacre in *The Wild Bunch*.

But these six are not patriots. Pike Bishop (Holden) and his gang are 1913 South Texas outlaws who've outlived their time and *their* time is up—and they know it. Deke Thornton (Ryan), a former saddle pal now working for the law, and in pursuit of the bunch, wishes "to God I was with them." Deke's pursuers are a motley seven while Pike's bunch are professional desperados, trying to stay loyal to one another, as Pike stresses: "When you side with a man, you stay with him; if you can't do that you're like some animal."

The film opens with children playing with a scorpion in a dusty village street. The film ends in a massacre. Symbolically, like the ants devouring the scorpion, the world of automobiles and Gatling guns is closing in on Pike and his bunch: Dutch (Borgnine), Sykes (O'Brien), Lyle (Oates), Tector (Johnson), Angel (Sanchez).

Fernandez plays Gen. Mapache, rival to Pancho Villa. Hopkins is "Crazy" Lee. Martin plays Coffer, Jones is T.C., and Dekker is Harrigan.

- Shot entirely in Mexico, at Durango and around Coahuila.
- The shootout climax took 12 days to film and editor Lou Lombardo made over 300 edits to piece together the massacre.
- Over 90,000 blank rounds of ammunition were used during production.
- The death march at the end was improvised by Peckinpah.
- Jerry Fielding and Sonny Burke did the music with its snare-drum and cymbal march-beat to certain death.
- The exploding bridge scene—the last shoot of the film—was done in one take; it was shot with six cameras; one fell in the water. Five stuntmen were used, each was paid $2,000.

Musicals

All That Jazz

1979, 20th Century-Fox, 123 minutes, Color.
Producer: Robert Alan Arthur. Director: Bob Fosse.
Cast: Roy Scheider, Jessica Lange, Ann Reinking, Leland Palmer, Erzebet Foldi, Deborah Geffner, Ben Vereen.

> "A masterwork An extravagant achievement that will be seen again and again."
> —Gene Shalit, NBC-TV

After this unusual film was shown at the Cannes Film Festival, the audience enthusiastically stood and applauded. As far as innovation in musicals is concerned, Hollywood won't get much better than this; after all, look who did it—the incomparable Bob Fosse. The semi-autobiographical musical-fantasy received an Academy Award nomination for Best Picture. Fosse was nominated for directing and Scheider, as choreographer/director Joe Gidion, was nominated for Best Actor.

However, the surrealistic film is about a rather unpopular subject—death, personified by a beautiful woman, Angelique (Lange). But there's a whole lot before life's final episode, like what goes into putting on a Broadway show, and the most erotic dance number ever screened: the nine-minute Air-otica Airlines routine led by statuesque Sandahl Bergman.

Reinking plays Kate, Joe's lover; Palmer is his ex-wife, Audrey. Foldi is their precocious adolescent daughter, Michelle. Geffner is Victoria, an easy-to-bed and not-very-good dancer. Vereen plays an annoying TV star, O'Connor Flood. They all participate in Gidion's deathbed hallucination ending, a spectacular musical odyssey that is not likely to be equaled or surpassed anytime soon.

Roy Scheider as Gidion and Jessica Lange as Angelique in *All That Jazz*.

- Fosse conceived the idea after his own brush with death, coronary bypass surgery.
- The title comes from Fosse's Broadway show *Chicago*, which eventually became an Oscar-winning movie.
- Fosse's real ex-wife was dancer/actress Gwen Verdon.
- Richard Dreyfuss was originally cast as Joe but quit during early rehearsals.

An American In Paris

1951, MGM, 113 minutes, Color.
Producer: Arthur Freed. Director: Vincente Minnelli.
Cast: Gene Kelly, Leslie Caron, Georges Guetary, Nina Foch, Oscar Levant.

> "One of Hollywood's most pleasing musicals...Splendid MGM production values...The final musical sequence remains unexcelled as a film ballet."
> —Leslie Halliwell, *Halliwell's Filmgoer's Companion*

Featuring a terrific 18-minute closing ballet, choreographed by Kelly, the popular musical is based on George Gershwin's symphonic tone poem of the same name. The film won the Oscar for Best Picture and also won

Gene Kelly, star and co-director of *An American in Paris*.

Academy Awards for score, screenplay, photography, sets, and costumes. (Kelly received a Special Academy Award.)

Kelly plays Jerry Mulligan, an American artist living in post-war Paris. He meets an attractive and wealthy woman, Milo Robbins (Foch), who becomes his patron; she buys his art but is unable to win his heart. That belongs to Lise Bourvier (Caron), a pretty shopgirl who happens to be engaged to a French nightclub entertainer (Guetary). Jerry is out to turn her affections around. Mulligan's pal in all this is pianist Adam Cook (Levant).

The words and music are by George and Ira Gershwin. There are four great Gershwin songs: "It's Wonderful," "Our Love Is Here To Stay," "Embraceable You," "I Got Rhythm." And Guetary does Goetz and DeSylva's "I'll Build A Stairway To Paradise" as part of his act.

- They wanted Chevalier over Guetary but Maurice was not available.
- The part of Lise was set for Cyd Charisse but she got pregnant. Kelly remembered seeing lovely Leslie dance in a Parisian ballet and offered her the part. She was just 20. Freed also thought it'd be good if the girl was actually French.
- It wasn't shot in Paris but on MGM sets, though there are a couple of Paris scenes that were taken without Kelly present.
- The big musical ending took a month to film.

The Band Wagon

1953, MGM, 112 minutes, Color.
Producer: Arthur Freed. Director: Vincente Minnelli.
Cast: Fred Astaire, Cyd Charisse, Oscar Levant, Nanette Fabray, Jack Buchanan.

> "It was not only a sophisticated tribute to all those innocent backstage movies that had preceded it, but was also a brilliantly double-edged tribute to its star, Fred Astaire...what could be considered his finest role in the best film he ever made."
> —*The Hollywood Musical.*

Fred and Cyd's "Dancing In The Dark" number is pure magic! And their "Girl Hunt" ballet, staged by Michael Kidd, is stunning—a super-

Cyd Charisse and Fred Astaire in the "Dancing In The Dark" number in *The Band Wagon*.

charged satire on 50s detective mysteries.

Other terrific songs by Howard Dietz and Arthur Schwartz: "By Myself," "That's Entertainment!," "Put A Shine On Your Shoes," "You And The Night And The Music," "I Guess I'll Have To Change My Plans," "A New Sun," "Louisiana Hayride," "I Love Louisa" and "Triplets"—in which Fred, Jack, and Nanette perform on their knees dressed as babies.

The story and screenplay by Adolph Green and Betty Comden has Charisse playing a ballet star, Gabrielle Girard, signed to do a Broadway show with Tony Hunter (Astaire), a Hollywood star whose film career has hit a snag. Levant and Fabray, Tony's friends, are hired to write the show. But an avant-garde director, played by Buchanan, turns the project into a mess and it's up to the old pro, Hunter, to save the day.

- The picture opens with an auction selling off some of Tony's nostalgic apparel, notably top hat and cane, purposely reminiscent of Astaire's *Top Hat*, making the film a self-parody of Fred.
- Fabray wore a hearing aid.
- Fabray cut her leg during "Louisiana Hayride" when she fell through the crate on which she was standing.
- The Fabray/Levant characters were based on Comden/Green.
- The title is from the 1931 Dietz and Schwartz Broadway musical which starred Astaire and sister Adele. The only songs that made it from the stage to the film are "Dancing In The Dark," "New Sun" and "I Love Louisa."
- Ava Gardner does a cameo near the beginning. The appearance had a dual purpose: it establishes that Fred's character was really a big star in Hollywood and it also served to promote Ava's new MGM film, *Mogambo,* also released in 1953.

Cabin in the Sky

1943, MGM, 100 minutes, B&W.
Producer: Arthur Freed. Director: Vincente Minnelli.
Cast: Eddie Anderson, Ethel Waters, Lena Horne, Rex Ingram, Kenneth Spencer, John Bubbles, Mantan Moreland, Butterfly McQueen, Louis Armstrong, Duke Ellington, Oscar Polk, The Hall Johnson Choir.

> "Forget Joseph Schrank's script and enjoy the precious footage of some of the most famous black performers at their peaks."
> —Danny Peary

It played for about three months on Broadway before Arthur Freed decided to make it a movie musical, and what a fine decision that was. It's a rare all-black musical, only three others challenge it as the best: *Stormy Weather, Green Pastures, Hallelujah.* And, wisely, Freed brought along the musical-fantasy's star, Waters, and director Minnelli, making his film debut. Ethel sings what are now pop standards: "Taking A Chance On Love" and "Happiness Is Just A Thing Called Joe."

Anderson, popular on radio/TV as Jack Benny's wisecracking butler, Rochester, stars as "Little Joe" Jackson, a good-for-nothing gambler who is adored, despite his faults, by wife Petunia (Waters). When Joe is

Eddie "Rochester" Anderson and Lena Horne in *Cabin in the Sky*.

shot and gravely wounded in a poker game, church-going Petunia prays super-hard to save him. But behind the scenes, spirit forces are at work to win over Joe's soul— Lucifer Jr. (Ingram) is battling an ambassador from Heaven (Spencer). To tempt Joe to the evil side, the Devil's disciple employs beautiful and sexy Georgia Brown (Horne), almost more than any man could resist, let alone lazy Joe.

McQueen (famous as Prissy in *GWTW*) is Lily, Moreland (the chauffeur in the Charlie Chan series) is The Idea Man, Bubbles plays Domino, and Polk is The Deacon. Adding wonderfully to the music scene is the Hall Johnson Choir, Louis Armstrong as The Trumpeter, and Duke Ellington featured with his fabulous orchestra.

- The tornado was footage from *The Wizard of Oz.*
- Ingram also starred in the Broadway production; he was the genie in the British production of *The Thief of Bagdad* (1940).
- Bill Bailey, Pearl Bailey's brother, does "The Moon Walk" later popularized by Michael Jackson.

The Gay Divorcee

1934, RKO Radio, 107 minutes, B&W.
Producer: Pandro S. Berman. Director: Mark Sandrich.
Cast: Fred Astaire, Ginger Rogers, Alice Brady, Edward Everett Horton.

> "It's one of their finest films, one that has great dancing and, though many don't agree, very amusing comedy."
> —Danny Peary

Astaire and Rogers had stolen the show the year before in *Flying Down to Rio,* even though they had supporting roles. This was their first film in which they co-starred, and it picked up an Oscar nomination for Best Picture. And it won the Oscar for Best Song: "The Continental"; the hypnotic production number was the screen's longest, 17 minutes, until Gene Kelly topped it with his amazing 18-minute ballet in *An American in Paris.*

The musical is based on the stage play, *The Gay Divorce,* but the Hays Office (Hollywood's censors) wanted an "e" added to thwart suggestions that a divorce might be a happy event. Mimi Glossop (Rogers) is getting a divorce from her peripatric husband and has retained the services of attorney Egbert Fitzgerald (Horton), befuddled friend of dancer Guy Holden (Astaire). Hortense (Brady) is Mimi's light-headed aunt. Egbert assures Mimi that the quickest way to get a divorce is for her to be caught with a man in a hotel room. But Guy accidentally stumbles into the set-up and is mistaken by Mimi as her lover, a role Guy prefers in reality.

The only Cole Porter song that made the transition from Broadway to Hollywood is the enchanting "Night And Day" which is beautifully danced by Fred and Ginger.

Fred Astaire and Ginger Rogers dancing "The Continental" in *The Gay Divorcee*.

- Astaire, not the credited Dave Gould, did his own choreography, assisted by Hermes Pan.
- Astaire insisted on being filmed with full-body shots to prove to the audience that his routines were complete and not interrupted by close-ups of fancy footwork inserted by an editor.
- This is the only film on which Astaire plays a role he originated on Broadway (in 1932).
- Betty Grable has a key part in the "Let's Knock Knees" number.

Gold Diggers of 1935

1935, Warner Bros., 95 minutes, B&W.
Producer/Director: Busby Berkeley.
Cast: Dick Powell, Gloria Stuart, Adolphe Menjou, Alice Brady, Winifred Shaw, Hugh Herbert, Frank McHugh, Gloria Farrell.

> "...*Lullaby of Broadway*...arguably the acme of Berkeley's remarkable career and his own favorite of all the numbers he created."
> —*The Hollywood Musical.*

The screen's greatest production number for group dancers, *Lullaby of Broadway* won Berkeley an Oscar nomination for Best Dance Direction

Busby Berkeley (third from left) director/choreographer for *Gold Diggers of 1935*, scanning a line of potential chorus girls.

(a now defunct category). The tune itself, by Harry Warren and Al Dubin, won for Best Song.

The sequence, a day and night in the life of a chorus girl, is really a film within a film, beginning with Shaw's face as a white speck on a black canvas, growing larger into extreme close-up, merging into a number featuring 100 men and women. Berkeley's busy cameras are angled from all directions—slanted, overhead, underneath, moving in and out, mingled with close-ups, capturing all sides of shapely women in precision with male partners, in geometric movement and design; a singular achievement in group tap dancing, a fantasy created over a series of stepped platforms; women in black with leather halters and bare midriff, men in waistcoats and black trousers; dancing feet atop a camera lens (on glass photographed from below).

The story itself—not much to behold, just another over-used plot about getting a Broadway show produced, but the numbers—amazing! Another number by Warren and Dubin, "The Words Are In My Heart," utilizes 56 girls and 56 miniature pianos.

Powell plays Dick Curtis, Stuart is Ann Prentiss, Brady is Matilda Prentiss, McHugh plays Humbolt Prentiss, Herbert is T. Mosley Thorpe, Farrell is Betty Hawes, and Menjou is Nicolai Nicoleff.

- The pianos move about the stage by 56 men inside.
- Martin the hotel desk clerk is played by Gordon Elliott who went on to become B-Western star Wild Bill Elliott.
- Stuart retired from the screen in 1946 but came back for a key part in *Titanic* over 50 years later.

Guys and Dolls

1955, Goldwyn/MGM, 138 minutes, Color.
Producer: Samuel Goldwyn. Director: Joseph L. Mankiewicz.
Cast: Marlon Brando, Jean Simmons, Frank Sinatra, Vivian Blaine, Stubby Kaye, Regis Toomey, Johnny Silver, Robert Keith, B.S. Pully.

> "It had been a great show and was a good film."
> —*The MGM Story.*

This top-flight musical was a major hit on-stage and just as big a hit on film: *Guys and Dolls* was the box-office smash of 1956! Based on a short

Frank Sinatra and Vivian Blaine in *Guys and Dolls*.

story by Damon Runyon, the movie also received several Academy Award nominations, for photography, sets, costumes, and score. And, over the years, it has gained followers as a cult film. Why? Because Brando sings and dances!—and does it quite well.

There's something about Miss Simmons that makes her perfectly cast as a sexually-repressed preacher. She does it wonderfully again five years later as evangelist Sister Falconer in *Elmer Gantry*. Maybe it has something to do with her being a brunette; pretty blondes and redheads don't seem to fit the image of a Salvation Army missionary, which is what she is here—as Sister Sarah Brown. She's taken for a ride by gambler Sky Masterson (Brando) who soon learns he's been converted—not to religion, but to falling in love with Sarah.

All the terrific Runyonesque gangsters and characters are here: Harry the Horse, Rusty Charlie, Society Max, Angie the Ox, Liverlips Louie—and, lest we forget, Big Jule (Pully).

Sinatra is crap-game promoter Nathan Detroit, Blaine is his long-suffering fiancée Miss Adelaide, Kaye is outstanding as Nicely-Nicely Johnson, Silver is Benny Southstreet, Toomey plays Brother Arvide Abernathy, and Keith is Lt. Brannigan.

And all the great Frank Loesser songs are here, plus a few extra: "Luck Be A Lady" is a big show-stopper with Brando shooting craps with the boys in a Broadway sewer; another equally great show-stopper is Kaye's confessional "Sit Down, You're Rockin' The Boat;" Blaine and the Goldwyn Girls rock the place with "Take Back Your Mink;" Sinatra leads the boys with "The Oldest Established Permanent Floating Crap Game" and "Fugue For Tin Horns;" and Brando and Simmons do duets on "A Woman In Love," "If I Were A Bell" and "I'll Know." A lovely tune from the stage show, "Bushel and a Peck," was not a part of the film—it was later recorded as a duo by Perry Como and Betty Hutton.

- Blaine, Kaye, Pully, and Silver did their roles on Broadway.
- "A Woman In Love" was added for the movie; it became a hit recording by a number of different artists.
- Rumor has it that Sky Masterson was based on frontier marshal Bat Masterson who moved to New York and became a sportswriter and expert on the horse track.

The Music Man

1962, Warner Bros., 131 minutes, Color.
Producer: Jack Warner. Director: Morton Da Costa.
Cast: Robert Preston, Shirley Jones, Buddy Hackett, Ronny Howard, Paul Ford, Hermione Gingold, Pert Kelton, The Buffalo Bills.

> "**** It's fun for the whole family, and what more could one ask?"
> —Steven H. Scheuer, *Movies on TV*

Meredith Willson's stage hit comes to the screen with the actor who helped make it a success on Broadway: Preston's Professor Harold Hill is

Shirley Jones and Robert Preston in *The Music Man*.

one of the all-time great characters in the lexicon of musicals. This truly is what a family musical should be: wonderful characters, a terrific plotline, marvelous songs, and happy moments to remember. It's all here in *The Music Man*, nominated for Best Picture.

Hill is a phony traveling salesman in the Midwest, pitching parents on creating a town band for their kids, but before the instruments and uniforms arrive, Hill is off to the next county—with their money. Fact is, Hill can't read music and has no intention of teaching the youngsters how to play. However, this time, in River City, Iowa, Hill gets stuck because he's fallen in love with the local librarian, Marian Paroo (Jones). Tar and feathering seems right around the corner…*unless*…somehow someway those crazy kids really do start to play, using Hill's "think system."

The songs include: "76 Trombones," "Till There Was You," "Trouble," "The Wells-Fargo Wagon," "Gary, Indiana," "Marian The Librarian," "The Sadder But Wiser Girl," "Pick-A-Little," "Sincere," "Goodnight My Someone."

Hackett is Marcellus Washburn, Hill's partner in double-dealing. Howard is Marian's non-talkative little brother, Winthrop. Kelton is Mrs. Paroo. Ford is Mayor Shinn, Gingold plays Mrs. Shinn. Also with barber shop singers The Buffalo Bills.

- Preston, who had never sung on-stage before, did 883 performances on Broadway and Willson insisted on Preston in the film—or no show.
- Kelton and the Buffalo Bills reprised their New York roles.
- Da Costa also directed the stage production.
- River City was really Mason City, Iowa, Willson's hometown, where the film's premiere took place.
- Jones became pregnant halfway through production but was shielded by sets, props, and special dresses.
- The USC and UCLA marching bands were used in the final scene.

My Fair Lady

1964, Warner Bros., 170 minutes, Color.
Producer: Jack L. Warner. Director: George Cukor.
Cast: Rex Harrison, Audrey Hepburn, Stanley Holloway, Wilfrid Hyde-White, Gladys Cooper, Jeremy Brett, Mona Washbourne.

> "A brilliant, stunning film. *My Fair Lady* is magnificent!"
> —*The New York Daily News.*

There's little doubt that Warner made a mistake in not giving the part of Eliza Doolittle to Julie Andrews, who dearly wanted it and had played it on Broadway. But there was no need for the Motion Picture Academy to get so offended: they didn't even nominate Hepburn for an Oscar while nominating Debbie Reynolds for *The Unsinkable Molly Brown*. (Now don't get me wrong, I love Debbie, I interviewed her backstage after watching her exuberant stage show; but Hepburn—wonderful as Eliza—clearly deserved at least a nomination.)

The film received 13 Academy Award nominations and won nine Oscars, including Best Picture, Best Actor (Harrison), and Best Director (Cukor's first). Cecil Beaton won two Oscars, for costumes and sets.

Harrison as Henry Higgins, the archetypical male chauvinist, was a role he made famous in a heralded six-year run on Broadway. Lerner and Loewe's musical about an English phonetics professor, Higgins, who bets he can turn a cockney flower girl, Eliza, into a lady, was adapted from the play *Pygmalion* by George Bernard Shaw.

Rex Harrison, Audrey Hepburn and director George Cukor on the set of *My Fair Lady*.

The marvelous songs quickly found an honored place in the lexicon of modern music: "I Could Have Danced All Night," "With A Little Bit Of Luck," "Show Me," "Just You Wait," "Wouldn't It Be Loverly," "On The Street Where You Live," "You Did It," "Get Me To The Church On Time," "The Rain In Spain," "I'm An Ordinary Man," "I've Grown Accustomed To Your Face."

Holloway reprised his Broadway role as Eliza's father, Alfred P. Doolittle. Hyde-White is Col. Pickering, Higgins' co-hort in the metamorphosis. Cooper plays Henry's mother, Mrs. Higgins. Washbourne is Mrs. Pearce, Henry's housekeeper. Brett is Freddy Eynsford-Hill, the young man who falls madly in love with Eliza.

- Hepburn's songs were dubbed by Marni Nixon.
- Because of Harrison's need to sing and talk the songs, they were unable to pre-record for lip-sync; so he wore a wireless mike under his tie.
- Cary Grant was considered for the role of Higgins but he vehemently refused: "It's Rex's show and if anyone but Rex plays the part I won't even bother to see the movie."

Oklahoma!

1955, Magna Pictures, 145 minutes, Color.
Producer: Arthur Hornblow, Jr. Director: Fred Zinnemann.
Cast: Gordon MacRae, Shirley Jones, Gloria Grahame, Gene Nelson, Rod Steiger, Charlotte Greenwood, Eddie Albert, James Whitmore.

> "Twelve years after it first took Broadway by storm…this watershed musical transferred triumphantly to celluloid."
> —*The Hollywood Musical.*

One of the greatest musicals of all time, both on-stage and on-screen, won Oscars for score and sound and got nominated for photography and editing, but it should have been nominated for Best Picture (one of the most egregious oversights in the history of Hollywood).

The Richard Rodgers-Oscar Hammerstein classic is about love in the wide-open territory looking to become the fortieth state, just as soon as the cowboys and farmers learn "to be friends." MacRae and Jones are perfect as the young lovers, Curly McLain and Laurey Williams.

The film is filled with great humor, both in plot and dance, choreography by Agnes DeMille. Grahame is a wonderful surprise as Ado Annie,

Gordon MacRae and Charlotte Greenwood in *Oklahoma!*

the "girl who just can't say no." Her boyfriend, Will Parker, is played by Nelson who does one of the screen's most memorable dance numbers: "Everything's Up-to-Date In Kansas City."

Songs include: "Oh What A Beautiful Morning," "Surrey With The Fringe On Top," "People Will Say We're In Love," "All Er Nuthin'," "Poor Jud Is Dead," "Many A New Day," "The Farmer And The Cowhand," "Oklahoma!"

Also with: Steiger as the evil Jud Fry, Greenwood as rubber-legged Aunt Eller, Whitmore as Annie's shotgun-toting father, and Albert as panhandler Ali Hakim.

- It was the first Todd-AO film; also shot in CinemaScope, which is the version most people saw in the theaters.
- It played on Broadway for 2,212 performances.
- The soundtrack album was one of the most successful sellers ever released.
- It was filmed in the San Rafael Valley of Arizona because Oklahoma had too many oil derricks, telephone poles, and planes overhead.
- The corn, "as high as an elephant's eye," had to be brought in from out-of-state and replanted.

Singin' in the Rain

1952, MGM, 103 minutes, Color.
Producer: Arthur Freed. Directors: Gene Kelly, Stanley Donen.
Cast: Gene Kelly, Debbie Reynolds, Donald O'Connor, Jean Hagen, Cyd Charisse, Millard Mitchell.

> "One of the best, and best written story-lines (by Betty Comden and Adolph Green) to grace a Hollywood musical…and a marvelous opportunity to take a lighthearted and often satirical look at the early days of talking pictures."
> —*The Hollywood Musical.*

This musical-comedy classic contains three of the greatest musical numbers ever produced: Kelly's four-minute "Singin' In The Rain" (hanging on a lamp-post, flipping an umbrella, splashing in the street-gutter), O'Connor's

Gene Kelly and Debbie Reynolds in a promotional photo for *Singin' in the Rain*.

"Make 'Em Laugh" (screwing up his face like it was made of plastic clay and somersaulting off the wall), and the 13-minute "Broadway Rhythm Ballet" (Kelly and Charisse in a number that is nothing short of spectacular).

But there's even more, including: "Good Morning" (Reynolds, Kelly, O'Connor), "Fit As A Fiddle" (Kelly, O'Connor), "Moses Supposes" (Kelly, O'Connor), "You Were Meant For Me" (Kelly, Reynolds), "All I Do Is Dream Of You" (Reynolds, flapper chorus), and "Beautiful Girl (chorus)—a parody of the Busby Berkeley musicals.

The plot is about the transition in Hollywood between silent and sound pictures. Kelly plays matinee idol Don Lockwood and O'Connor is his friend, pianist, and idea man, Cosmo Brown. Hagen is Lina Lamont, a pretty but dumb-blonde actress with a squeaky voice which Monumental

Pictures producer R.F. Simpson (Mitchell) tries to hide by dubbing in the voice of novice actress Kathy Selden, played by Reynolds in her first starring role: she was 19.

- They had to mix milk with the water in the "Singin' In The Rain" sequence because the rainwater wasn't showing up properly for the camera.
- Betty Royce dubbed Debbie's singing voice—which means Betty was dubbing Debbie dubbing Lina.
- Debbie's tapping sound was dubbed by Kelly's feet.
- Debbie's feet were bleeding after rehearsing "Good Morning" hundreds of times.
- Reynolds said Kelly was a taskmaster and sent her to dance lessons eight hours a day for three months with three teachers including Carol Haney.
- O'Connor was bedridden with exhaustion for three days after doing "Make 'Em Laugh."

The Sound of Music

1965, 20th Century-Fox/Argyle Enterprises, 174 minutes, Color.
Producer/Director: Robert Wise.
Cast: Julie Andrews, Christopher Plummer, Eleanor Parker, Richard Haydn, Peggy Wood, Charmian Carr.

> "…as a piece of old-fashioned popular entertainment with both eyes firmly on the box-office cash registers of the world, it was a shrewdly professional piece of work, stunningly presented, and crafted with awesome expertise."
> —*The Hollywood Musical.*

Financially, it is the most successful movie musical of all time, grossing nearly $600 million (adjusted for inflation), #5 on the list of top moneymakers. And critically, it also has its special place in cinematic history—nominated for 10 Oscars and winning five, including Best Picture and Best Director.

The popular family film is based on a true story, originally told in a book by Howard Lindsay and Russel Crouse which, in turn, was made into

Julie Andrews and Christopher Plummer in *The Sound of Music*.

a successful Broadway production; Mary Martin starred on-stage with music by Richard Rodgers and Oscar Hammerstein II. The story is about Maria and Baron von Trapp and their singing family's flight from Nazi-occupied Austria into Switzerland in 1938. In real life, just as in the film, Maria, her husband and the seven children hike over the Austrian Alps to make their escape from Hitler's forces. In the movie, Andrews plays Maria and Plummer is her husband, the strict Captain Georg. Maria, at the age of 20, had left a Salzburg convent to become governess for the motherless children of the Baron. She and the decorated ex-naval officer fell in love and married a year later.

The memorable songs include: "Do-Re-Mi," "My Favorite Things," "Climb Every Mountain," "Maria," "Sixteen Going On Seventeen," "Edelweiss," plus the title song.

Parker plays the Baroness; Haydn is the family friend, Max Detweiler; Wood is the Reverend Mother, and Carr is Liesl, the eldest child.

- It was shot on location in and around Salzburg; the film opens with an extended helicopter-camera view of the beautiful Austrian countryside.
- Mary Martin, as one of the co-producers, made multiple millions from the film.
- William Wyler was originally assigned as director but pulled out of the project so he could do a thriller he liked very much, *The Collector*.
- Marni Nixon, famous for dubbing the songs for Audrey Hepburn in *My Fair Lady*, Deborah Kerr in *The King and I*, and Natalie Wood in *West Side Story*, makes her only screen appearance as nun-in-training Sophie. She was the wife of composer Ernest Gold (*It's a Mad, Mad, Mad, Mad World*), and mother of singer/composer Andrew Gold.
- Angela Cartwright, as Brigitta, was one of the stars of TV's "Lost in Space."
- The real Maria died at 82 in 1987 in a hospital near the Trapp Family Lodge, an Austrian chalet-style resort on an 800-acre estate in Stowe, Vermont.

That's Entertainment!

1974, MGM, 132 minutes, Color/B&W.
Producer/Director: Jack Haley, Jr.
Cast: (as hosts/narrators) Fred Astaire, Bing Crosby, Gene Kelly, Peter Lawford, Liza Minnelli, Donald O'Connor, Debbie Reynolds, Mickey Rooney, Frank Sinatra, James Stewart, Elizabeth Taylor.

> "Sparkling compilation of show-stoppers from over 70 MGM musicals, from *The Hollywood Revue of 1929* to 1958's *Gigi*."
> —*TV Guide*.

Other studios did musicals, but none did more or did them better than MGM. This film is more than a series of musical numbers edited together; it's a history lesson for movie buffs about the golden years of

Esther Williams in one of the giant water production numbers in *That's Entertainment!*

moviemaking. The picture is great fun for those of us who lived through those glorious years but it's also a primer for the modern generation who may have never heard of Nelson Eddy-Jeanette MacDonald operettas, or swimming sensation Esther Williams, or nightclub icon Jimmy Durante, or Deanna Durbin (Judy Garland's teenage rival), or Eleanor Powell (what dancing legs!), the greatest tap dancer the screen has ever known (notwithstanding Ann Miller).

Among the clips are Garland as an early member of the Gumm Sisters, Garland and Durbin in a 1936 short, Crosby in "*Going Hollywood*," Kelly and the fabulous Nicholas Brothers from *The Pirate*, the great voice of Mario Lanza singing "Be My Love" to Kathryn Grayson in *The Toast of New Orleans,* Astaire and Kelly dancing together (their only time) in *Ziegfeld Follies,* and Garland doing her version of "You Made Me Love You"—(Dear Mr. Gable) sung to a picture of Clark Gable.

There's more, *lots* more. So much so that Haley (son of The Tin Man in *The Wizard of Oz)* produced two sequels.

- The DVD/video ranks with *Gone With the Wind* and *The Wizard of Oz* as MGM's top-sellers.

- Sinatra said *The Hollywood Revue of 1929* was the first talking musical; not so—*Broadway Melody* was released nine months earlier.
- In fact, that is not Dennis Morgan's voice in *The Great Ziegfeld* clip; it was dubbed by Allan Jones.
- This was the last film shot on the MGM backlot; it was torn down after the shoot. They put in a housing development.

West Side Story

1961, United Artists, 151 minutes, Color.
Producers: Robert Wise, Saul Chaplin; Directors: Robert Wise, Jerome Robbins.
Cast: Natalie Wood, Richard Beymer, George Chakiris, Rita Moreno, Russ Tamblyn.

> "Nothing short of a cinema masterpiece!"
> —*The New York Times.*

Winner of 10 Academy Awards, including Best Picture, the hit musical has some of Broadway's most famous music ("Tonight," "America," "I Feel Pretty," "Maria") and is loosely based on Shakespeare's "Romeo and Juliet." The excellent music is by Leonard Bernstein with lyrics by Stephen Sondheim. Ernest Lehman's fine screenplay is taken from the highly successful stage show by Howard S. Prince and Robert E. Griffith. For the film, as for the New York show, Robbins handled choreography.

The 1950's love story between a white boy and a Puerto Rican girl in New York City is played out against the backdrop of two street gangs: the Jets and Sharks, heading for an all-out fight—a street rumble. Wood plays the girl, Maria, and Beymer is the boy, Tony.

Supporting Oscars went to Moreno (Anita) and Chakiris (Bernardo). Tamblyn is Riff, the leader of the Jets.

- Wood's singing is dubbed by Marni Nixon.
- Carol Lawrence played Maria on stage and was very disappointed that she didn't get the movie.
- Wise actually wanted Elvis Presley to play Tony.
- Actual street gang members visited the New York outdoor sets and Wise hired some of them to do crowd control.

Musicals 471

Jerome Robbins and Robert Wise co-directing *West Side Story*.

- Originally the plot was planned as a Catholic boy falling for a Jewish girl, which would have made the title East Side Story.

Yankee Doodle Dandy

1942, Warner Bros., 126 minutes, B&W.
Producers: Jack Warner, Hal B. Wallis; Director: Michael Curtiz.
Cast: James Cagney, Joan Leslie, Walter Huston, Rosemary DeCamp, Richard Whorf, S.Z. Sakall, Jeanne Cagney.

> "...the best musical of 1942 and one of the best biopics to come out of Hollywood...Cagney's performance, both physically and temperamentally, captured to perfection the appearance as well as the essence of the man."
> —*The Hollywood Musical*

Now a perennial Fourth of July favorite on television, Cagney's impersonation of Broadway great George M. Cohan (1878-1942) provided Cagney with a Best Actor Oscar and the film was nominated for Best Pic-

James Cagney as George M. Cohan in *Yankee Doodle Dandy*.

ture. Pugnacious Jimmy is positively electrifying in the role of the song-and-dance man, dancing off stage walls and dominating every scene. The story takes Cohan from his young world as a member of The Four Cohans to fame and fortune as the biggest star on The Great White Way.

Cohan (who died the year of the film's release and who personally chose Cagney to play him) wrote 35 plays and 500 songs in his 55-year career and some of the best of those songs are here: "Give My Regards to Broadway," "Mary," "Harrigan," "Over There," "45 Minutes From Broadway," "It's A Grand Old Flag," and "I'm A Yankee Doodle Dandy."

Leslie, who was just 17 at the time, plays Mary, Cohan's sweetheart/wife. Huston is Jerry Cohan, George's father; DeCamp is the mother.

Jeanne Cagney, Jimmy's real sister, plays George's sister. Whorf is producer-partner Sam Harris. Sakall is Mr. Schwab, the show backer.

- It was Cagney's favorite film.
- In retirement, Cagney, who started out as a "hoofer," lamented that he had not made more musicals.
- Cohan, actually born on July 3, preferred to say he was born on the fourth to promote his patriotic productions.
- Huston was only five years older than Cagney and DeCamp was 15 years younger, though they played Cagney's mom and dad.
- Leslie said she and Cagney did the duet number "Harrigan" in one take.
- Eddie Foy, Jr. does a cameo as his famous father.

About the Author

George McManus spent 40 years as a broadcast journalist, most of it in California, where he covered the Academy Awards backstage.

His time in radio/TV also provided him the opportunity to interview, at length, dozens of filmmakers, often while they were on a book or movie promotion tour. These experiences not only inspired this book, but also enhanced the author's knowledge/appreciation of the films that grace these pages.

Mr. McManus lives with his wife and their children in Northern California. He hosts The Midnight Movie on the local community access channel.

Acknowledgments

Academy of Motion Picture Arts and Sciences ("Oscar" and "Academy Award" are registered trademarks and service marks of the Academy)
Allison Baeza
American Film Institute
British Film Institute
Prof. Richard Brown
Charles Champlin
The Chicago Daily News
The Chicago Tribune
Mike Clark, *USA Today*
Entertainment Weekly
Exhibitor Relations Company
The Film Quarterly
Jack Garner, Gannett News Service
Dan Hess
Hollywood Foreign Press Association ("Golden Globes" is a registered trademark and service mark of the Association)
The Hollywood Reporter
Internet Movie Database, Inc. (www.imdb.com)
KCBS
KSFO
The Los Angeles Herald-Examiner
The Los Angeles Times
Dick Mason, VIP Tours, Burbank Studios
Michael Medved
Movies Unlimited
Newsweek

The New York Daily News
The New Yorker
The New York Times
Robert Osborne, *Turner Classic Movies*
Premiere
Andrew Sarris, *The Village Voice*
Gene Shalit, *The Today Show*
TIME
Peter Travers, *Rolling Stone*
TV Guide
US Magazine
Variety
The Wall Street Journal
The Washington Times

Photo Credits

The illustrations in this book come from the personal collection of the author. Many pictures are from stills issued to publicize films made or distributed by the following film companies, organizations, or individuals. Although every effort has been made to trace the present copyright holders, we apologize for any unintentional omission or neglect.

Jerry Ohlinger's Movie Material Store, The Movie Market, The Kobal Collection, Cinemabilia, National Film Archive, The Estate of Frank Capra, The Estate of Charles Chaplin, The Estate of H.G. Clouzot, The Estate of Merian C. Cooper, The Estate of Dino De Laurentiis, The Estate of Cecil B. DeMille, The Estate of Federico Fellini, Victor Fleming Trustees, The Estate of John Ford, The Estate of Sam Goldwyn, The Estate of Howard Hawks, The Estate of Alfred Hitchcock, Howard Hughes Trustees, The Estate of John Huston, The Estate of Buster Keaton, The Estate of Akira Kurosawa, The Estate of Fritz Lang, The Estate of David Lean, The Harold Lloyd Estate, The Estate of Jean Renoir, The Estate of Hal Roach, The Estate of David O. Selznick, The Estate of George Stevens, The Estate of Francois Truffaut, The Estate of Hal B. Wallis, Jack Warner Trustees, The Estate of John Wayne, The Estate of Billy Wilder, The Estate of William Wyler, Allied Artists, Associated British Studios, Cineguild, Cineriz, Columbia Pictures, Fantasy Films, London Films, Lucasfilm, Magna Pictures, MGM, Orion/TIG Productions, Paramount Pictures, Pennebaker Productions, Pixar, Rank Film Distributors, Republic Pictures, RKO Radio Pictures, Romulus-Horizon, Seven Arts, South Australian Film Corp., Svensk Filmindustri, 20th Century-Fox, United Artists, Universal, The Walt Disney Company, Walt Disney Pictures, Warner Bros., Cinema Retro Magazine, Myron Ross Photos, Sy Sussman Photos.

Bibliography

Agan, Patrick. *The Decline and Fall of the Love Goddesses.* Los Angeles: Pinnacle Books, 1979.

Agee, James. *Agee on Film.* New York: McDowell, Obolensky, 1958.

Alleman, Richard. *The Movie Lover's Guide to Hollywood.* New York: Harper & Row, 1985.

Arce, Hector. *Gary Cooper.* New York: William Morrow, 1979.

Associated Press Library, Editor: Thomas Simonet. *Oscar: A Pictorial History of the Academy Awards.* Chicago: Contemporary Books, 1983.

Bacon, James. *Made in Hollywood.* New York: Warner Books, 1977.

Baxter, John. *Sixty Years of Hollywood.* Cranbury, N.J.: A.S. Barnes Co., 1973.

Bergman, Ingrid. *Ingrid Bergman: My Story.* New York: Dell, 1980.

Brown, Jay A. & Consumer Guide. *Rating the Movies.* New York: Beckman House, 1985.

Brownlow, Kevin. *The Parade's Gone By.* New York: Ballantine Books, 1968.

Capra, Frank. *The Name Above the Title.* New York: The Macmillan Company, 1971.

Davis, Bette with Whitney Stine. *Mother Goddam.* New York: Berkley Books, 1983.

Dolan, Edward P., Jr. *History of the Movies.* Greenwich, Conn.: Bison Books, 1983.

Eames, John Douglas. *The MGM Story.* New York: Crown Publishers, 1979.

The Paramount Story. New York: Crown, 1985.

Earley, Steven C. *An Introduction to American Movies.* New York: New American Library, 1979.

Ebert, Roger. *Roger Ebert's Movie Yearbook 1999.* Kansas City: Andrews & McMeel, 1998.

Roger Ebert's Video Companion. Kansas City: Andrews & McMeel, 1995.

Edelson, Edward. *Great Movie Spectaculars.* Garden City, N.Y.: Doubleday, 1976.

Everson, William K. *Classics of the Horror Film.* Secaucus, N.J.: Citadel Press, 1974.

Finler, Joel W. *All-Time Movie Favorites.* Norwalk, Conn.: Longmeadow Press, 1975.

Flamini, Roland. *Scarlett, Rhett and a Cast of Thousands: The Filming of Gone With the Wind.* New York: Macmillan, 1975.

Fonda, Henry with Howard Teichmann. *Fonda: My Life.* New York: Signet, 1981.

Franklin, Joe. *Classics of the Silent Screen.* New York: Bramhall House, 1959.

Frazer, George MacDonald. *The Hollywood History of the World.* New York: William Morrow, 1988.

Gardner, Gerald and Harriet Modell Gardner. *Pictorial History of Gone With the Wind.* New York: Bonanza Books, 1983.

Graham, Sheilah. *Hollywood Revisited.* New York: St. Martin's Press, 1985.

Griffith, Richard and Arthur Mayer. *The Movies.* New York: Simon & Schuster, 1970.

Halliwell, Leslie. *Halliwell's Filmgoer's Companion.* London: Paladin, 1985.

Halliwell's Harvest. London: Grafton Books, 1986.

Halliwell, Ruth and John Walker. *Halliwell's Film Guide*. New York: HarperCollins, 1991.

Hardy, Phil. *The Western*. New York: William Morrow, 1983.

Harmetz, Aljean. *The Making of the Wizard of Oz*. New York: Alfred A. Knopf, 1977.

Harvey, James. *Romantic Comedy*. New York: Alfred A. Knopf, 1987.

Higham, Charles and Joel Greenberg. *The Celluloid Muse*. London: Angus & Robertson, 1969.

Higham, Charles. *The Films of Orson Welles*. Berkeley: University of California Press, 1970.

Hirschhorn, Clive. *The Columbia Story*. London: Octopus, 1999.

The Hollywood Musical. London: Octopus, 1981.

The Universal Story. New York: Crown, 1983.

The Warner Bros. Story. New York: Crown, 1979.

Hutchinson, Tom and Roy Picard. *Horrors: A History of Horror Movies*. Secaucus, N.J.: Chartwell, 1983.

Hyams, Joe. *Bogie*. New York: Signet, 1965.

Jewell, Richard B. *The RKO Story*. London: Octopus, 1982.

Kael, Pauline. *The Citizen Kane Book*. New York: Bantam Books, 1971.

5001 Nights at the Movies. New York: Holt, Rinehart & Winston, 1982.

Karney, Robin and Joel W. Finler. *Chronicle of the Cinema*. New York: DK Publishing, 1995.

Katz, Ephraim. *The Film Encyclopedia*. New York: HarperCollins, 1994.

Lambert, Gavin. *GWTW: The Making of Gone With the Wind*. Boston: Little, Brown & Co., 1973.

Lasky, Jesse L., Jr. with Pat Silver. *Love Scene*. New York: Thomas Y. Crowell, 1978.

Leventhal, Albert R. *The Movie Makers*. Secaucus, N.J.: Derbibooks, 1974.

Libby, Bill. *They Didn't Win the Oscars.* Westport, Conn.: Arlington House, 1980.

Lucaire, Ed. *Celebrity Trivia.* New York: Stein and Day, 1986.

Magill, Frank N. *Magill's American Film Guide.* Englewood Cliffs, N.J.: 1983.

Magill's Survey of Cinema. Farmington Hills, Mich.: St. James, 1999.

Maltin, Leonard. *The Disney Films.* New York: Crown, 1984.

Leonard Maltin's Movie and Video Guide. New York: Signet, 1998.

Manchel, Frank. *Great Science Fiction Films.* New York: Franklin Watts, 1982.

Nash, Jay Robert. *Zanies.* Piscataway, N.J.: New Century, 1982.

O'Hara, Maureen with John Nicoletti. *'Tis Herself.* New York: Simon & Schuster, 2004.

Peary, Danny. *Cult Movies.* New York: Dell, 1983.

Cult Movies 2. New York: Dell, 1983.

Guide for the Film Fanatic. New York: Simon & Schuster, 1986.

Rebello, Stephen and Richard Allen. *Reel Art.* New York: Abbeville Press, 1988.

Reynolds, Debbie and David Patrick Columbia. *Debbie.* New York: Pocket, 1988.

Rosenblum, Ralph and Robert Karen. *When the Shooting Stops...the Cutting Begins.* New York: Viking, 1979..

Sadoul, Georges. *Dictionary of Films.* Berkeley, Los Angeles: University of California Press, 1972.

Scheuer, Steven H. *Movies on TV.* New York: Bantam, 1983.

Schickel, Richard. *The Men Who Made the Movies.* New York: Atheneum, 1975.

Shipman, David. *Movie Talk.* New York: St. Martin's, 1988.

Spada, James. *Grace.* New York: Dell, 1987.

Stanley, John. *Creature Features Movie Guide.* Pacifica, Calif.: Creatures at Large, 1981.

Strauss, David P. and Fred L. Worth. *Hollywood Trivia.* New York: Greenwich House, 1981

Thomas, Bob. *Walt Disney: An American Original.* New York: Simon & Schuster, 1976.

Thomas, Tony, and Aubrey Solomon. *The Films of 20th Century-Fox.* Secaucus, N.J.: Citadel Press, 1985.

Thomson, David. *A Biographical Dictionary of Film.* New York: William Morrow, 1981.

Tyler, Parker. *Classics of the Foreign Film.* New York: Citadel, 1962.

Van Gelder, Peter. *That's Hollywood.* New York: Harper Perennial, 1990.

Vermilye, Jerry. *The Great British Films.* Secaucus, N.J.: Citadel, 1978.

Wlaschin, Ken. *The Illustrated Encyclopedia of the World's Great Movie Stars and Their Films.* New York: Harmony, 1979.

Worth, Fred L. *The Trivia Encyclopedia.* Los Angeles: Brooke House, 1974.

Zinman, David. *50 Classic Motion Pictures.* New York: Crown, 1970.

www.ingramcontent.com/pod-product-compliance
Lightning Source LLC
Chambersburg PA
CBHW071621230426
43669CB00012B/2030